AF251620

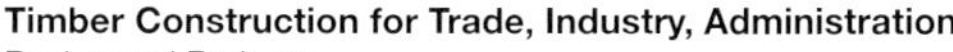

Timber Construction for Trade, Industry, Administration
Basics and Projects

Wolfgang Ruske

TIMBER CONSTRUCTION
for Trade, Industry, Administration

Basics and Projects

Birkhäuser – Publishers for Architecture
Basel · Boston · Berlin

A CIP catalogue record for this book is available from the Library of Congress, Washington D.C., USA.

Bibliographic information published by Die Deutsche Bibliothek. Die Deutsche Bibliothek lists this publication in the Deutsche Nationalbibliografie; detailed bibliographic data is available in the Internet at http://dnb.ddb.de.

This work is subject to copyright. All rights are reserved, whether the whole or part of the material is concerned, specifically the rights of translation, reprinting, re-use of illustrations, recitation, broadcasting, reproduction on microfilms, or in other ways, and storage in data banks. For any kind of use, permission must be obtained of the copyright owner.

This book is also available in a German language edition (ISBN 3-7643-7050-5).

© 2004 Birkhäuser – Publishers for Architecture, P.O. Box 133, CH-4010 Basel, Switzerland Part of Springer Science + Business Media

Translation into English:
James Roderick O'Donovan, Vienna
English Copy-editing: Janice Zawerbny, Toronto
Layout/Graphic design: Continue, Basel

Printed on acid-free paper
Produced from chlorine-free pulp. TCF ∞

Printed in Italy

ISBN 3-7643-7008-4

9 8 7 6 5 4 3 2 1

www.birkhauser.ch

Our World of Work

Human culture has deep-rooted connections with work and the world of work. The wish to be involved in shaping society and, through this involvement, to earn the means of maintaining oneself and one's family is a fundamental dream. This attitude stands in contrast to the threats felt by employees in our modern working world, fears such as mobbing or unemployment, while the business owner is subject to constant economic pressure. Our age is one of change. Changes in values, prosperity and new poverty, consumption and leisure, industrialised countries and the Third World are indicators of global social developments that must lead to a rethinking and redesign of our world of work.

Planning and building for business and industrial clients must satisfy requirements that are more demanding than those made by many other commissions, while also taking into account special problem areas. Company buildings are integrated in a dense network of relationships in the contexts of people – world of work – environment.

Human relationships are formed between business owners, their staff and suppliers, customers, financiers, shareholders, representatives of the authorities and the general public. The image and status of the company are not formed exclusively by public relations, human relations, internal relations, community relations, financial relations and other patterns of relationships but, quite literally, by its image, that is, by looking at the external appearance of the company – at its buildings.

In an age dominated by image, corporate design is a decisive factor in a company's future development. It is therefore hardly surprising that, in many of the projects presented in this book, the company's image was highly influential in choosing which wood would be used as the building material. Using wood in corporate design also means the incorporation of all three contextual factors: people – world of work – environment. After all, what material is better suited to creating a humane, ecologically oriented and economically based work environment than wood? While future-oriented industrial and commercial building does not inevitably mean building in wood, it always requires a humane and economical approach to building.

Wolfgang Ruske

CORPORATE DESIGN

Industry and commerce: why build in timber today?

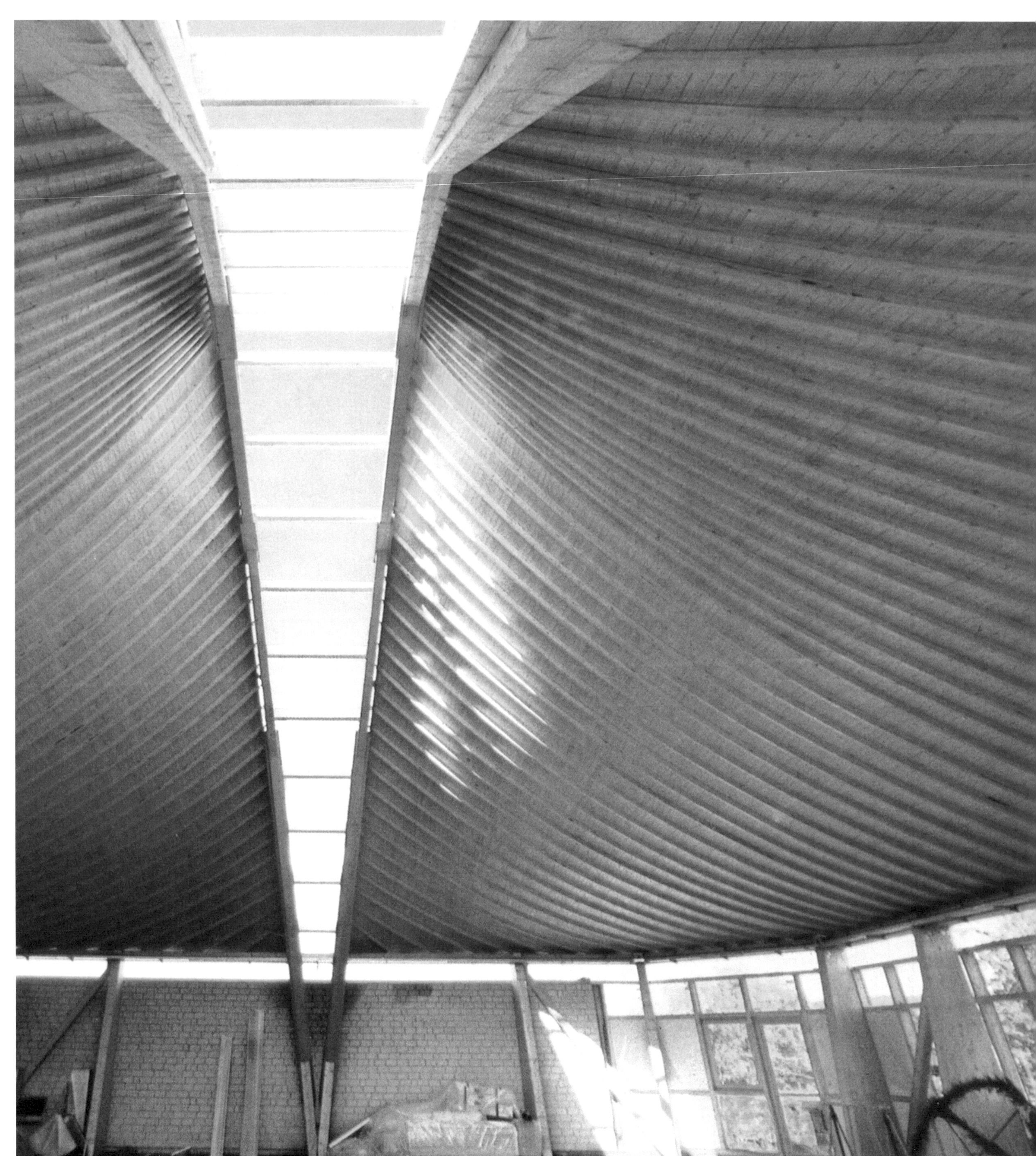

Architects plan only a small percentage of industrial architecture. In the opinion of the Hamburg architect Meinhard von Gerkan, one consequence of this fact is that buildings in industrial areas throughout the world are "aesthetic rubbish". His Munich colleague Christoph Hackelsberger goes so far as to speak of "luridly coloured excrement". When businessmen such as Klaus-Jürgen Maack (ERCO, Germany) have the feeling "of never being quite properly noticed," the unease caused by the arbitrary nature of one's own buildings leads to an attempt to create a company image with the aid of corporate design. In an age when products are interchangeable, the presentation of the company, including its architectural appearance, becomes a method of business communication, which justifies the expenditure involved in economic terms. This is particularly true whenever corporate design leads to a corporate identity, that is to say, when people feel so good in their workplace that they start to identify with the aims of the company. Productivity increases and the staff becomes in a sense, an advertisement for the company. For reasons that will be explained in this book, building with an alternative material like wood has a greater likelihood than other materials of being noticed and accepted in the right context. This applies to all those who communicate with the company.

Entrepreneurial flair under timber roofs

"Building involves responsibility to the future. A building stands in the landscape and exerts an influence, it challenges its surroundings and the people who deal with it." This statement was not made by an architect, but by client and businessman Fritz Hahne, chairman of the board of directors of the office furniture manufacturer Wilkhahn in Bad Münder (Germany). Hahne, whose timber-built production hall has been awarded a number of architecture prizes, "is delighted when people feel good and the staff council can stand back and say proudly and happily: that's us!"

Wilkhahn is one of the few medium-sized businesses that can claim to have understood the idea of corporate identity at a time when the notion did not even exist in Germany. The approach, activities and management style of this company are – according to Theodor Diener, chairman of the board of management – determined by two factors: first, by the quality of the design and the product, and second, by the social partnership combined in a single term that he calls truthfulness. Conveying this business philosophy or, to put it another way, the identity of the business – both outwards and inwards – is a precondition for the establishment of what is referred to today as entrepreneurial culture.

The architecture of their building is a visible expression of Wilkhahn's entrepreneurial culture. Their close collaboration and involvement with architects, designers and customers who demand quality led Wilkhahn to set high standards for their own buildings and complexes at an early stage. "We view industrial building as a matter of design and are of the opinion that it has no special right to be ugly. If you measure a realistic picture of modern commercial and industrial buildings against this concept then you soon begin to have serious doubts," says Theodor Diener.

"Is this due to the fact that we tend to view industry and commerce as an evil necessary to satisfy the requirements of our existence? From this viewpoint, if one compares the urban development and the architecture of non-industrial buildings with the architectural envelopes produced for industry and trade, this disdain, if not to say contempt, is made particularly clear in their lack of architectural quality. This leads one to recall," Theodor Diener continues, "that in an age when industrialisation was still celebrated as social progress, this esteem was also expressed in the aesthetic of industrial buildings. Even as late as the 1920s, far more buildings indicated the importance of what went on inside them through their design than is the case today. This is also an aspect of entrepreneurial culture!"

Wilkhahn's timber production pavilions are small, comprehensible manufacturing units that match the highly skilled work that goes on inside them. Upholstering and sewing do not have to be carried out in gigantic sheds – even though many planners of these kinds of premises seem to view such buildings as the most rational system. The basic decision to use manageable work groups that reflect the sequence in which the work is carried out was made at a very early stage. Not only were the planners of the manufacturing processes involved in this decision, but also the staff association, which represents all of the workers in the entire building. Many discussions were held about who would work where, including which direction they would be oriented in, and who would work together with whom, and opposite whom. Questions about the facilities required in the workplace, for example, whether underfloor heating for the seamstresses or a view outside was needed, were also discussed. This entire process could not have run more smoothly, especially when one takes into account how truly difficult it is to demand from the individual workers a kind of estimate or concrete idea of a workplace that does not yet exist.

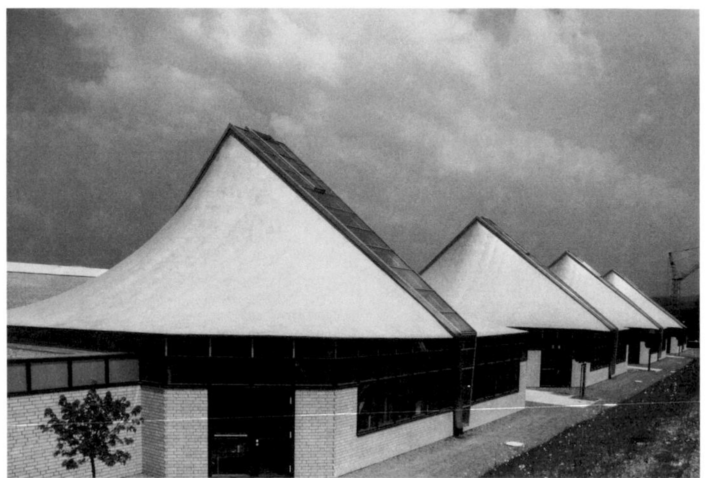

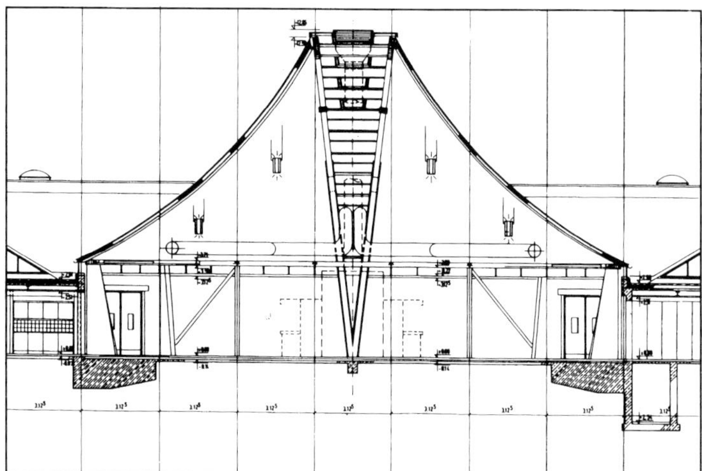

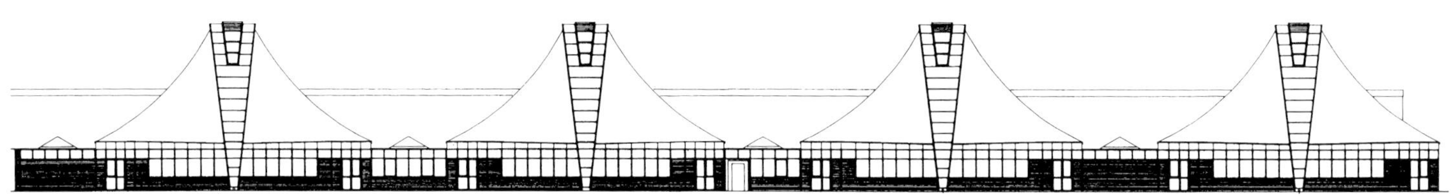

Wilkhahn pavilions

The concept of the wooden tents is also an indication of the way the Wilkhahn company thinks and acts. "It shows that we make a serious effort in both our work environment and in our products to take ecological, social and aesthetic demands into consideration. After just a year, it was clear that productivity and quality had risen," concluded Diener.

Porsche AG built its casino and office building in 1985 using a wooden structure that was left visible – offering the explanation that it must "reflect the future-oriented dynamic spirit of the building".

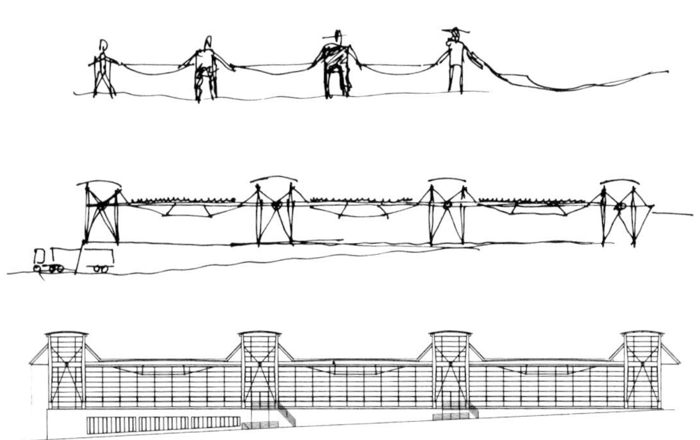

Determining the design: in a second building phase in 1992, new production buildings were erected for the office furniture manufacturer Wilkhahn in Bad Muender (Germany).

When a company that produces a high-tech product with dynamic, future-oriented perspectives such as a Porsche sports car builds in wood, it automatically raises the issue of the material's traditional image. A revolution of sorts appears to have taken place here: from the image of an improvisational, cheap building material to a high-tech material with an added ecological value that can be and is used as a way of enhancing the company's image. In addition, there are technical advantages that can be of particular interest to business users, including those in so-called niche markets with specific requirements.

Planning preconditions

In planning industrial, commercial and office buildings, close collaboration is necessary between the client, architect, specialist engineer, planning authorities, town planners, building physics specialists, operating planners, management consultants, building contractors and supply companies. The inclusion of the staff in the planning process is a way of establishing a feeling of trust and identification with the new company building and the work processes that take place there. Staff suggestions about how to create a pleasant work environment and work patterns that will allow them to enjoy personal accomplishments can be integrated into the design. This is the only approach that enables the sociological, technical and economic system represented by a modern-day industry to be set up in a way that is both functional and economical.

Location and ties

Creating ties between company buildings and the existing infrastructure and buildings, as well as incorporating the site's topography, is a planning approach that can lead to architectural and social integration. For example, the furniture company Vitra, in southern Germany, organised a workshop with the town planning authorities, regional and international architects and designers, and students to generate ideas for the overall urban design of the company's buildings and to create a link with the local town of Weil am Rhein. The international timber-based products company, Holzwerkstoffkonzern Glunz, built the Glunz Dorf in Hamm for its administration, a collection of timber frame buildings around a communications centre at the hub of a large designed biotope.

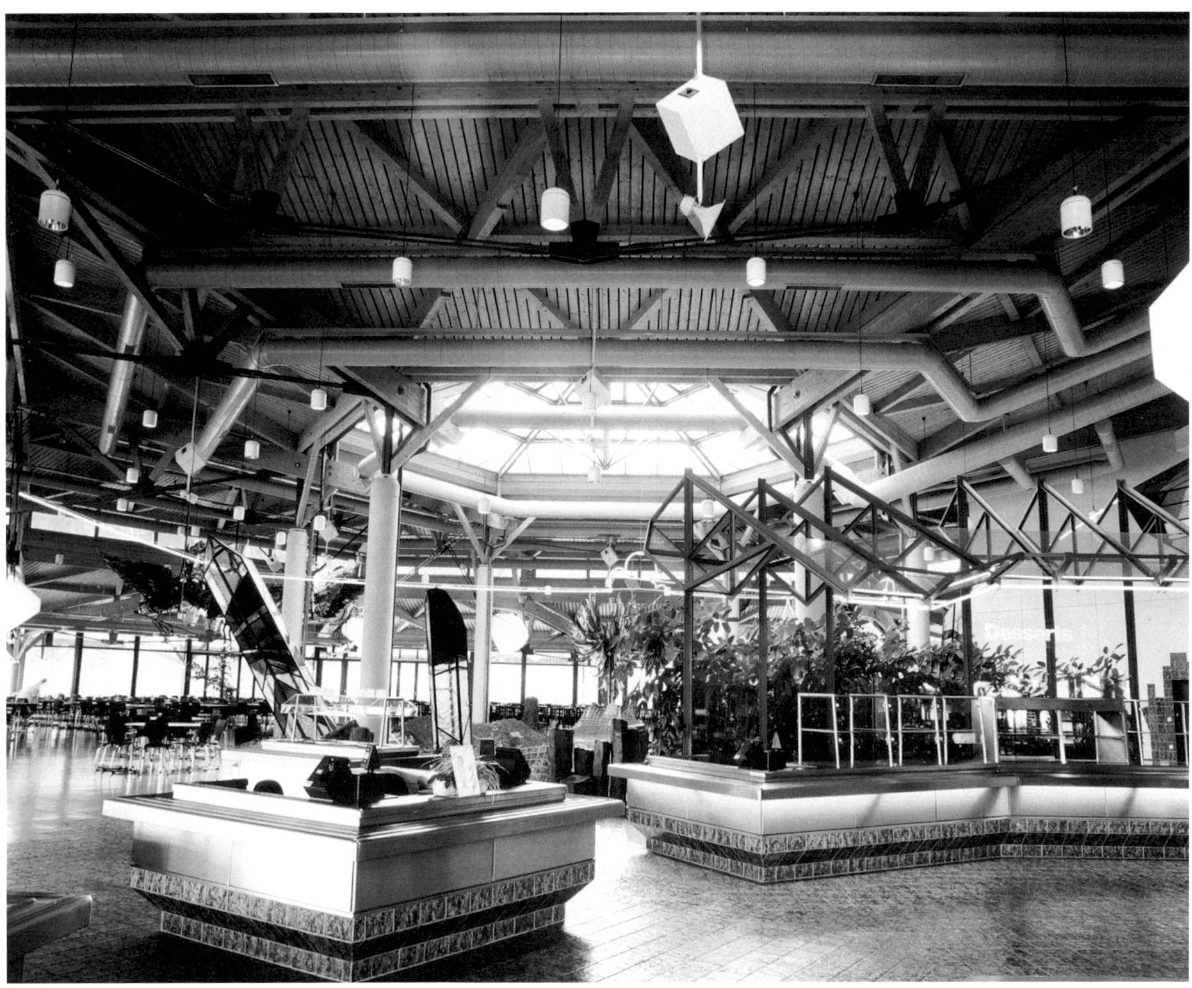

Casino of Porsche AG in Stuttgart (Germany)

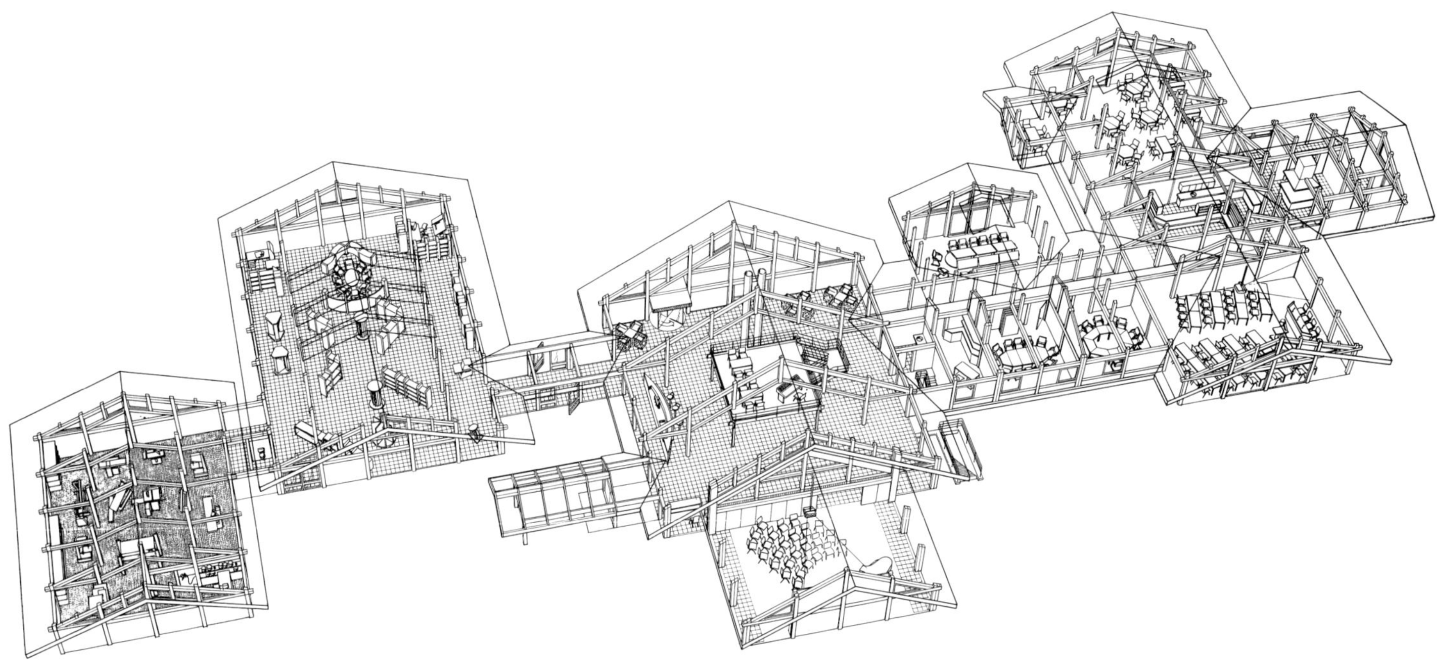

The communication centre of the wood-based products manufacturer Glunz at the centre of the *Glunz Dorf* (Glunz Village) in Hamm (Germany). A collection of timber frame buildings around a large biotope, 1990

Function

The function of the building that houses the company's production facilities must be the primary starting point for the design. Wood is a material that allows considerable freedom in design. The function of a building can also dictate its most appropriate form and optimum structure, particularly in cases where the entrepreneur does not just opt for one of those "empty shells" (Prof. Dr. Degenhard Sommer, Technische Universität Wien), which are often employed for buildings with undefined functions. It is perhaps self-evident that, for example, in the case of warehouses for bulk goods, a structure with a conical cross-section should be used. The flexibility of the system employed is another important aspect of the design of a building and its construction. The introduction of new uses, building extensions and the demounting of existing structures should be technically feasible and economically reasonable.

People – Design – Environment

Responsible building that is flexible enough to deal with future requirements is based on the principles of sustainability, changeability, protection of users' health, efficient use of energy, clarity of the building layout, and the technology and sequence of processes conducted in it. This holistic view of the building also takes into account ecological, social and economic factors. In Germany, the federal government has established guidelines for sustainable building to be applied to state building projects. In the future, industrial and commercial building will also have to be oriented according to the premises of sustainability. These include the use of energy-saving, environmentally friendly materials that do not pose a danger to health, avoiding compound materials that are difficult to separate, the use of solar energy sources for heating, cooling, and air conditioning, as well as controlled dismantling of structures to allow recycling or thermal use. These criteria all favour building in wood.

Timber construction

As a building material, wood fulfils all the demands of sustainable building and sensible handling of resources. Nowadays, in most forests in the temperate regions of the world, more timber is grown than is used, which means that sufficient material resources are available. The tree uses solar energy to grow, in the process storing carbon dioxide and emitting oxygen into the atmosphere. Little energy is required to transport and process wood. The tactile material appeals to people's senses, psyche and intelligence when used in a way that reveals its load-bearing function. In the design of buildings, wood can also meet the technical requirements for economic structures covering large spans.

Characteristics of the material

The anatomical structure of fibres and cells, as well as the chemical composition of the wood, determines its technical qualities. The structure of wood is anisotropic, which is to say that the qualities of the material are dependent upon direction: along the grain, wood has one hundred times greater tensile strength and four times greater compressive strength than at right angles to the grain. A cube with sides of 4 cm can carry a load of 4 t – more than standard concrete – with a relatively low dead weight. In contemporary timber building, specially improved timber-based materials are generally used, allowing for roof spans that have long since exceeded the 100-m mark.

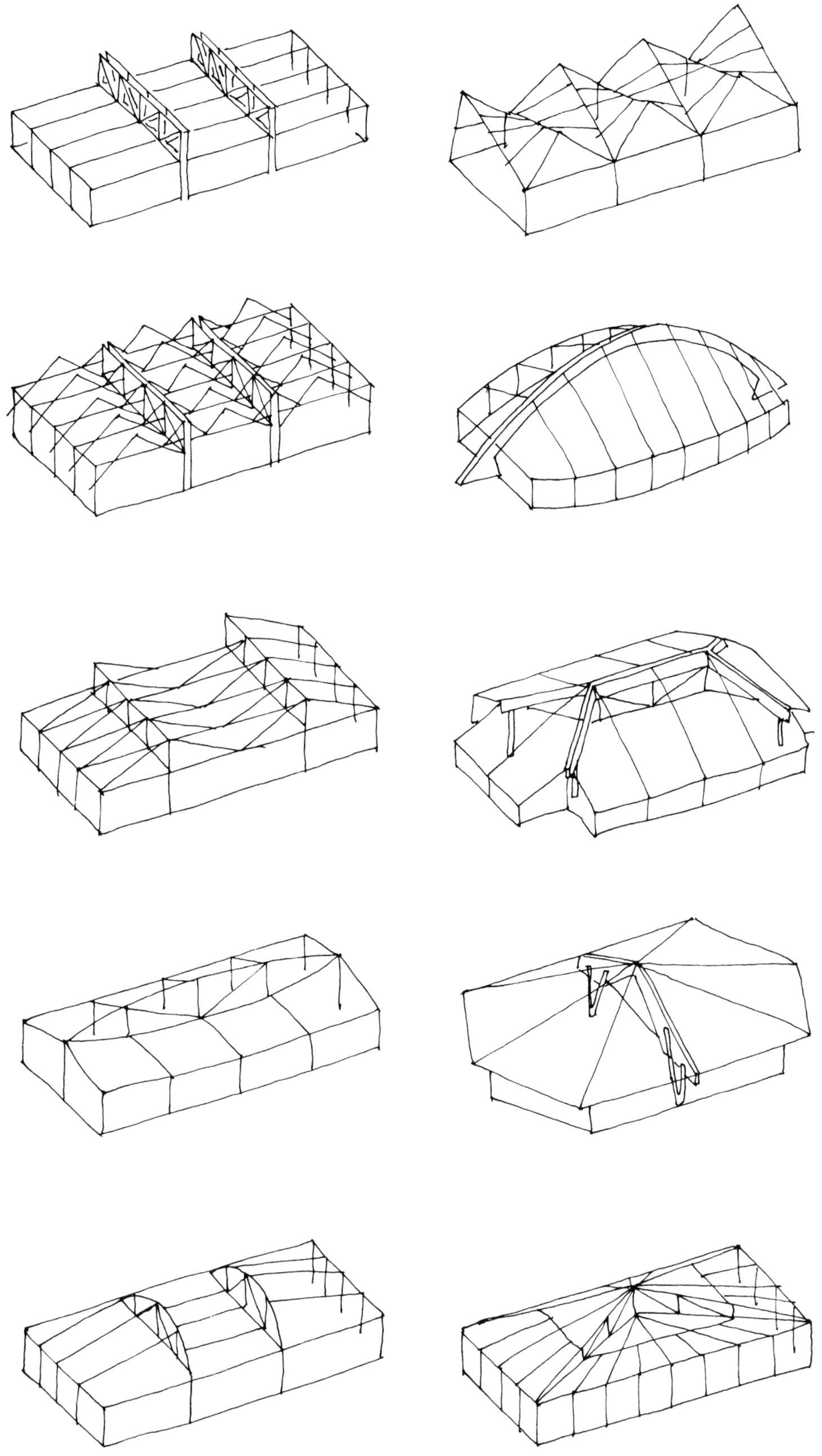

In timber construction, determining the building form is influenced by the nature of the site, the functional requirements and the possibilities of natural lighting.

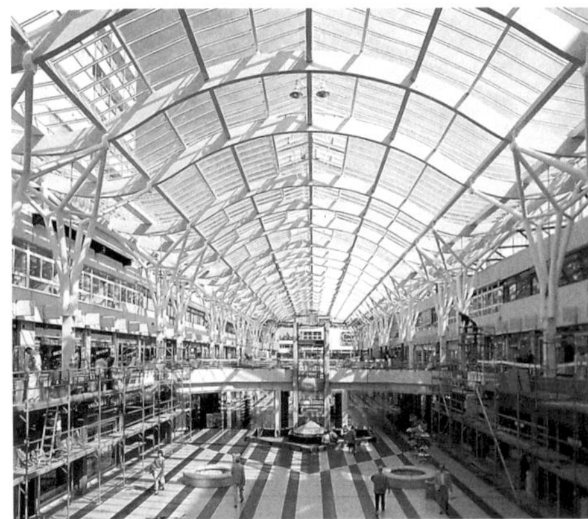 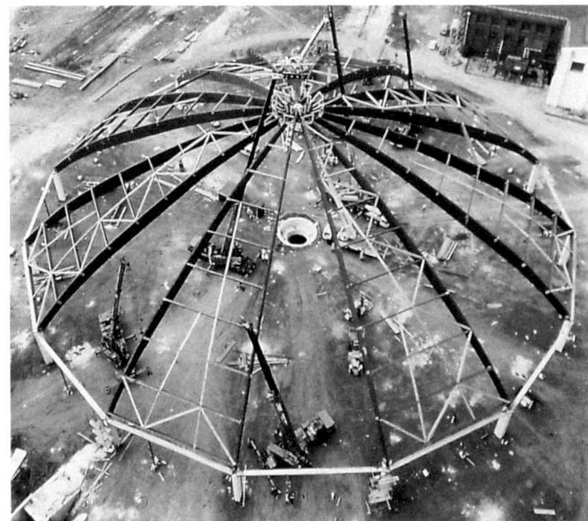 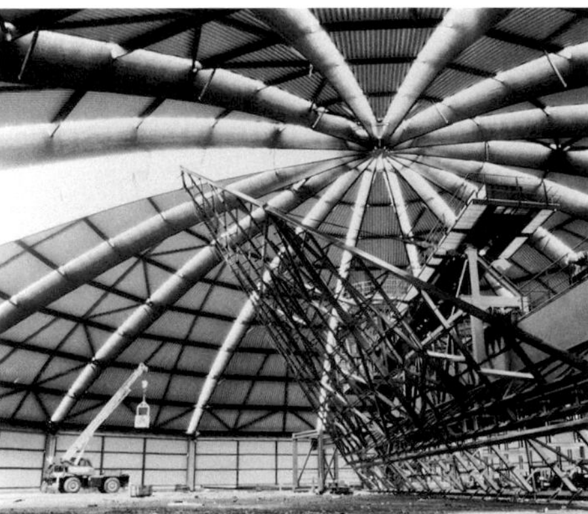

Nordwest-Einkaufszentrum (shopping centre) in Frankfurt am Main (Germany) 1985. Roof over a pedestrian zone with a floor area of 10 000 m^2, using wave-shaped beams made of glue laminated timber with glass roofing.

Coal mixing plant of Ruhrkohle AG in Bottrop (Germany). Arched beams made of glue laminated timber with a span of 100 m.

Reaction to chemicals

In comparison to other materials, wood is highly resistant to acids, bases, salts and other chemicals. When timber structures are used in chemical industries, paint factories, tanneries, galvanising workshops, accumulator workshops, salt warehouses, sewage treatment plants, waste and recycling buildings, etc., care must be taken so that the connecting materials are also resistant to corrosion.

Wood preservation

Fungi that attack wood require permanent humidity of more than 25 percent and insects, such as the common furniture beetle and the house longhorn, flourish in conditions of timber humidity between 28 and 30 percent. The best method of protecting timber structures is therefore to use dry wood and to keep the construction dry. The danger of insect attack is generally exaggerated. In the case of wooden elements under a roof that are accessible on three sides and under a roof, chemical protection treatment is not necessary. Structural timber preservation methods are a part of the detail planning and include all measures necessary to prevent constant moisture penetration, including the danger of vapour condensation in the cross-sections of the elements.

Earthquake safety

In Anchorage (Alaska), a 20-m-high office building was to be built above an earthquake fault-line. The building authorities insisted that timber frame construction be used for reasons of safety, in case of earthquakes. Regions subject to earthquakes are spread throughout the world. In such areas, wooden structures with special wall panels that take over the transfer of loads and the dissipation of energy can be erected, offering a high degree of safety in case of earthquakes and tremors.

Flexibility

Timber building has a long tradition of prefabrication. Most of the primary structural work and part of the detail fitting can be carried out independent of weather conditions in the workshop or the joining shed of the timber construction company. The use of CNC-controlled joining systems is standard these days: it allows economic production of individual building parts and structures with the maximum of precision. The assembly of the load-bearing structure generally takes just a few days. Thanks to their flexibility, timber buildings allow unproblematic extensions horizontally and, generally, also vertically, and permit production to be subdivided into sections or levels. Wooden structures can be re-planned, reduced in size, taken down and rebuilt at a different location, and also can be recycled in an environmentally responsible manner. Crane runways, suspended galleries or other installations can be built-in after completion.

Maintenance and servicing

The life span of professionally designed timber buildings is practically limitless; used properly, wood in an interior requires no special care. Depending on the climate and the type of surface finish chosen, paintwork and coatings on facades must be renewed in a rhythm of several years or decades; untreated facades made of long-life woods make painting unnecessary. Repair work to the construction can be carried out without major difficulty; defective parts can, generally, be easily replaced.

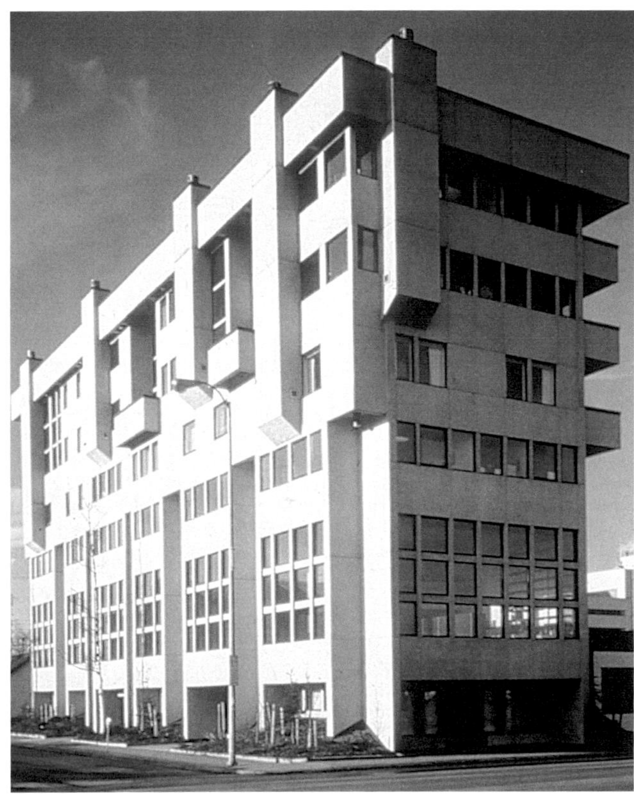

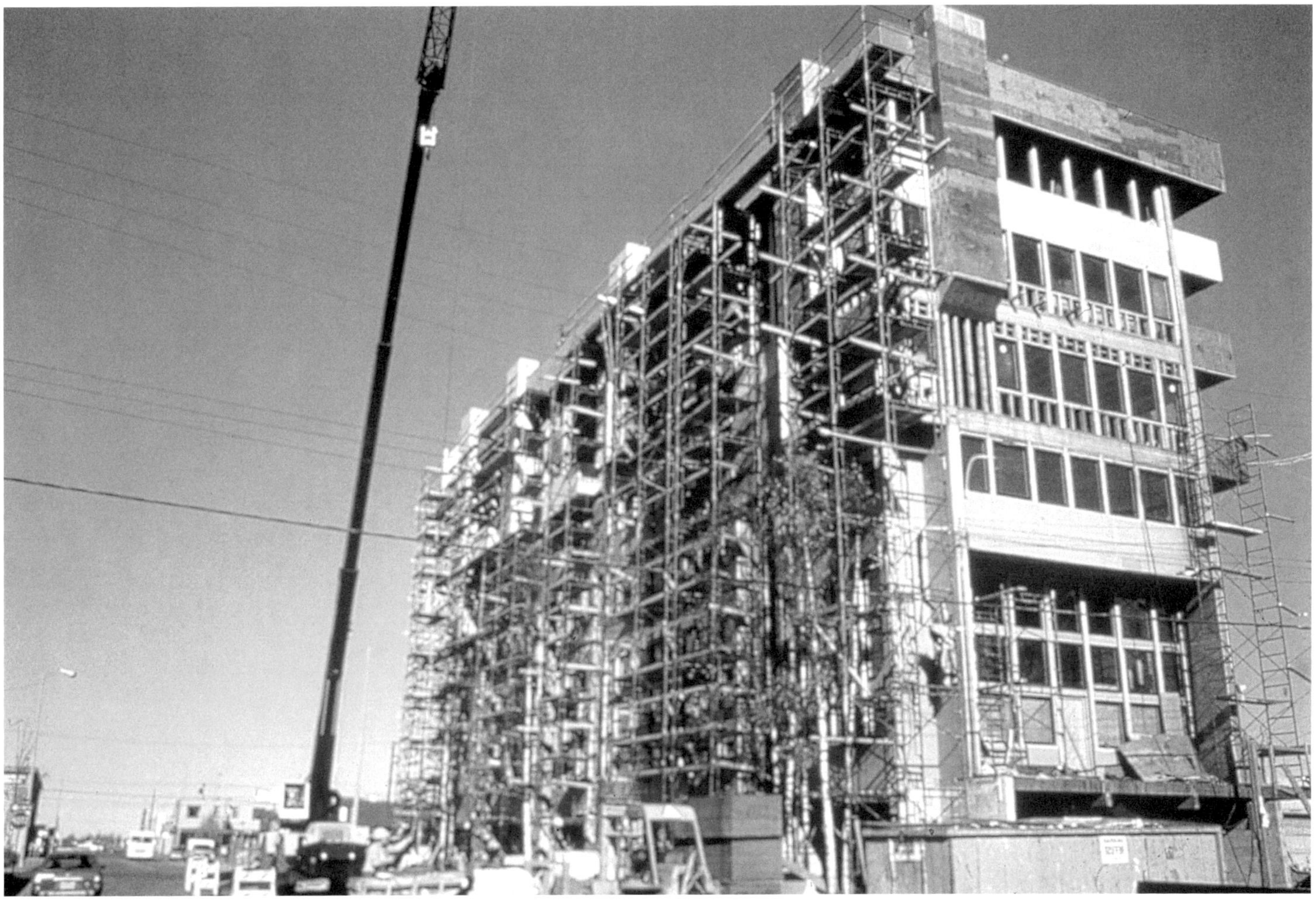

In Anchorage (Alaska, USA), a 20-m-high retail office building was erected over an earthquake fault-line. For reasons of earthquake safety, building authorities required a timber frame building.

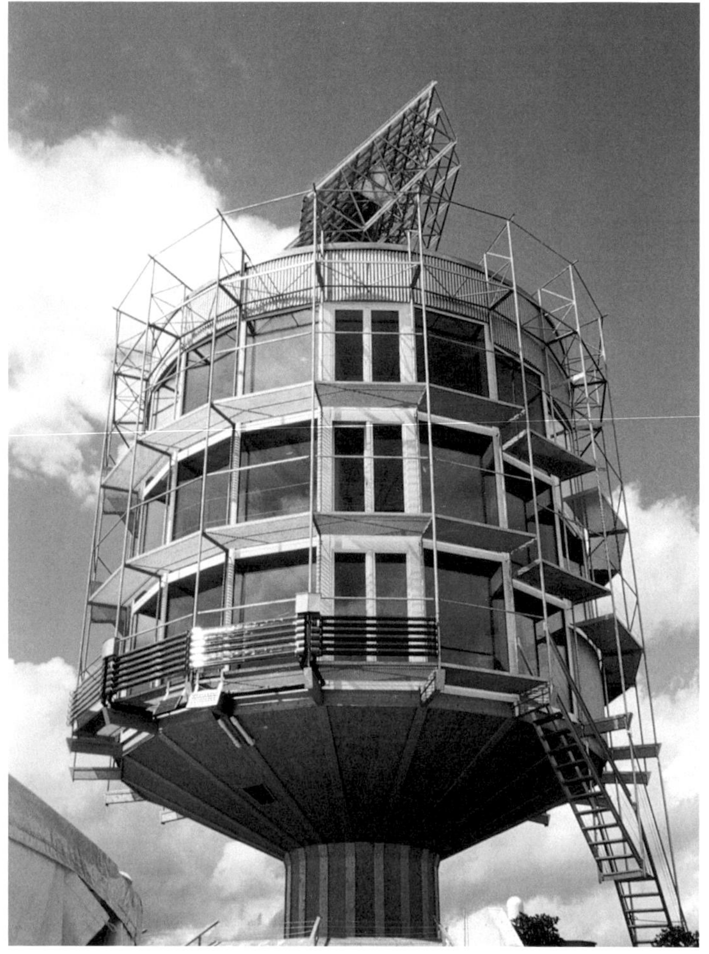

Solar energy tower of the bathroom fittings manufacturer Hans Grohe in Offenburg (Germany) used as an exhibition building

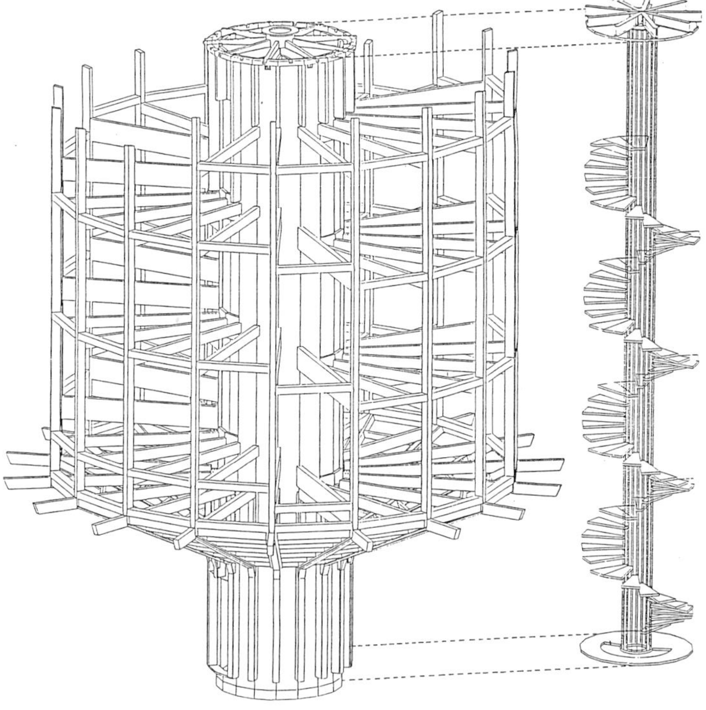

Solar energy tower, isometric illustration of the skeleton timber frame with staircase tower

Building costs and cost effectiveness

For the entrepreneur, cost-effectiveness is a central concern in industrial, office and commercial buildings. It is measured according to the construction costs and the costs of maintaining and running the building in accordance with its function. A cheap "empty shell", seemingly suitable for many different uses, may initially satisfy the obvious requirements but can turn out to be expensive when the production structure, the logistics or the spatial requirements of the company change. The importance of the construction costs alone becomes relative when one considers that, in long-term company cost accounting, they generally amount to only a fraction of the labour costs and, furthermore, include numerous factors whose value is impossible (or very difficult) to calculate: image forming (corporate design), humane atmosphere (productivity), consequential costs (environmental impact).

Wood is a light-weight building material with a considerable load-bearing capacity, a fact that reduces the costs of making foundations, of transport and of assembly (even in extreme construction conditions). Prefabrication and short construction periods also reduce the costs of financing. If the amount of thermal insulation is increased (which is simple to do with wooden structures), the cost of heating and cooling can be cut drastically. The relative thinness of the walls of a timber building yields about 10 percent more useful space (or smaller overall building dimensions with the same floor area). Entrepreneurs who look to the future will, even at the planning stage, keep an eye on factors such as dismantling and disposing of materials with minimal or no pollution because not only will environmental consciousness become more expensive in the future, it will be something that companies and their owners will have to clearly demonstrate.

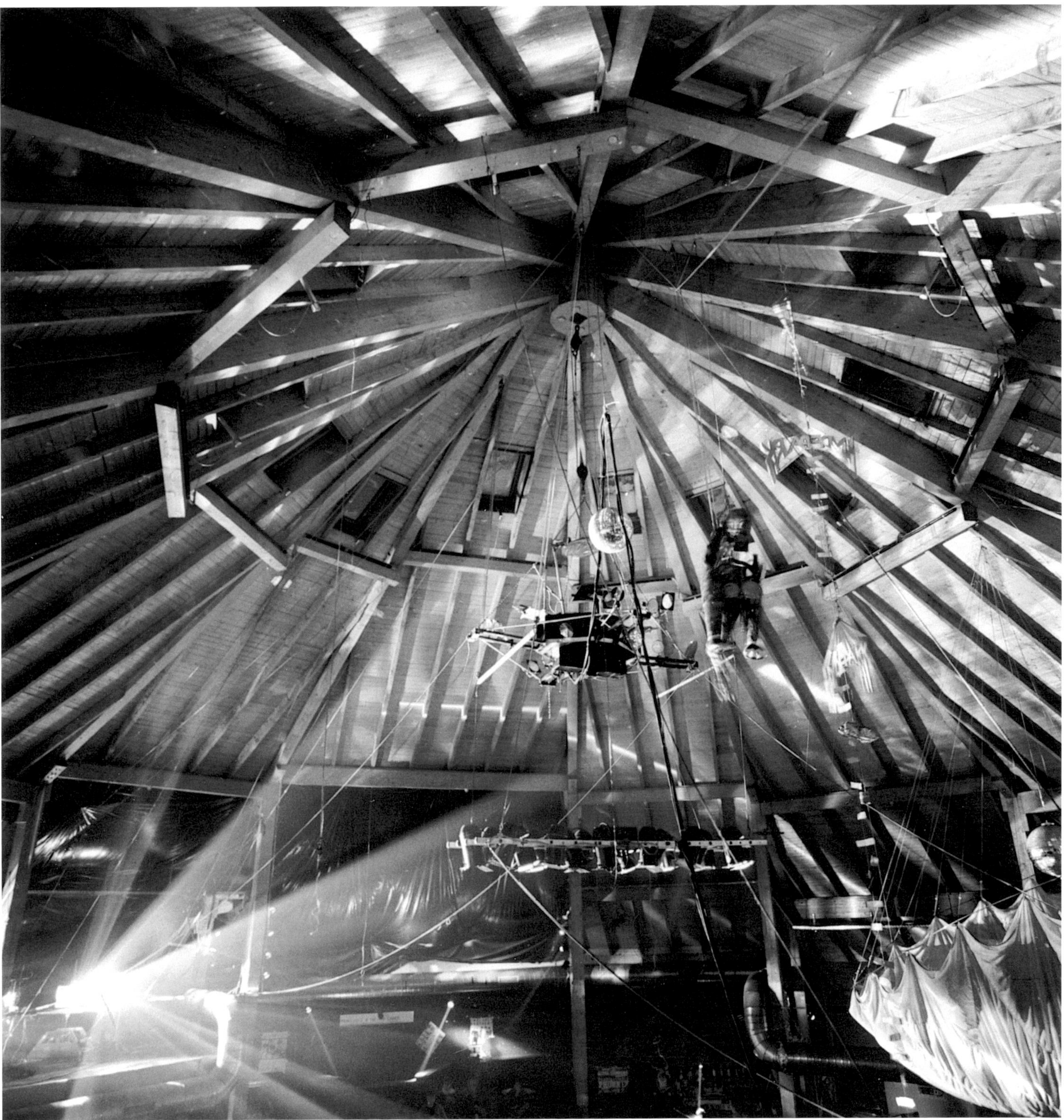

Discothèque in Osnabrueck (Germany), 1985

ENVELOPE

Timber construction methods used in the enclosure of space

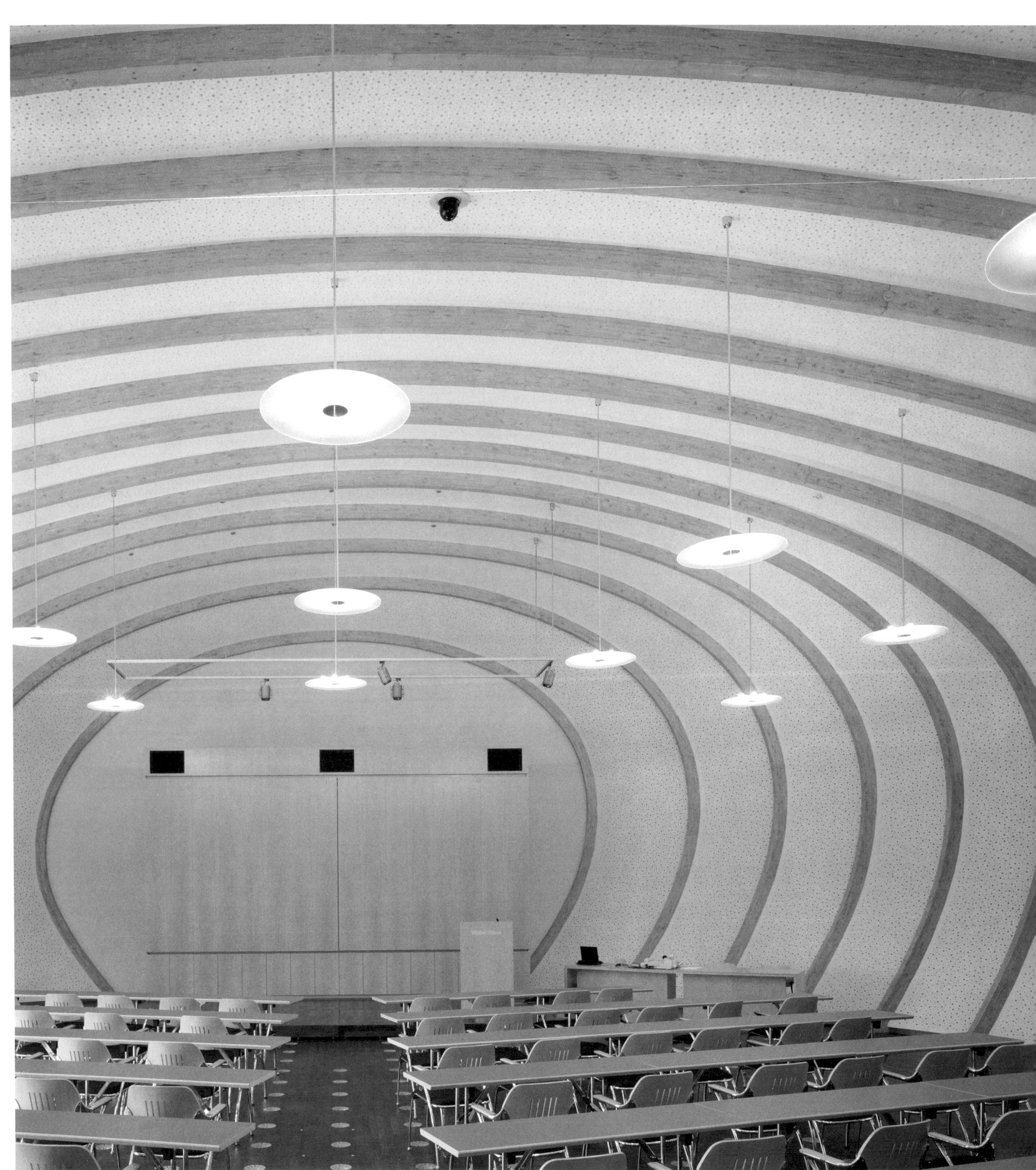

Classic methods of timber construction

Log buildings

The log building system, one of the oldest timber building systems, has an important tradition. This system was used not only for dwelling houses but also for towers, churches, bridges and other buildings up to five storeys in height. The traditional corner connections using interlocking, plain and cross-lap or dovetail joints have essentially survived down to the present day, but thanks to the use of precision machinery they can now be made more precisely. In addition, modern corner joints allow corners to be made with angles other than 90 degrees. The softwood beams or logs, which can be round or edge sawn, are profiled, for example, with tongue and groove. To improve the stability of the beams and the settlement of the walls, timbers glued vertically or beams glued at right angles to each other are used.

A distinction is drawn between a solid log wall and a layered wall construction with additional thermal insulation. A disadvantage of using solid timber sections is the settling of the construction, which makes settlement joints necessary at the windows, doors, and lintels, and at the connections to brickwork or masonry. The settling is due to the fact that wood shrinks as it dries. The degree of shrinking is related to the amount of moisture in the wood at the time it is used in the building, which should not exceed an average of 20 percent. Modern timber elements such as glued laminated timber (gluelam) have a moisture content of 15+/−3 percent or less, which means that the problem of shrinking is less significant when it is used. Concealing service runs in log construction is also a problem; on the other hand, the wood mass offers advantages in terms of internal climatic conditions and its positive environmental features. The disadvantages of log construction – the high level of settlement, changes in dimensions, the problems with ducting and cabling for services – can be avoided through the use of hierarchical separation (see "Oekotop principle" on page 25).

Plank construction

In plank construction, the time-consuming corner connections of log construction are avoided by the use of corner uprights that are joined to the horizontal wall elements. Thus, plank construction is a mixed construction form. This building method, however, is rarely used. The uprights are channelled at the sides to take the planks so that various types of connections, including those using an independent wooden "tongue", are possible. In modern applications, sandwich construction with internal thermal insulation is used instead of solid timber planks.

Traditional timber frame construction

This traditional building method was particularly widespread in Central Europe and is still used today in individual cases. The development of computer-controlled processing machines means that the handmade connections used in traditional timber frame building can now be produced economically. As these connections reduce the cross-sectional area of the timbers, the structural elements are generally oversized. The construction of sole plates, posts, beams and struts is erected storey-by-storey, and the struts should be placed at the corners of the building so that wind forces are directly transferred to the sole plates.

The walls between the timber uprights can be made using different materials. Generally speaking, these materials alone do not provide the levels of thermal insulation required nowadays so that a wall cladding – either internal or external – with additional insulation is necessary. The timber frame system is prefabricated and is a rigid system. Instead of using tenons or notched connections, new timber frame buildings are often built using modern steel connectors. This is unfavourable since – in the case of small elements – the joints are not subject to much stress and the vertical loads are transferred directly by the contact between the wood elements.

The classic timber building methods of enclosing space

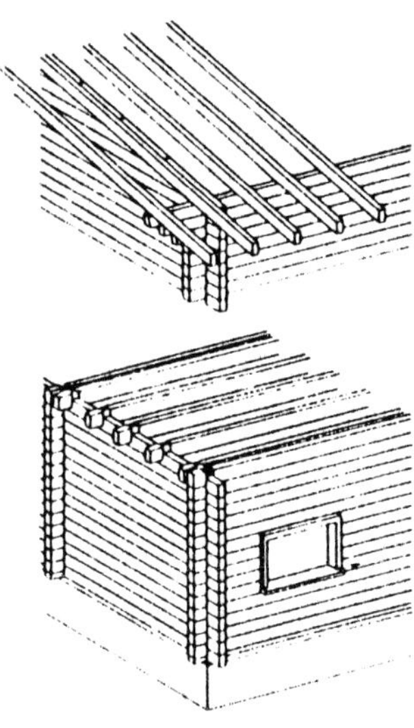

Log construction

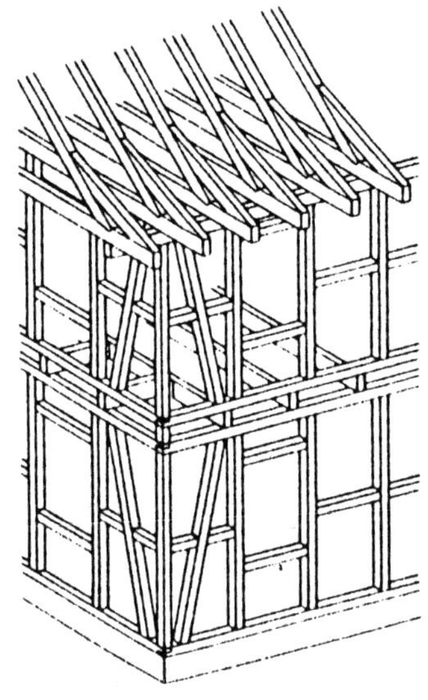

Traditional timber frame (half-timbered) construction

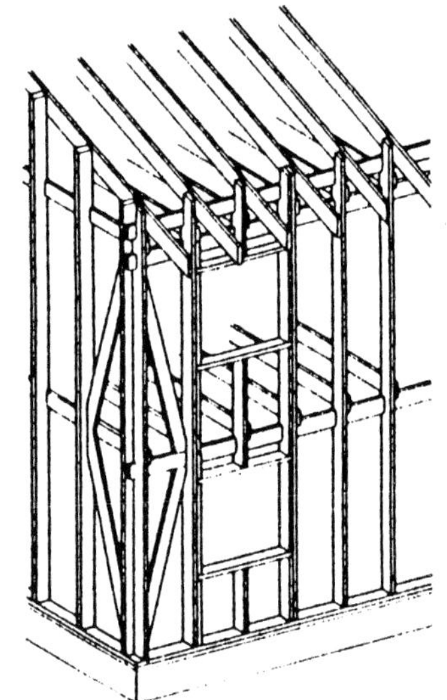

Balloon frame construction

These three traditional building methods are still used today on a limited scale for industrial companies which, due either to their origins or their products, have a particular relationship to traditional timber construction. These include agricultural companies, wineries, cooperatives, handcraft companies and warehouses for ecological and biological products.

Skeleton frame construction

In a timber skeleton frame building, the structure generally is left visible. The elements forming the walls are usually placed between the uprights (often as areas of glazing) or enclose the structure as a seamless envelope. The load-bearing skeleton frame of columns and beams, as well as the floor and roof timbers, can be laid out on a grid of up to 8 m. This allows considerable freedom in designing the floor plans and means changes can be made easily. The large spans involved in timber skeleton frame building mean that glued laminated elements are primarily used, as they can be produced in the dimensions required and can also be made in various forms (circular columns, for example). In addition, they have high strength levels, resist cracking and offer an impressive resistance to fire.

The following systems in timber skeleton building are defined according to the number and arrangement of columns and beams:

Columns and double beams
The double beams can be connected using steel dowels or can rest on steel brackets. If steel dowels are used, the cross-sectional area of the beams must be dimensioned to compensate for the weakening of the wood caused by the holes made for the dowels.

Beams between double columns
The floor beams can be fixed between the columns by notching the beams and uprights. Where continuous beams are used, the space between the uprights is filled with a glued timber piece. In both versions the connections are made using screwed bolts.

One-part beam and column system
In this system one must distinguish between single- and two-storey construction systems. There are several possible ways of connecting the beams and posts using steel or wood connecting systems. In the case of single-storey buildings, the secondary beams or joists generally rest on primary beams that in turn rest on the columns. In multi-storey buildings, the beams rest between the continuous uprights. The joists are either placed between the beams, creating a kind of grid, or rest on the beams.

Platform frame

Approximately 95 percent of timber buildings in North America are built using the platform frame system whereby external claddings are often employed to suggest a solid building. The platform system, with its principle of storey-by-storey construction, is used in North America for buildings of up to eight storeys in height. It has also been adapted to suit European conditions and has established itself in Central and Northern Europe as an economical timber building system.

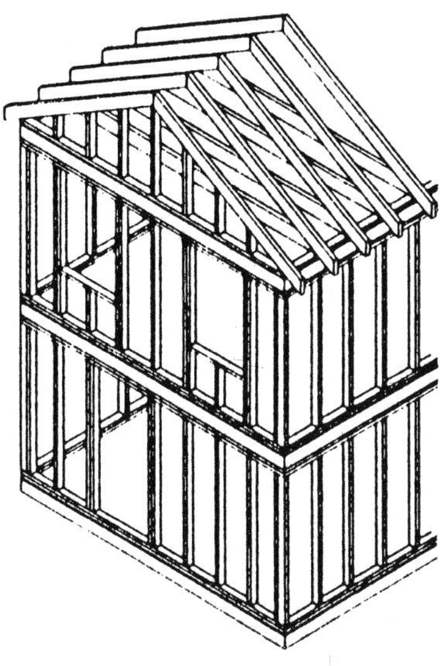

Platform frame construction

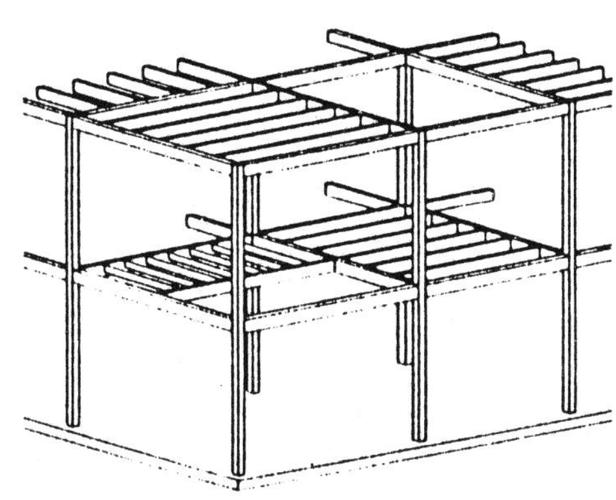

Skeleton frame construction

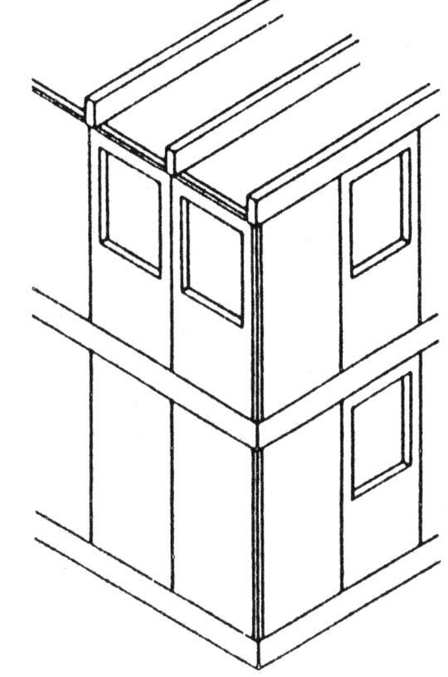

Panel / plate construction system

The platform system construction principle is simple: storey-height uprights placed at relatively small centers of 62.5 cm, together with the sole plates and the wall plates, form the wall frame, which is stiffened on both sides by sheeting made of plywood, OSB or chipboard. The advantages of this system lie in the small range of standardised solid timber sections used and the simple nailed connections. The insulation plane lies within the structural plane, creating an internally insulated system. Additional claddings are required both internally and externally. The standard cross-sections provide efficient exploitation of the wood and keep the costs of processing low. In Europe, solid structural timber with a moisture content of 15 percent is generally used.

Platform frame construction is particularly suitable for multi-storey buildings – for example, office buildings – as the erection of such buildings takes place floor by floor. The method has two major advantages: first, one floor serves as a work platform for the erection of the next floor, and second, there is reduced settling from the shrinking wood as it dries. Generally speaking, wood with a moisture content of around 18 percent and higher is used. During use, the wood dries to reach an equilibrium moisture content of around 9 percent, causing the individual sections to shrink. In the direction of the grain, this shrinking is negligible, but in horizontal building elements at right angles to the grain, it is a serious factor. In one- and two-storey buildings, if the settlement is even and building parts with different deformation patterns are joined elastically or using settling joints, no problems will result.

But the problem of shrinkage in multi-storey buildings remains. It is clear that the effect of settling of a single floor is multiplied according to the number of storeys in the building. In addition, the loading of the building causes deformation. In the case of a four-storey frame building that is about 12 to 13 m high and made of solid timber, sections of shrinkage and the accompanying settlement – once the wood has reached an equilibrium moisture content of 9 percent – amounts to around 5 to 8 cm. If we add the deformation due to loading to this figure, we arrive at a minimum figure of 8 to 13 cm. If laminated veneer lumber (LVL) of lesser thickness is used instead of solid wooden sections – which have a tendency to deform when loaded at right angles to the grain – then the amount of settling is considerably less, since laminated veneer lumber is reduced to a moisture content of under 10 percent in the manufacturer's workshop or warehouse.

Laminated veneer lumber also stands up to greater compression stress at right angles to the grain. Sole plates and wall or top plates in LVL have a permissible load-bearing capacity one and a half times that of solid timber. For example, in a four-storey timber frame building 12 m high with horizontal building elements (sole plate, top plate and the edge beams of the intermediate floors) made of LVL, there is relatively negligible settling of 2 to 3 cm; this value is about the same as that of massive construction buildings.

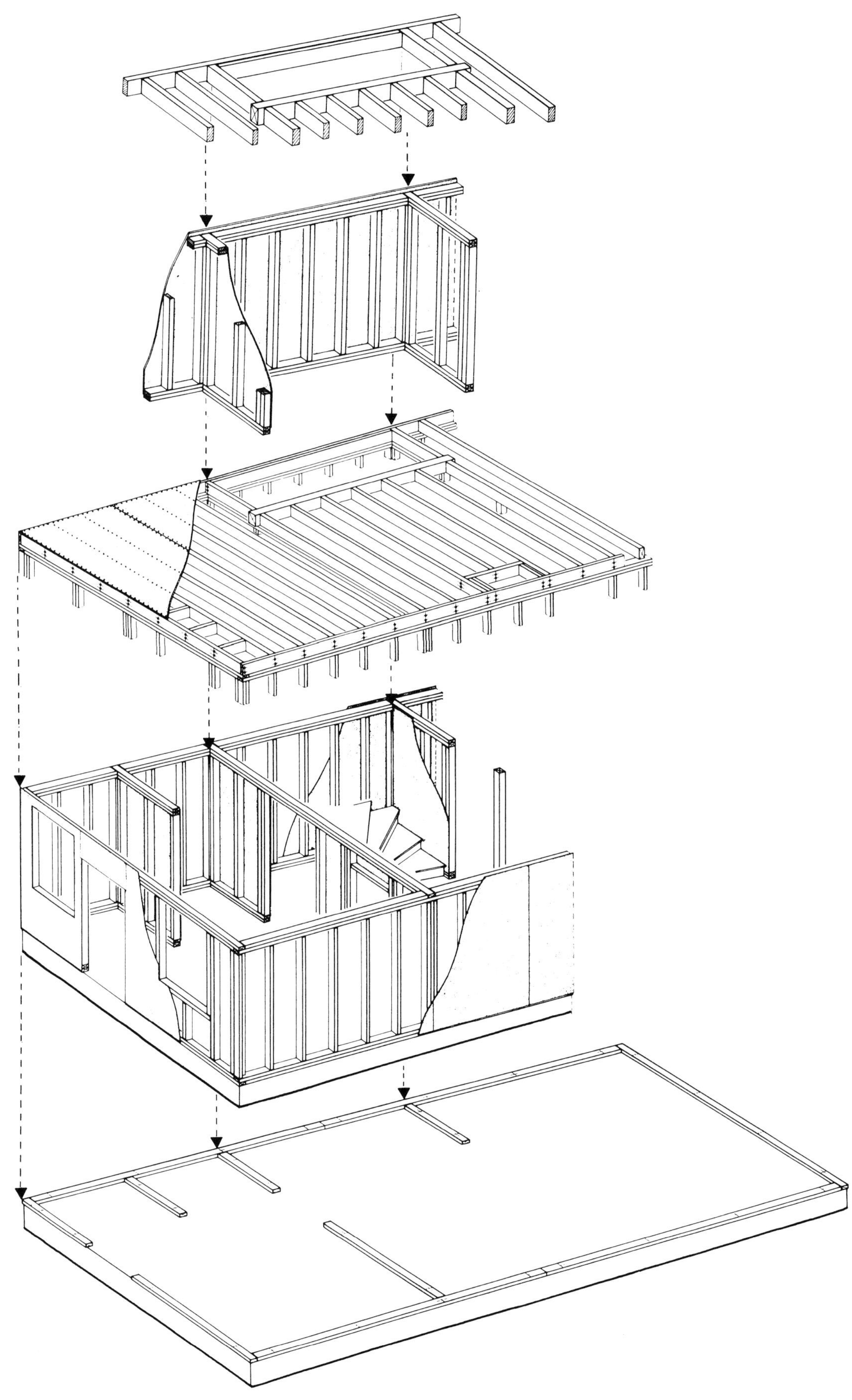

In North America, Scandinavia and other regions, timber frame construction, especially the system of erecting a complete storey at a time, is widely used. It has also established itself in Central Europe as a simple and economical form of timber construction.

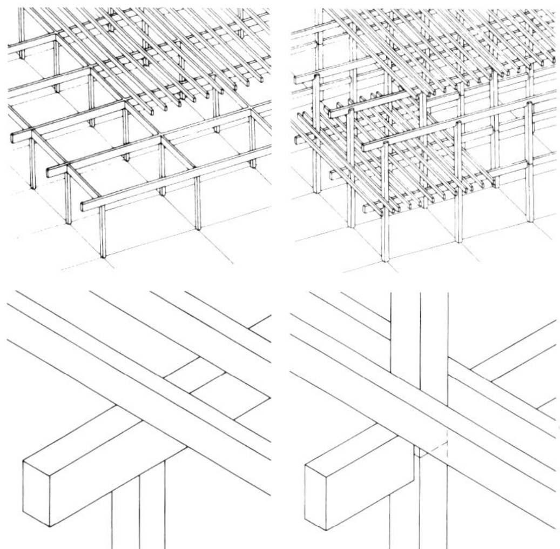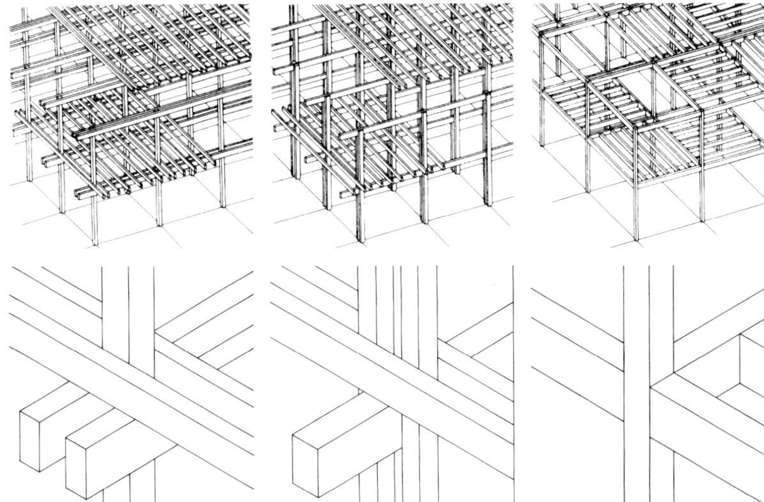

Variations on the timber skeleton frame system

Timber frame (balloon frame)

This is a kind of timber frame construction in which the uprights of the wall construction continue through two or more storeys. This system – in which the sole and top plates form the top and bottom – is known in North America as balloon frame construction. Use of this system is relatively insignificant in Europe.

Panel building construction systems

Whereas a timber frame building is generally constructed by hand on the building site, panel elements, also using the frame building principle, are produced in the factory. They are produced in the size of a wall, insulated and sheeted, and can thus be fitted on-site, in the briefest of periods. This is the familiar principle of prefabricated construction that was developed in Europe after the Second World War. The wall panels can be small in size or the entire width of a facade. The doors and windows are usually integrated before the panels are delivered to the building site. The use of this system is generally restricted to office buildings and smaller commercial businesses.

Cellular building systems

In order to further increase the degree of prefabrication, the building elements are assembled in the factory to make spatial units enclosed on two, three or four sides, with floors and ceilings. They are then delivered to the building site and joined together to make the building. This use is restricted to administration buildings (offices) and housing units for workers on the building site (temporary use). One example of a creative use of this system is the office building of the lift manufacturer Schindler (see p. 158).

New timber building systems

Stacked plank system

The idea of placing planks beside each other, on edge, then nailing or dowelling them together and using them as panel elements, is as simple as it is ingenious. This idea is already several decades old but has been rediscovered in recent years and developed into the stacked plank system. It has already been used for numerous projects, including warehouses and industrial buildings in which the walls, roofs and ceilings are made using stacked planks. One example of the use of this system is the training centre of a paint manufacturer (see p. 62).

The continuous nailing creates a wooden building element of any width required. It is important that dried boards be used in order to reduce the transverse deformation caused by shrinkage and swelling of the wood due to changes in moisture levels. Stacked plank elements are generally manufactured in a workshop in order to shorten the construction period but they can be made by hand on the building site (see training centre p. 62).

Today, the stacked plank system meets the requirements of modern economical timber building systems:
– It is simple and can be made by every manufacturer; the know-how is freely available.
– Stacked plank units can be manufactured in the workshop or factory, regardless of weather. The system offers the opportunity to prefabricate an entire building in the workshop as a series of building elements, which can then be assembled on-site in the shortest of periods.
– No special demands are made in terms of the strength class of the wood (however, minimum strength classes should be observed). Lower quality side planks can be used.

- Stacked plank building elements can be used in numerous ways: exposed rough cut, planed and surface treated, or insulated on one or both sides and sheeted.
- Using relatively thin walls, high load-bearing capacity and good insulation values can be achieved, making the system economical in terms of usable floor area. The option of erecting a weather-tight primary structure in a short period, which can then be completed by the clients themselves, is of particular interest to businesses with limited financial resources.
- The wood surface, with its surface temperature specific to the kind of wood used, creates a pleasant working climate at relatively low temperatures.
- Solid wood building elements offer protection against overheating in summer.
- Solid timber systems have a balancing effect on the humidity of the internal spaces that is coupled with the ecological effect of binding carbon dioxide.

Laminated veneer lumber elements

Laminated veneer lumber elements, glued to form large surfaces, are nowadays produced in lengths of up to 20 m, widths of up to 2.3 m and in thickness of 6 to 24 cm. These elements are suitable for walls, floors, ceilings, and roofs and can be used in all areas of a building.

Layered board elements

Elements of this kind are characterised by solid cross-sections, by solid timbers glued to each other at right angles and by their large scale. At present, the maximum element thickness is 29 cm, 14.8 m is standard length, up to 20 m is possible, and element widths of up to 4.8 m can be manufactured. With elements of this size, four-storey external walls can be made in one piece.

The build-up of the panel is always symmetrical; the minimum number of layers is three. The composition of the elements influences the stability and rigidity of the panel. The building elements are wind-proof and allow construction that is open to diffusion without a foil layer.

Wood block panels

Wood block panels consist of three to seven layers that are glued to each other at right angles, with distances between them so that cavities are produced in the wall. The system includes wall and floor panels built up on a grid system. Glued sole and wall plates are required for erecting the walls; corner posts and parapet sections complete the system.

Steko-Module

The core of this wall construction system is a wood module using inter-locking pieces that can be assembled, in a very simple manner, to create entire walls. This system is designed so that all standard floor and interior fitting-out elements can be easily used with it. The "building blocks" are "locked" pieces (i.e., they are glued at right angles) and thus form dimen-sionally stable elements. Service cables can be run in the cavities of the modules. If filled with loose insulation, the thermal insulation is improved; heavier filling materials improve the acoustic insulation. The surfaces can be left untreated, or additional insulation and facade cladding can be applied to the exterior, while decorative treatments can be used in the interior.

Hollow box elements

By connecting several elements to each other, hollow box beams made of glued boards are used to create large-scale construction units for long spans and high loads that avoid excessive construction thicknesses. The voids can be exploited for service runs and for all the requirements of building physics (thermal insulation, acoustic insulation, heat storage mass, etc.). Their use for wall, floor and roof elements has been tried and tested.

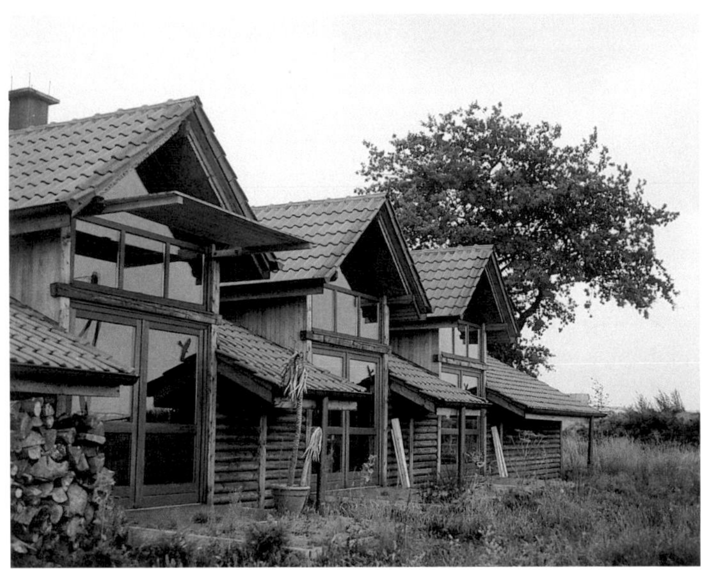

Retail building for organic food in Coesfeld (Germany), log construction

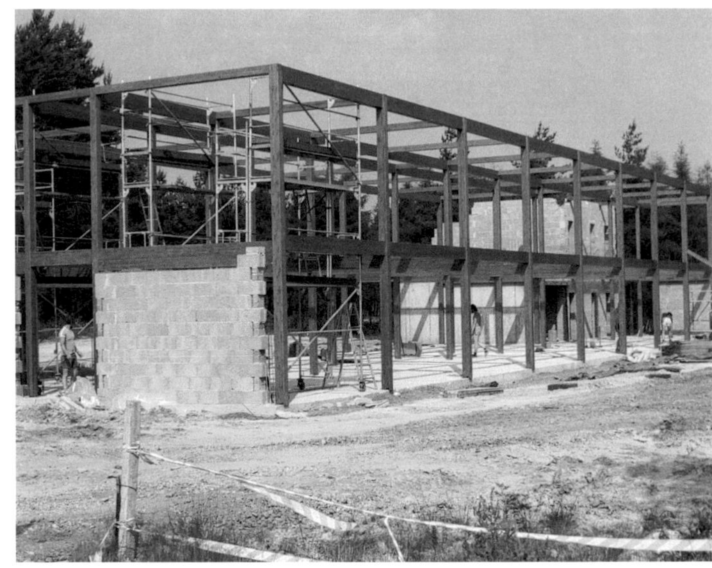

Commercial building of timber skeleton frame construction

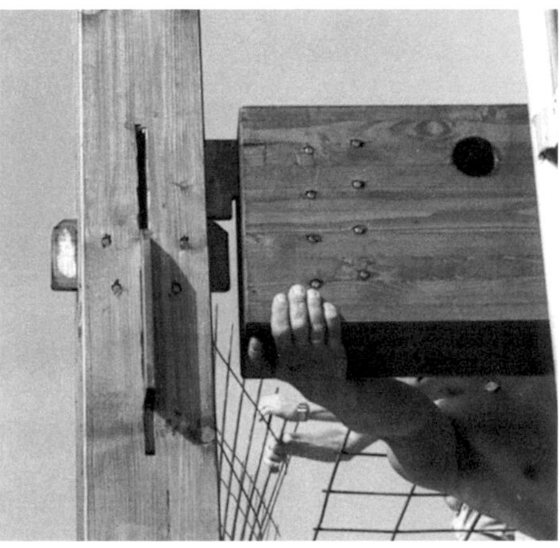

Connecting system for timber skeleton frame parts inserted into the wood

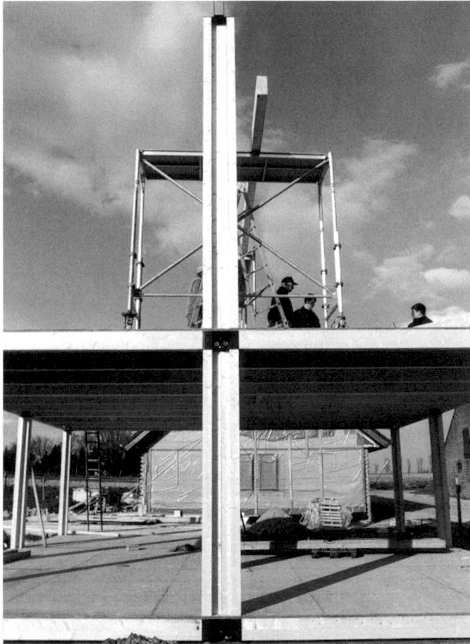

Skeleton frame building using four-piece beams and *Induo* junctions

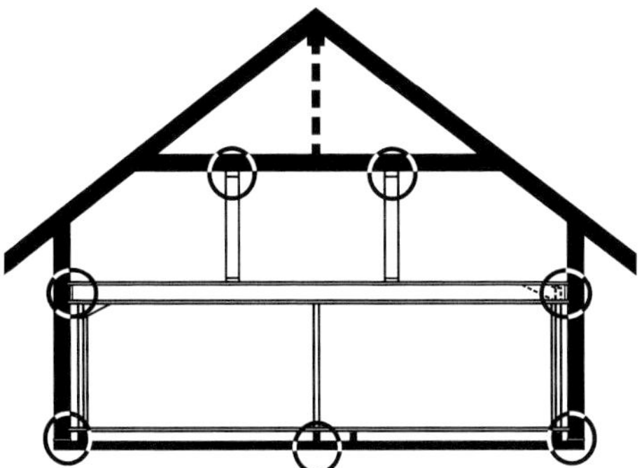

The principle of separating all relevant parts of a building solves all the problem areas in timber building and creates the framework for a new standard in building with wood. External shell: timber log wall; internal structure: timber frame

Oekotop principle

Wood is a building material with very positive features (ecology, healthy living, attractiveness, thermal insulation, stability, etc.), but it has one major disadvantage that is particularly evident in solid timber construction: its dimensions change in response to the (air) humidity. This can create a variety of problems and defects in completed buildings. What is essentially a very simple principle, namely the isolation of all the relevant parts of the building, consistently solves this problem in timber construction and creates the basis for new standard in building with wood. With this so-called hierarchical, modular separation of the entire external shell from the internal construction, changes in dimensions of the wood become irrelevant. The use of different materials for the external walls, in combination with an internal structure made of wood, is also advantageous.

The principle of the hierarchic modular isolation means that all building parts are isolated from each other in constructional terms (elastically, thermally), even in the case of the internal wall, all the way down to the last screw, in order to create a construction that has no joints and no thermal or acoustic bridges.
The individual isolations:
– foundation from the floor slab and the walls
– external envelope from the internal construction
– internal walls from each other
– internal walls from the floor slab
– internal walls from the ceiling
– internal walls from the roof slope
– building elements within the internal walls
– floors/ceilings from the external walls
– building elements within the floors and ceilings

This process, registered under the name "Prinzip Oekotop", represents a breakthrough that will be used extensively in the future, in numerous areas of timber construction.

HAT

Roof structures for office buildings and halls

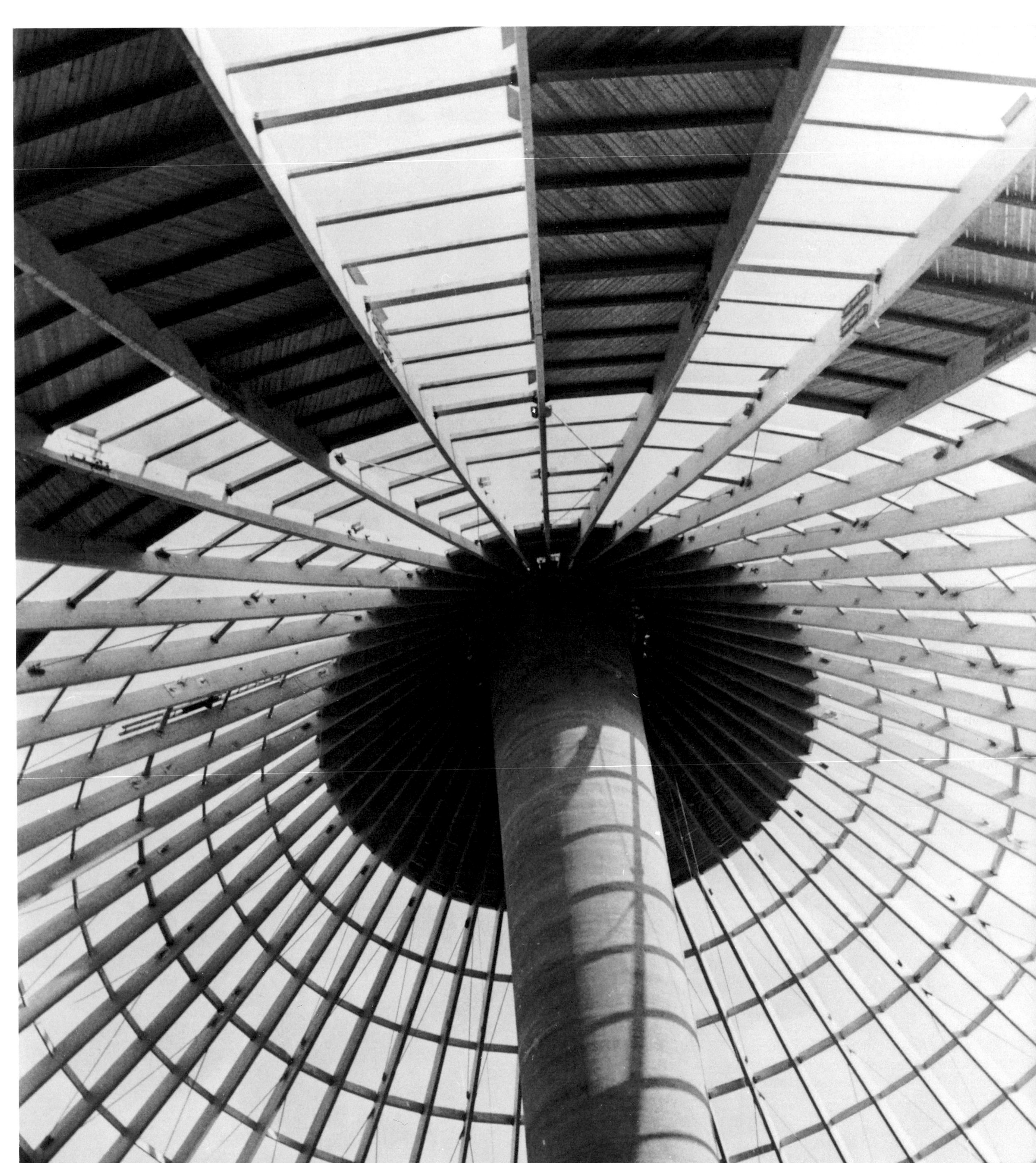

The decisive advantage of wood as a construction material lies in its low weight in relation to its load-bearing capacity. This relative lightness means that foundations, wall construction, transport and assembly are all easier. Prefabrication and joinery work have a long tradition in timber building, allowing precise assembly to be carried out quickly and relatively independent of the weather conditions. Innovative uses of wood such as glued laminated timber, veneered laminated timber and parallel strand timber enable use of large spans and new roof forms.

Roofs can be divided into different categories, according to the following criteria:
– use (house roof, hall roof, special forms such as cantilevered roofs)
– form (gable roof, mono-pitch, hipped, mansard, shed, tent, curved, domed, folded plates and shells)
– roof pitch (inclined, flat)
– construction (supported, free-spanning)
– structural design (determinate, indeterminate)
– treatment in terms of building physics (ventilated, unventilated, insulated)
– roof elements used (types of beams, surface elements, three-dimensional structures, space frames)
– span

Roof structures

The basic pitched-roof types that have been handed down by traditional craftsmanship are the purlin roof and the rafter roof. The purlin roof in its simplest form can be used as a flat roof.

Purlin roofs

Purlin roofs consist of foot, middle and ridge purlins (or ridge beams), the roof trusses on which the middle and ridge purlins lie, and the rafters. This structurally simple system can be used for all kinds of roof forms and plan types. With a purlin roof, the loads are carried principally by the internal walls. The external walls are only moderately loaded.

Flat roofs, as well as simple and compound mono-pitch roofs made using inclined rafters, can be regarded as the simplest forms of purlin roof. According to the size of the roof and its span, purlin roofs can be constructed with a simple standing roof truss (in the long direction, as a support for the ridge purlin and without middle purlins), and go up to a quadruple standing roof truss over three roof levels. In the latter case, struts can also be used.

Rafter roofs

Rafter roofs span a roof space without internal supports and are suitable for roof pitches of between 30 and 60 degrees. The rafters are connected at the ridge to create a triangular, structurally determinate construction. The roof loads are transferred exclusively to the external walls, which makes the construction of the points, where the rafters rest, more complicated. Rafter construction is less suitable for roofs with cut-out sections, roofs with dormer windows, hipped roofs or roofs over angled floor plans.

Collar-beam roofs

Collar-beam roofs are essentially rafter roofs with a horizontal tie (collar) below the level of the ridge. Using timbers of the same cross-sectional area, they support larger spans than the simple rafter roof.

Flat roofs

To avoid pooling of water on the roof surface, flat roofs should have a minimum slope of 2 percent. Solid timber joists used as single-span beams are suitable for spans of up to 4.5 m, and as continuous beams for spans of up to 6 m. For longer spans, the use of glued laminated beams or other laminated or compound elements is recommended.

Bracing

The bracing for a roof in the transverse direction is provided by the roof structure itself. In the long direction, braces are needed to take up the wind loads and the stabilising forces from walls and supports. These can be in the form of wind braces or panels made of a timber-based material.

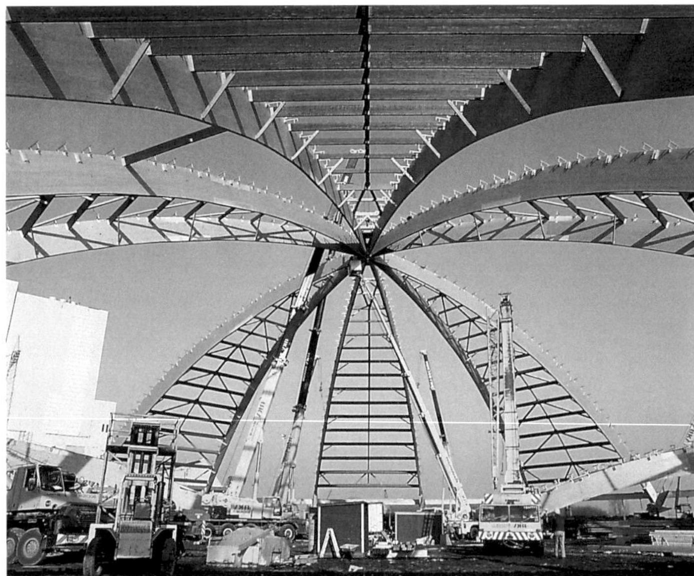

A structure adapted to its function: bulk material storage shed for coal

Hall roofs

There are various systems of primary and secondary timber-built structures that can be used to economically bridge medium to large spans. These building elements can be made of solid timber, laminated layers (glued laminated timber, veneered laminated timber, parallel strand timber), compound cross-sections (web beams, box beams) or using trusses (different kinds of trusses, three-dimensional systems). The methods used to join these building elements range from conventional nails to innovative steel nodes. Each of these structures has a particular span range that is determined by the laws of statics, the building regulations and the dictates of economy.

Flat-roof structures

Flat roofs are frequently used in industrial and commercial buildings for reasons of economy. Inexpert working of the roof skin and roofing materials, whose long-term performance had not been adequately researched, has led in the past to expensive repairs, making the initial savings appear relative.

The following constructions are suitable for flat roofs:
– structural timber sections, solid timber sorted according to strength, double and triple built-up beams and Kreuzbalken (Kreuzbalken are produced by sawing a log into four quarters, turning them 180 degrees so that the curved sides of the quarter beams all face inwards, then gluing them together, leaving a hole running lengthways at the centre of the beam). All such beams have improved structural qualities: spans of up to 7 m

– glued laminated timber: spans of 7 to 40 m
– parallel-chord trusses: spans of 5 to 50 m
– parallel-chord trusses made of glued laminated timber: spans of 20 to 80 m
– supported beams: spans of 8 to 80 m
– grid lattices: Grid lattice structures are built up of beams that meet at a particular angle. They are either rigidly connected to each other at these junctions or continue, stiffened, through the junctions. By connecting the elements together they all work to transfer the load.
– space frames: In a simple truss, each joint is formed by two rods meeting on the same plane, whereas in a space frame the junctions consist of three rods meeting on different planes. A spherical jointing piece is required to form this junction. If timber rods are used (laminated rods are also an option), a light filigree structure that can be used for various roof types, ranging from canopies to manufacturing and warehouse buildings, can be produced.
– planar shells: Normally a roof structure consists of primary and secondary beams. If panel-like materials with a high load-bearing capacity are used instead, the size of the structure can be reduced. The panels transfer the vertical traffic loads and the stiffening forces. The panels are laid at right angles to the main load-bearing system. The joints in the long direction are positioned over the beams. If the cross-section of the roof surface is broken up into a compression zone (panel material) and a tension zone (steel tension cables or rods), a kind of three-dimensional frame is created. This spoked-wheel effect allows larger spans to be roofed with relatively thin timber-based panels without the use of internal supports.

Description	Structural system	Sketch	Span l (m)	Depth of beam	Distance between beams	Roof pitch $(\alpha)°$
Trusses	triangular-shaped truss		7.5 to 30	$h \geqq \dfrac{l}{10}$	4 to 10 m	12 to 30°
			7.5 to 20	$h_m \geqq \dfrac{l}{10}$	4 to 10 m	12 to 30°
	trapezoid-shaped truss		7.5 to 30	$h \geqq \dfrac{l}{12}$	4 to 10 m	3 to 8°
			7.5 to 30	$h_m \geqq \dfrac{l}{12}$	4 to 10 m	3 to 8°
	parallel-chord truss		7.5 to 60	$h \geqq \dfrac{l}{12} - \dfrac{l}{15}$	4 to 10 m	–
			7,5 to 60	$h \geqq \dfrac{l}{12} - \dfrac{l}{15}$	4 to 10 m	–
			7.5 to 60	$h \geqq \dfrac{l}{12} - \dfrac{l}{15}$	4 to 10 m	–
Trussed frames	three-hinged frame		structural timber frame 15 to 30; frame with gluleam supports 25 to 50	$\dfrac{l}{12}$	structural timber frame e = 4 to 6 m; wide-span frame e = 6 to 10 m	20°; –
	three-hinged frame single-sided		10 to 20	$\dfrac{l}{12}$	e = 4 to 6 m	3 to 8°
	two-hinged frame		structural timber frame 15 to 40; frame with gluelam members 25 to 60	$\dfrac{l}{12}$	structural timber frame e = 4 to 6 m; wide-span frame e = 6 to 10 m	3 to 8°; –
Box beams	box beams with web panels (parallel cross-section)		nailed: up to 20 glued: up to 40	up to 1.5 m	5 to 7.5 m	–
	box beams with web panels (dual-pitched roof beams with a horizontal bottom chord)		nailed: up to 20 glued up to 40	up to 1.5 m	5 to 7.5 m	3 to 8°
	box beams made of gluelam		up to 40	up to 1.5 m	5 to 7.5 m	–
Glulam beams	single-bay beams		10 to 35	$\dfrac{l}{17}$	5 to 7.5 m	–
	single-span beams with dual-pitched roof form		10 to 35	$\dfrac{l}{16} / \dfrac{l}{30}$	5 to 7.5 m	3 to 8°
	single-span beams with dual-pitched roof form, underside folded upwards		10 to 35	$\dfrac{l}{16} / \dfrac{l}{30}$	5 to 7.5 m	max. 12°
	single-bay beams mono-pitched form		10 to 35	$\dfrac{l}{18} / \dfrac{l}{25}$	5 to 7.5 m	8 to 12°
Grid of beams made of gluelam	grid of beams made of gluelam		up to 25	$\dfrac{l}{18} / \dfrac{l}{25}$ of the shorter span	–	–

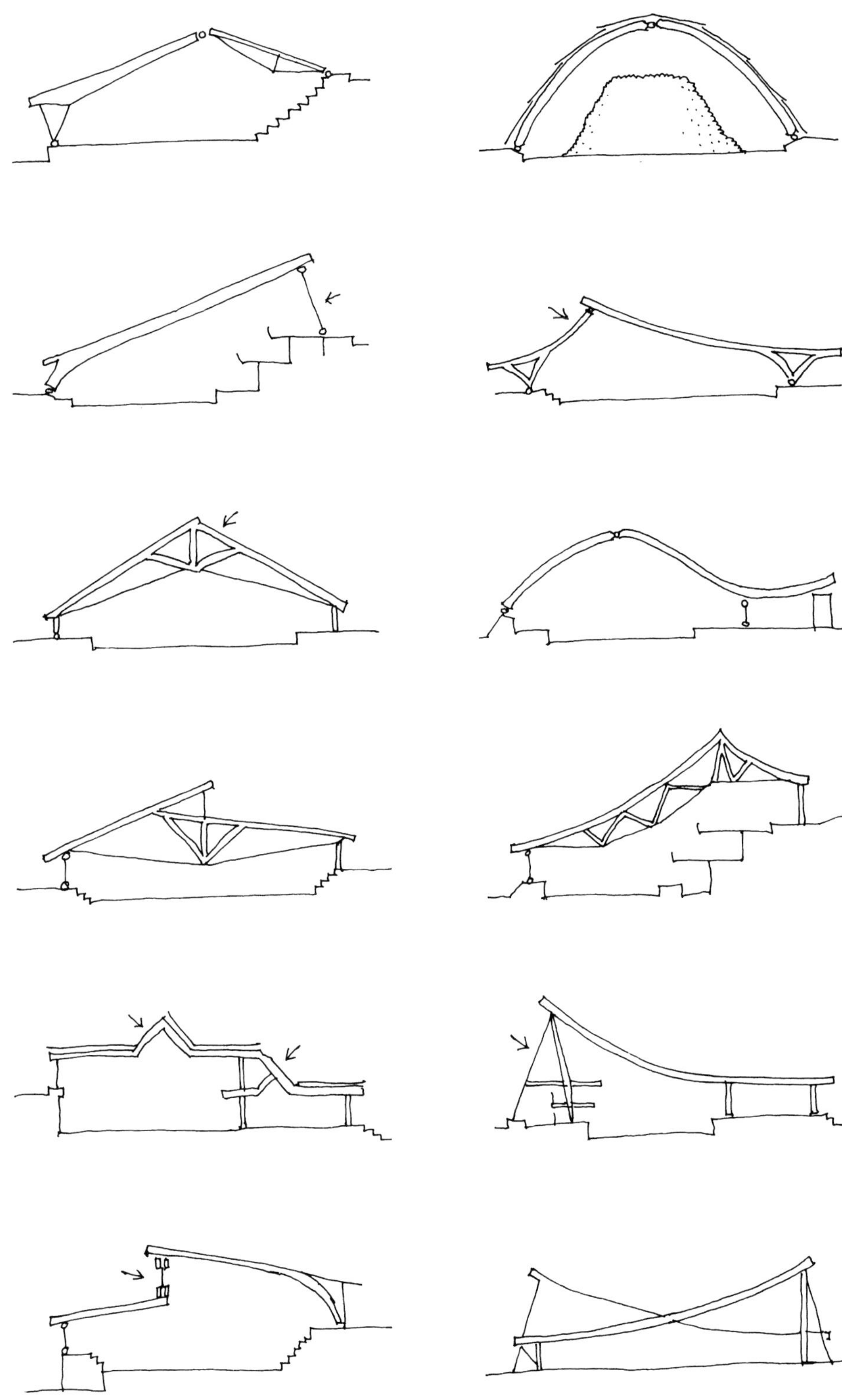

Examples of the adaptation of timber structural systems to various design situations, such as adaptation to the terrain, function (bulk materials) or lighting.

Gable (duo pitch) roofs

The classic rafter, collar, and purlin roofs with pitches of between 30 and 60 degrees and maximum spans of 10 m are suitable for smaller buildings, offices and workshops. In the area of hall construction, where greater spans are involved, specially treated wood-based materials and/or composite timber elements are used.

For gable roofs the following structures are suitable:
– gluelam trusses with inclined top chords (trapezoid beams): spans 12 to 30 m
– pitched-roof trusses: spans 7.5 to 30 m
– pitched-roof trusses with raised eaves: spans 20 to 50 m
– three-pin trusses: spans 20 to 70 m
– two-pin lattice frames: spans 10 to 60 m
– three-pin trusses of gluelam and other building elements: spans 15 to 35 m
– three-pin gluelam frames: spans 15 to 40 m
– two-pin gluelam frames

Mono-pitch roofs

The mono-pitch roof is less problematic in terms of construction than the flat roof. All structural systems that can be used for flat roofs are, in principle, suitable for mono-pitch roofs as well.

Structures with:
– timber joists, structural timber sorted according to strength, double and triple built-up beams and Kreuzbalken (see note on Kreuzbalken above under flat roofs on page 78): spans up to 7 m
– gluelam: spans 7 to 40 m
– parallel-chord trusses: spans 5 to 50 m
– parallel-chord trusses made of gluelam: spans 20 to 80 m
– mono-pitch trusses: spans 7.5 to 20 m
– mono-pitch trusses with raised eaves: spans 7.5 to 35 m
– supported beams: spans 8 to 80 m

Barrel-vaulted roofs

Simply curved roofs are suitable for large free-spans (fair buildings) and for halls that, because of their particular function, need a certain clear internal cross-sectional area.

The structures suitable for barrel-vaulted roofs include:
– gluelam trusses (two-pin arches): spans 20 to 100 m
– gluelam trusses (three-pin arches): spans 20 to 60 m
– arched trusses: spans 40 to 120 m
– rhomboid grid shell structures: The variations of the so-called Zollinger-Lamellenbauweise (Zollbauweise), at times made using gluelam, allow greater spans and are made with small uniform elements that are fixed together using screwed joints. This means that these roofs can also be taken down again easily. The individual lamellas, or fins, are cut curved on one side to fit the shape of the roof, while the ends are cut off at an angle. Examples include the fair halls in Rimini (see p. 82) and Friedrichshafen (see p. 90).

Domes, suspended structures, folded plates and spatial shells

Roofing large spaces without internal supports is in the domain of engineered timber construction. Here, surface structures have particular advantages as they offer a high load-bearing capacity and define space with a particular aesthetic effect. In addition, a wide range of different forms is possible. Domed structures can be made of individual rods in the form of a lattice or gluelam ribs arranged in a radial pattern. Folded plates consist of planar materials that are connected to each other in a way that increases the shear resistance. One or two dimensionally curved shell structures can be created by lattices made up of rods and/or wood-based panels.

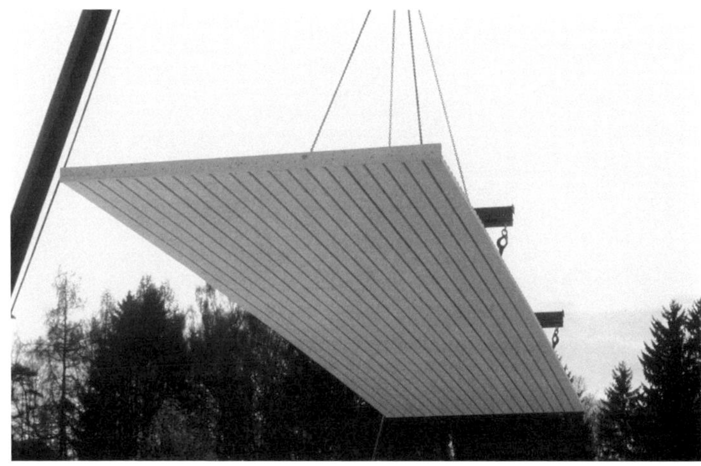

The fixing of prefabricated *Lignotrend* – acoustic elements for roof and ceiling

Roof structure systems possible in timber construction, with their different methods of transferring loads

Load transferred by:	**1** Beam	**2** Members	**3** Frame
forces at bearing points under vertical loads	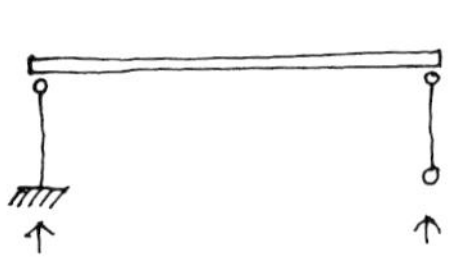	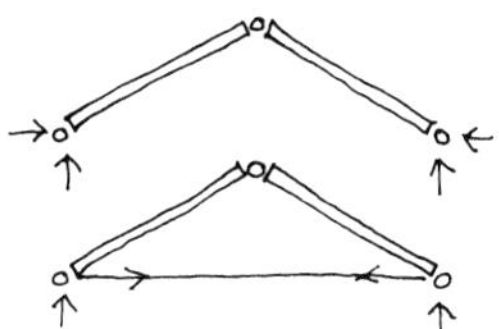	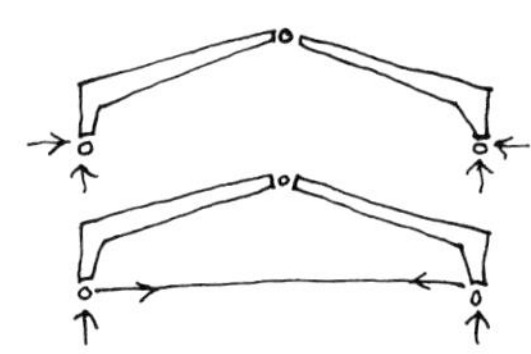
predominantly subject to compression stress	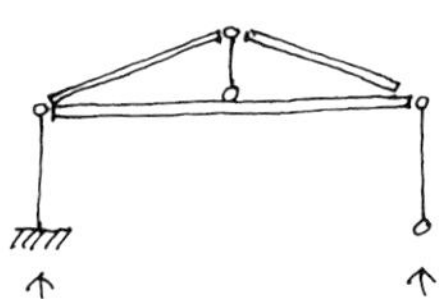	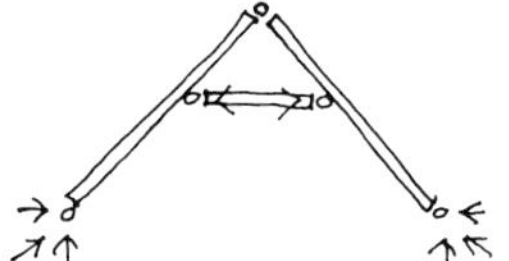	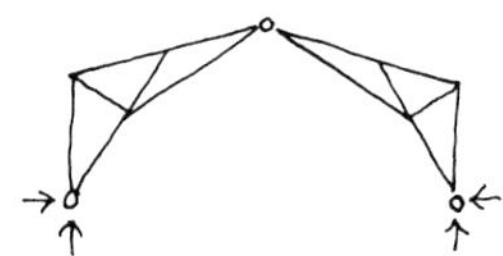
predominantly subject to tensile stress	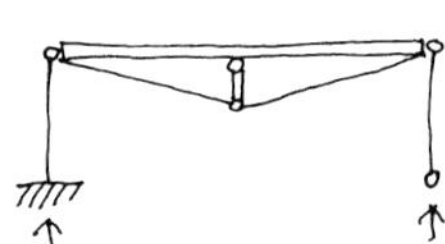	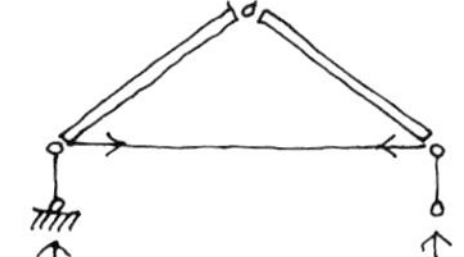	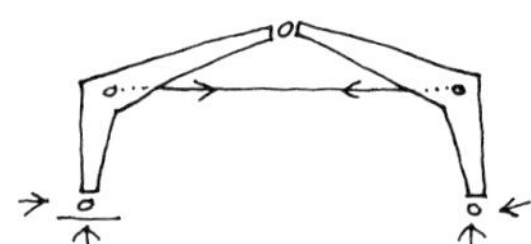
predominantly subject to tensile and compression stresses	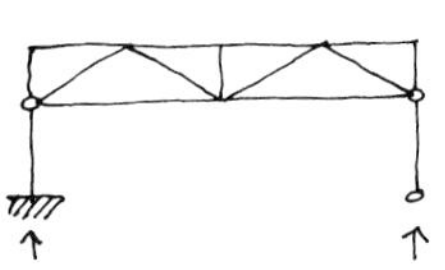	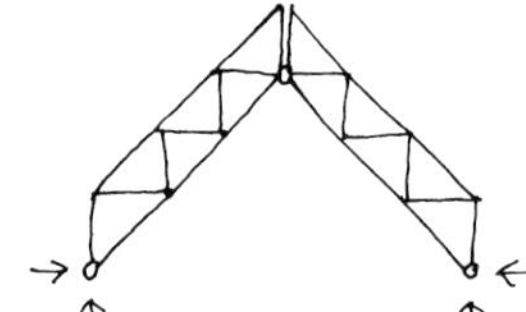	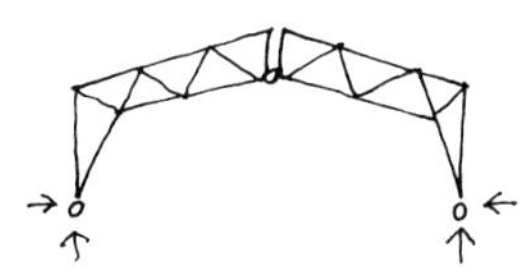
predominantly subject to bending	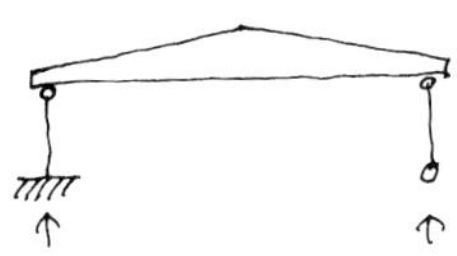	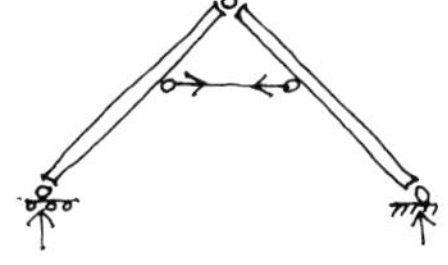	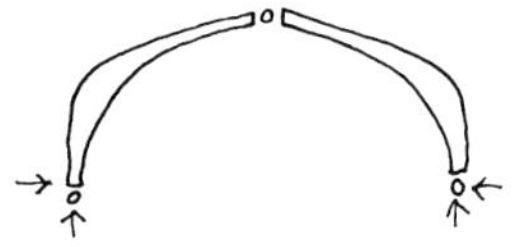
arranged radially	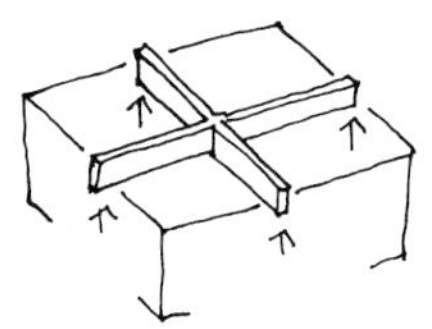	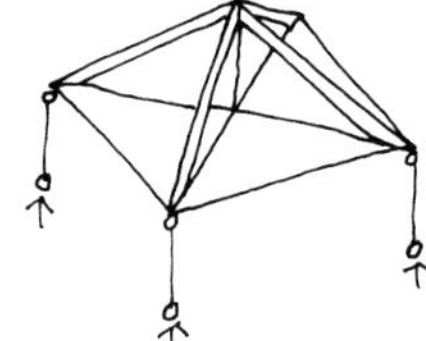	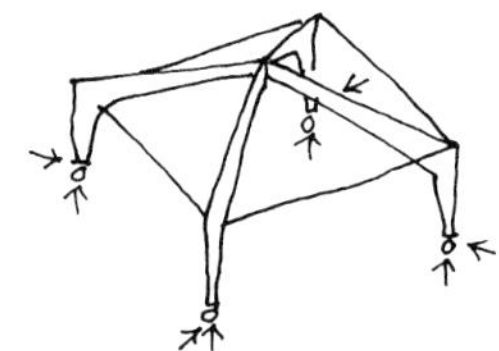
made up of surfaces put together	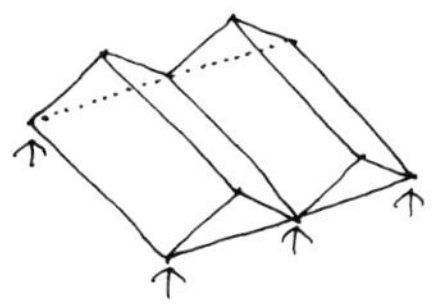	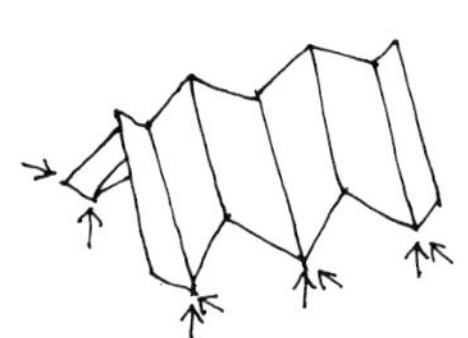	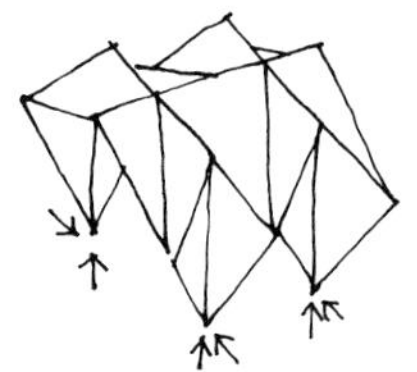

4 Arches   **5** Cantilever arm (based on 1–4)   **6** Hanging systems (based on 1–4)   **7** Suspension systems

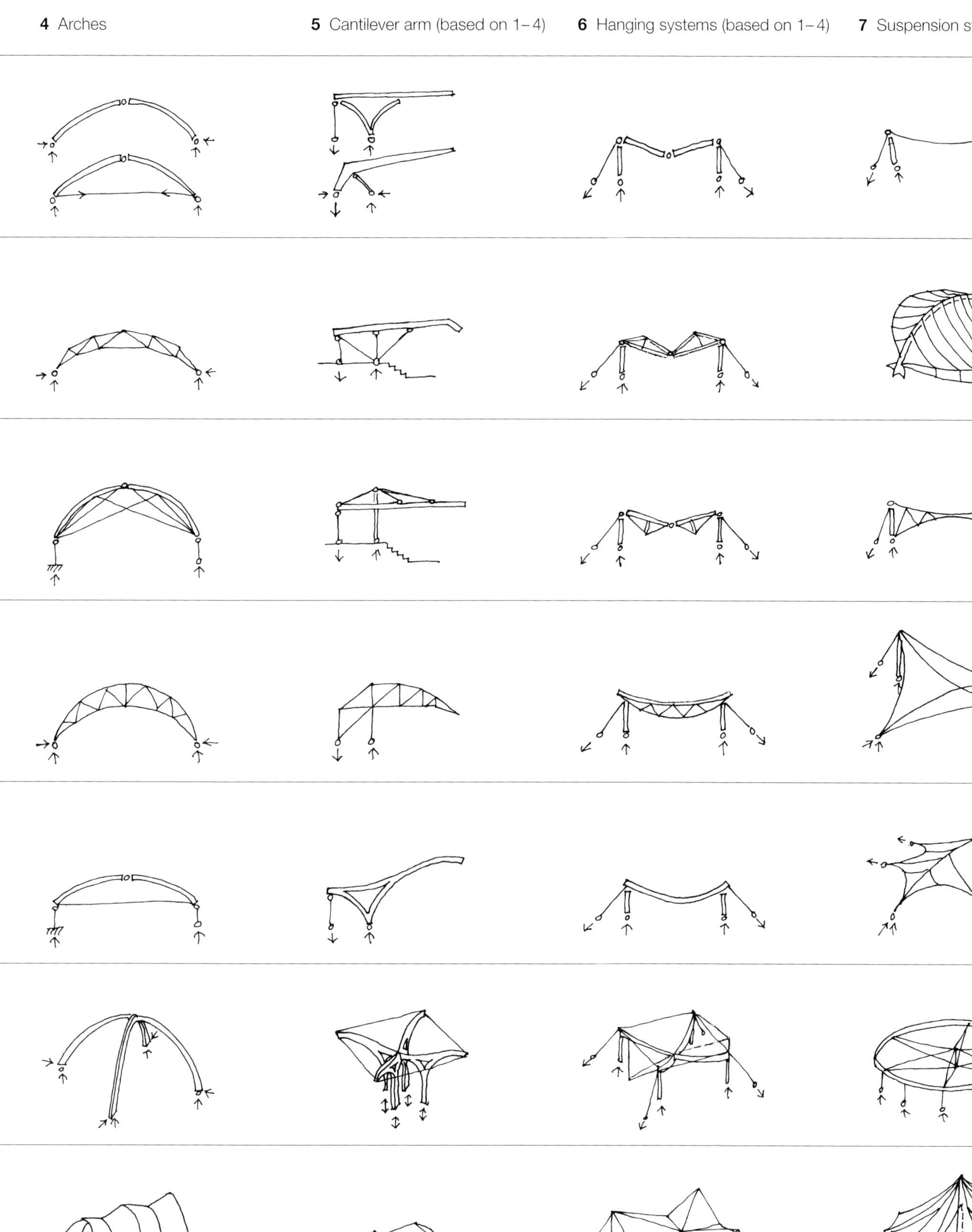

FACE

Facades made of wood-based materials

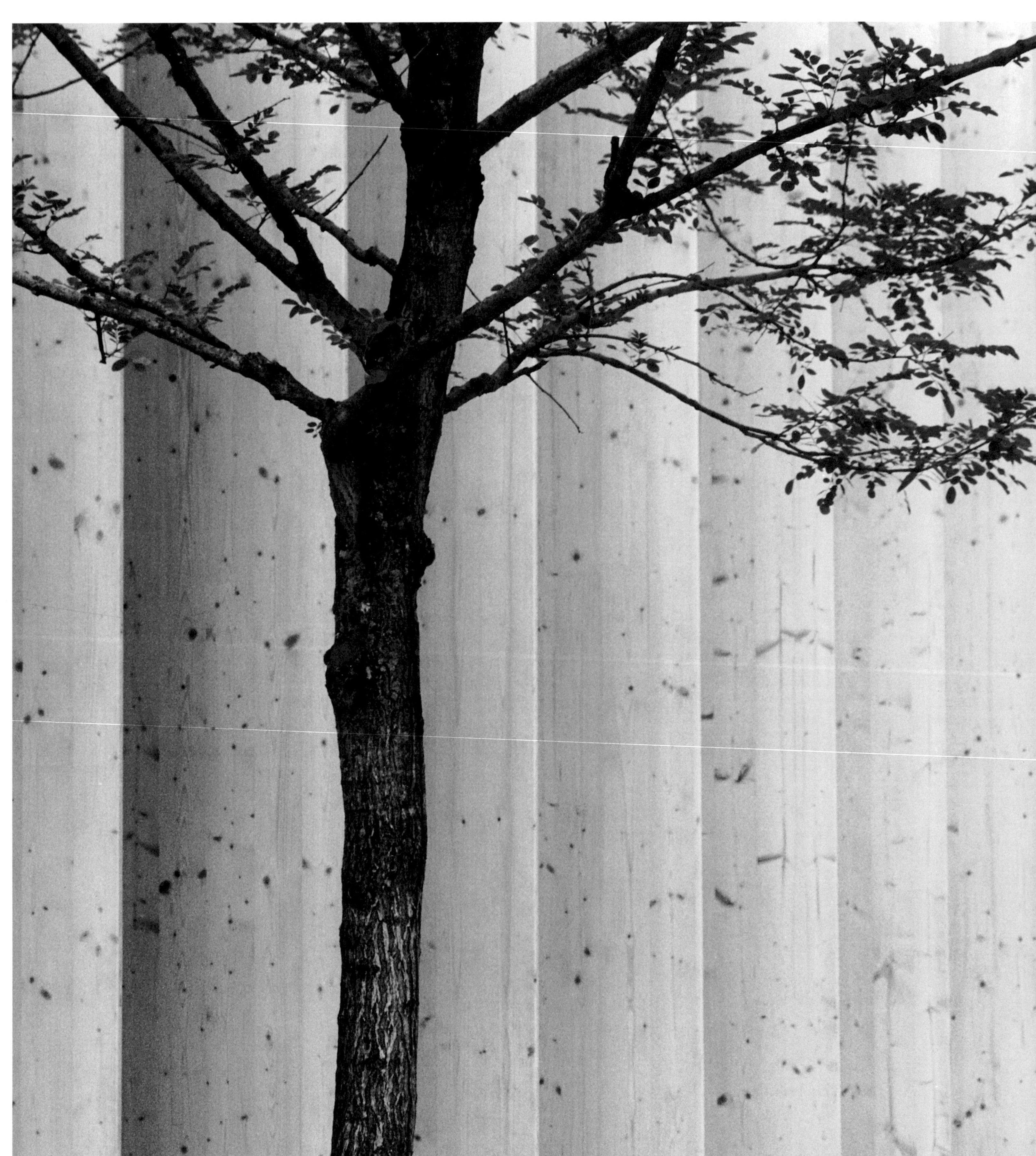

The facade cladding, the outermost layer of the building wall, is what largely determines the appearance of a building. In addition, the external cladding must provide protection from the elements. Wood and wood-based materials are well-suited to this task, as they have a pleasant visual appearance and, if employed properly, have a long life. In addition, in case of damage (for example, damage by vehicles), individual parts of the cladding can be easily replaced. In planning and building facades, criteria such as selection of the right wood, wood preservation, fire safety and surface treatment must all be taken into account.

Materials

Solid wood

Most wooden claddings are made out of sawn wood, solid boards that, according to their cross-sectional form and profile, require a specific method of fixing and produce different surface effects.

Organic materials such as wood possess qualities that are based on their anatomical cellular structure. Due to their naturally grown structure, the mechanical and biophysical qualities and values of wood differ according to direction of the grain. This anisotropic quality is illustrated clearly in the characteristics of swelling and shrinking, which must be taken into consideration when using wood externally. Wood is hygroscopic and thus always seeks to reach a balance with the surrounding air by absorbing or releasing moisture. Up to its fibre saturation point – which on average lies at a wood moisture content of around 28 percent – the structure of wood expands when it absorbs moisture and shrinks when it loses moisture. In the direction of the grain this shrinkage is insignificant; radially, it is 4.3 percent and, tangentially, it is 8.3 percent, on average. The extent of the change in dimensions is dependent on the kind of wood and its gross density, as well as its anatomical and chemical composition. These alterations in dimensions should be taken into account when selecting a particular wood, in the fixing method used and, finally, in the treatment of the surface. A rule of thumb for suitable cross-sections for façade boarding is: minimum thickness 18 mm, maximum width 160 mm. The moisture content of wood at the time of fixing should be around 18 percent ± 6 percent and should, as far as possible, match the expected equilibrium moisture content.

Shingles

Wooden shingles are made, in various shapes and sizes, out of fir, larch, oak, and western red cedar. Conically and parallel sawn and split shingles or shakes are available. They are generally fixed overlapping, with the joints staggered, at a distance of a few millimetres from a substructure of battens placed at close intervals or a wood sheeting. The use of wooden shingles in commercial buildings is particularly widespread in North America.

Wood panels

Today, alongside solid wood products, predominantly wood-based materials are used as external panels, and complete systems with special sections for every detail are available. They are more dimensionally stable than solid wood and offer greater design possibilities. Three- and five-ply panels of softwood with thicknesses of between 16 and 75 mm have proved successful as a facade material. The layers, glued at right angles to each other, are generally made of larch or Douglas fir, durable woods suitable for external use that do not require any surface treatment. Large-scale facade claddings can be produced using this material.

Plywood sheets

Building veneer plywood is regarded as weatherproof when it is produced with a water-resistant adhesive. But the term "weatherproof" is not a guarantee of suitability for use outdoors because differences in tension between the covering layer and the second veneer layer at right angles to it or the layer of adhesive beneath can lead to partial peeling. In the case of facade plywood, only those products expressly recommended by the producer of facades (and with the appropriate guarantee) should be used.

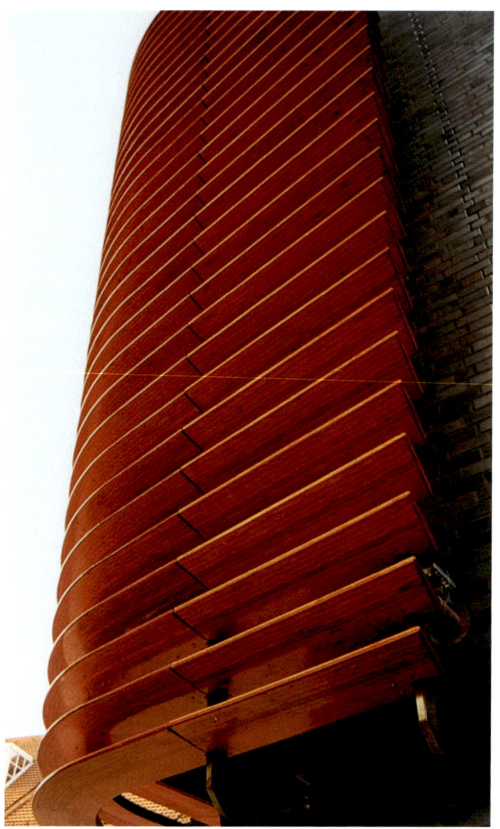

Salamander shoe shop in Muenster (Germany), 1993. Sun-shade lamellas made of laminated veneer panels with a high-solid polyurethane coating

Laminated veneer timber

With a sheet width of 2.5 m, laminated veneer timber offers new possibilities in the design of large facade areas. Made up of veneer layers that are not always glued at an angle of 90 degrees to each other, in many products the grain of all the layers runs in the same direction, or only a few layers have the grain running in the transverse direction. In comparison with plywood, laminated veneer timber offers greater tolerance of bending in the long direction of the veneers. The gluing together of the layers effectively distributes any weaknesses in the timber construction, which increases the stability. The cross banding effect makes this sheet material relatively stable in terms of form; even in cases of one-sided or intensive exposure to moisture, the dimensions hardly change at all. This is particularly important for external claddings. The material can be curved using an appropriate radius.

Cement-bound chipboard

Chipboard and fibreboard panels that use cement as a binding agent are very durable and have low flammability so that they can be used where low distances to neighbouring buildings prohibit the use of other wood-based materials, or in multi-storey buildings where the spread of fire must be hindered. Changing humidity levels cause only slight warping. However, they are more difficult to work than either solid wood or laminated timber materials. Cement-bound wood panels are available untreated, sanded and with coloured surfaces. They can be coated with the standard paint and render systems.

Substructure and fixing

Whether a back-ventilated substructure is necessary when timber is used externally is a matter of debate in expert circles. The main concern is that driving rain should not be able to penetrate behind the facade. If back-ventilated claddings are specified, then counter battens are generally necessary. In the case of staggered vertical boarding, the back ventilation is provided by a substructure of transverse battens. For the substructure roof battens measuring 24–48 mm and 30–50 mm as well as timber sections from 40–60 mm upwards are suitable and should have a maximum moisture content of 20 percent. The distance between the battens depends on the thickness of the boards. 18-mm-thick boards require battens at 40-cm intervals, while if the cladding is 22 mm thick, the battens only need to be at 55-cm intervals. In the case of large-scale panels, particular attention should be paid to a secure substructure and fixing. Ventilation openings should be provided with protective grilles against pests.

Solid profiled sections can be fixed invisibly to the substructure with special clamps or visibly fixed using nails or screws made of rust-free austenite steel or aluminium. Smooth-edged boards and panels of wood-based materials are generally screwed visibly using self-boring screws. But even with this type of screw, pre-drilled holes should be made to prevent splitting the wood. Wood-based sheets can be fixed invisibly using split battens or a system of metal sections.

Arrangement

Water run-off is less problematic with vertical board claddings than it is with horizontal ones. The systems available include tongue-and-groove boarding, staggered vertical boarding, vertical boarding with cover battens, or vertical boarding with open joints over counter battens. Each system has its own attractions in design terms. Claddings using boards and battens – screwed in a way that does not prevent changes in the dimensions of the wood – offer the advantage of parts that can be easily replaced without damaging the entire cladding. For horizontal cladding, profiled boards (tongue-and-groove) are used (whereby the tongue is always at the bottom to prevent accumulation of water) as well as various kinds of overlapping claddings that are preferable to the former because they are more efficient in leading off water. Rebated and non-rebated weatherboarding is laid with the boards overlapping; this overlap should be at least 12 percent of the covering width of the board.

Grids or lattices of wooden louvers, fixed at a distance from a substructure, have become fashionable in recent times and offer delightful alternatives with visual functions such as the deflection of light and the provision of shade. In such cases, a second layer must be provided that leads off the water.

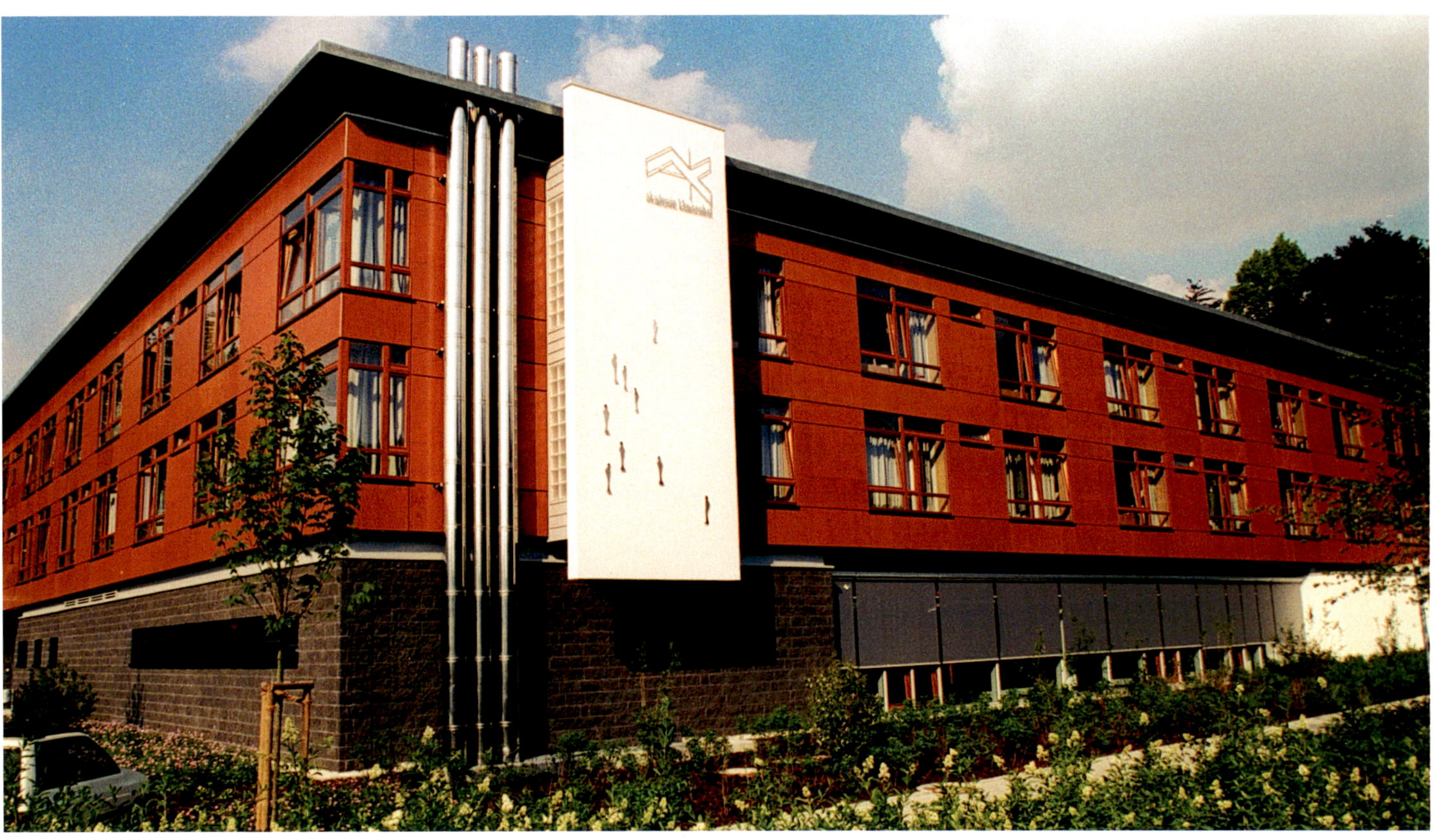

Klausenhof academy building in Rhede (Germany), 1995. Facade of multi-laminate wood panels with high-solid polyurethane coating

Protection of wood through building measures

Under certain conditions of climate and time, fungi and insects can attack an organic material like wood. When used externally, in addition to the constructional methods of protecting wood that aim to lead water off quickly and prevent uncontrolled insect damage, chemical wood protection measures must also be considered, particularly when woods without natural resistance to such attacks are used. Certain substances in wood are not only responsible for its natural durability but also for its colour. Water-soluble substances in wood can lead to discolouring when it is painted. This can be prevented by the use of an isolating primer coat. (See below)

The construction-based methods of wood protection for a facade include: an adequately projecting roof; covering projecting horizontal edges with Z-shaped metal sections; sealing exposed end grains of timbers; and maintaining sufficient distance from the ground (at least 30 cm) to provide protection from rain water bouncing upwards. In general, measures need to be taken that prevent the penetration of water into the ends of the wood, avert water from gathering in the construction and facilitate the rapid run-off of moisture. The joint is not only a design element in the facade but a technical detail that must be carefully designed. The number of horizontal joints should be kept to a minimum. Overlapping and metal sections help to lead off water. Vertical joints can be either backed with a batten or covered with a cover strip.

Untreated surfaces

Without surface treatment wood used outdoors ages in a gradual, dignified way. This aging process has almost become a trademark of wood and involves the wood turning grey (due to the effects of ultraviolet light and the weather), the development of fine cracks and a gradual roughening of the surface. Like the irregularities in natural wood, the aging process is accepted by the client if it does not mean a shorter life span. The changes in untreated wood caused by weathering are never uniform. They depend on climatic conditions, orientation, protective overhanging roofs, shadow and planting, and can differ even within a single facade. The changes of colour (patina) range from light silvery grey to brownish black.

Chemical wood preservation

Monitoring agencies in various countries not only regulate the stability (statics) of buildings, but often examine building elements that are neither load-bearing nor have a stiffening function, because their incorrect use could pose a threat to general safety. One example is the failure to protect external claddings from damage caused by fungus or insect attack. In this case, many clients insist upon chemical preservation methods. Wood elements can be impregnated with environmentally friendly, chromate-free, wood preservation materials using a pressurized tank process.

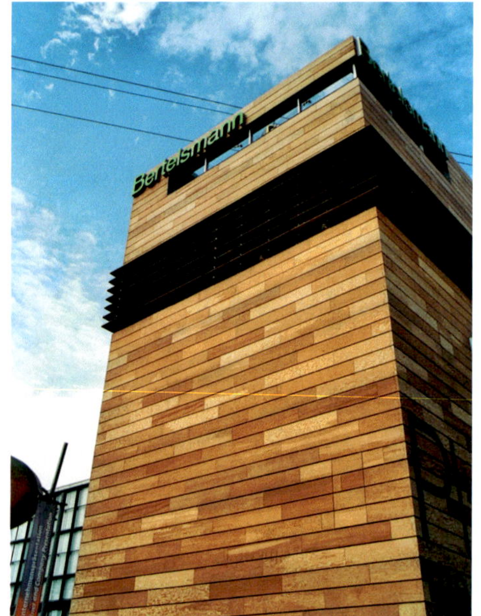

Bertelsmann exhibition pavilion in Hanover (Germany), 2000. Facade cladding of American facade plywood panels, relief-brushed and glazed

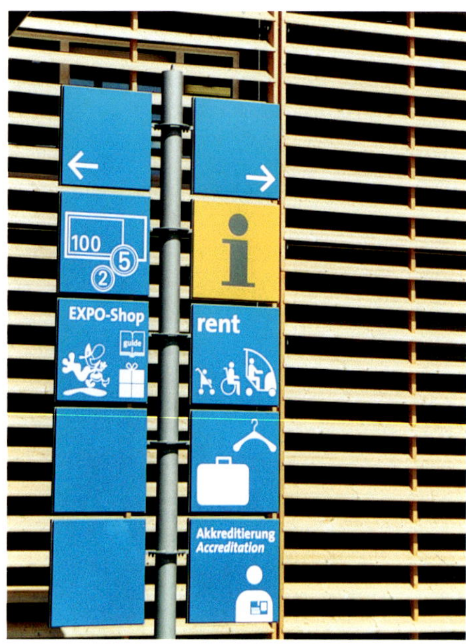

Restaurant in Hanover (Germany), 2000. Facade cladding is of profiled pine boards, with natural finish

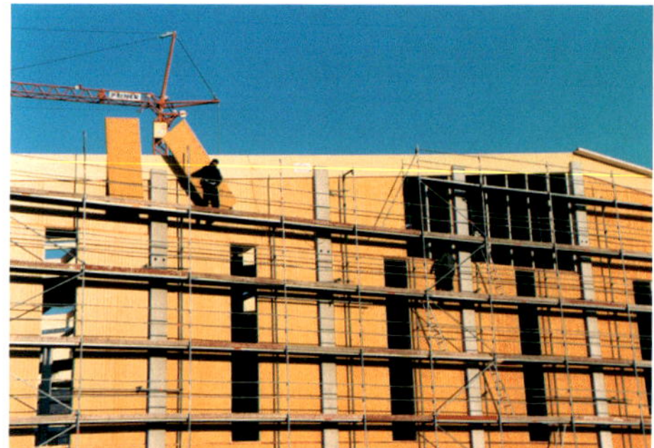

South facade of the Dold-Logistikzentrum in Buchenbach (Germany). Fitting Dold three-ply laminate panels in spruce with a pine finish

Surface treatment

When used externally, wood does not need any surface treatment. However, if one wishes to avoid the natural aging process (which does not represent a technical defect), only coatings containing pigment offer protection against UV light. The more pigment the coating contains, the more protection against UV damage it provides. Therefore, clear varnishes and colourless glazes – with the exception of highly elastic, high-solid coating systems on a polyurethane base – are not suitable for wood surfaces that are exposed to weather and sunlight. The intensity of the weathering process depends on the geographic location, the orientation and the climatic conditions that the building element is exposed to. The coating system employed should be selected according to these criteria.

The method of working the wood surface also affects the effectiveness of coatings, both from a decorative point of view and in terms of the durability of the coating. Good ground for coatings is provided by smooth (sanded or hydroplaned) wood surfaces without roughened, exposed fibres. Sawn surfaces are highly absorptive and offer good binding qualities for thin (low viscosity) coating systems. With high viscosity coatings, the adhesiveness is reduced, as tiny air cushions on the surface negatively affect the durability of the coating. When such systems are used, edges should be rounded off in order to improve adhesion in these extreme areas.

Primer
The primer is the element in a coating system that has the function of ensuring the adhesion of the coating. In addition, there are primers that contain fungicides against blue stain fungus or mould and primers that provide a protective layer against discolouring by substances contained in the wood. They are generally colourless but are also available with pigment.

Glazes
The characteristic of glazes is their semi-transparency with a binding agent content that, in thin film glazes, is around 30 percent and in thick film glazes ranges between 30 and 60 percent. High solid coatings have about 85 percent solid body content and can be applied in a single stage process. The lower the pigmentation the more clearly the grain of the wood is revealed. Low pigmentation glazes and colourless glazes are, however, not suitable for building elements exposed to the weather. Thin coat glazes provide a dry film thickness of 20–60 µm with thick film glazes the figure is 60–80 µm. This dry film thickness is sufficient for dimensionally stable building elements. Glazes are available in various wood tones and a series of colours, as either solvent- or water-based systems.

Paint systems
Once they have hardened, opaque coatings (with an alkyd resin or acrylic resin base and other synthetic resins) form a protective layer over the wood; they are applied over a primer that forms part of the system. Nowadays, water-based paints are used almost exclusively. According to the particular requirements of the job, either diffusion paints with a diffusion resistance µ-value below 5,000 (wood claddings) or diffusion resistant coating systems (µ-values over 12,000) can be used for windows and other dimensionally stable elements. The variety of colours available is almost limitless and any shade required can be mixed.

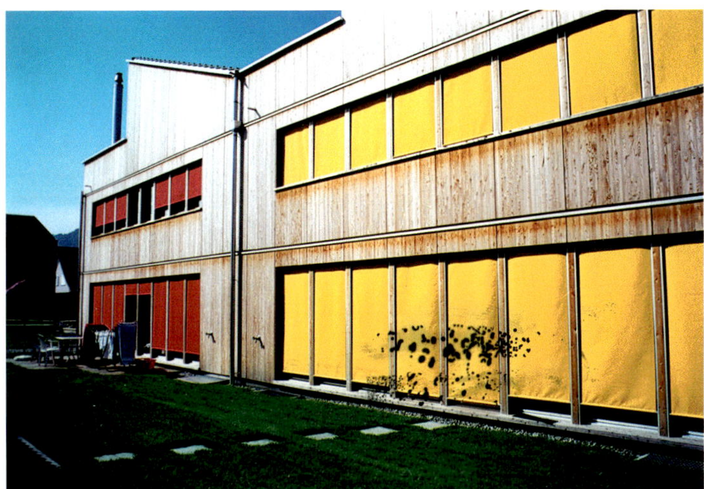

Facade cladding of *Kaufmann-K1-Multiplan*, three-ply laminate panels in larch. The untreated surface of the wood begins to turn grey after a number of years; the extent of this process depends on the weather and the direction the facade faces.

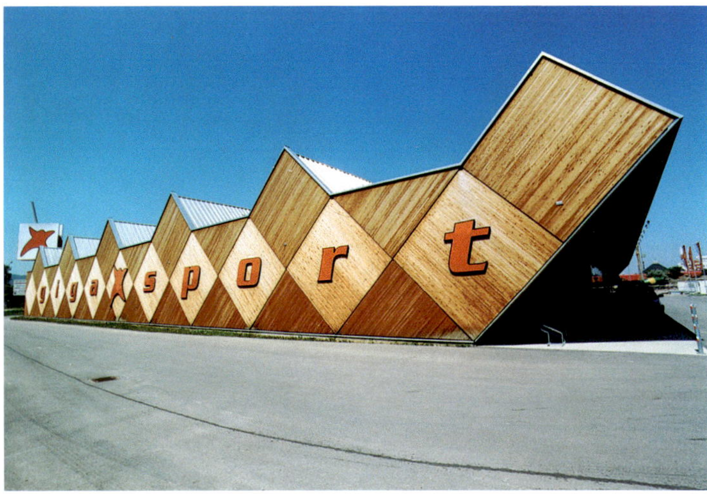

Facade of a shop of the Giga-Sportcenter chain in Austria. Facade cladding of *Kaufmann-K1-Multiplan*, three-ply laminate panels in larch

Fire protection

Generally speaking, facade materials with normal degrees of flammability can be used in lower buildings. This means that wood-based materials of all kinds can be employed. In the case of taller buildings, the use of low flammability materials is required in a number of countries. In such cases, cement bound chipboard or wood panels impregnated with flame-retardant materials can be used. Despite these regulations, buildings can be granted exemptions in individual cases, particularly when certain conditions have been met with regard to construction, the spread of fire, the escape routes or the distance to other buildings.

Preservation

There is no material that does not react chemically with air and water, the ultraviolet radiation of sunlight, or that is not damaged by the mechanical influences of the weather. Paints and coatings are no exception. When facade elements are expected to maintain their function over a long period of time, they must be examined at regular intervals and, when necessary, renovated. Maintenance refers to the preservation of the existing condition, while renovation means restoring the original functional condition.

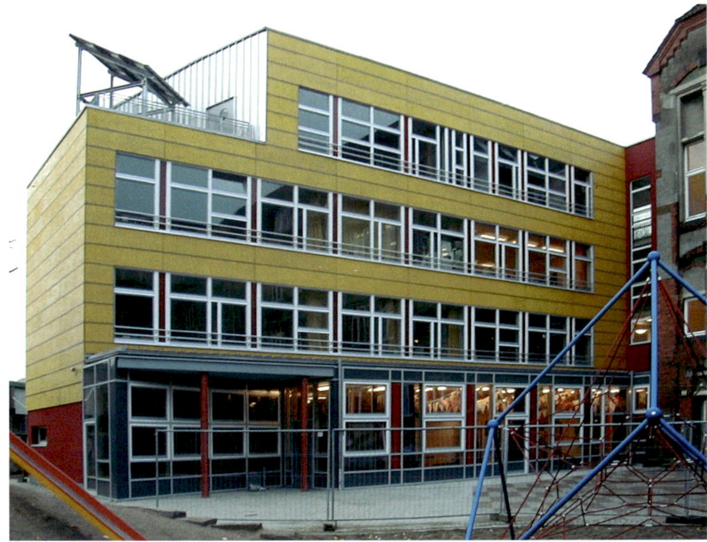

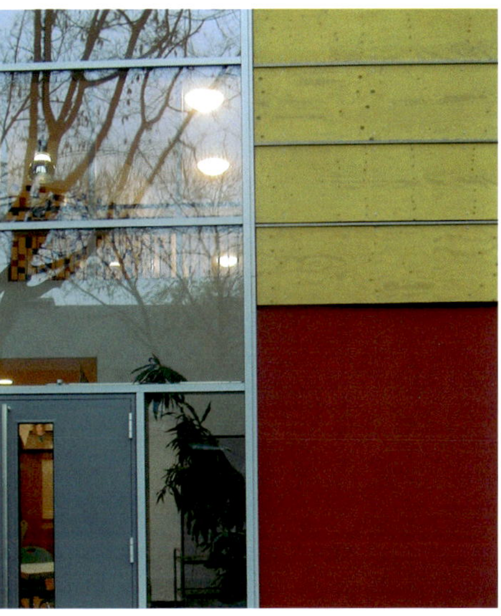

Training building in Hamburg (Germany), 2001. Facade design with *Merk-Igniplan* fire-resistant (F 30 B) treated veneered timber panels in yellow and red

FIRE!

Fire protection in timber building

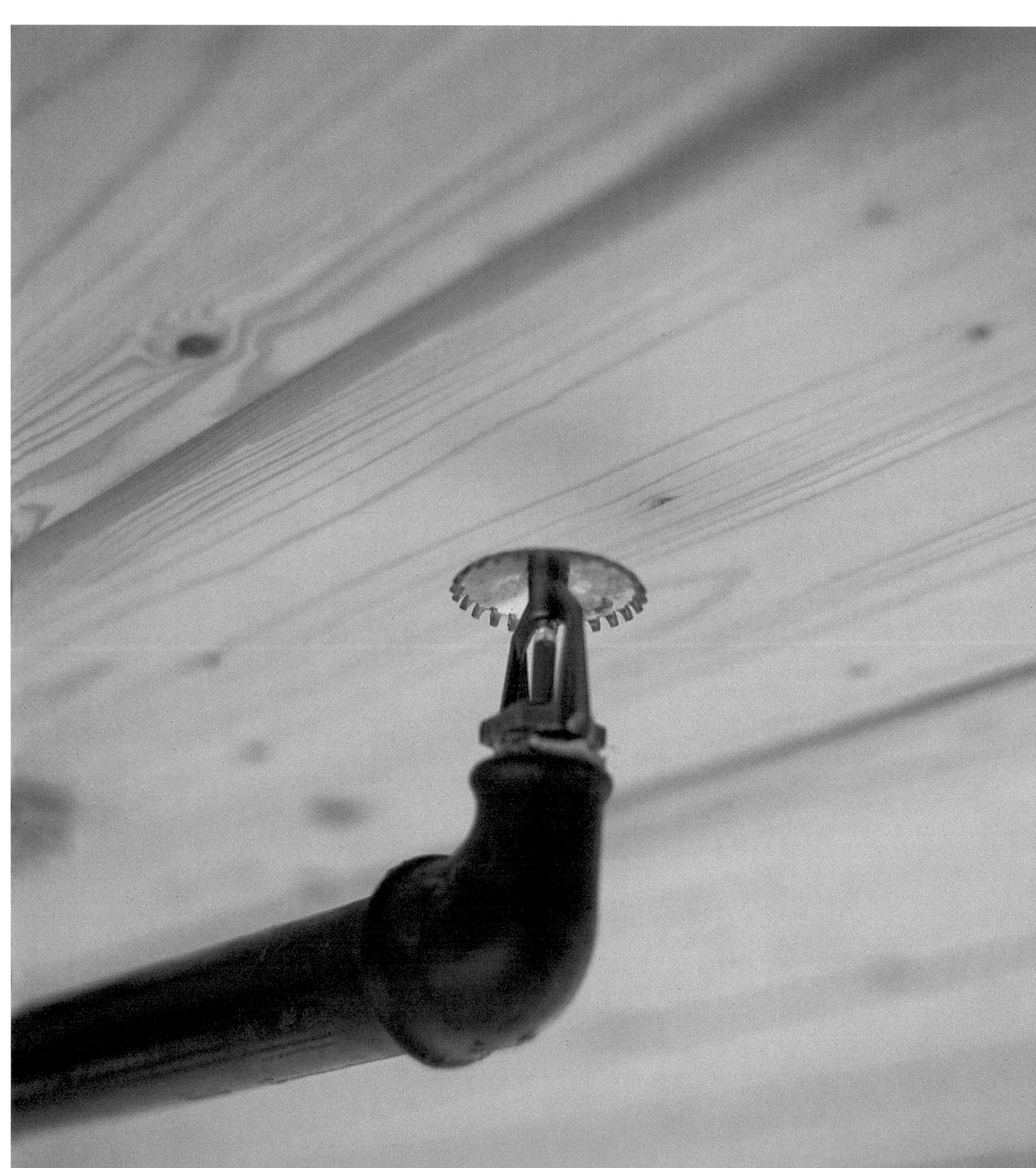

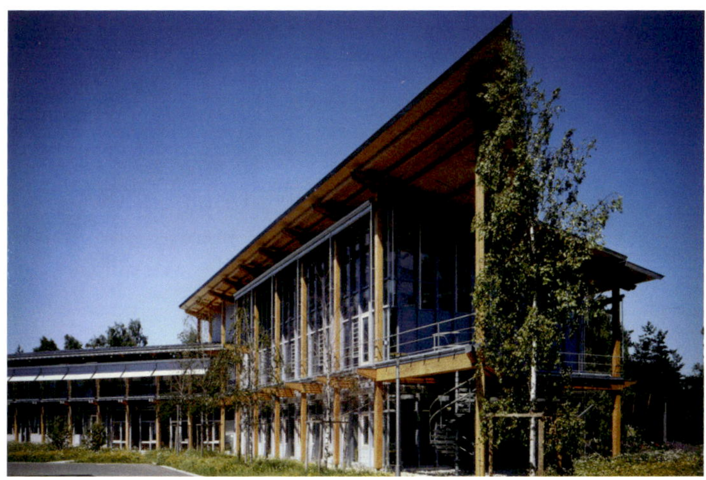

Office building of the Lux timber building company in Georgensmuend (Germany), 1993. No fire prevention requirements were imposed on the glue laminated timber skeleton frame, as the continuous maintenance balconies with access to the garden offer a quick means of escape in case of fire.

How should we interpret the fact that a number of new fire stations in Germany have been built in timber? After all, we all know that timber is a flammable material and it is subject to numerous regulations that define certain (often unjustifiable) boundaries within which its use is permitted. A certain change of approach in evaluating the performance of timber, and timber buildings, in the case of fire has become apparent. The simple awareness that timber is flammable is not the sole deciding factor in assessing the material's behaviour in a fire. For instance, taking into account the amounts of damage and danger to life, health and goods resulting from a fire, the fire prevention office in Munich arrived at the conclusion that the extent to which wood is used is immaterial. In contrast to the other phenomena that occur parallel to a fire, timber is relatively harmless. These factors, such as the smoke density and toxicity resulting from the fire, are decisive in terms of injury to people, which means that, from the point of view of the fire-fighting services, timber performs favourably in comparison to many other building materials. Many tests conducted on building materials do not correctly assess all the risks they involve, thus placing wood at a disadvantage.

Fire prevention legislation throughout various regions indicates that a standard of protection in buildings can be achieved by a number of different fire protection measures. Generally speaking, buildings with long halls can be separated by firewalls into individual fire compartments (for example, of 40 m in length) in order to prevent the rapid spread of fire and smoke. However, a subdivision of this kind is not always possible. Continuous shed spaces are a required for joinery halls in the timber building industry and for airplane hangars, for example. But fire prevention

concepts have also been worked out for buildings with specialised functions as well, which allow them to be built in timber. For instance, an aircraft hangar at Cologne-Bonn airport in western Germany was built as a composite system with an exposed timber roof structure. The local building legislation required that the main timber trusses spanning 94 metres should have a fire exposure rating of thirty minutes (F30-B). The client wanted a higher rating of 60 minutes (F60-B), which was achieved by increasing the cross-sectional size of the timber elements. The fire rating of the secondary trusses made of gluelam, and of the rest of the timber construction, was the required F30-B.

The behaviour of timber building elements in a fire

Organic building materials such as wood disintegrate at high temperatures (pyrolysis). The temperature at which they ignite depends on the moisture content of the wood and the length of time it has been heated. Distinctions are drawn between three different kinds of fires: the smouldering fire is a slow pyrolysis without flames in which the building material

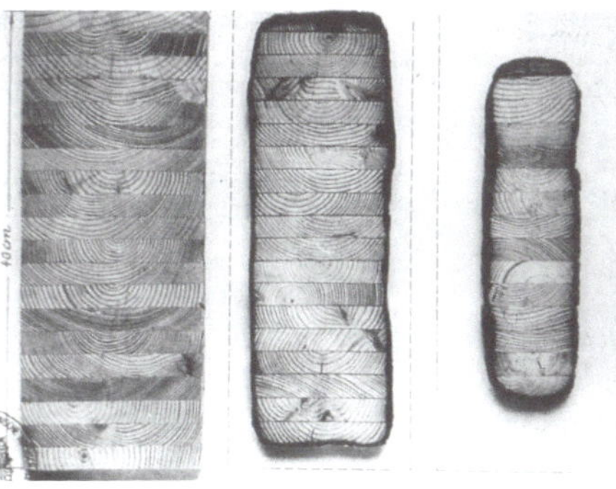

Cross-section through a glue laminated timber beam after 30 minutes and after 60 minutes of exposure to a fire. As the rate at which wood burns is known, the calculation of simple rectangular sections presents no problems.

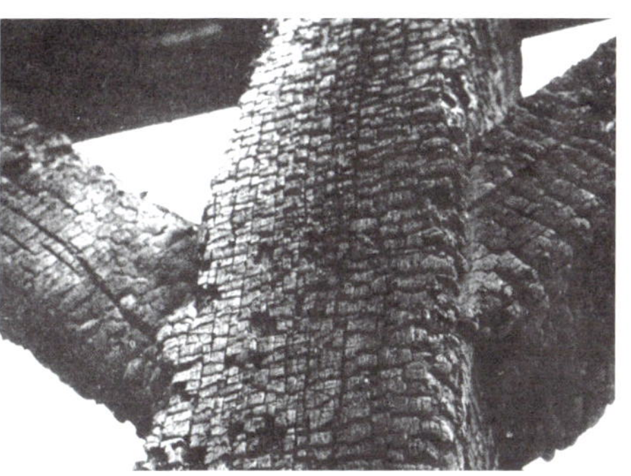

Solid timber column with angle struts after 40 minutes of exposure to fire

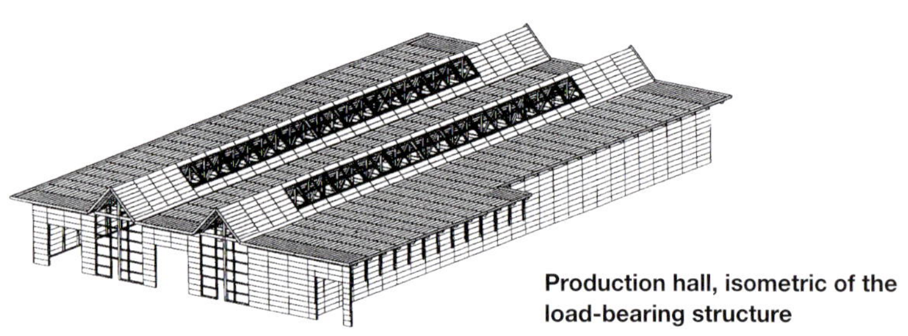

Production hall, isometric of the load-bearing structure

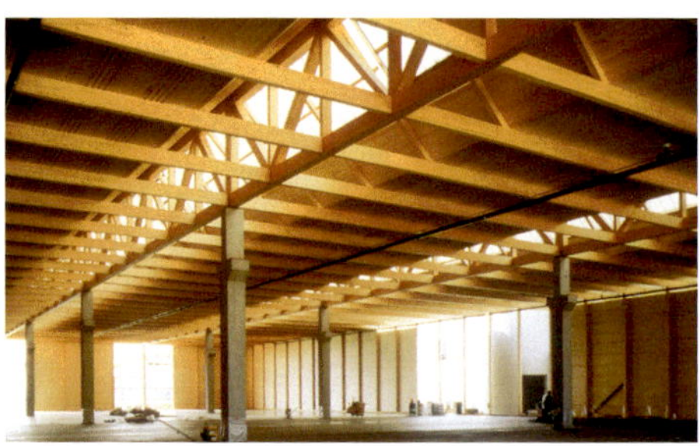

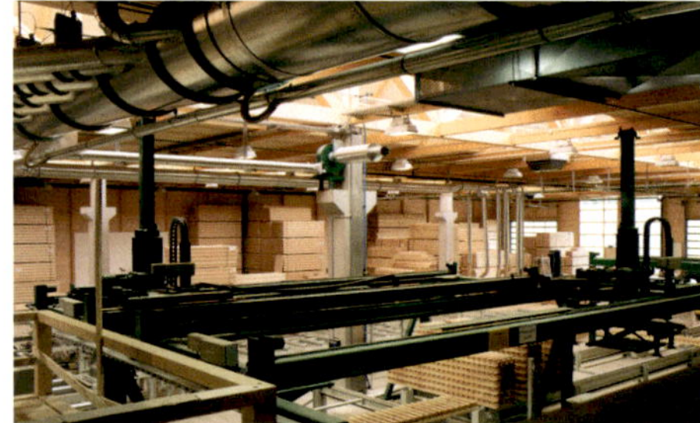

Production hall. The roof construction consists of 3.4-m-high, glue laminated timber lattice trusses. Four of the trusses span the entire 80 m length of the hall.

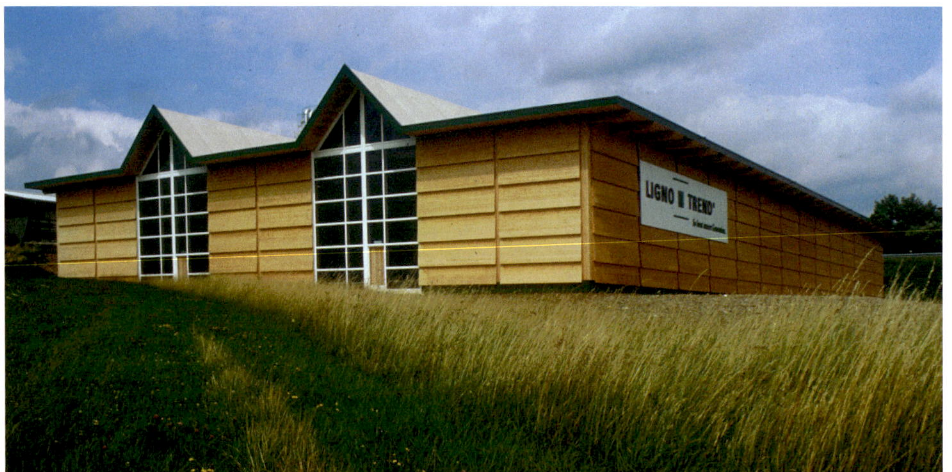

Production hall for *Lignotrend* wooden block panels in Weilheim-Bannholz (Germany), effective area 3 500 m²

chars and emits smoke; if sufficient air reaches the pockets of embers in charred wood, a glowing fire results; while an open fire with flames can develop through spontaneous or deliberate combustion in cases of continuous heating at around 200 °C.

Evidence of how materials and building elements relate to fire are obtained through tests conducted by authorized material testing stations and institutes and are, generally speaking, documented by a test certificate. When classified materials and building elements are used, this is no longer necessary. In addition, using an approved calculation method, it is possible to calculate the load-bearing, cross-sectional area of timber's structural elements remaining within the charred outer layer. The rate at which softwood and beech wood burns is 0.8 mm per minute in the case of solid timber and 0.7 mm per minute in the case of gluelam. Hardwood (with the exception of beech) burns at a rate of 0.56 mm per minute.

Minimum thermal expansion

Although it is a flammable material, timber is suitable for fire-resistant building elements. Here, the advantages of wood over other materials – such as its poor thermal conductivity and its almost negligible thermal expansion – are decisive. These factors play a significant role in safety considerations in terms of the overall stability of buildings. In a fire, the surface of a timber element changes into charcoal, reducing the rate at which it burns up by over 50 percent. The greater the cross-sectional area, the longer the period of resistance to fire, which can theoretically

be up to two hours. Only a cm beneath the surface, the timber retains its load-bearing capacity, regardless of whether the fire temperature is 600 °C or 1200 °C. The connections and the steel used to form them are generally the weakest link in a timber structure with regard to fire safety. Thus, where deemed necessary, connecting systems that are concealed within the timber sections must be used or the connecting elements themselves must be clad with wood.

Chemical methods of fire protection involve impregnating wood and are used primarily for thin wood claddings. Depending on what system is selected, the flammability of wood is reduced by painting it or soaking it in a bath. Protective coatings that produce foam when heated can be transparent or opaque.

Fire protection concepts

The goal of an effective fire safety concept is ensuring the protection of people, goods and buildings. This includes preventive fire protection, that is to say, all those measures that can prevent a fire from starting and hinder it from spreading, as well as the provision of safe fire escape routes. Firewalls, fire detectors, sprinkler systems, smoke and heat extraction systems and secure escape routes can produce a tailor-made fire safety concept. The building regulations for different countries and regions are often a matter of interpretation and allow alternative solutions if it can be proved that the safety goal has been achieved. Numerous examples in the following section of this book provide an indication of this fact.

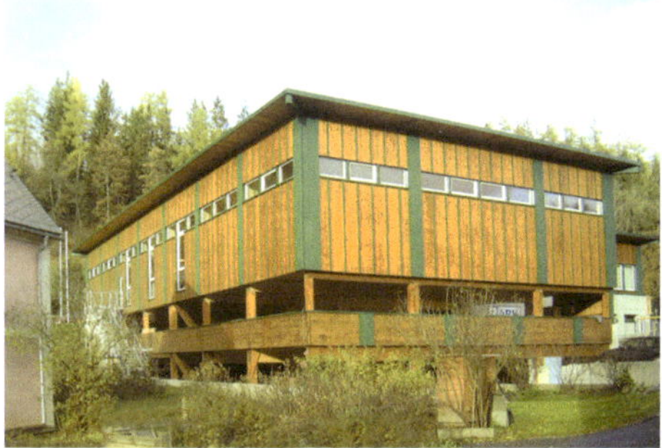

1

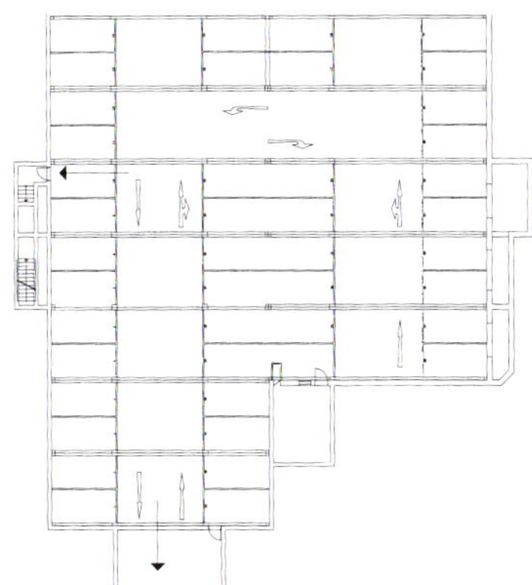

2

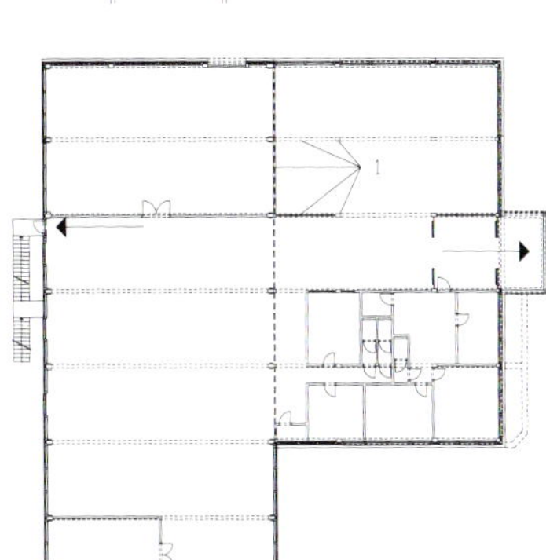

3

1 Commercial building over two car-parking levels in Murau (Austria). All three storeys are built in timber using glue laminated timber for both columns and beams. The fire resistance rating required for the car-parking building was F 30, which meant that timber construction was allowed. Under the regional building regulations, the use of the top floor as a shop required more stringent fire safety measures. F 30-B (30 minutes fire resistance) was required for the roof and F 90-B (90 minutes resistance to fire) for the floors, columns and beams.

2 Interior view of the car-parking deck

3 Floor plan of the lower car-parking deck and the upper retail floor (below). Essentially, the fire protection concept is based on having adequate fire resistance in the timber construction and the existing escape routes. A fire alarm system is directly connected to the fire brigade.

4 Temperature gradient for timber cross-section exposed to fire on four sides

5 In a timber beam ceiling covered with boarding that encloses a space, during a fire the timber beams are exposed to flames on three sides, the boarding on only one side.

6 The degree of exposure of columns in the case of a fire depends on their position. From above: free-standing – exposure to fire on four sides; in front of a wall – on three sides; in a wall – on two sides; in a wall – on one side.

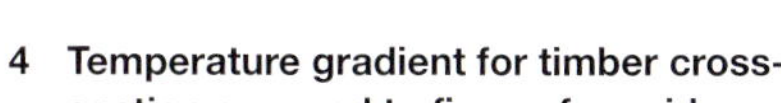

4

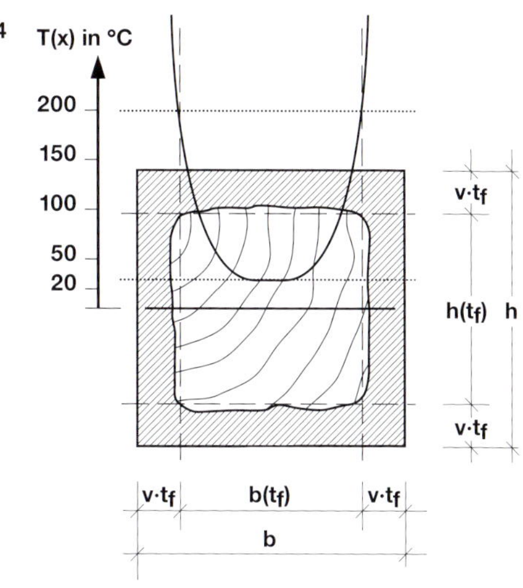

5

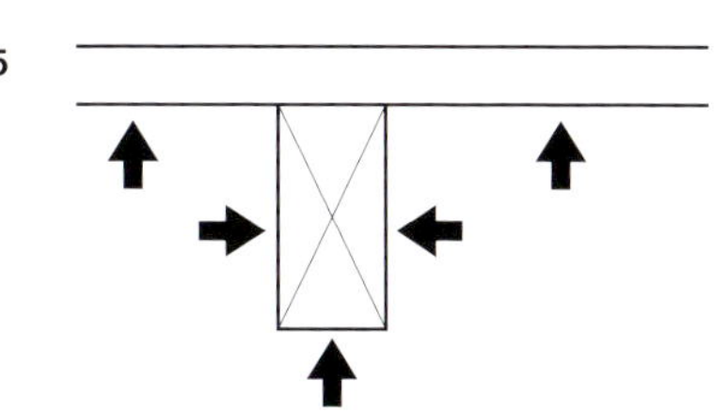

6

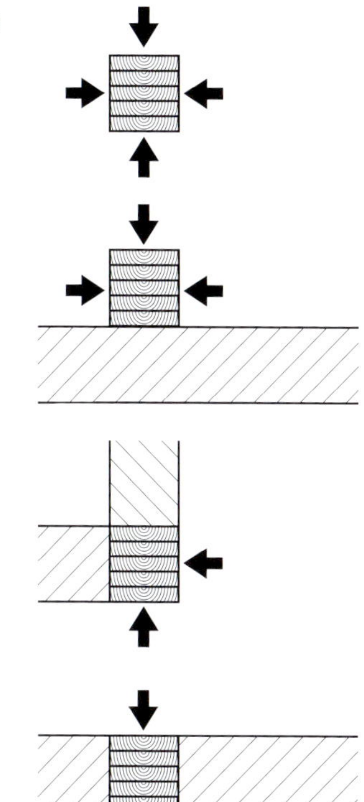

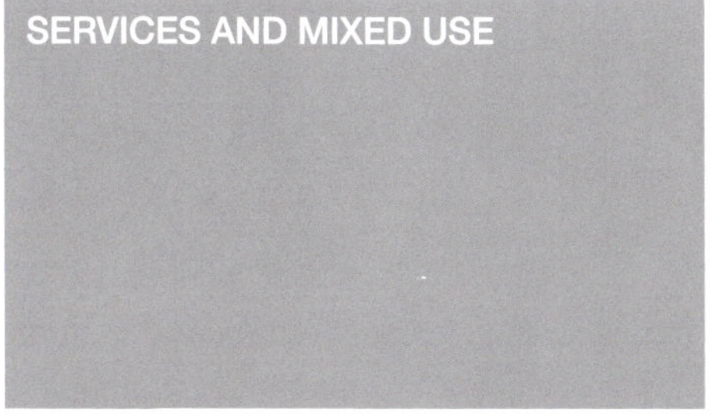

SERVICES AND MIXED USE

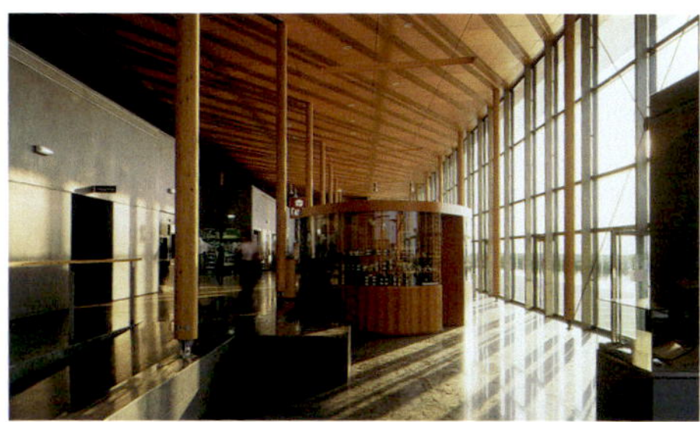
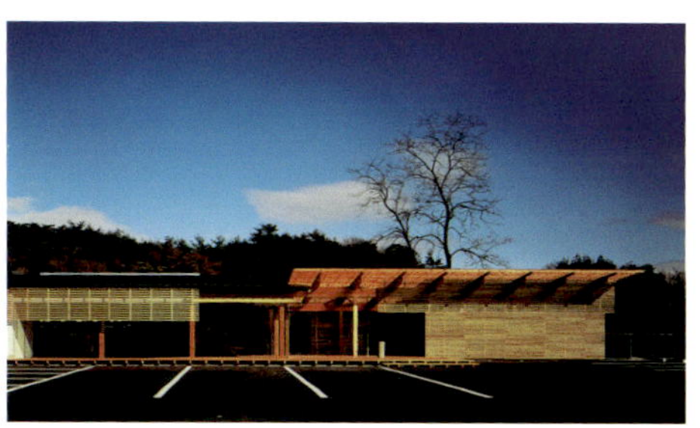
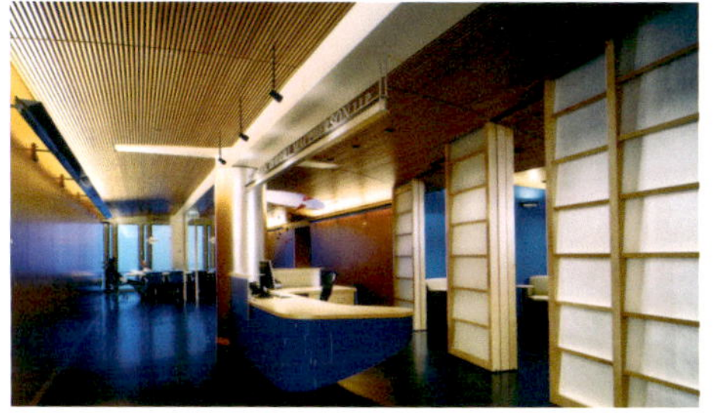
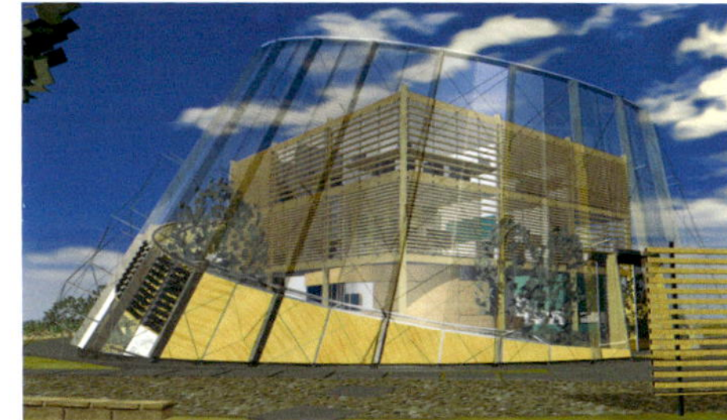
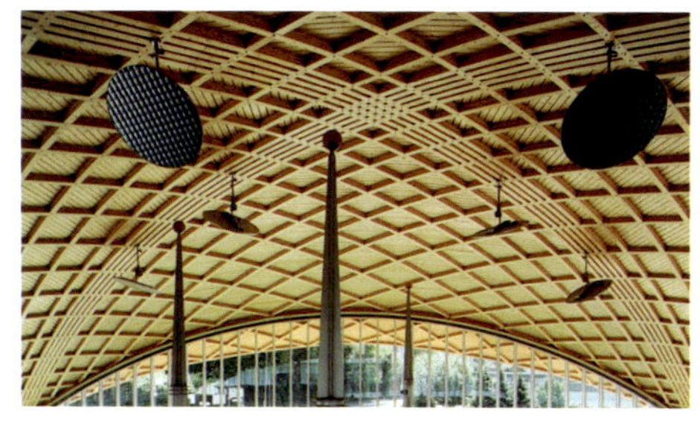
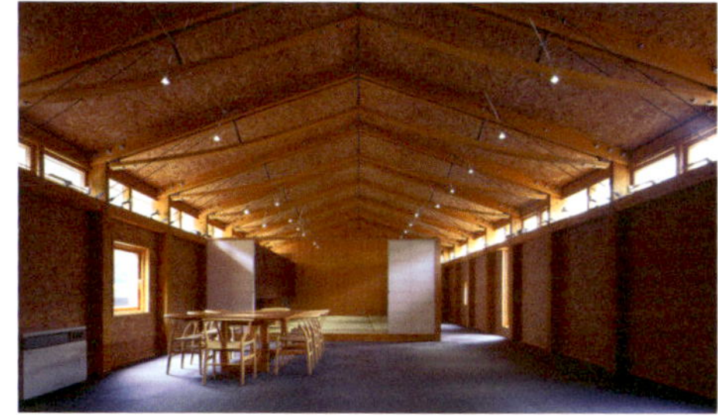
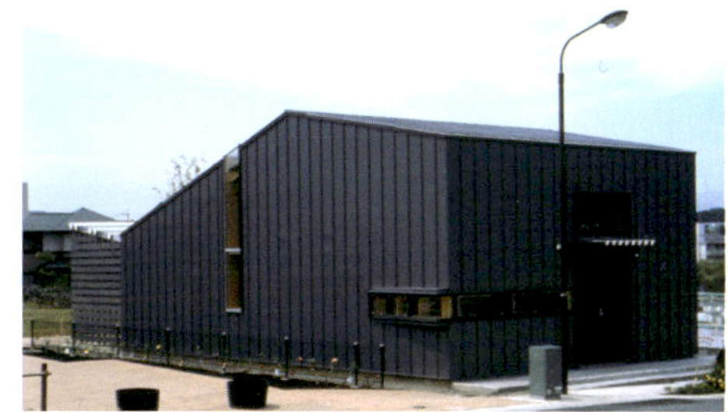
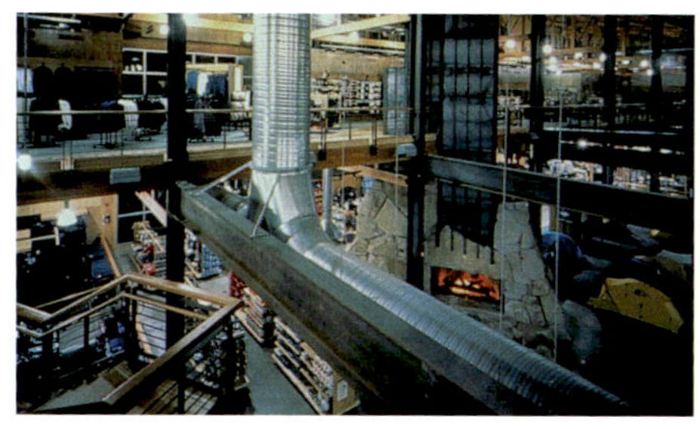
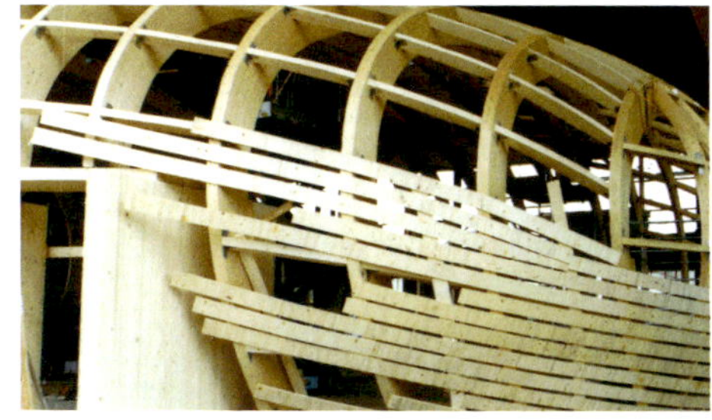
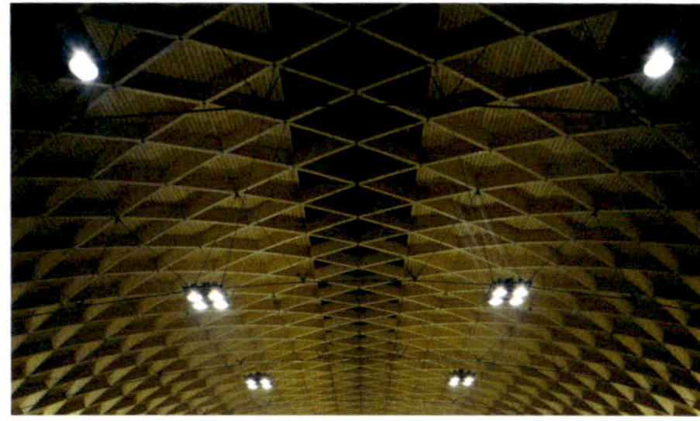
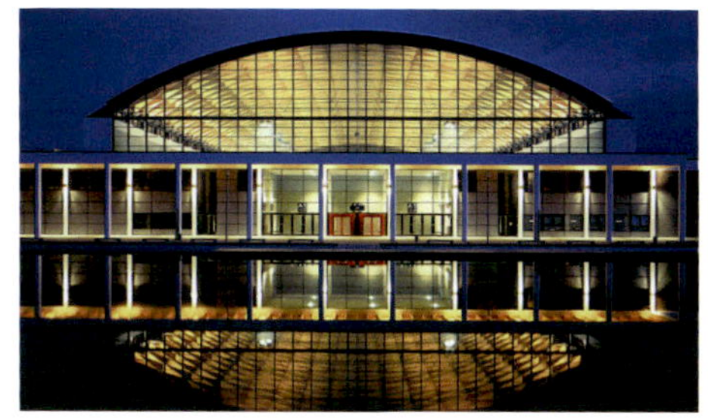

Bruno Mader Architect

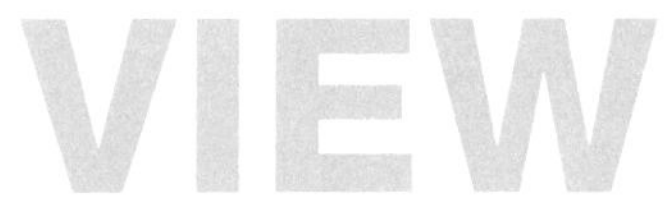

Motorway service area Baie de Somme / France

In northern France between the River Somme and the English Channel, the rest stop Aire de la Baie de Somme on the A16 near the town of Abbeville offers a broad view of the landscape that stretches flatly towards the horizon. The nature of this plain inspired the client and the designer to create a kind of theme park that would focus on the natural world of this region, instead of the usual rest stop consisting of a filling station with a snack bar.

Bringing nature closer

The complex is integrated into the layout of the fields and is planned in such a way that it is screened as far as possible from the highway traffic. The approach roads are placed at the outside edges of the site, the car parking area is at a lower level and separated by narrow canals. Thus the cars do not interrupt the view of the landscape. The canals – not unusual in this marshy landscape – are fed with rain water that is collected along the highway and in the rest stop; they also serve as a water reservoir in case of fire.

The individual service areas of the rest stop are organised under a broad timber roof. Opposite the filling station are three concrete cubes that accomodate the sanitary facilities, the cash desks for the filling station and the kitchens for the self-service restaurant. The spaces between these building elements are like picture frames for a landscape painting of Picardy. The restaurant, which offers local specialities and has a space for exhibitions, also gives travellers a brief opportunity to make themselves familiar with the region in a number of different ways, particularly where the side facing the marshy landscape is generously glazed. The visitors can then deepen their understanding of the region by going across a large terrace that opens onto the landscape and into a round exhibition building. In the interior of this cylinder, the fauna and flora of the Baie de Somme are presented on screens. In addition to this electronic provision of information, visitors can also enjoy a commanding view over the landscape from the roof terrace.

Wood, concrete, gravel

The timber roof, an element made of natural materials connecting the road and the landscape, is supported by four rows of round columns made of glued larch wood. They echo four rows of ash trees that are planted along the lines of the timber columns. The columns seem to penetrate the roof and recall the posts of the oyster banks along the nearby English Channel coast. The structure of the roof is made of glued laminated timber beams, between which laminated purlins are placed. The roof construction consists of thermally insulation corrugated metal sheeting 120 mm thick (0.5 W/m²K), on which timber sections are placed that support a final 25-mm-thick layer of larch. The ends of the posts are protected with metal caps. In the interior, a plywood acoustic ceiling veneered with Okoumé wood forms the soffit.

The walls of the service blocks are made of concrete; the exposed sides are covered with grey gravel from the estuary of the Somme and form a contrast to the smooth wooden ceiling. This detail is intended as a reference to both the raw nature of the landscape and the traditional vernacular architecture of the region.

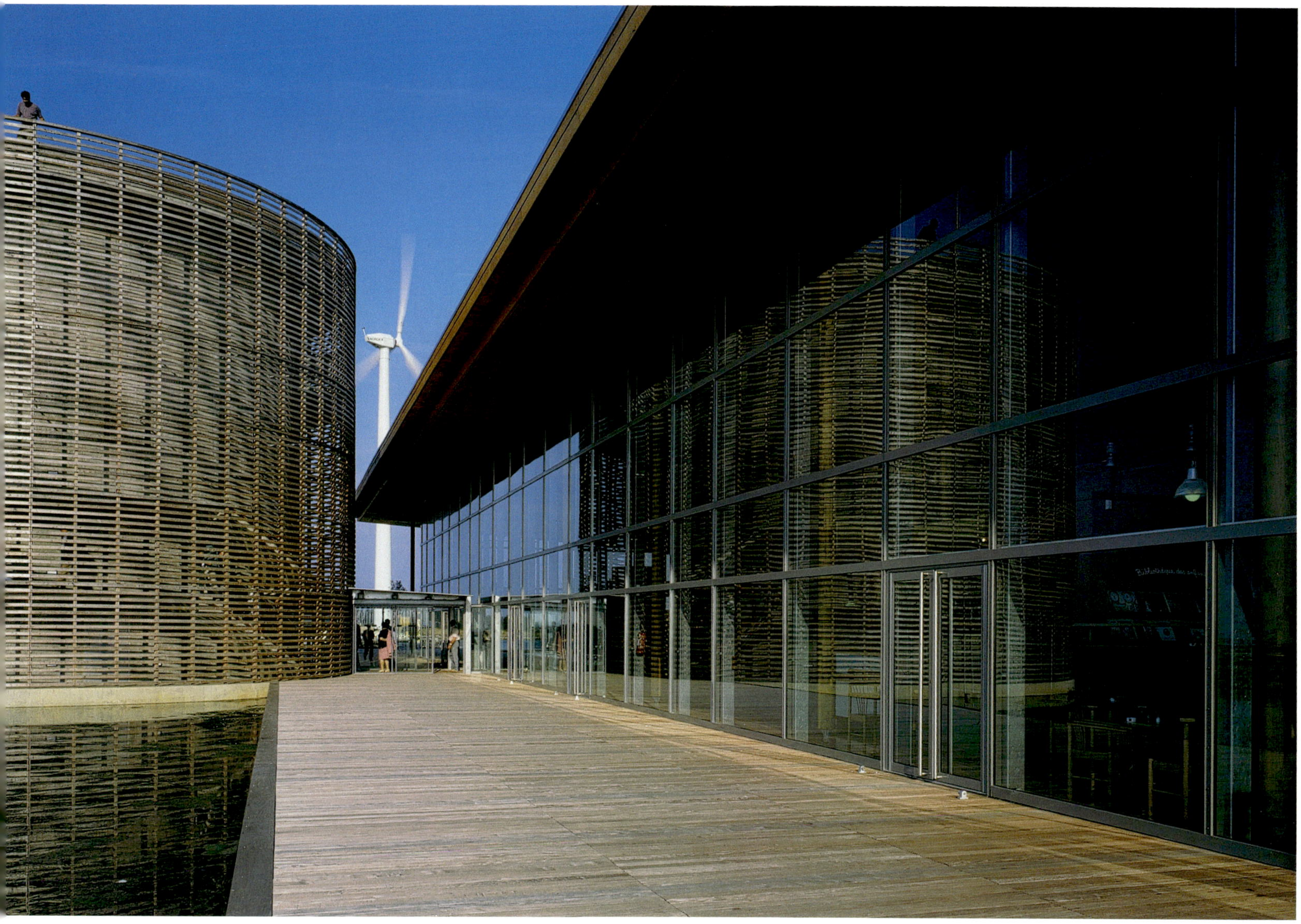

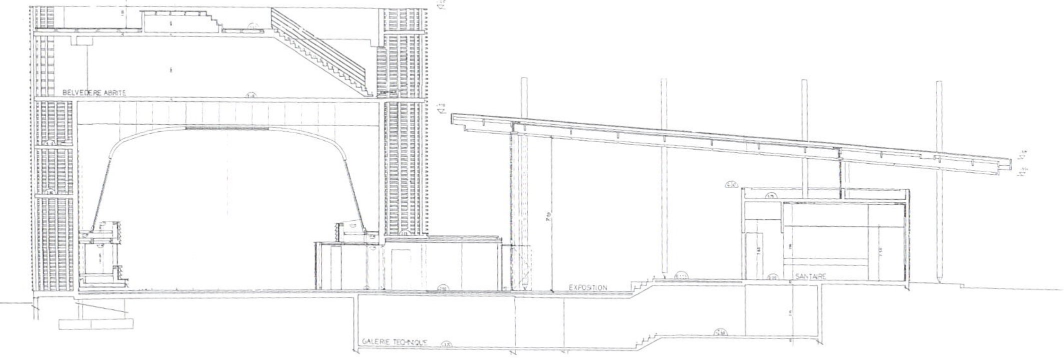

Cross-section with the rest stop and viewing (lookout) tower

Southeast elevation

Northwest elevation

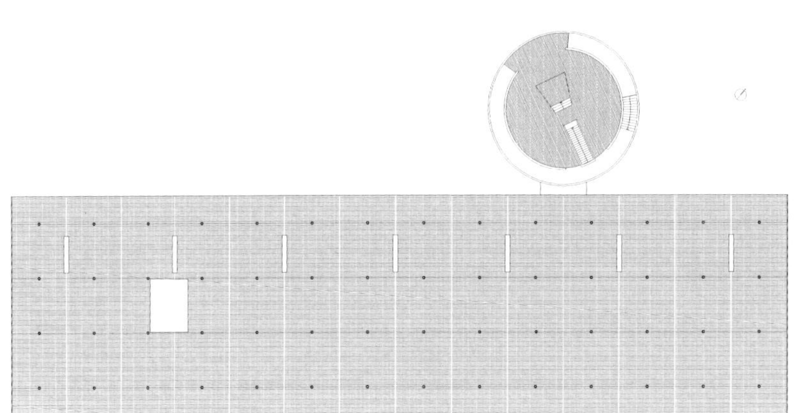

Top view

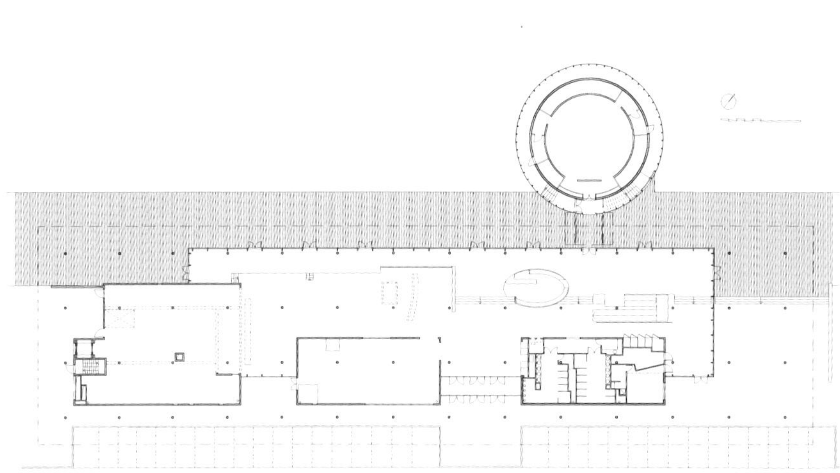

Floor plan

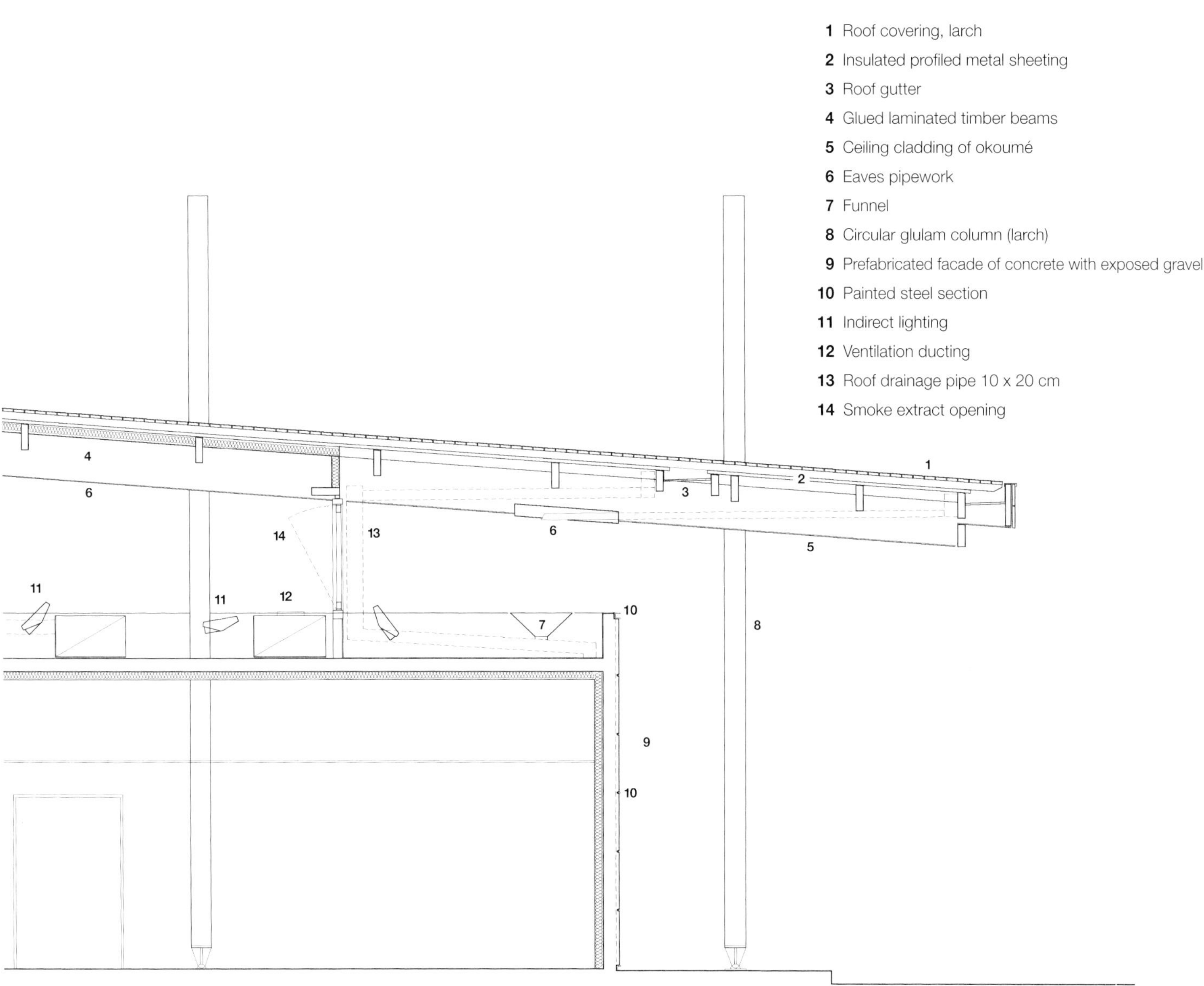

Partial section showing the roof drainage and indirect lighting

The viewing tower or lookout also has a cylindrical core made of concrete. The outer skin that surrounds the passageway around the inner core is made of rough-cut larch boards that are mounted with a gap between them and will, in the course of time, age to a grey colour. The viewing slits between the boards offer a panoramic moving view of the landscape as the visitors ascend the steps around the core.

Wind energy supplies the power

The wooden structure of the roof is braced by the concrete cubes and a single steel cross-brace. The indirect lighting, the ventilation system and the roof drainage are all integrated into the roof construction. The water is led via spouts to the canals referred to above. The structural details and technical fittings are effective but simple, as suits the building and its relationship to the landscape. The filling station is also adapted to these constraints in design terms.

The curtain wall facade of double glazing with aluminium frames has a U-value of 2.6 W/m²K and is shaded by the projecting roof. The layer of wood on the roof improves the circulation of air and prevents overheating in summer. The controlled supply and extraction of air uses a heat recovery system. At the lower area of the glass facade, a blower system can be used to prevent condensation on the glass. Half a million kWh of electricity produced annually by a wind energy generator meets the electricity requirements of this building. Excess energy is fed into the local electricity network. At night the paths and the water canals are part of a light show that guides visitors to the information tower.

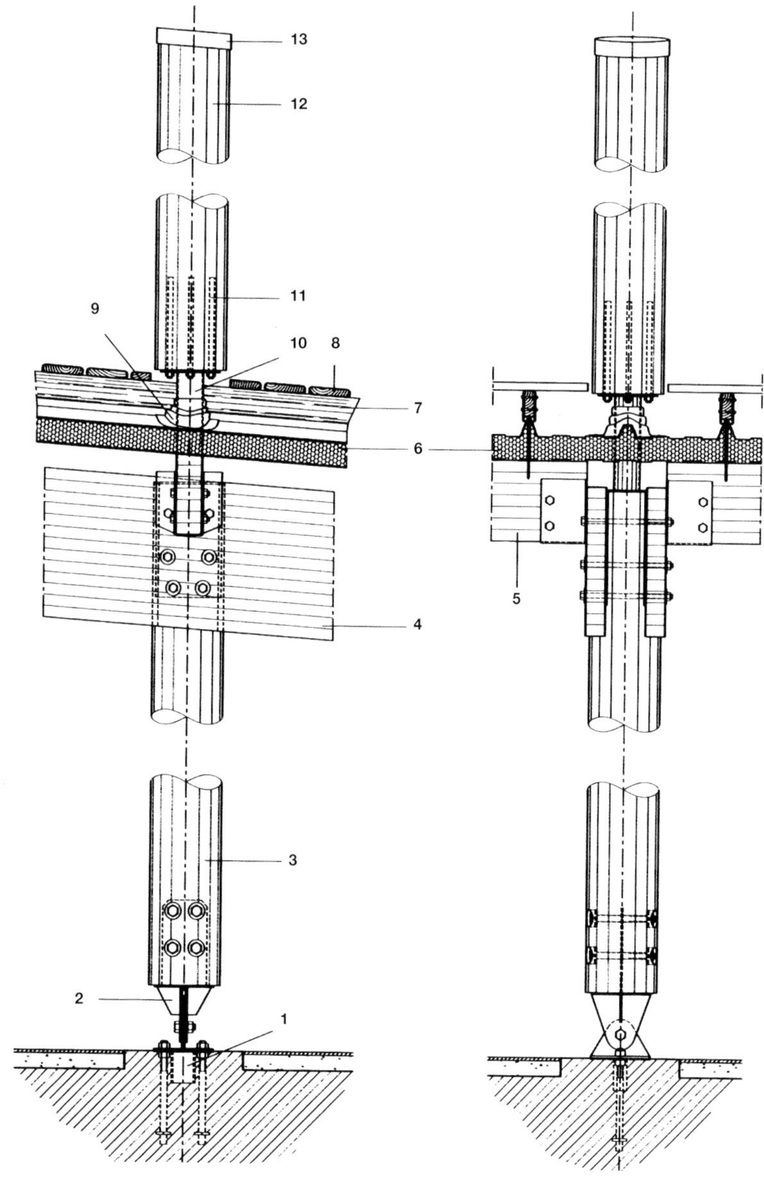

1 Steel anchoring with joint connection
2 Column foot
3 Circular column of glued laminated timber, diameter 240 mm
4 Glued laminated timber member
5 Purlins
6 Profiled steel sheeting with 120 mm thermal insulation
7 Structural timbers
8 Boarding, larch wood 25 mm
9 Sealing collar
10 Column anchor
11 Glued-in threaded rod to secure the anchor plate
12 Circular column made of glued laminated timber, diameter 240 mm
13 Zinc capping on the columns

Structure, front and side view

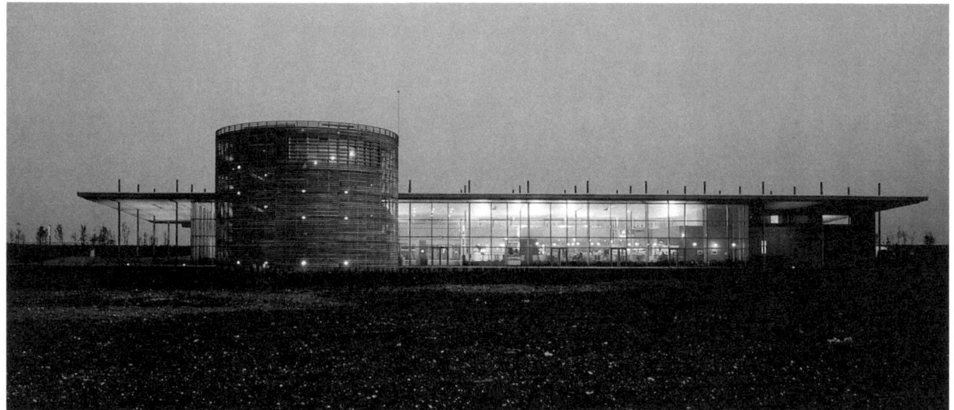

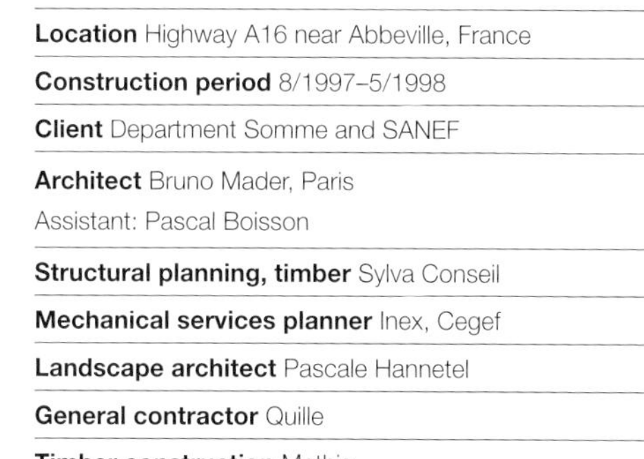

Location Highway A16 near Abbeville, France

Construction period 8/1997–5/1998

Client Department Somme and SANEF

Architect Bruno Mader, Paris
Assistant: Pascal Boisson

Structural planning, timber Sylva Conseil

Mechanical services planner Inex, Cegef

Landscape architect Pascale Hannetel

General contractor Quille

Timber construction Mathis

Floor area 4,828 m²

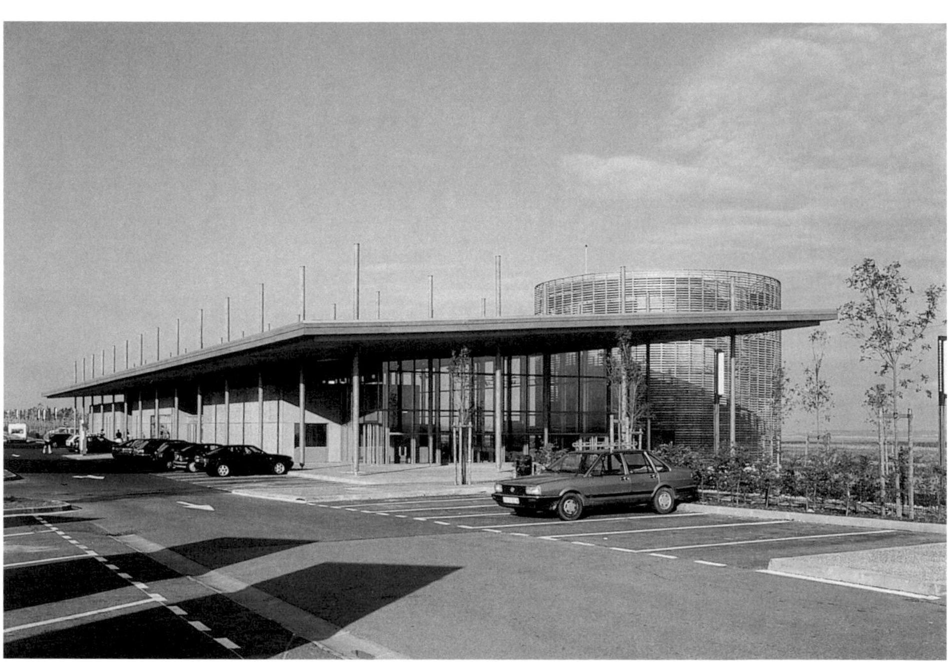

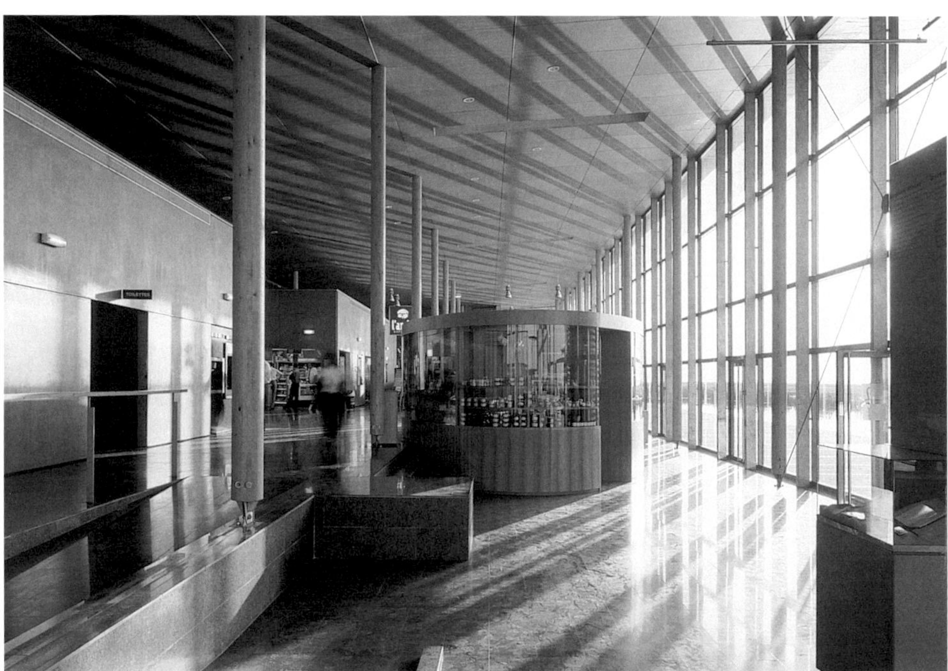

Noodle factory with restaurant in Fukushima / Japan

FILTER

Kengo Kuma & Associates, Architects

Kengo Kuma is not the kind of architect who offers a superficial presentation of himself, but is rather an analyst of tradition who has the calm of Zen-like concentration, the courage to experiment and the modesty of a wise man.

This new noodle factory with adjoining restaurant was built at a location that is typical of the rural areas in Japan. Part of the site is characterised by the natural scenery of the waterfall of the River Abukama, while the other part is turned towards the approach road to Fukishima airport and the city of Suga. The building is therefore located at a precarious interface between unspoiled nature and the highway, and functions as a filter between these two opposites. The architect demonstrates this effect through four different elements on the facades made of wooden battens. The wooden pieces of the grids have different cross-sectional areas and the distances between them also differ. These four different wooden lattices complement each other; they overlay and penetrate each other visually, creating fascinating effects.

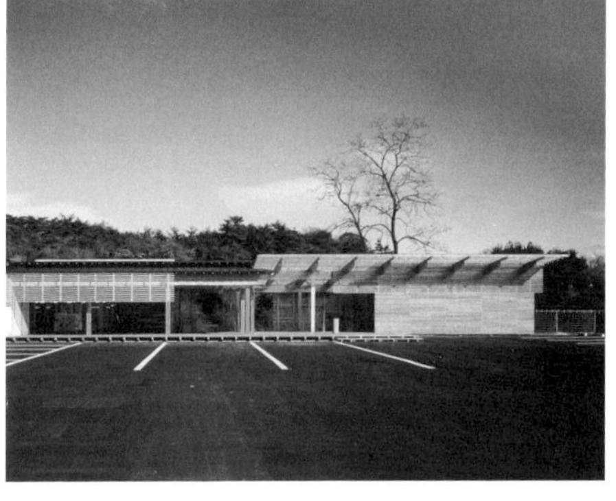

Grid of lines

As you walk along the building you can follow a play of open and closed areas. The degree of permeability of the facade changes constantly through the structure of the lines.

The main parts of the building lie below ground level. Above it, at ground floor level, are the car parking spaces. The building appears to dissolve as it rises upwards, an impression that is strengthened by the "filter function" (i.e., the wooden structures in the vertical plane that are permeated by light and air). At ground floor level there is a foyer, a shop and a restaurant with an outdoor terrace whose rooms extend to the upper floor. The kitchens for the restaurant and the work spaces of a small noodle factory

are also located at this level. The lower level is built in concrete; the structure placed upon it is made of wood.

An existing building had to make way for this new design. Kengo Kuma replaced it with an architecture that reacts sensitively and appropriately to the characteristics of the place. His architecture is free of outdated concepts and therefore frees the viewer from the constraints of habitual ways of seeing. The architecture of the noodle factory, which the architect himself calls "River Filter", uses the characteristics of the materials – with all their constructional and sensual qualities – to achieve a new interplay between architecture and environment, and between tradition and a contemporary modernism.

Location Tamakawa, Fukushima, Japan

Construction period 1994–1996

Architects Kengo Kuma & Associates, Tokyo

Structural designers Aoki Structural Engineers

General contractor Ando Architecture Design Office

Total floor area 925 m²

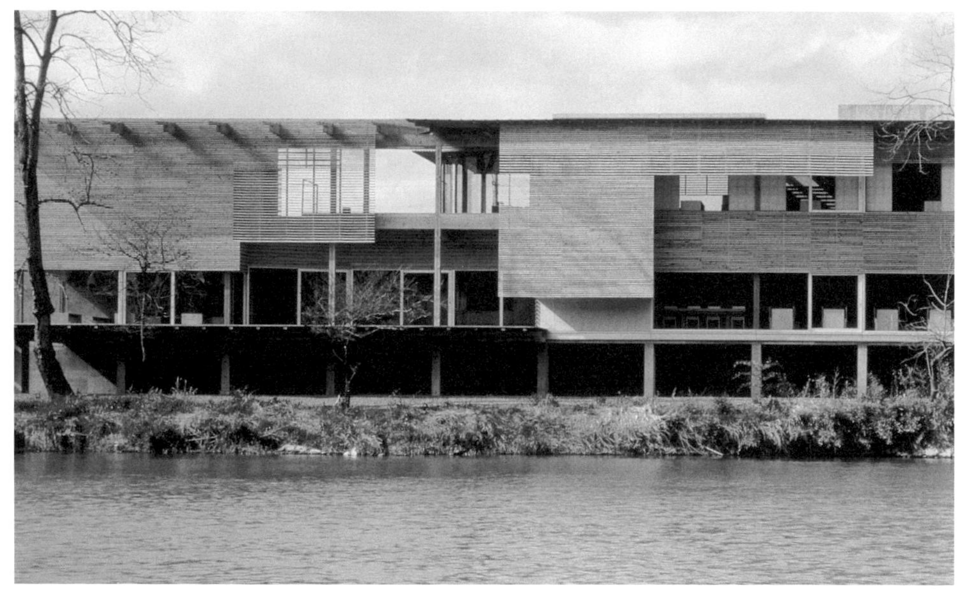

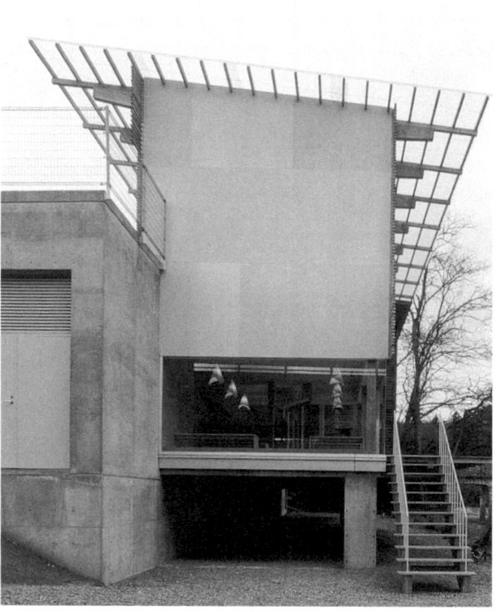

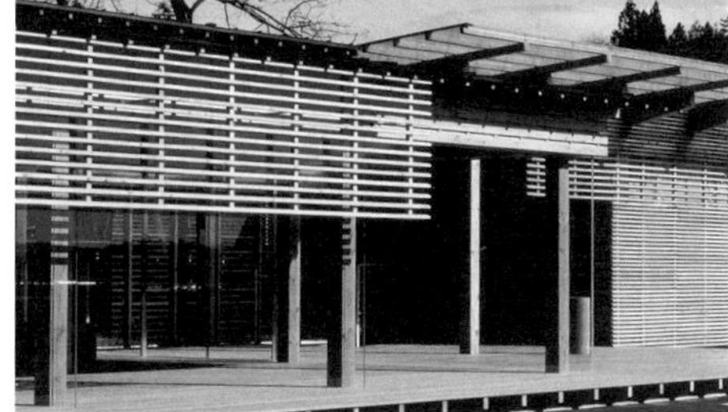

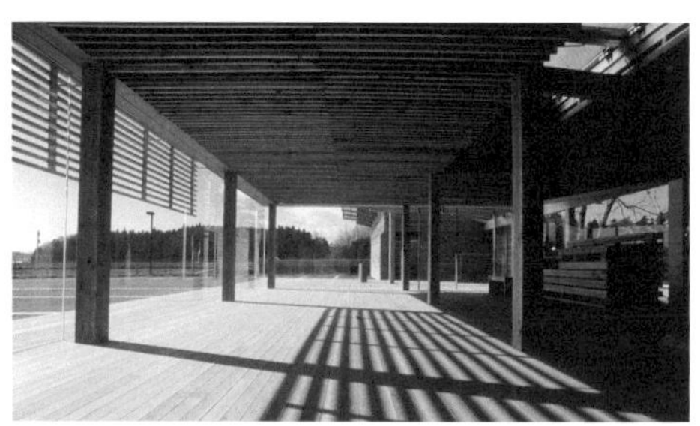

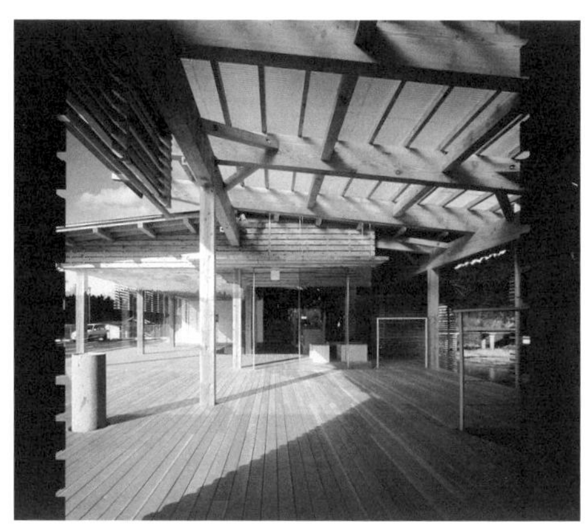

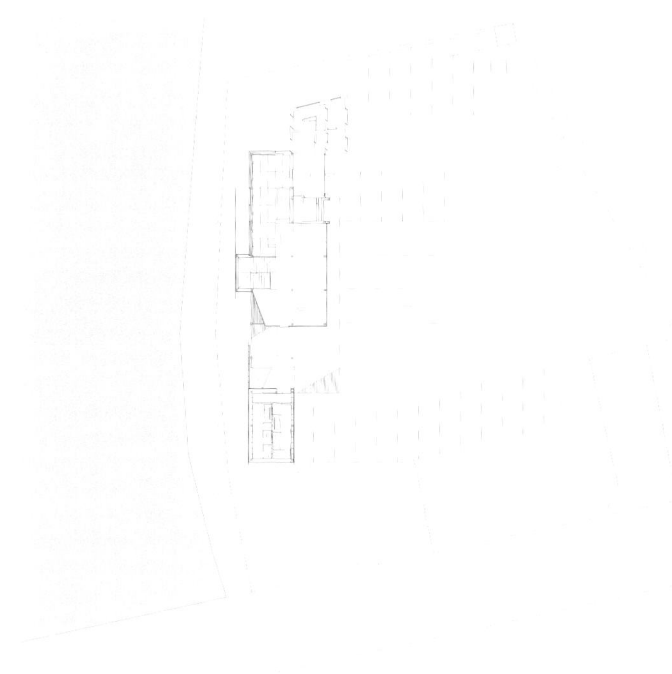

Floor plan

AERIE

Law practice in San Francisco / USA

Turnbull Griffin & Haesloop, Architects

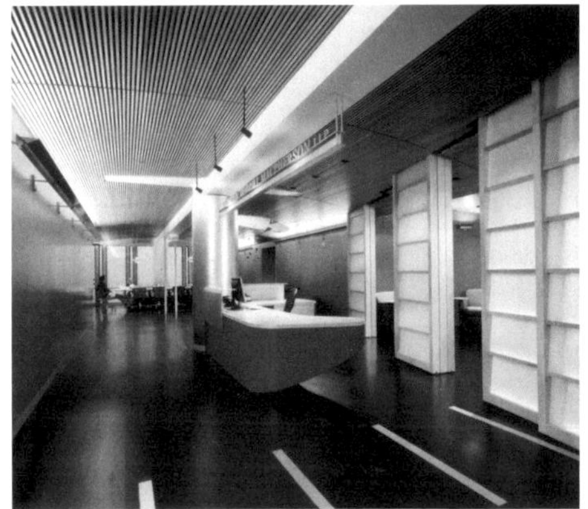

This law practice, which specialises in patent law in the high-tech industry, required a new home for its rapidly expanding office in San Francisco. When the practice was offered the upper floor of the Embarcadero Building – previously also occupied by a law office – it decided to move in there. The space was suitable in terms of the floor area it offered, but the floor plan and the fittings were too cramped and dark for this practice, whose focus is, in every respect, on openness and cooperation.

The challenge for the architects was, on the one hand, to preserve as many functions of the original office as possible while, on the other, redesigning the entrance area as an open and impressive reception lobby suited to the entre-preneurial culture represented by this practice.

The planners opened up the wall across the entire width of the storey, creating a spatial situation that eliminated the cramped, ill-lit atmosphere that had previously dominated the reception area and the corridors. The new lobby is opposite the lift and is flanked by seating groups and dominated by a large translucent light-wall. Combining indirect lighting and a skylight (the light entering though it emphasises a small seating group) a soft atmospheric ambiance was created. The new conference rooms on either side of the lobby have spectacular views of central San Fran-cisco and the northern Bay area which can be enjoyed by visitors and staff alike. The former waiting area was remodelled as the file archives of the new practice. By opening up moveable partitions, extra space for receptions and other events can be created.

The materials used underscore the bright and friendly atmosphere that results from the way light is handled in this design: blue doors and desks, flooring of dark wood with maple stripes and a curved ceiling of maple sections that makes the spaces seem higher than they actually are.

Client Skjerven Morill LLP., San Francisco, USA

Architects Turnbull Griffin & Haesloop, Architects, Berkeley, CA.

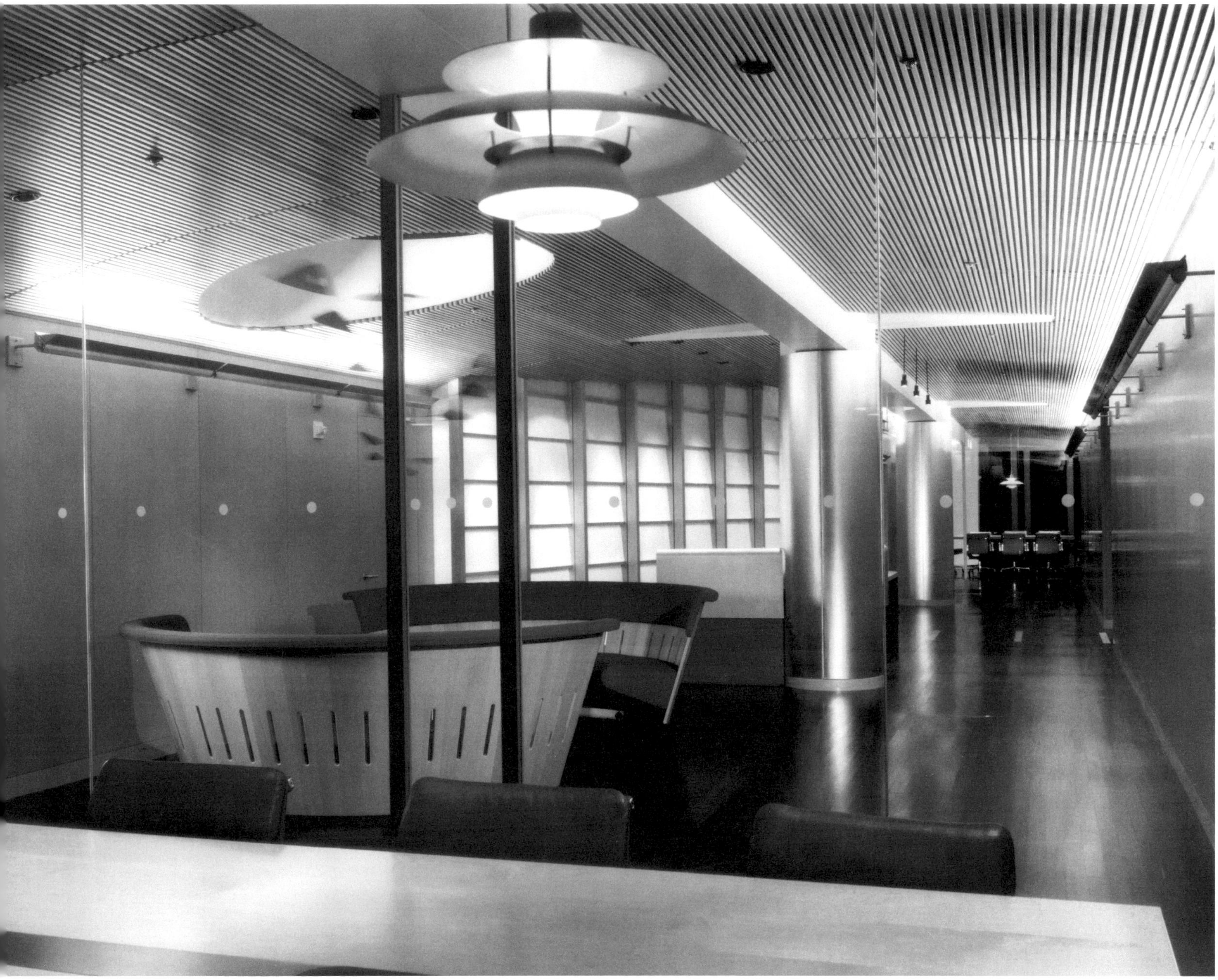

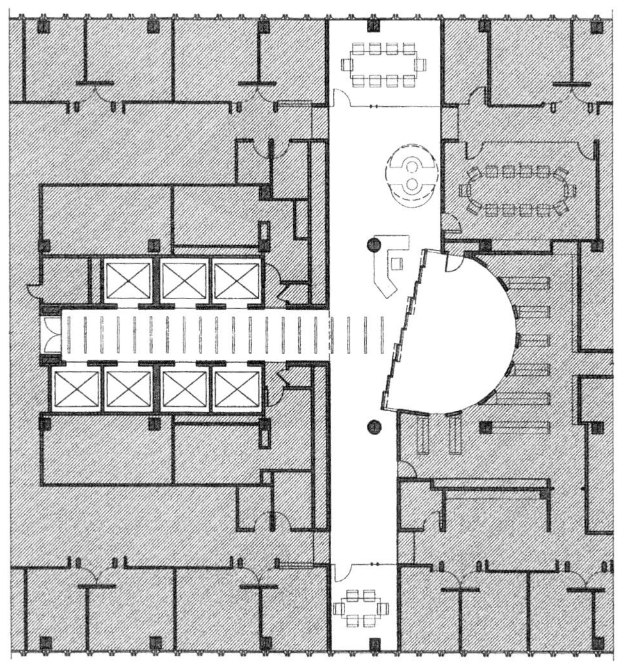

Floor plan

Forest ecology centre in Scottsdale, Tasmania / Australia

TREE STUMP

Morris-Nunn & Associates Architects

The forest ecology centre in Scottsdale consists of two interlocking buildings and is, so to speak, a "building within a building". It was planned with the explicit aim of achieving substantial energy savings (well below normal use levels) throughout its entire life span. The planning process focused on energy efficiency, and the demonstration of sustainably produced plantation wood as a source of energy savings, in particular the Radiata pine, was an integral part of the project.

The basis of the design

The architectural impression made by the forest ecology centre is characterised by a radical departure from the traditional form of office buildings. Its exterior form was determined by the wish to provide the greatest possible usable volume in the interior. The conical shape provided a practical alternative to the ideal form of the sphere and also maximised the available floor area at ground level. The building is tilted towards the north in order to exploit the winter sun, while the south-facing rear of the building is thermally insulated.

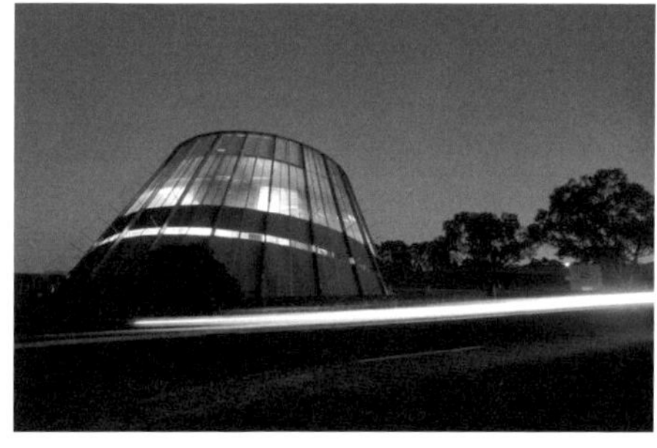

The forest ecology centre is a cone made of pine that represents a tree stump, in a sense a symbol of the business of forestry. At a time of global environmental crises, this building – along with its symbolic tree stump – is intended to demonstrate the importance of sustainably managed forests and the raw material wood, whose ecological significance in the reduction of CO_2 and as a supplier of CO_2-neutral energy cannot be emphasised often enough.

Energy concept

The forest ecology centre in Tasmania illustrates an important step in the creation of energy-saving buildings. The conservation measures aim at using only 20 percent of the energy normally required by a modern office building. In the forest ecology centre, two building

elements are interlocked, creating a buffer zone for the inner building that is formed by a curved facade of translucent polycarbonate panels and a special Teflon-coated, two-layer membrane roof. The external form of the conical stump is turned towards the sun.

The energy-saving concept uses the principle of the glasshouse. The inner building is warmed by solar energy, which enters through the transparent walls and transparent roof of the outer skin. When overheating appears likely, large areas of blinds are opened to allow the exchange of air. The blinds are controlled by a central computer system that uses sensors to automatically regulate the flow of air. In winter, warmth is stored in the building and distributed by a ventilation system. In summer, the blinds are used in combination with the effects of natural convection.

Despite the webbed polycarbonate panels and the two layers of roof membrane, the building cools down during winter nights. The workplaces are initially heated in the morning by the

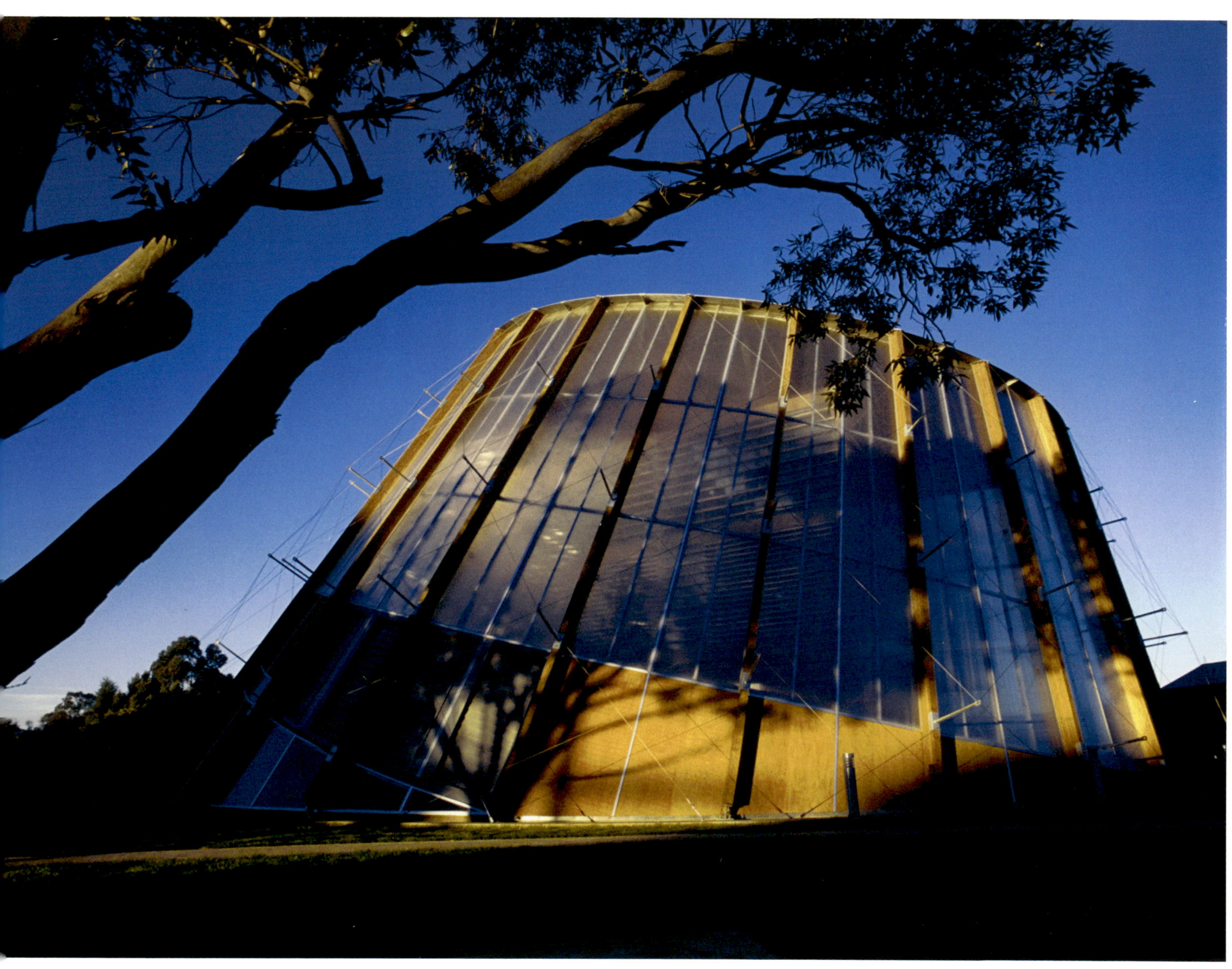

use of electric air heaters that are turned off automatically as soon as the sun begins to heat up the air in the space. The offices are lit almost entirely by natural light.

The building's internal control computer regulates the ventilation system, operates the blinds, the ventilator, the heating and the office lighting. Internal and external sensors measure the light intensity, temperature, air humidity, and amount of rainfall, as well as the concentration of CO_2 in the air at various positions and heights.

The innovative use of wood

This building is not a purely timber structure. Instead, wood is used where it is appropriate and where the possibilities offered by plantation softwoods, in conjunction with other materials, can be demonstrated. The goal was also to show that, despite the costly "building within a building" system used, it is still possible to build very economically, in terms of both construction and maintenance. The fact that this goal has been achieved while using a highly unique architectural form emphasises the role of design in energy-saving buildings using natural materials.

The innovative structure of the building is made of glue laminated timber sections measuring 300 x 70 mm and structural steel elements that are connected by a network of galvanised steel tubes. These elements support the polycarbonate skin and the membrane; the closed parts of the facade are made of plywood treated with oil in order to slow down the natural aging process. The plywood sheets are mounted on an insulated frame that is sheeted internally with MDF panels veneered in pine.

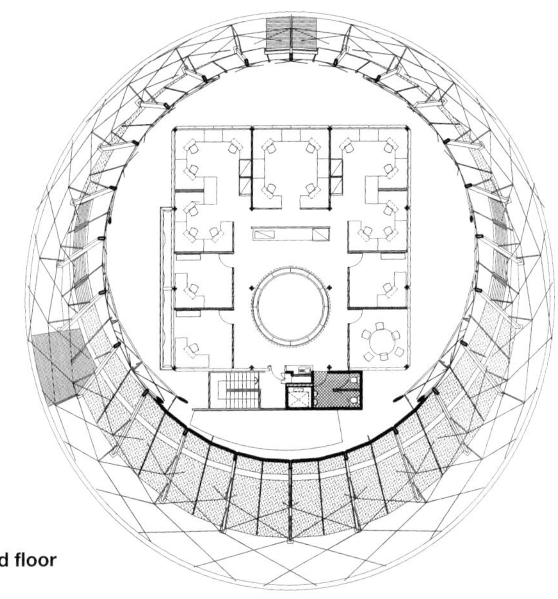

Second floor

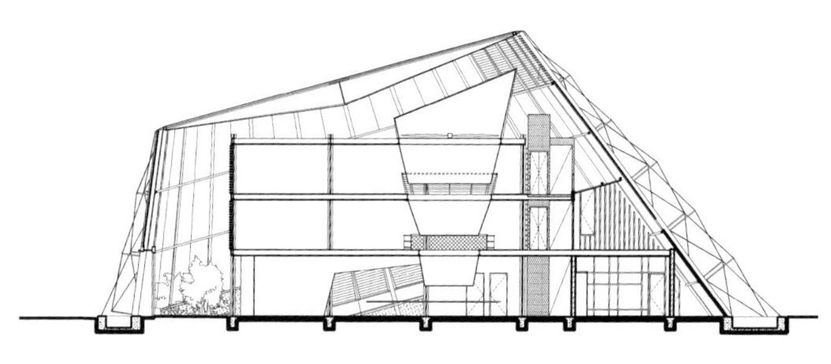

Section

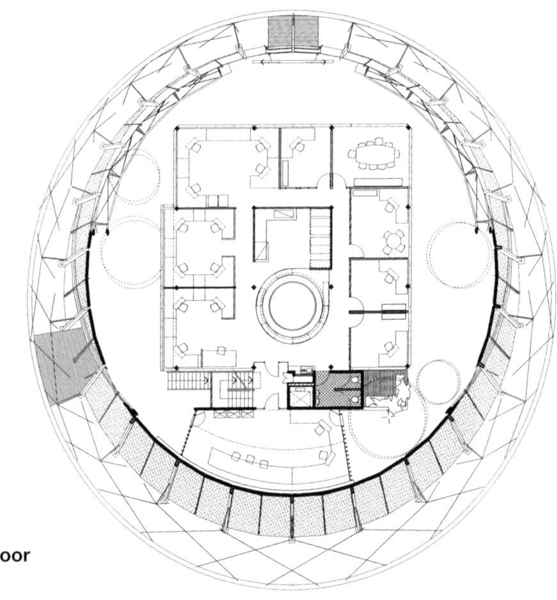

First floor

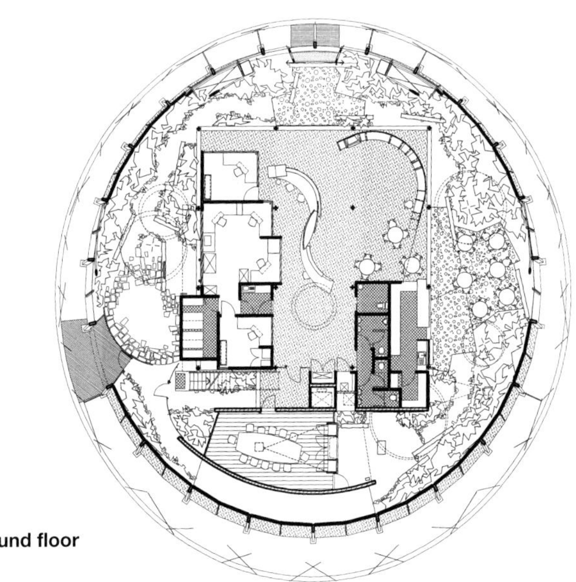

Ground floor

Although current building legislation in Tasmania requires the use of traditional massive construction systems for a three-storey building, the forest ecology centre consists primarily of wood and steel. Laminated timber was used to protect steel elements in the case of fire. The building's performance in a fire was evaluated through a computer simulation. As a result of the "building in a building" design, the smoke rises upwards through natural convection along the outer face and leaves the building. This led to a positive assessment of the building by the fire safety engineers.

The grid of horizontally arranged pine battens in the inner building is not just a visually striking feature but also provides a screened private area in the offices.

In the buffer zone between the two facades, native Tasmanian plants were planted to symbolise wood as a renewable resource. This "green layer" also improves the quality of the air in the interior through the process of photosynthesis.

Costs

The major success of this building is the fact that it is an economical building system in which the use of native woods played an important role. Thus the forest ecology centre cost only 88 percent of the price per square metre of a standard office building with a comparable floor area, built around the same time, and in the same neighbourhood. In comparison with other similar buildings in different areas of Australia, the cost framework, despite the expensive computer simulations used during the design phase, is about 78 percent of the normal cost. In addition, there is the factor

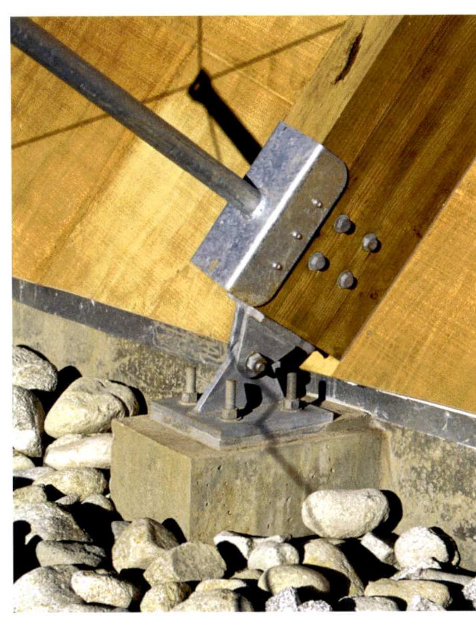

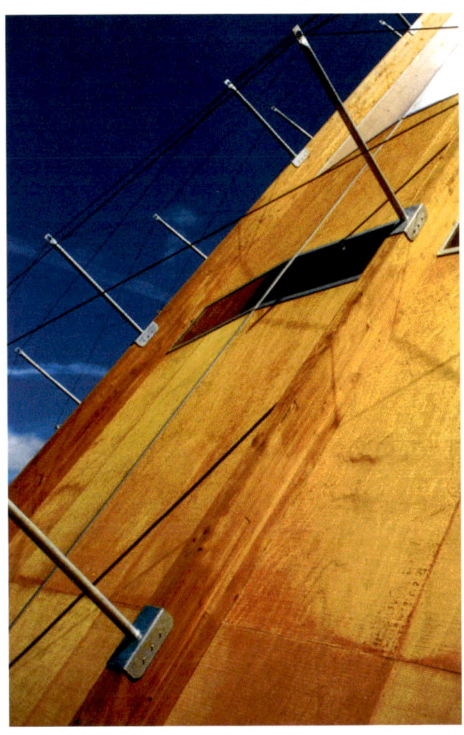

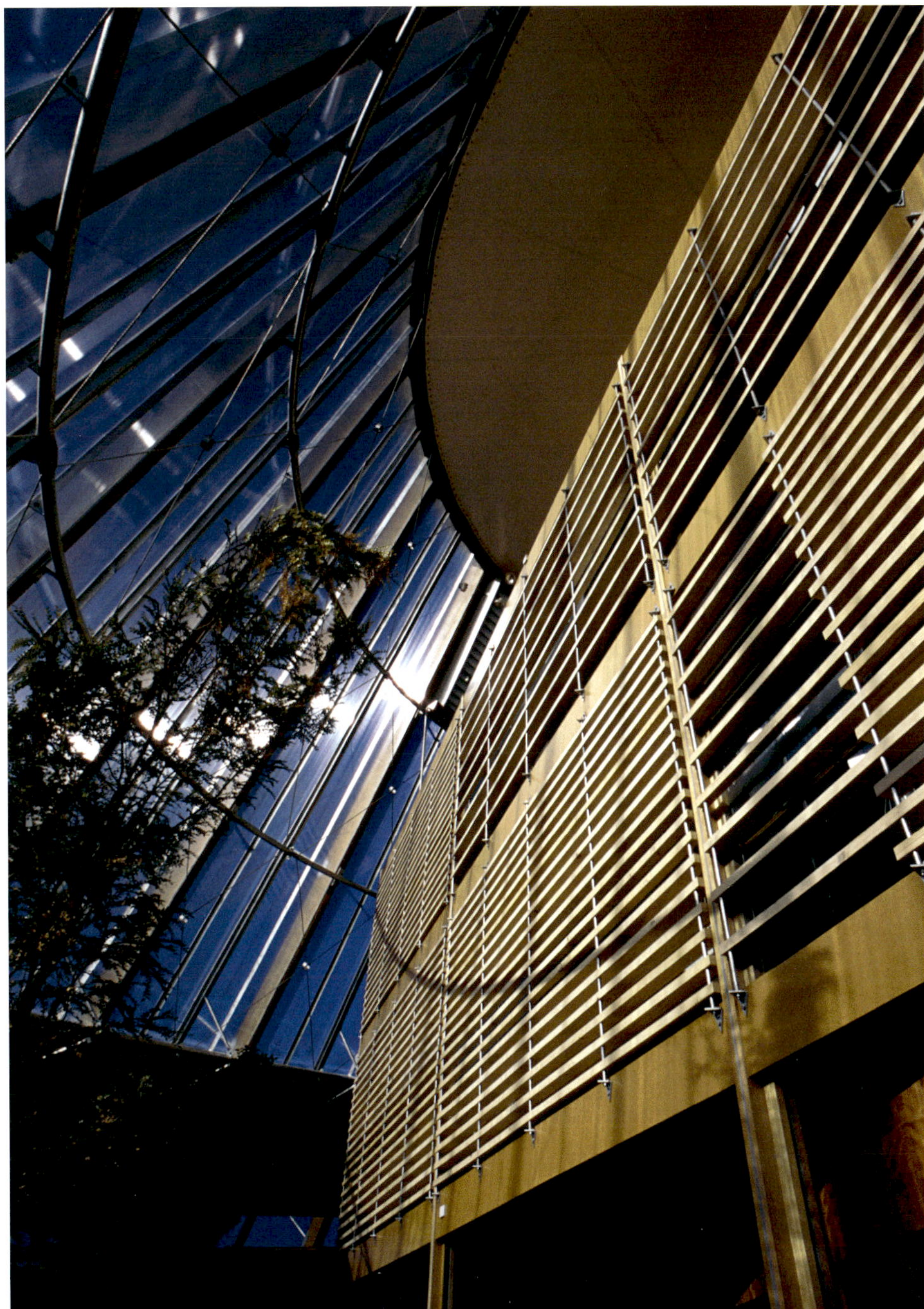

of future energy savings that, it is calculated, will amount to about 80 percent in comparison to similar standard-construction buildings. The energy use is continuously monitored and recorded.

Computer Aided Design

This project could never have been built without the use of the computer. The architects used a sophisticated ArchiCAD package to create a virtual 3D model. The first major tasks were the simulation of climatic conditions (use of solar energy and cooling) in which climatic information data from a nearby airport was used. The analysis of the building form using an airflow simulation programme confirmed the function of the air circulation in the inner building.

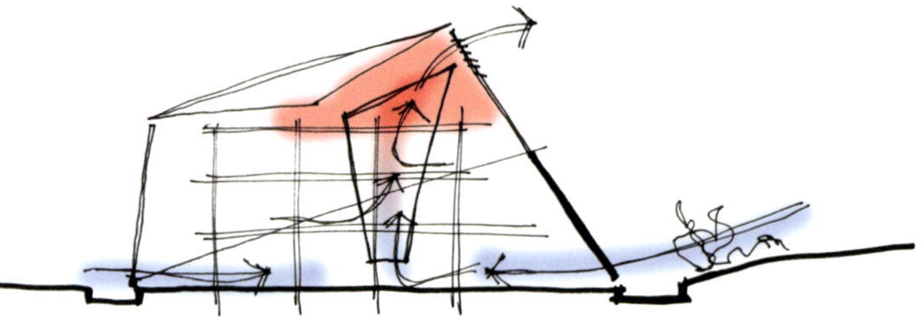

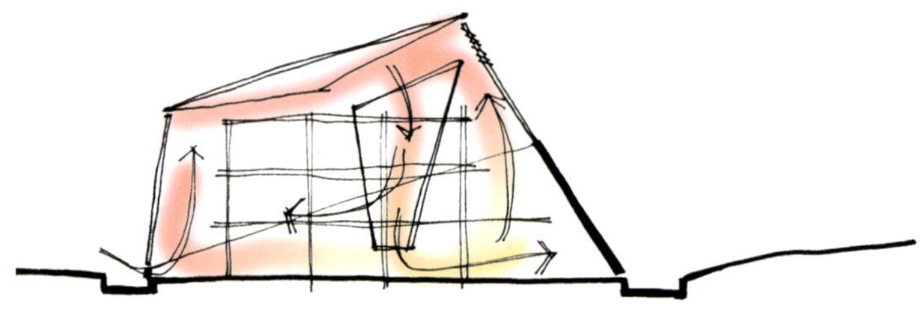

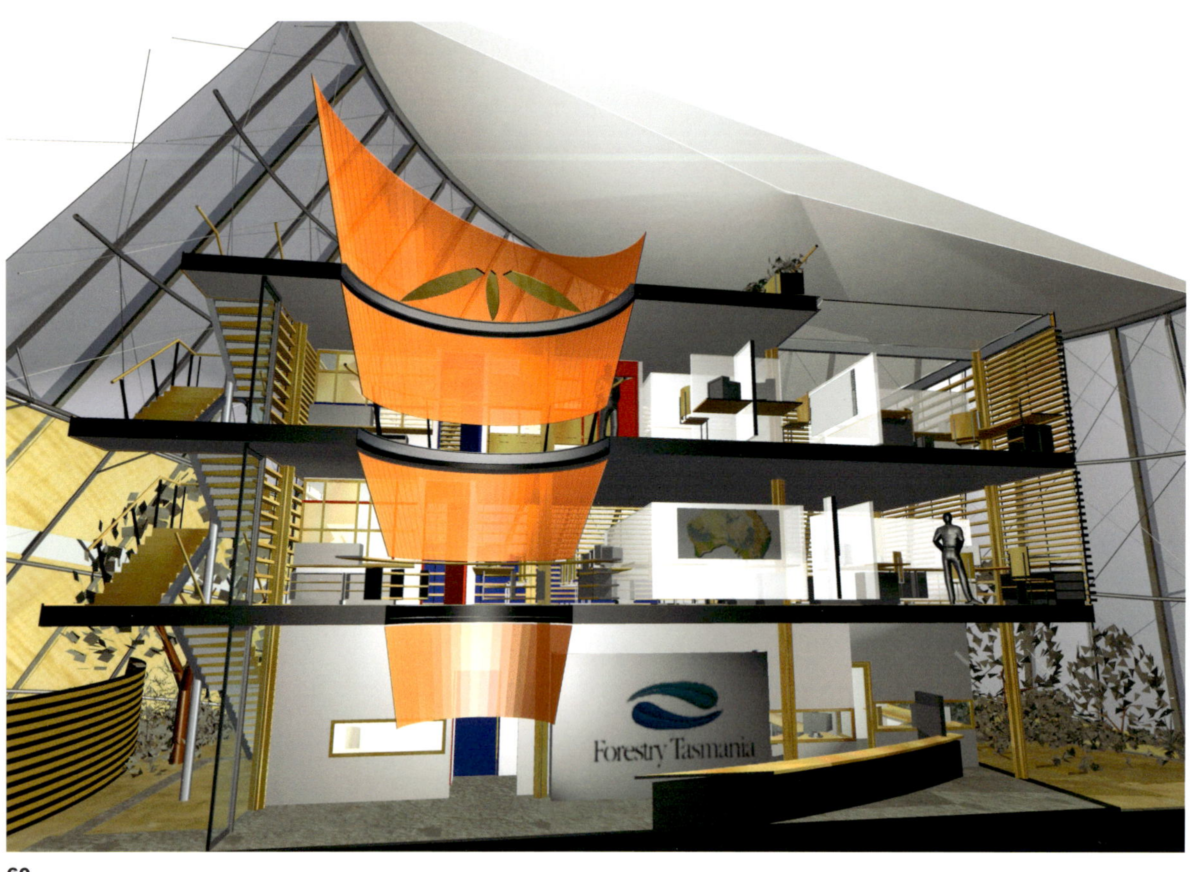

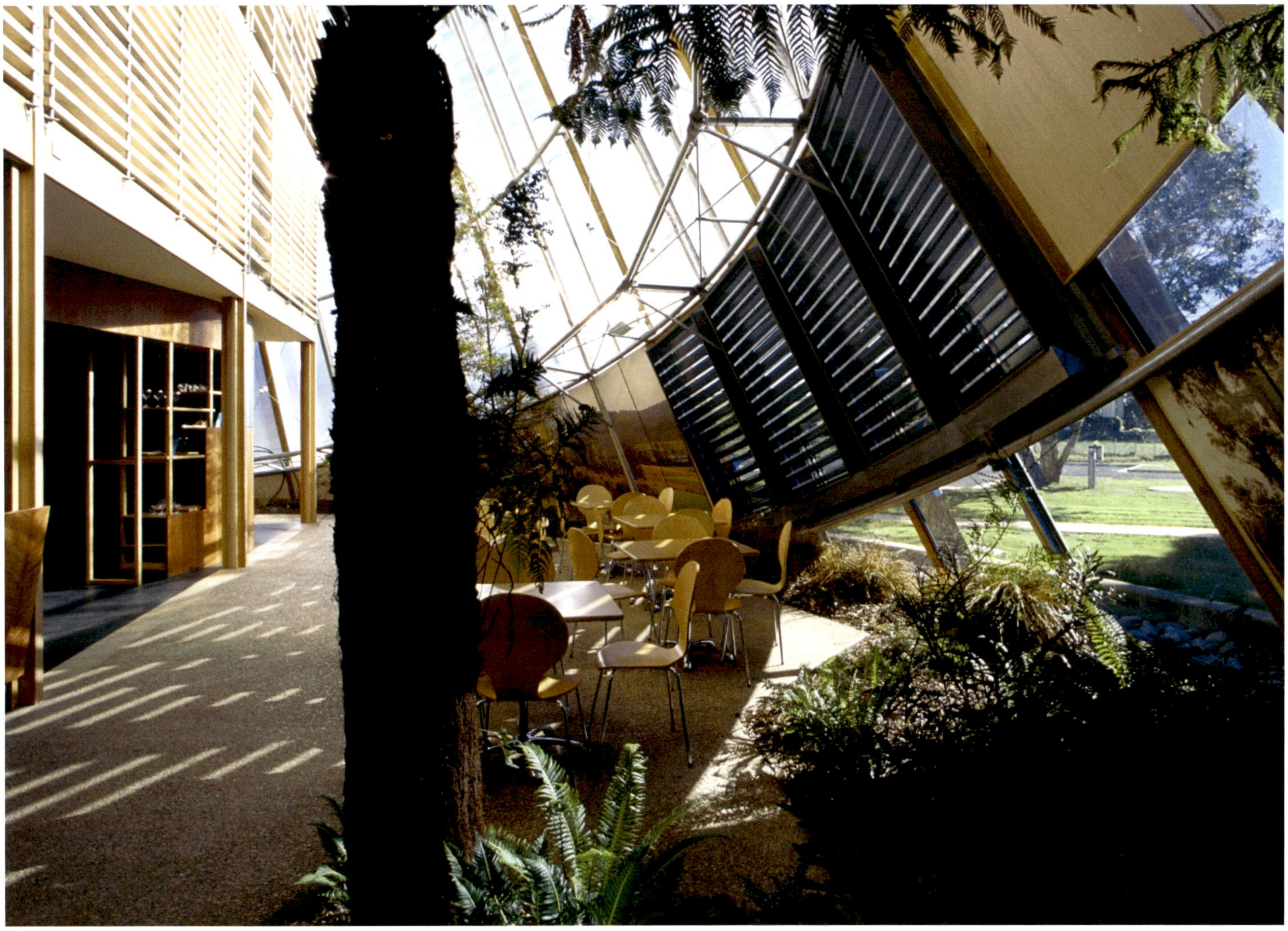

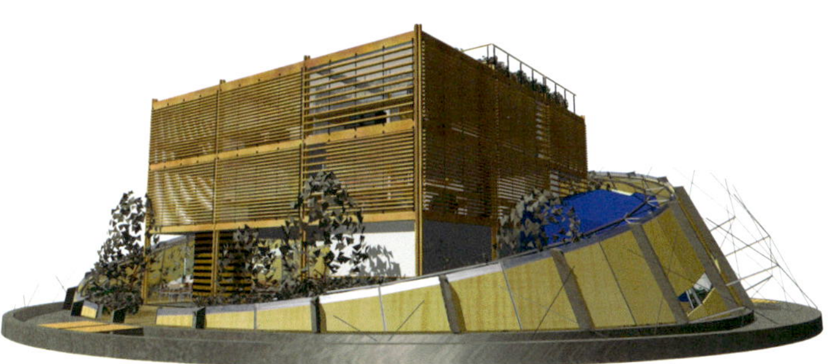

Location Scottsdale, Tasmania, Australia

Construction period 2000–2001

Client Forestry Industry of Tasmania, Scottsdale

Architects Morris-Nunn & Associates Architects, Hobart; Robert Morris-Nunn, Peter Walker

Structural planners Gandy and Robert; Jim Gandy

Planning: heating, air conditioning, ventilation Advanced Environmental Concepts; Che Wall, Nicholas Lander

Electrical services planner Tasmanian Building Services; John Calder, Gosta Blichfeldt

Fire protection ARUPS; Per Ollson, Jan Ottosson

Cost control Stanton Management Group; Patrick Stanton of Davis Langdon Aust.

Building contractor Fairbrother Pty Ltd.

Training centre in Ober-Ramstadt / Germany

HANDCRAFTS

Architects: Heinz Braun, Gerd Ehrlicher, Tillo Schmidt

In Ober-Ramstadt, a community on the edge of the Odenwald, a new information and training centre for crafts people represents a communication platform extending across the different building trades, set up by Germany's largest manufacturers of paints and protective coatings for the building industry. The business chose for its "Haus des Handwerkes" ("Handcrafts House") an unusual construction that immediately attracts the eye. Under the curved roof there is a timber construction system that has never been used before. The building lived up to its name during the construction period, as it was built using a high level of craftsmanship and not as an industrialised prefabricated building. The choice of wood and colour enter into an exciting relationship with each other and are used together as a way of reflecting the company's business.

A stage for paints and protective coatings

Modern seminar and meeting rooms of different sizes, as well as an Internet cafe for use during breaks, complement the 20 x 25 m hall under its domed structure. The core of the complex is a triangular two-level presentation stage that can accomodate single or parallel demonstrations of the application and use of the company's products. Ceiling floodlights with warm and cold lamps, as well as spotlights with reflector mirrors, simulate all imaginable lighting conditions in order to demonstrate the various surface finishes.

The main access is through the entrance hall, which also contains cloakrooms and sanitary facilities. Beside the entrance hall is a foyer giving onto a tea kitchen and an administration office. The training room with stage as well as the presentation hall can both be reached from the foyer. The training room can be opened up to the foyer and the presentation hall. A small service room, with separate access from outside, houses the electro-technical services and equipment used for lectures and presentations. The domed building allows presentation surfaces of different heights to be set up. A seminar room and a conference room with a mobile partition wall are separated from the training room by chair storage. There is a changing room next to the conference room. At the southwest of the building there are two further small service rooms for the heating plant and electrical switchboards.

Roof shell using a stacked board construction system

The unusual construction of the training centre is, in structural terms, a shell. In order to achieve the required room height, the shell rests on columns. The wooden ribs and the seven layers of boarding form a stable structure. Filigree tension chords transfer the horizontal thrust to the four bearing points.

The "Handcraft House" is built using the stacked plank system (see ENVELOPE chapter). In this simple but highly contemporary method, individual boards are combined to form a spatial structure by simply nailing them together. Since it allows the use of lower quality wood, this system is economically attractive; in addition, it permits a considerable degree of prefabrication, which means that the building period can be drastically reduced. Thus the primary shell – the structure – is also exposed to form the interior and its shape determines the character of the hall. The colours used are also signals, with a significance and effect that the company wanted to particularly emphasise here. Although applied only as a thin coating both inside and outside, colour cannot be overlooked and determines the nature of the form, "reaching" the viewer and the visitor from afar. This reasonably priced opportunity to

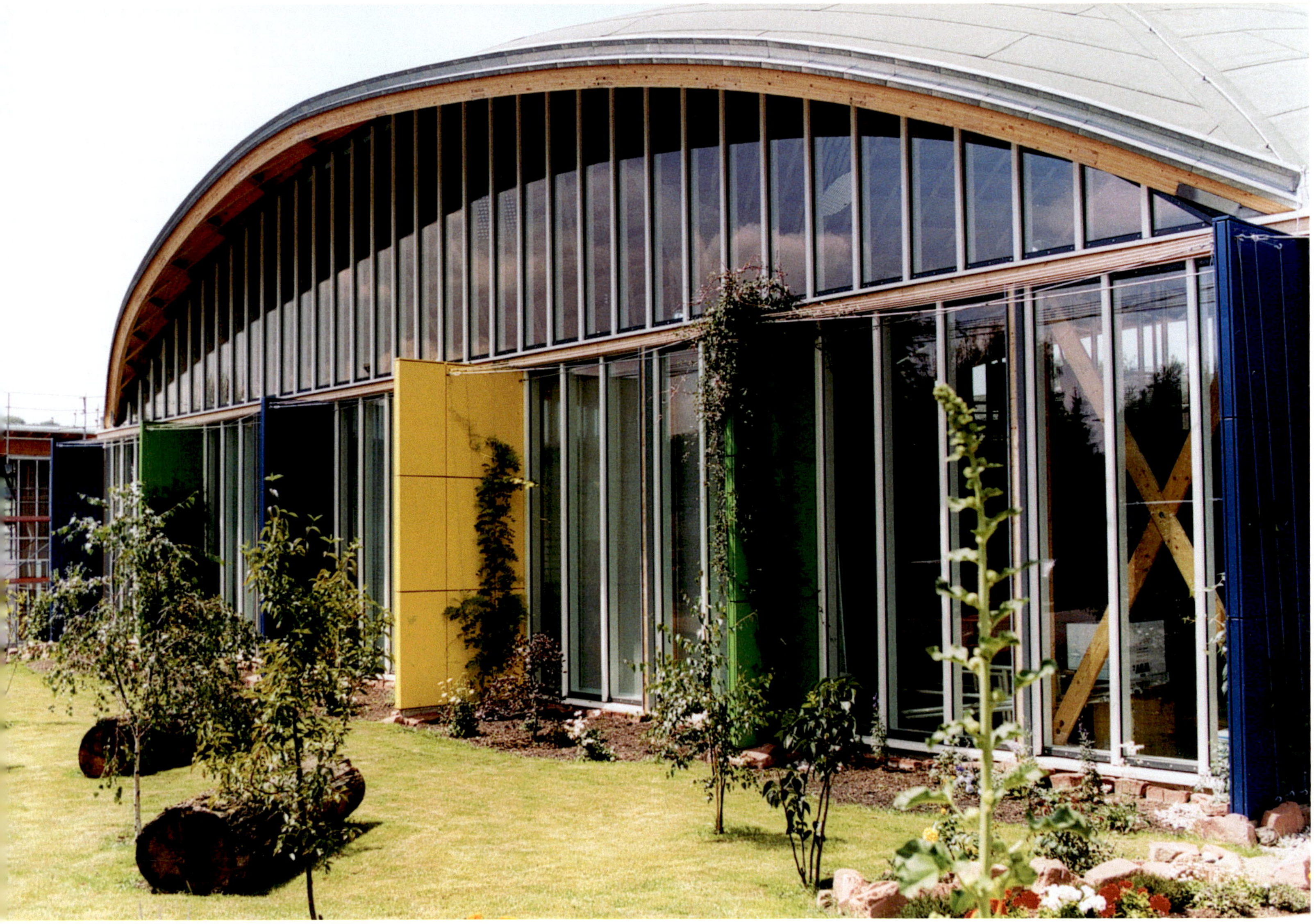

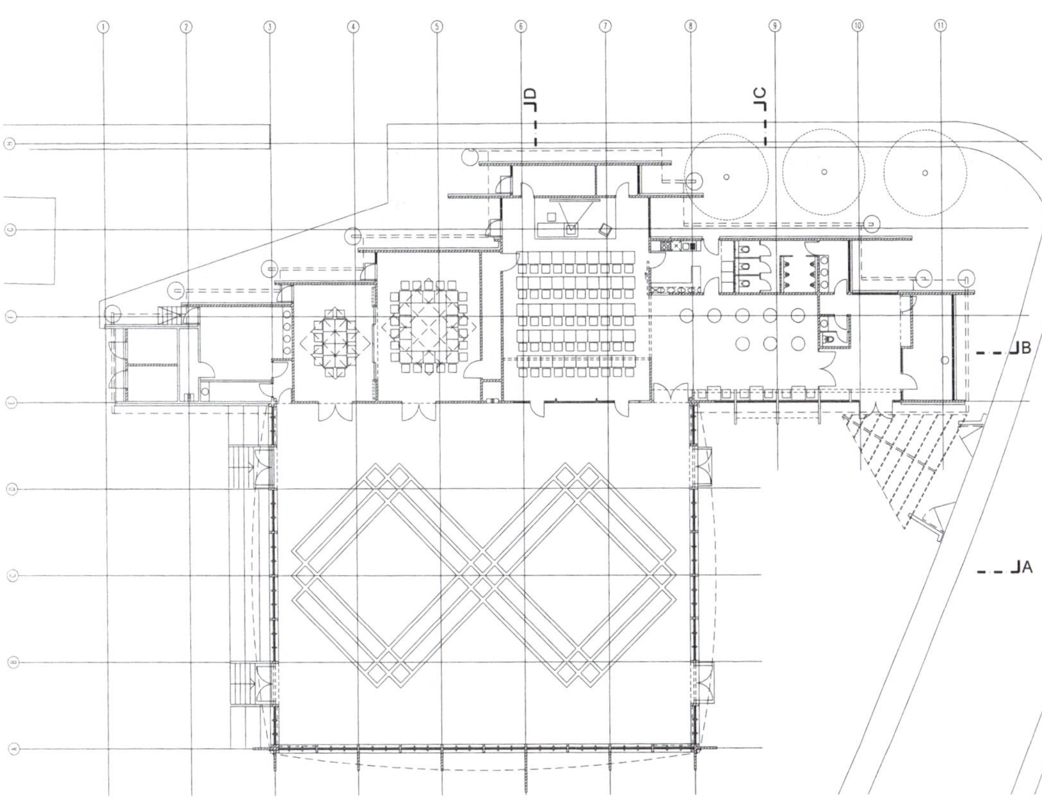

Ground floor

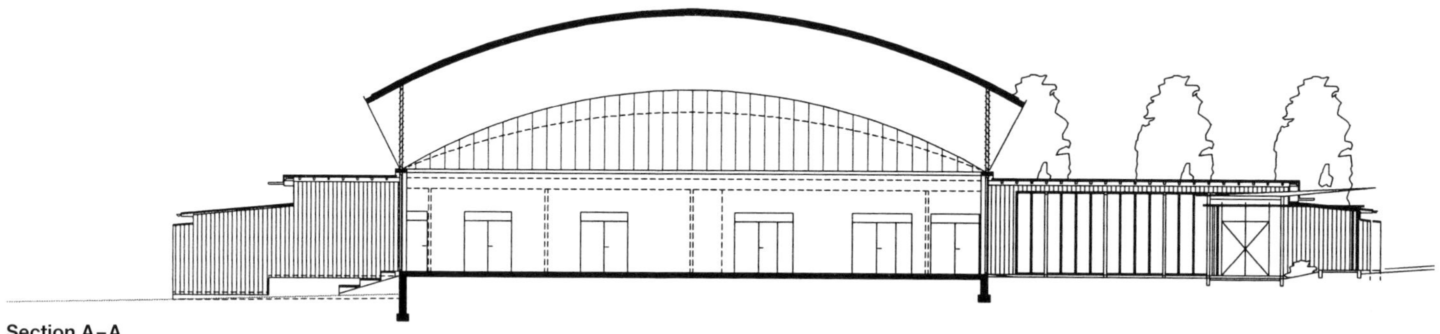

Section A–A

deliberately and sustainably influence form demands a considerable degree of knowledge and a keen feeling for the particular context. The "Handwork House" is therefore not only a place where this knowledge is handed on but is also an object where the company's own products are demonstrated, providing examples of the possibilities of surface coatings in the most varied applications.

Construction and fitting

For the erection of the dome it was necessary to create a falsework as a negative form, which was simply and cheaply made using nailed panels and timber trusses. The individual trusses were braced against each other to form a structure of their own. The roof shell was designed precisely using a 3-D CAD programme. The special aspects created included the development of suitable bearings for the four corner points where the forces are extremely concentrated. The outcome is a bearing point at which seven ribs meet, two of which serve as verge ribs.

The shallow dome spans a rectangular floor plan of 20 x 25 m. This means that the board ribs are inclined differently, a fact that had to be taken into account in making the bearings. Two different kinds of bearings had to be made, designed as mirror images of each other. For safety reasons, models were made and tested. The roof shell, on the other hand, was designed entirely using CAD. The carpenter received the CAD data from the architect, checked them and then constructed his falsework.

The roof shell is carried by 4-m-high glued laminated timber columns. The corner columns were constructed as three-part pinned columns (with a space for a rainwater pipe) and consist of three individual beams measuring 18 x 18 cm. Between the corner columns, at a distance of 2.5 m, posts were inserted that, due to their dimensions of 8 x 48 cm, work effectively as panels. Their broad side was set at right angles to the facade so that they can divert wind loads. Steel wind braces were provided in the corner bays to ensure stability. For fire safety reasons, they were later clad in timber. The fixing was made using bolts, the heads of which are filled with wooden plugs, also for reasons of fire safety. The horizontal forces from the roof shell are taken up by a laminated timber tension band (15 x 48 cm in cross-section) running around the roof. This tension band is fixed to the panel columns using slotted metal plates and is mitred at the corners. After the bearing points had been fixed, the ribs of the shell-shaped roof structure could be constructed. Starting from the bearing points, this structure was mounted by hand, board by board. Each wooden lamella was handmade on site. This approach was simpler that having to design thousands of different lamellas on the computer. Each arched rib consists of spruce lamellas that were curved and screwed in four layers over the falsework. The arched ribs were laid closer together at the diagonals to the

dome, creating an attractive pattern. The glass facade is attached to the ribbed arches that run almost parallel to the edge ribs. The boarding used as an exposed soffit helps to stabilise the structure and, at the same time, carries the thermal insulation and the roof skin. By leaving a distance joint of 1 cm between the exposed boards, the effect of an acoustic ceiling was achieved. The dome has a height from the top of the tension band to its topmost point of 6.4 m, the height from the floor to the top of the dome is 10.6 m.

Location Ober-Ramstadt, Germany

Construction period 6/1997–6/1998

Client Deutsche Amphibolin-Werke of RobertMurjahn GmbH & Co. KG, Ober-Ramstadt

Design Tillo Schmidt, Freiburg

Architects Architekturbüro Heinz Braun, Darmstadt; Gerd Ehrlicher, Griesheim

Structural designer IEZ Internationales Entwicklungszentrum für Holzkonstruktion, Julius Natterer, Saulbarg/Wiesenfelden

Timber construction Ingenieurholzbau Heinz-Werner Ochs, Kirchberg

Volume (hall with dome): 4420 m³

Surface area of dome 530 m²

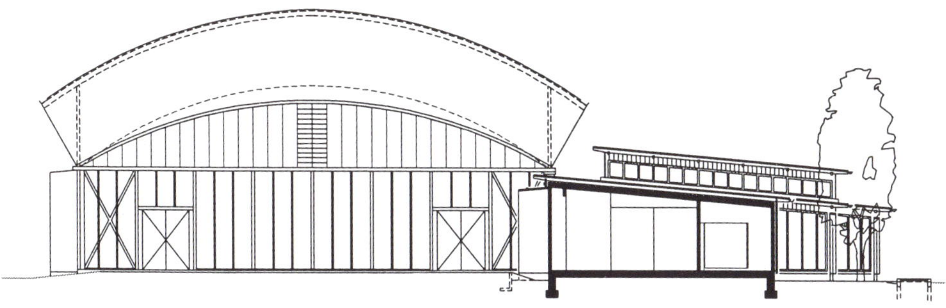

Section C–C

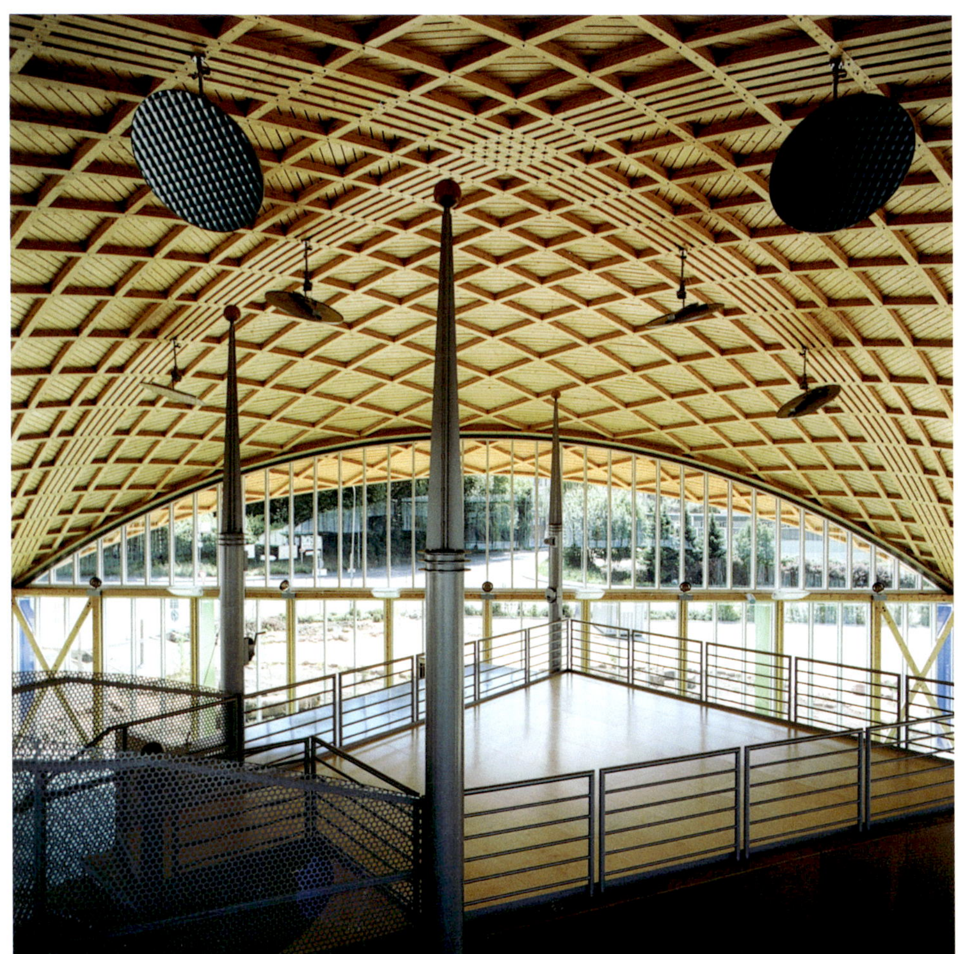

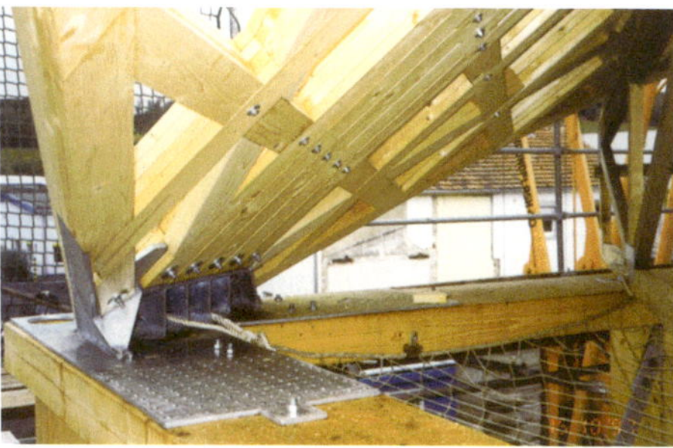

One of the four bearing points of the roof shell

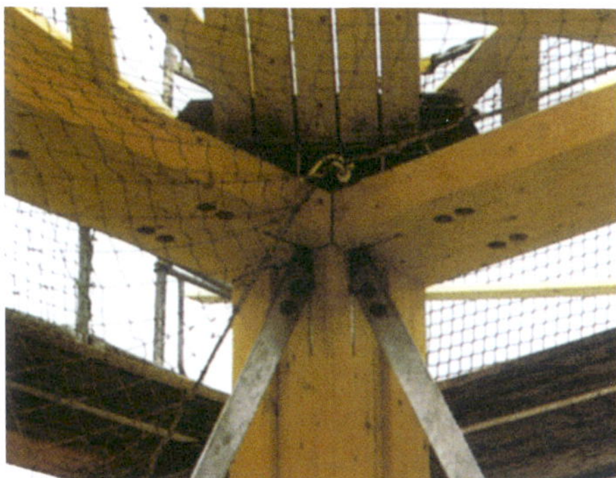

Detail of column – tension bands – bearing point
– wind-bracing made of steel

IIDA Archiship Studio

Forest Club in Nagano / Japan

FORESTRY

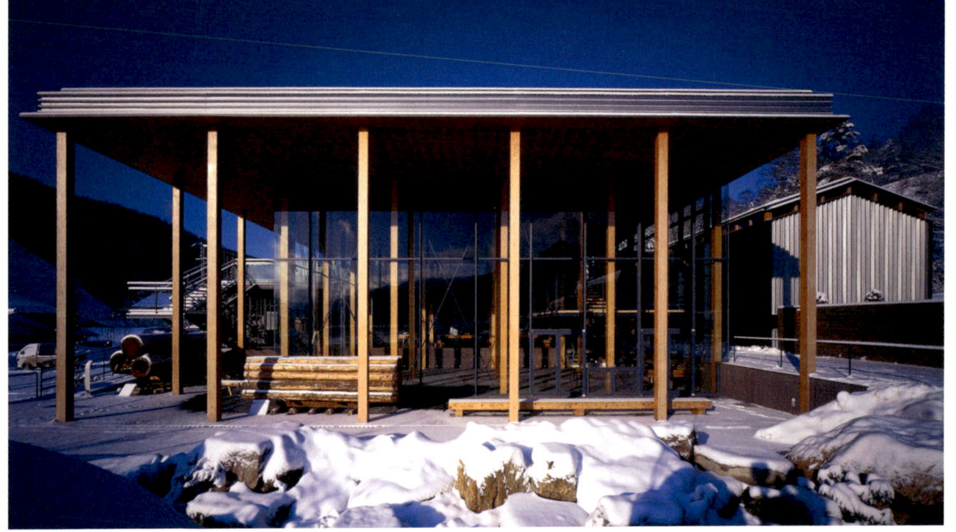

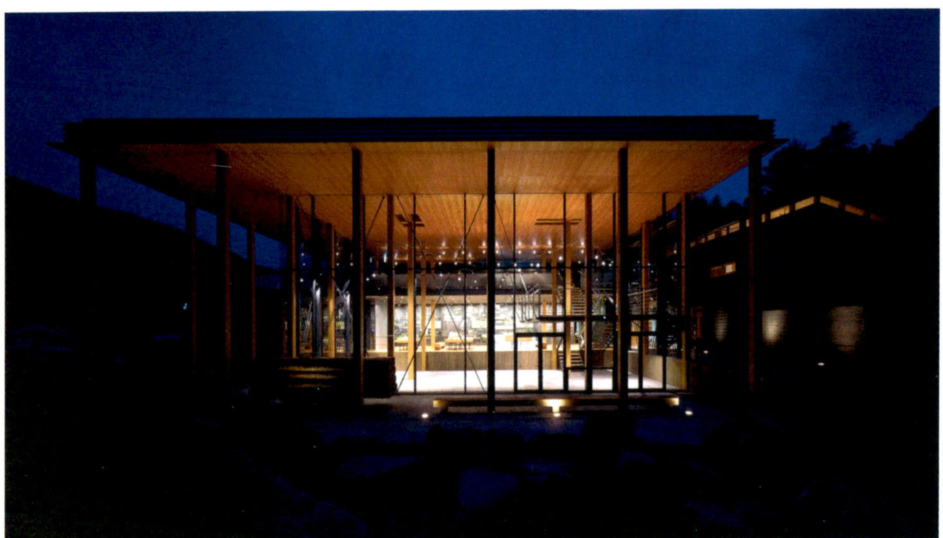

The Kawakami Forest Club is a facility of the forestry business that offers seminars and lectures for the further training of its members. The club is, however, also used for public relations work. It is intended to encourage cultural exchange between the forestry business and the local population, to develop an understanding of the work done in the woods, and to explain the complex processes involved in sustainable forestry as well as the economic context of the use of wood.

The brief for this two-storey building with timber skeleton frame construction includes a training and conference space, a hall for travelling exhibitions, a permanent gardening exhibition, a club room for the forestry engineers, a restaurant with kitchen and outdoor terrace, and a foyer. The building was primarily built in larch wood, which is the predominant type of wood in the region. Emphasis was laid on contemporary design and the use of innovative timber elements.

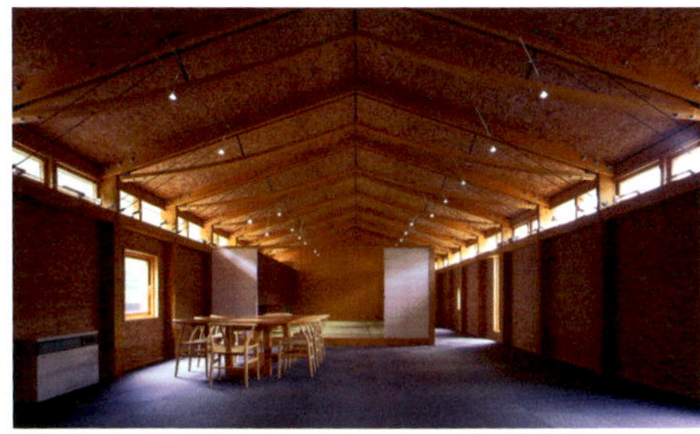

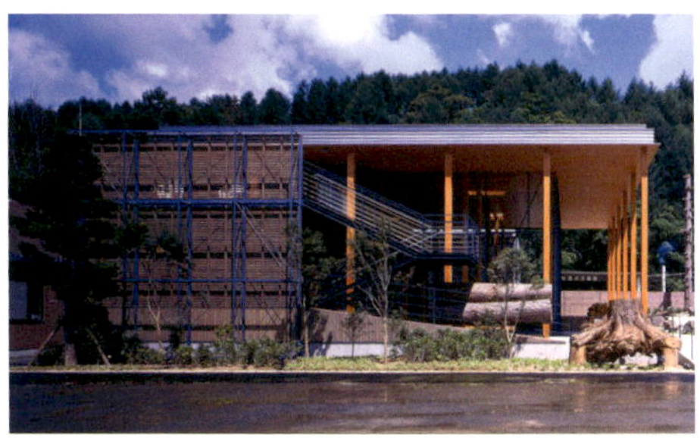

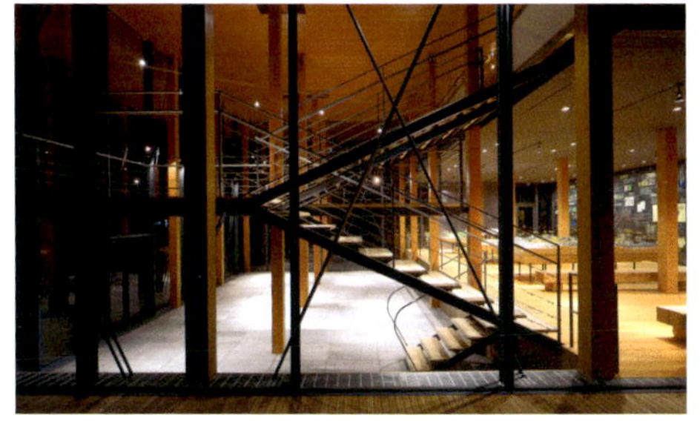

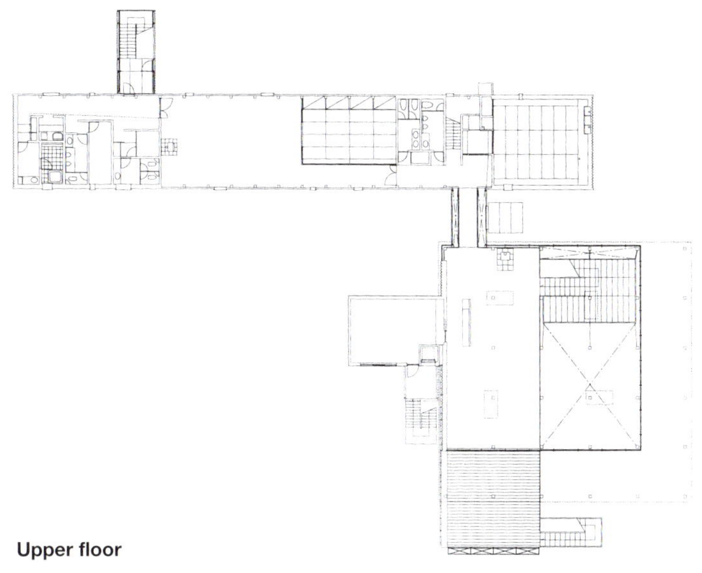

Upper floor

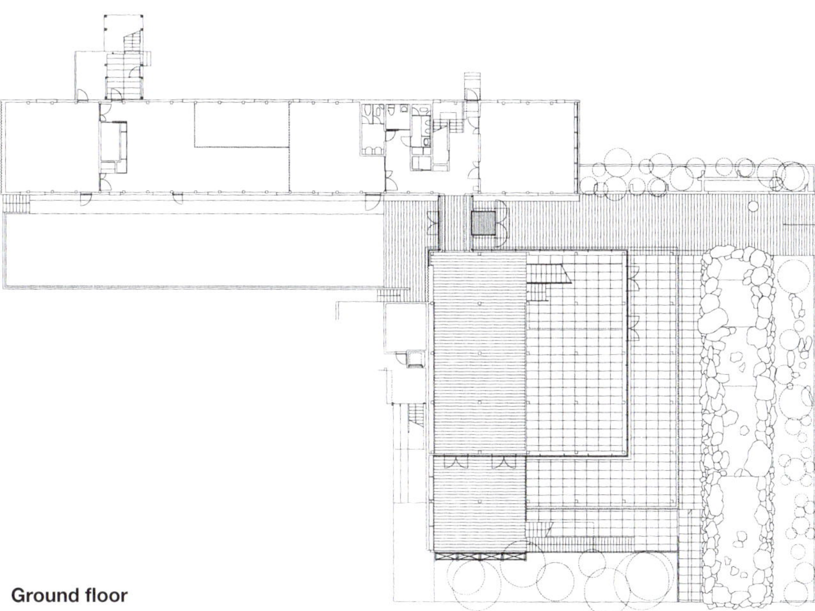

Ground floor

Location Nagano, Japan

Construction period 9/1996–5/1997

Client Forest industry Nagano

Architects IIDA Archiship Studio Inc., Kanagawa

Floor area 990 m²

Clubhouse in Tokyo / Japan

WESTWARD

Architects: IIDA Archiship Studio

This small clubhouse was built for the residents of a suburb of Tokyo. The single-storey building has a simply proportioned sequence of spaces. Essentially, it consists of three rooms: the outer doma, the inner doma and a multi-purpose room that can be used for various different kinds of activities. The doma is a traditional earth-floor space that is used as an entrance area, workshop or communications area. In addition, the service spaces include a kitchen and a lavatory.

The roof of this building uses a stacked plank system (see ENVELOPE chapter, page 18), made up of timbers of a standard cross-sectional size 2 inches x 12 inches (38 mm x 286 mm). These timbers are connected with nails and bolts to form an element resembling a panel, consisting of glued layers of boards. The coffered walls were built using the same standard timbers, whereby vertical louvers are connected with horizontal ones. Through the combination of these walls with the stacked plank roof panel, there was no need to use internal columns. This allowed the entire building width of 7.5 m to be flexibly exploited in terms of dividing up the internal space.

Location Tokyo, Japan	
Construction period 11/2001– 3/2002	
Architects IIDA Archiship Studio Inc., Kanagawa	
Floor area 89 m²	

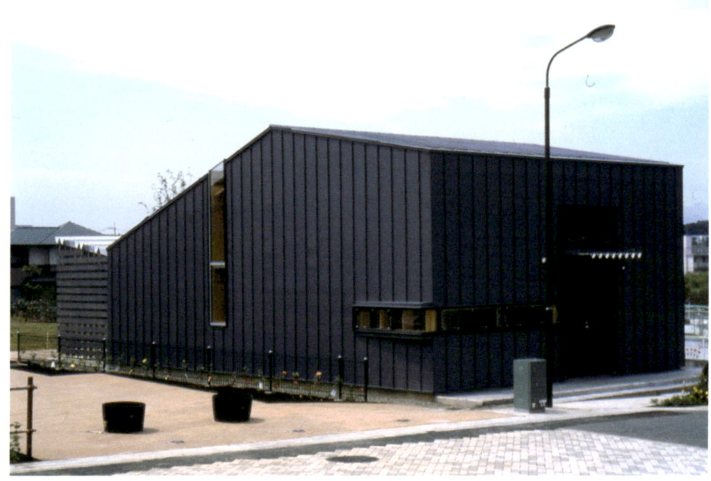

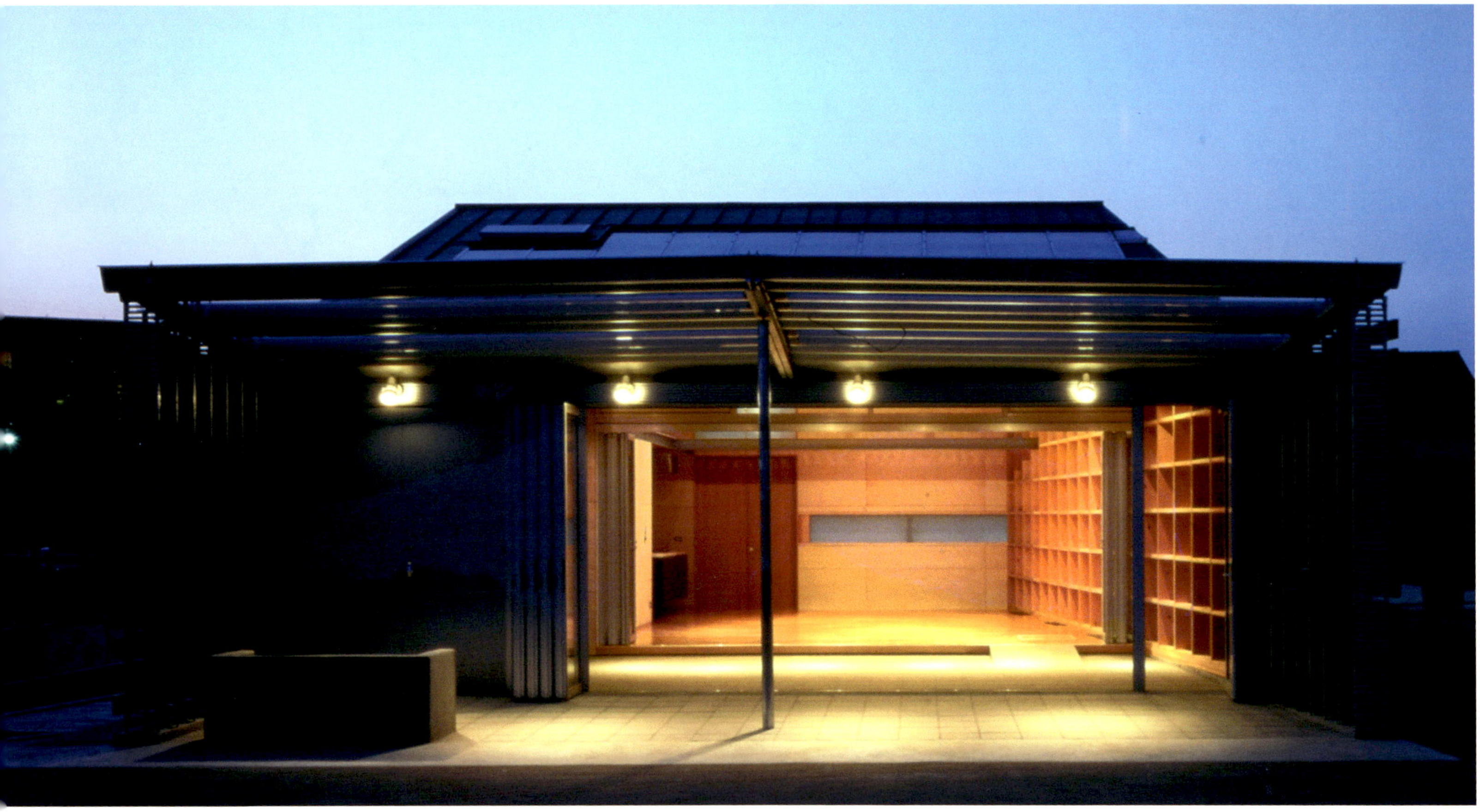

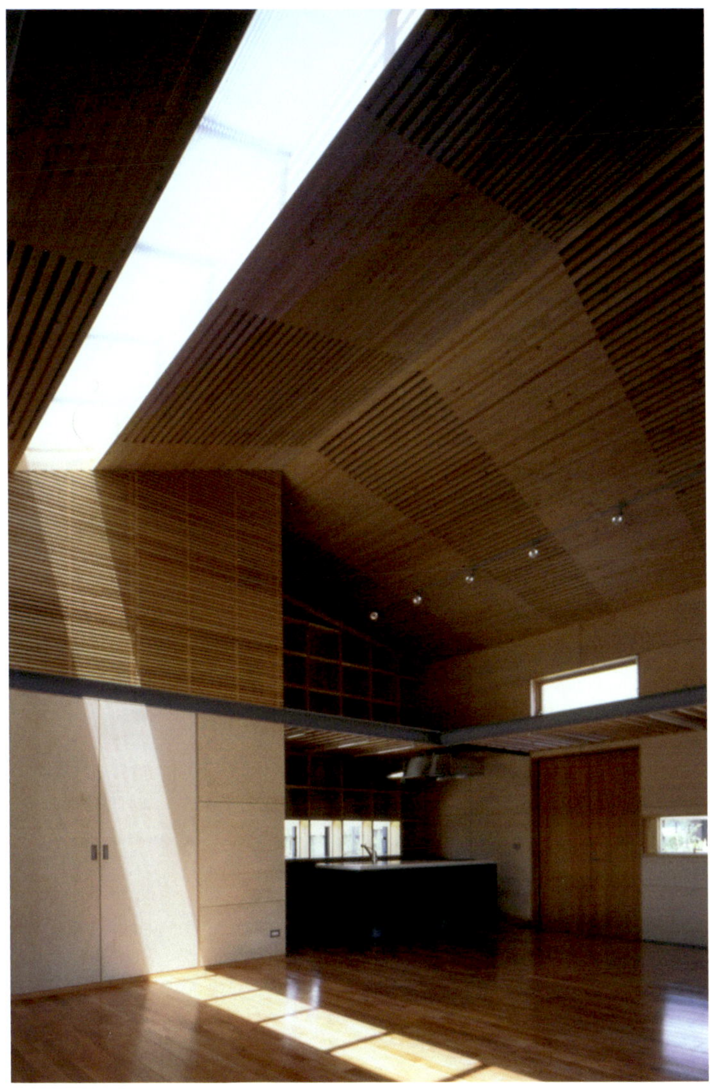

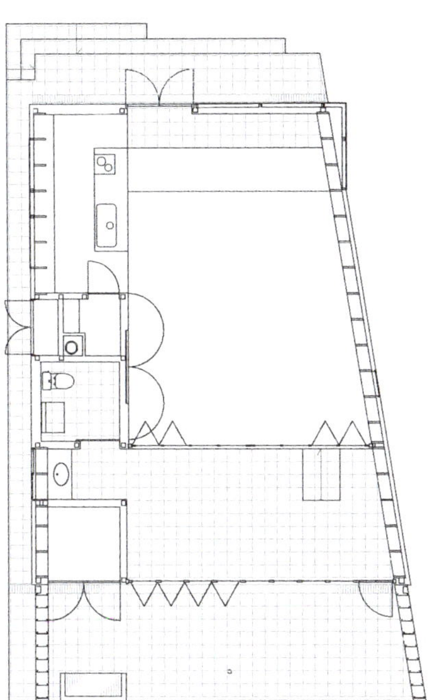

Floor plan

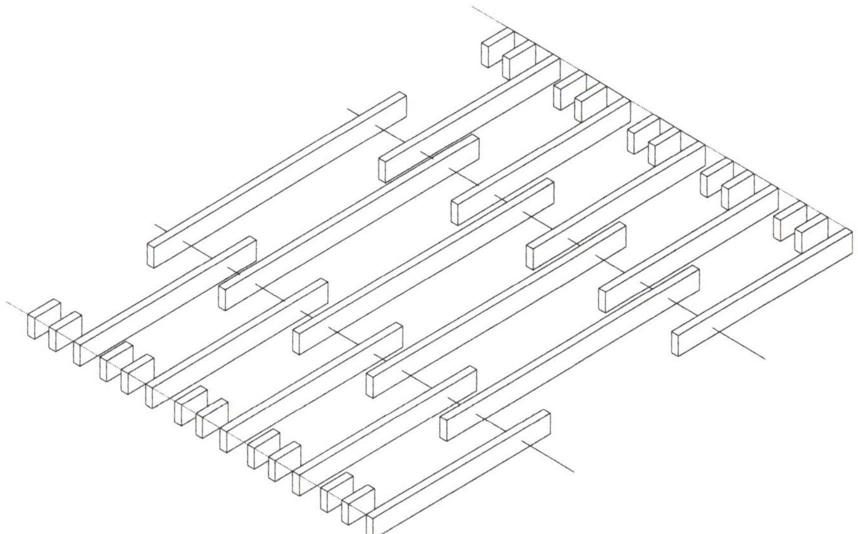

Arrangement of timbers for
the stacked plank roof panel

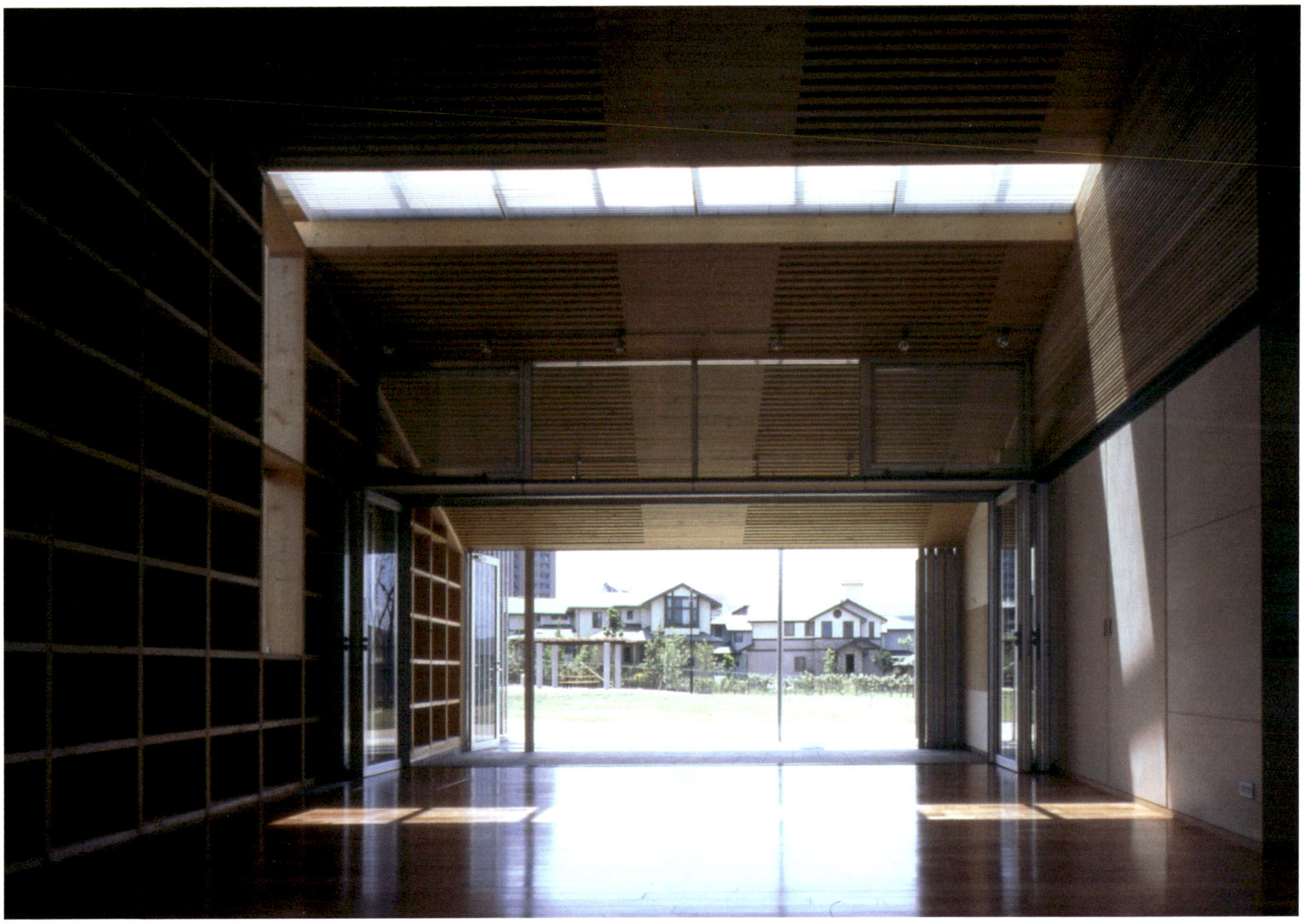

View outside from the multi-purpose room, looking through the doma

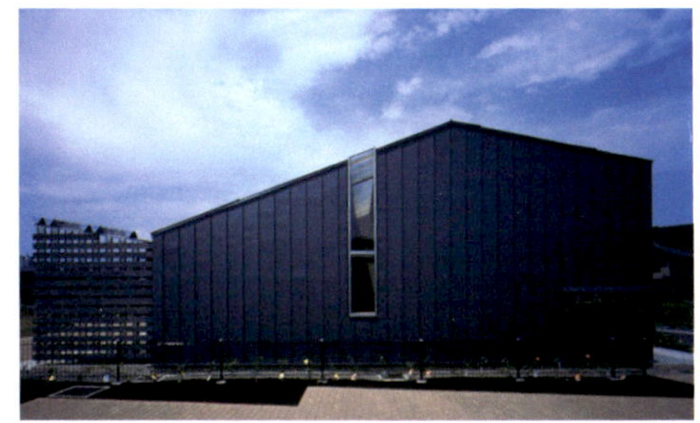

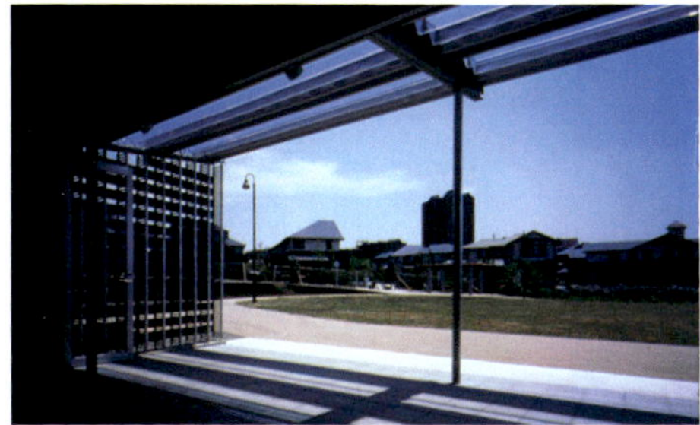

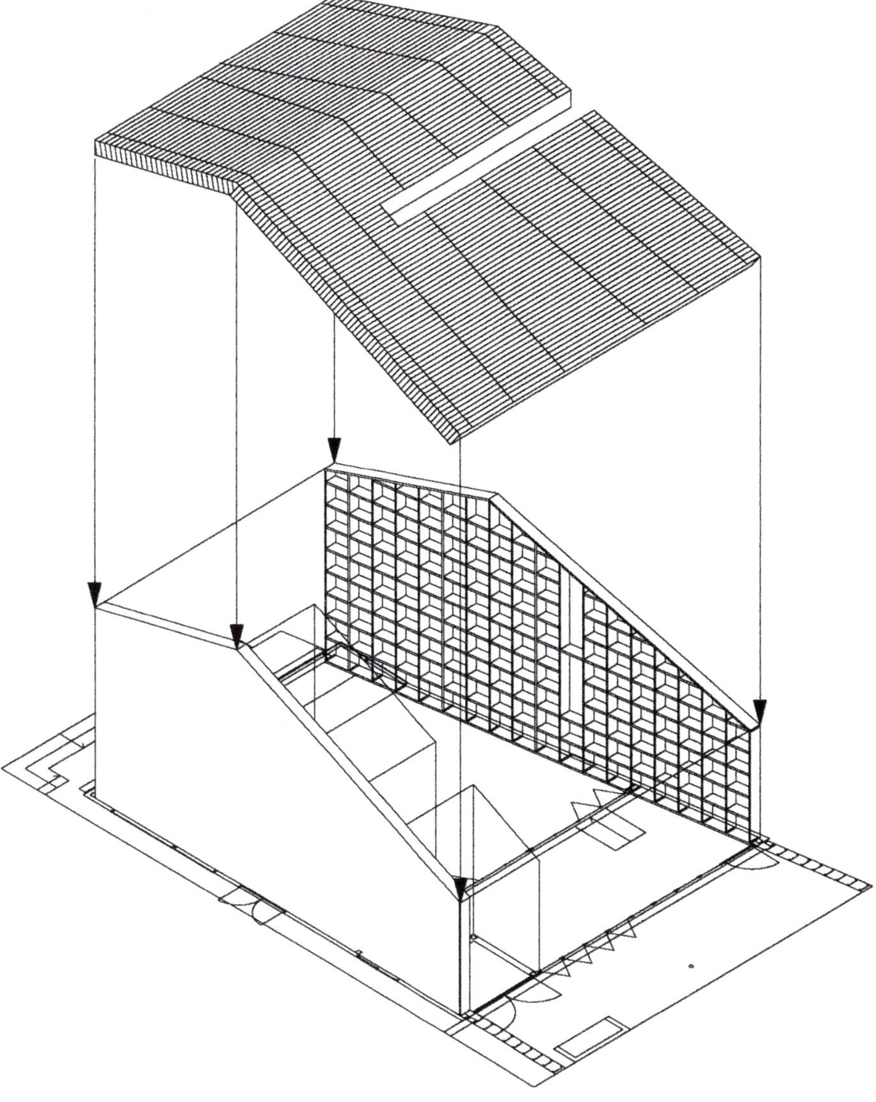

Isometric with stacked plank roof lifted

Outdoor store in Seattle/USA

EQUIPMENT

Mithun Partners Architects

The light, decorative sales space of Recreational Equipment Inc. (REI), retailers of outdoor sports goods in Seattle (Washington State), received an international award as store of the year. On three floors, this shop offers customers the sensual experience of a shopping world that perfectly displays a wide range of sports goods in the surroundings in which they will be used. The attractive and environmentally conscious timber construction is successfully combined with steel, concrete and glass components and thus ideally suits the theme of high-tech sports goods for outdoor use. The shop is regarded as a kind of "clubhouse", and many see it as part of a "peaceable northwest experience". In this sense the building is a "present" to the city of Seattle, as it makes a definite contribution to the identity of the region.

A cooperative of sportspeople

REI not only offers the largest range of quality equipment and clothing for outdoor sports in the United States (i.e., equipment for camping and mountaineering, touring and cycling, climbing, winter sports and water sports), but is also the leading supplier worldwide of outdoor equipment. A mail order service and adventure travel agency round out the range of services offered. Recreational Equipment Inc. is a unique business; this American retailer of quality

outdoor sports equipment and clothing, with over four million partners, is one of the largest consumer cooperatives in the world. Founded in 1938 by a group of climbers who wanted to obtain quality equipment from Europe, this cooperative is famed for finding reasonable prices and at the same time guaranteeing optimum quality, a service that did not exist at that time in the United States. The emphasis on

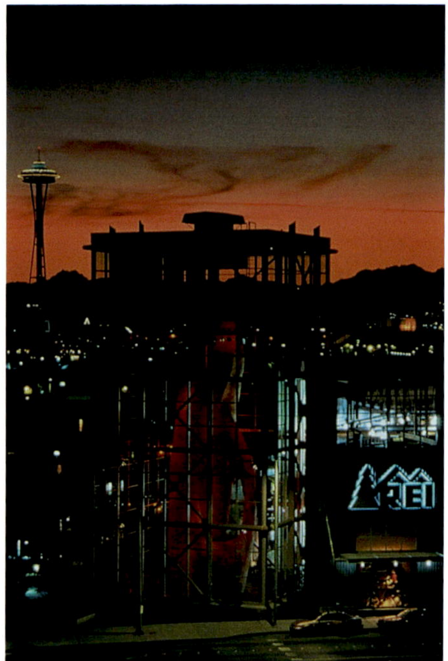

quality, service and the members' involvement in decision-making still has top priority; a major portion of the profits is returned to the members in the form of a yearly dividend.

World of experience

In this context it was a particular challenge for the architects to combine the character of a modern specialist store for open-air sports equipment with cost-effective, environmentally conscious aspects, the exploitation of the available resources in terms of site and materials, and a sensually perceptible, enclosed shopping environment. Their aim was to create a world of experience in which all the designed areas, such as outdoor space, entrance area, staircases, sales rooms and displays, harmonise ideally with each other and perfectly display the current range of high-tech sports products.

The wooden structure, which was completed after only a fifteen-month building period in the autumn of 1996, is ideally suited to its location on the west coast of North America, a region that lies in an earthquake zone. It offers an area of 8,900 m² on three floors for various different kinds of outdoor sports. In addition, the building includes a repair and equipment hire department, office spaces, a large conference and lecture room with seating for 250, a children's

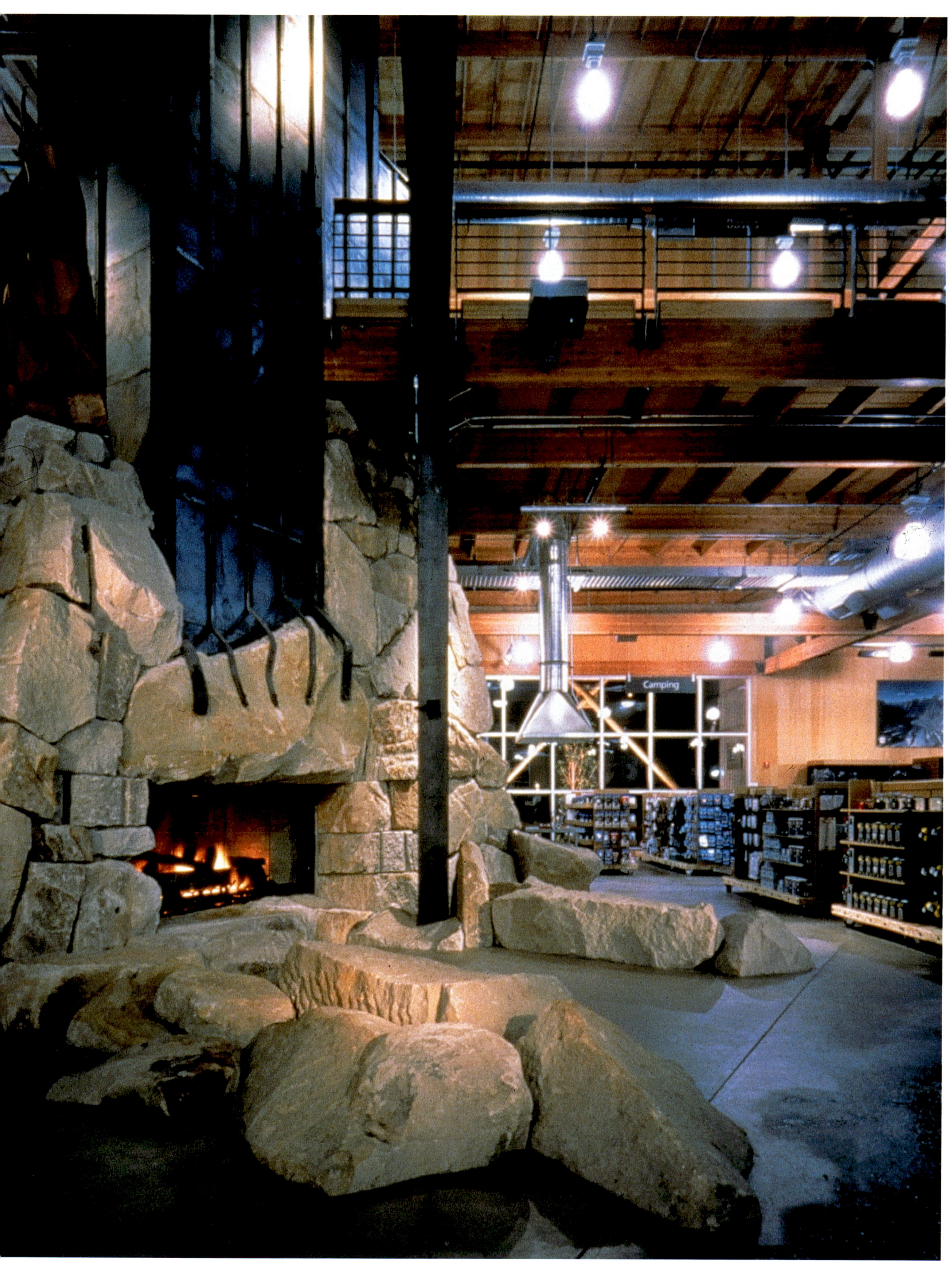
Camping

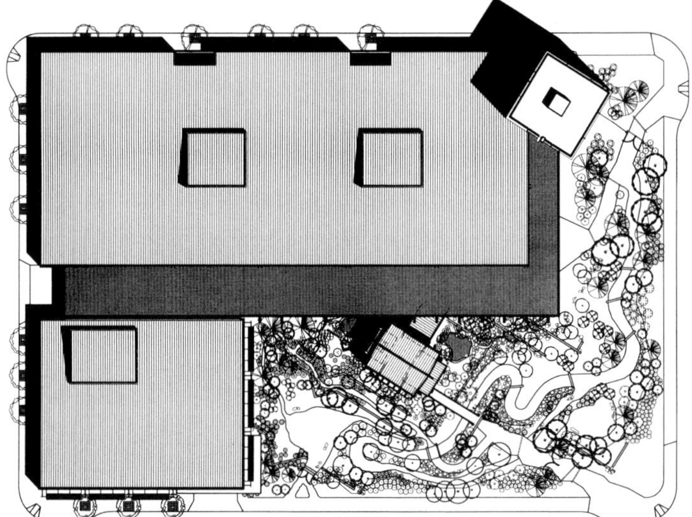

Top view

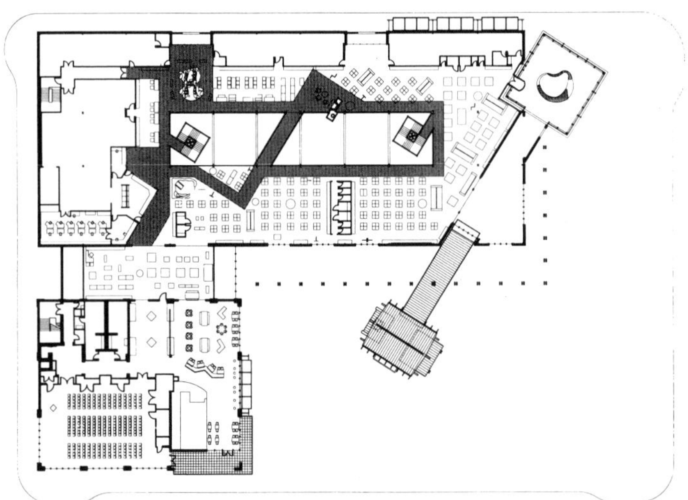

Upper floor

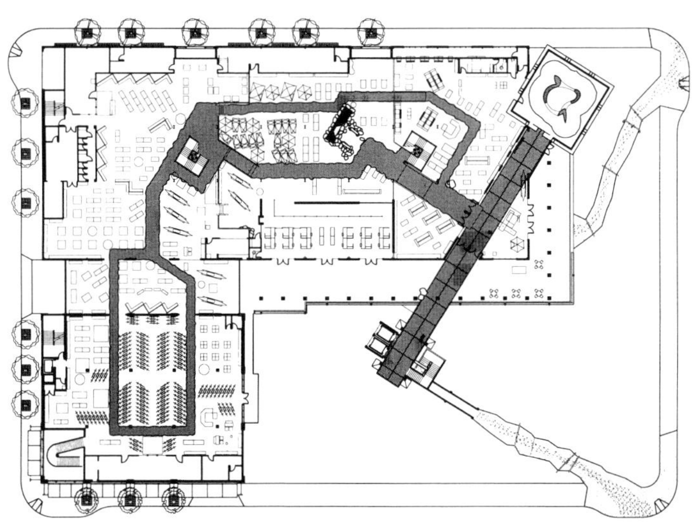

Ground floor

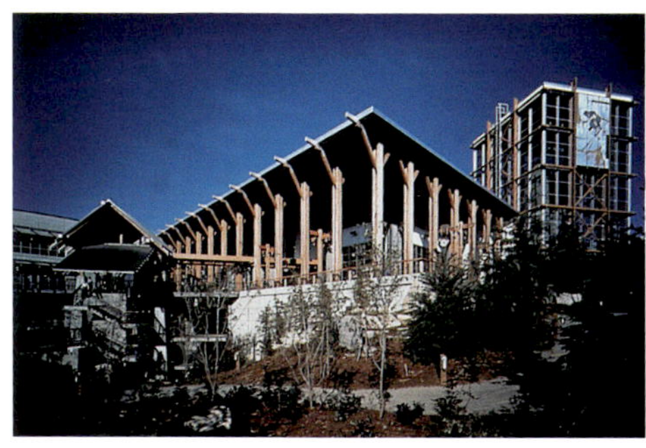

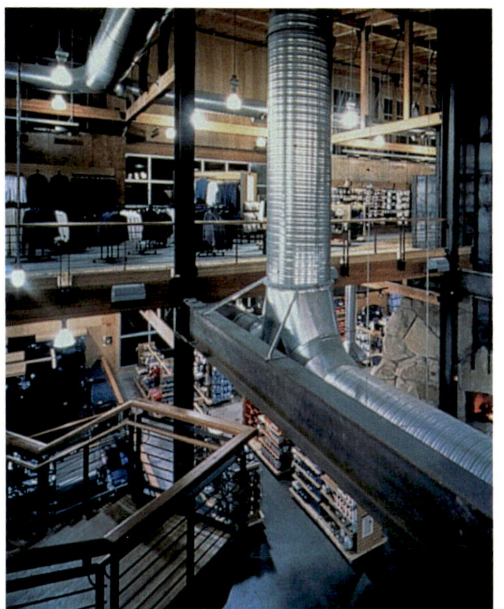

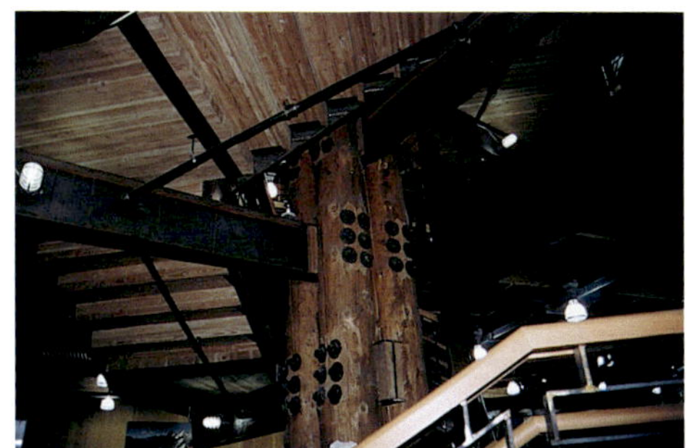

play area, an art gallery, and a café with seating for 100, as well as an underground garage with 456 parking spaces. With a 20-m-high rock face (the largest free-standing indoor climbing facility in the world), a running track for trying out running shoes, an indoor rain room, a gigantic landscaped courtyard with mountain bike testing area, a nature trail and a waterfall, the customers are able to test products in the surroundings they will be used in, and are offered a world of experience that appeals to all the senses and motivates them to become active themselves.

Since wood is ideally suited to the design of a natural environment and light atmosphere and, at the same time, symbolises environmentally conscious building, it was decided to use gluelam trusses for the roof and floors as well as for the staircases. The load-bearing columns are made of rusted steel, rough-sawn wood (rustically treated or even left in the form of logs) or concrete, depending on the aesthetic and structural demands. Plywood panels have a structural role in the walls and ceilings. OSB panels were used as decorative wall cladding for the displays and as demarcation for the cash desk areas. The plywood and OSB panels have five coats of naturally coloured glaze, giving them a shiny marble-like appearance. The roof structure is a combination of gluelam with steel trusses and Douglas pine timber sections. In order to give the building a light character, the plywood lining of the roof structure is left exposed. The wood, steel, concrete and glass components of the building can be seen as an entirely successful combination of nature and high-tech that ideally complements the range of sport products on display.

The restriction to just a few basic materials in both the construction and the interior remains true to the traditions of this business and serves as a symbolic connection between indoors and outdoors. It stands for a sensible exploitation of existing energies and for environmentally conscious building. Three quarters of the materials used here (for example, wood and windows) came from earlier REI buildings and were used again here. The recycled materials and objects range from shop counters to the rocks used in the outdoor landscaping. Rainwater is collected and led to a waterfall at the entrance that provides a visual and aural attraction for the visitors, in addition to drowning out the noise from the nearby motorway.

The pronounced awareness of both materials and energy that the architects displayed is reflected in the design as a whole. It integrates natural light, energy-saving lighting, the use of solar energy and environmentally sound building materials. The generous and open entrance and sales areas, as well as the natural and environmentally compatible timber building system, reflect the philosophy of outdoor enthusiasts: respect towards the environment and admiration of the beauty of nature.

Location Seattle, WA, USA

Construction period 6/1995–9/1996

Client Recreational Equipment Inc., Sumner, WA

Architects Mithun Partners Inc., architect & interior design, Seattle, WA; Assistants: Bert Gregory, AIA, design supervision; Thom Emrich, AIA, building administration; Rob Deering, project architect; Casey Huang, architect; Ken Boyd, architect; Bill McKnight, interior design

Structural planners RSP/EQE structural engineer

Mechanical engineering consultant MacDonald-Miller mechanical design/builder

Electrical services McKinney & Associatese; Madsen Electric

Lighting design Candela

Landscape architecture The Berger Partnership, P.S.

General contractor GLY Construction, Bellevue, WA

Floor area 8900 m²

Customer centre for a producer of houses in Rheinau/Germany

WORLD OF EXPERIENCE

Günter Hermann Architects

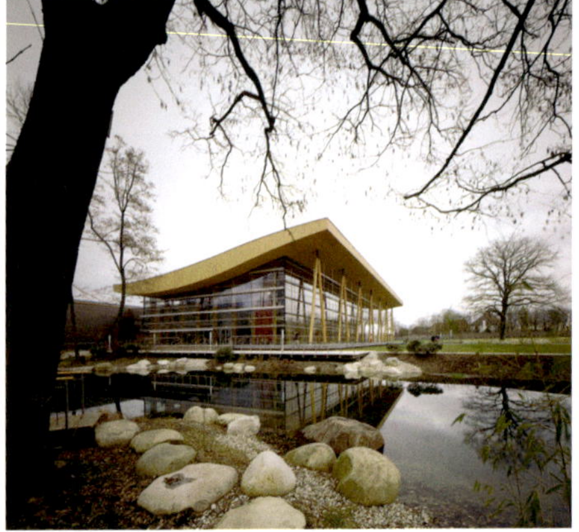

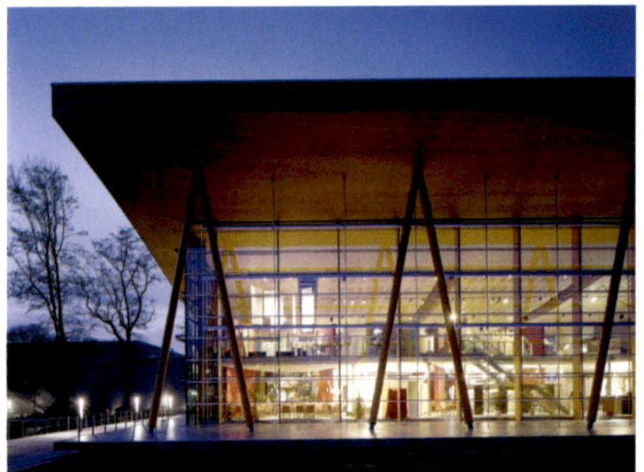

The plan was to build an extensive customer centre beside the headquarters of one of the largest producers of prefabricated homes in Germany; the company supplies high-quality houses with tailor-made plans, some of which are fitted out by customers themselves. Behind this centre was the idea of leading customers into a world of experience that accompanies them on a journey through domestic culture over the centuries.

The concept

The customers move through a park landscape with mature trees in which the houses are displayed and the customer centre is integrated. The complex consists of an exhibition hall with a conference room as a platform for presentations of products, a so-called "black box" with the "world of living" through which customers can take both a literal and figurative journey; first, a trip through different ways of living over the centuries and, second, a stroll through the park of alder trees to view the houses produced by the company.

The foyer

The main entrance is oriented towards the existing development. From an internal company street, one crosses a few steps to arrive under a large roof made of timber and steel that shelters the matt black forecourt. The laminated veneer ribs of the roof construction are threaded along metal tubes, and the main and secondary beams lie on the same plane. Internally, the two-storey foyer is functionally simple with white walls, a grey slate floor, a suspended gallery level and bright yellow cylinders that are inserted for special functions.

Exhibition hall

The timber building of the exhibition hall "floats" on a thick stony slab on the former flood plain of the Rhine. The slab serves as a base for the exhibition hall and offers visitors an elevated position from which they have a view across the park landscape. Identically structured matt black flooring connects the interior with the outdoors. Internally, an unpolished Porto slate is used, while externally, due to the danger of frost, concrete paving slabs are used with the same surface finish, which is achieved by imprinting the wet concrete with slate.

The curved wooden roof is supported by timber columns and also serves as a canopy for the main facade. At the sides and soffit, the construction is clad with naturally coloured Siberian larch wood panels that have internal areas with slits to improve the acoustics. In the completely glazed hall, there is an exhibition of fittings and furnishings and a customer advice centre.

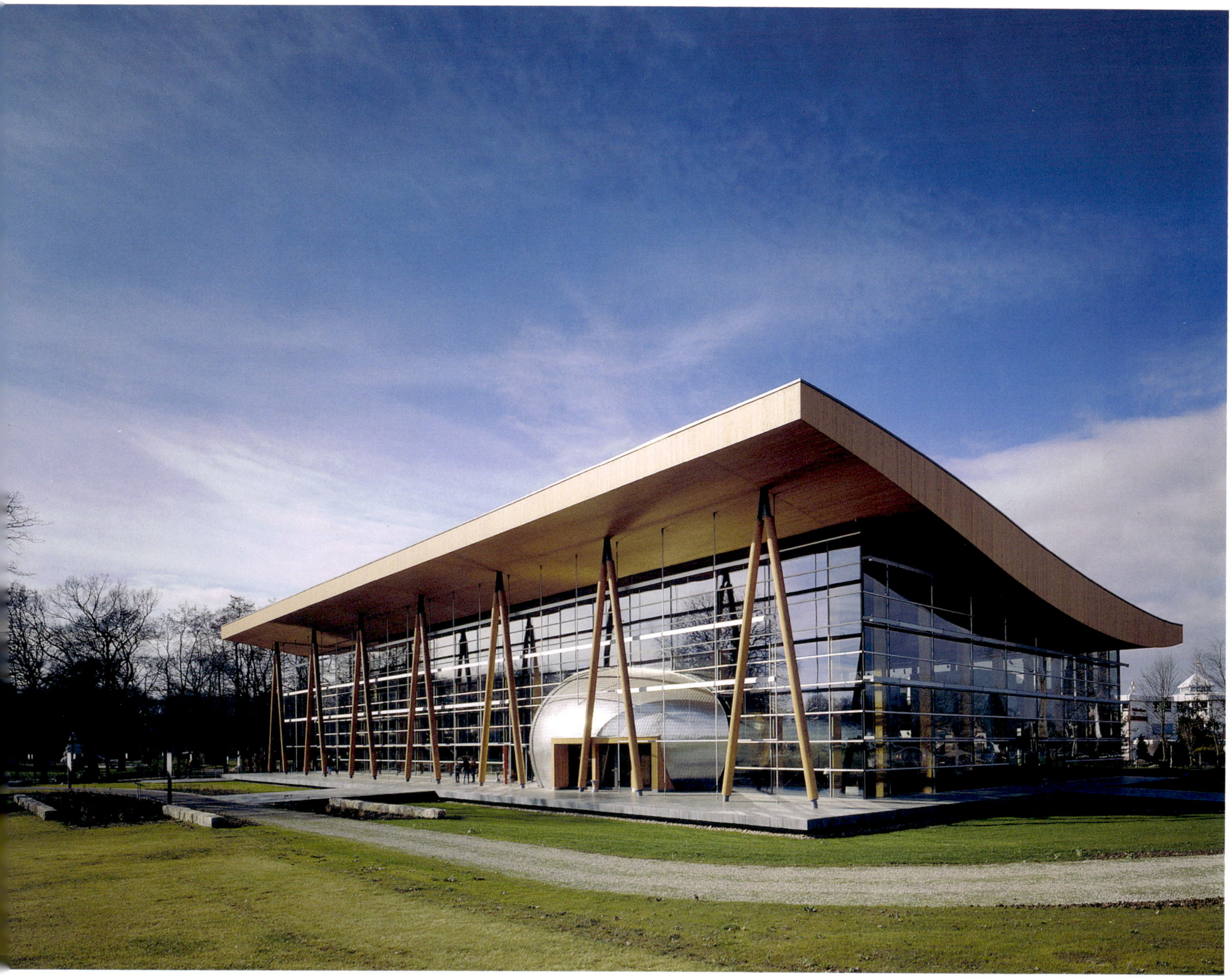

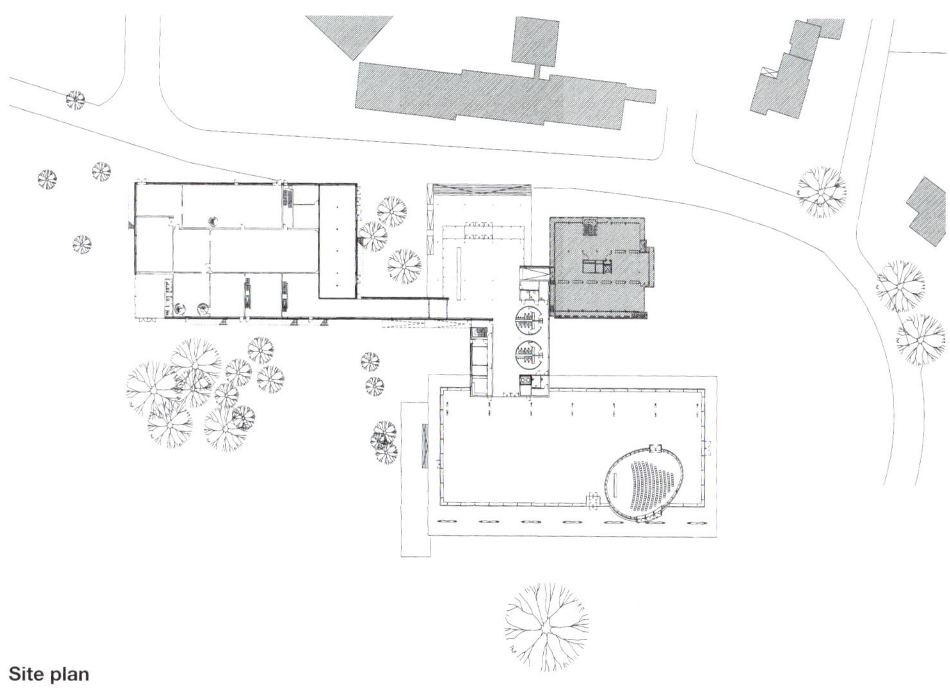

Site plan

The conference room

The conference room is part of the exhibition hall. With a shiny silvery skin made of tin-plated copper scales, the amorphous space slides through the main facade of the hall. Inside, the beams emerge out of the perforated plasterboard ceiling like the ribs of a skeleton. The floor is strip parquet made of smoky oak.

The black box

The grey steel building of the "black box" is on one side. It is used to store the sets and equipment for the event planners and set builders. The facade of the box is completely closed and clad with horizontally structured metal sheeting. Daylight is not required as the atmosphere on the sets is created using artificial lighting effects.

The timber structures

The structure of the exhibition hall
The timber construction of the roof structure spans a floor area of 66 x 30 m, without internal supports. In the transverse direction, gently curved fish-bellied, glued laminated beams are placed at intervals of 11 m. They each consist of two individual beams 20 cm wide and with a height that varies from 80 to 230 cm. At both of the long sides of the hall, these beams cantilever up to 8 m beyond the columns. The fish-bellied form of the beam reflects the trajectory of the bending moment. In the long direction of the hall, laminated timber purlins measuring 12 x 48 cm were placed at distances of 90 cm to take the roof boarding. The longitudinal purlins are hung as single bay beams between

the main beams. The purlins cantilever about 5 m at both gable ends. The tension and compression forces of the fixed end moment are diverted through the main beams by adjustable steel elements.

The roof decking, made of 33-mm-thick, three-ply blockboard panels, forms a shear bay that braces the hall horizontally. The A-shaped supports to the hall are made of circular section laminated timber columns, 40 cm in diameter. They work as a three-point frame and provide the vertical bracing of the hall. The load-bearing structure of the glass facade consists of slender laminated veneer sections that span freely between the floor slab and the roof plate, and are trussed with steel cables to prevent them from tilting.

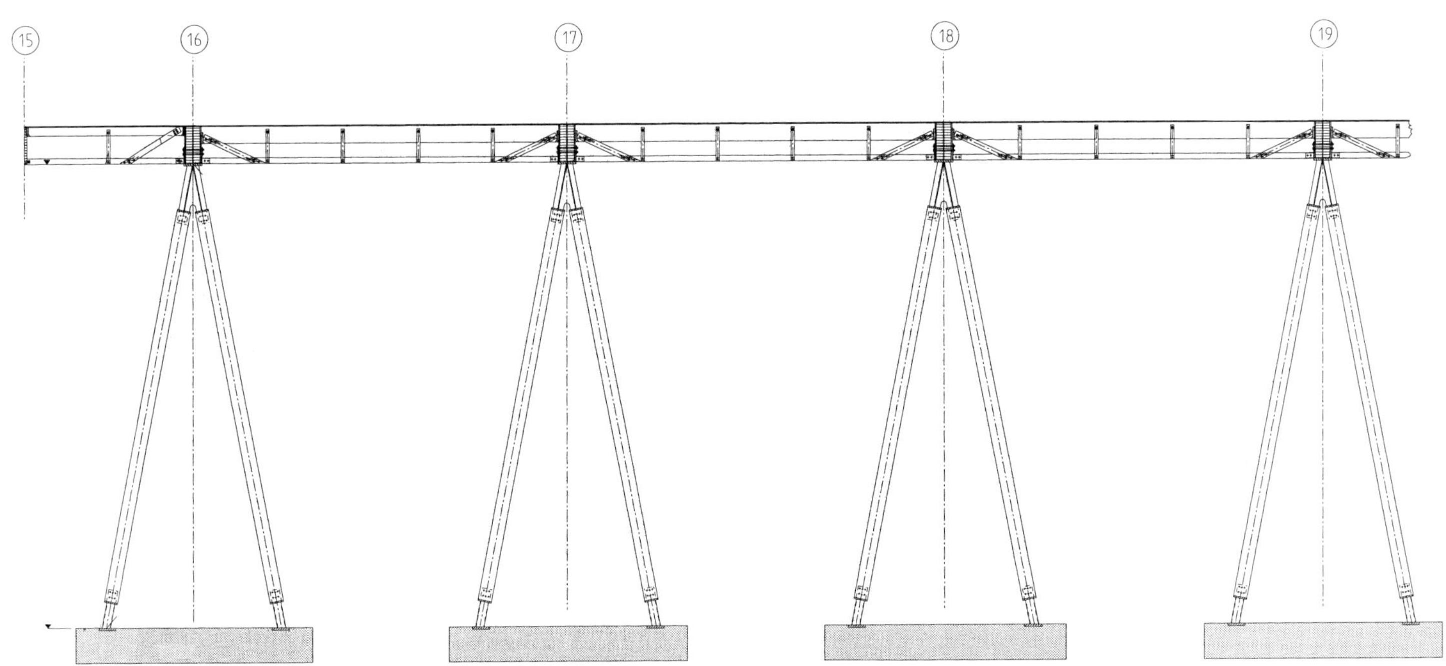

View of support frames in the exhibition hall

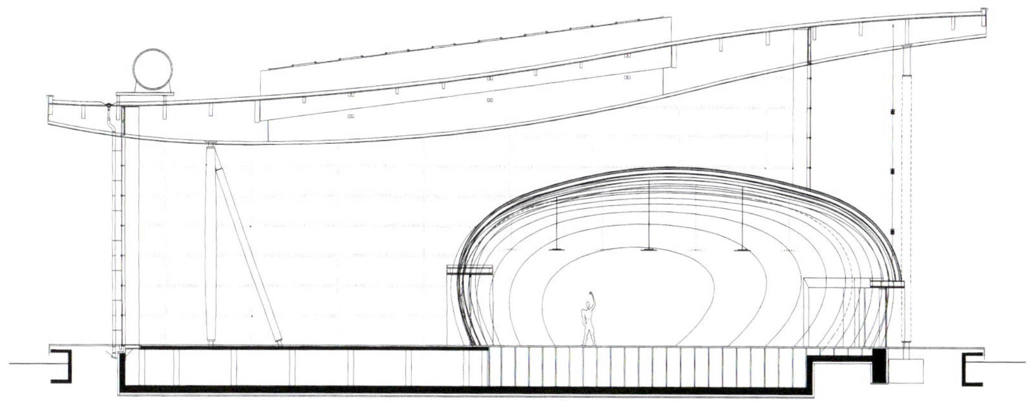

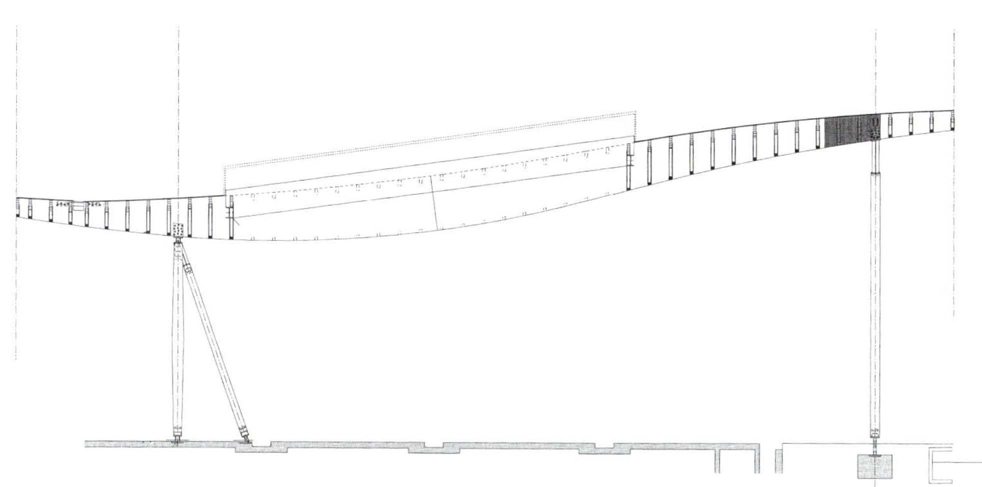

Cross-section through the timber structure of the exhibition hall

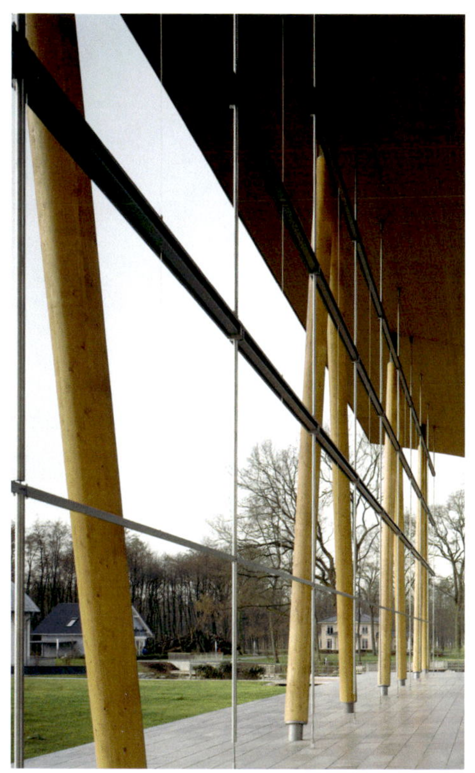

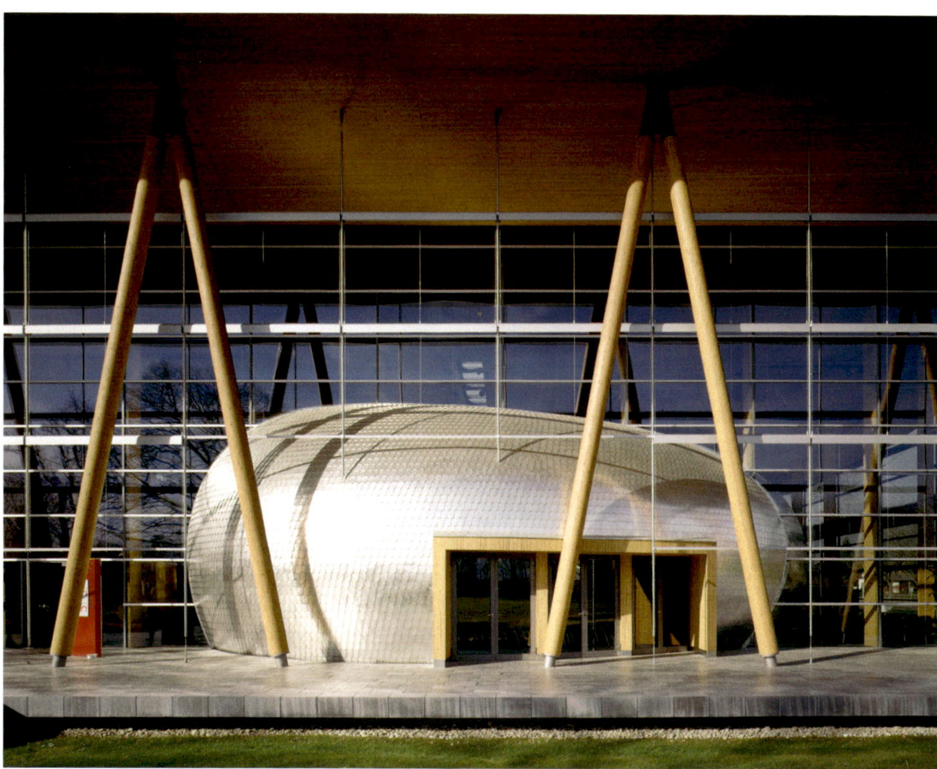

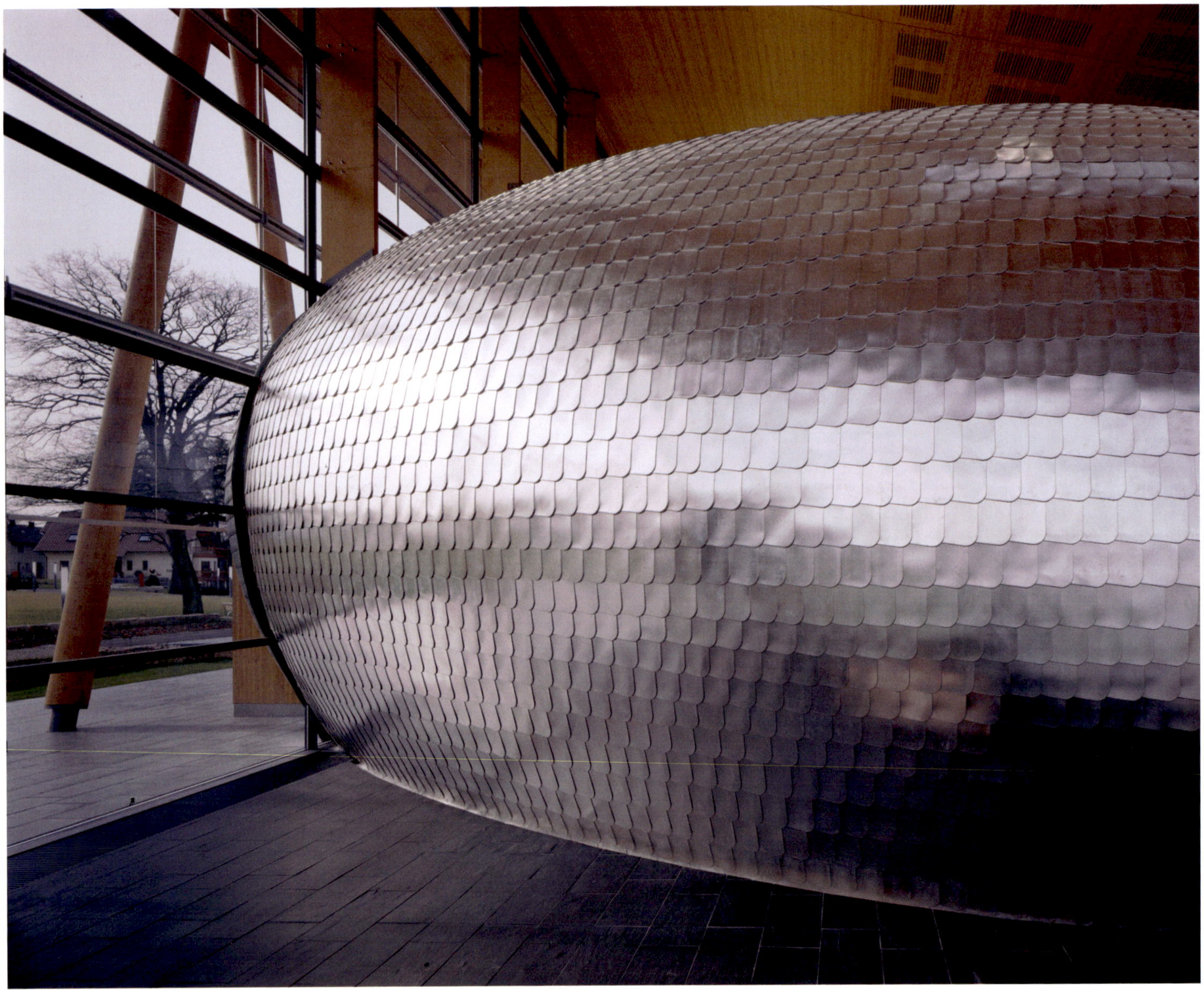

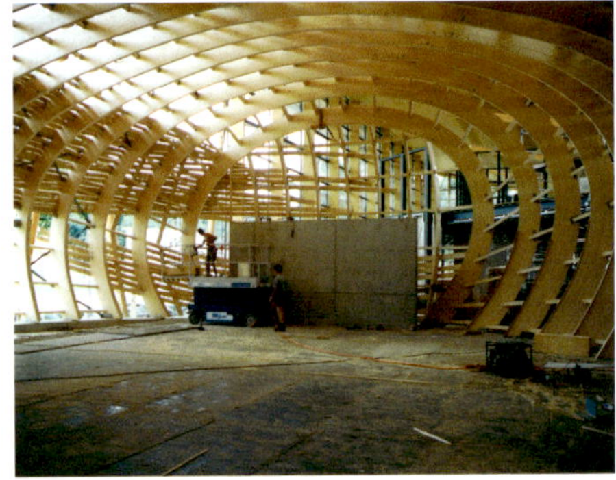

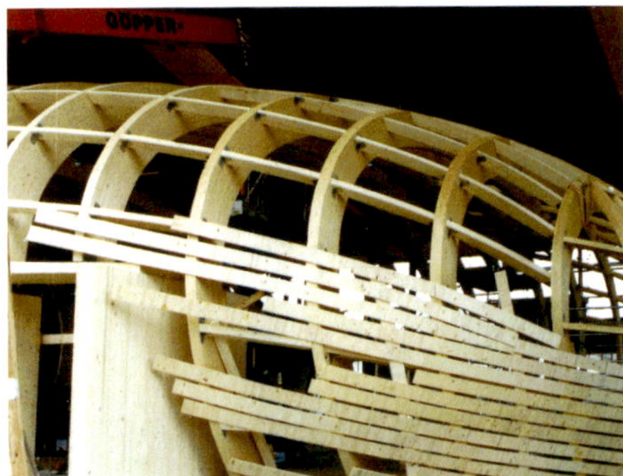

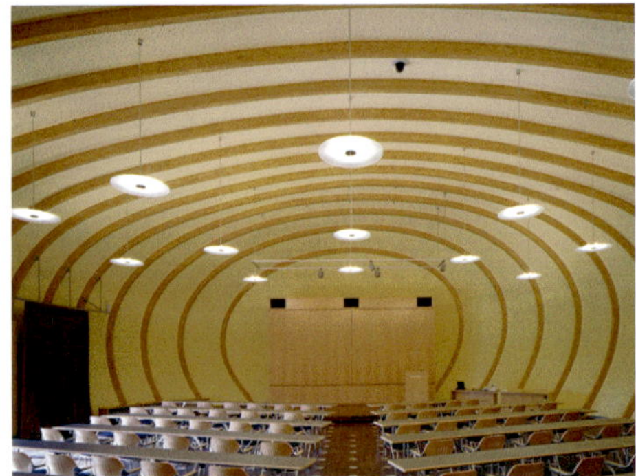

The conference room

The conference room is like the upturned hull of a ship constructed of transverse and longitudinal ribs. The form of the structure was discovered by using a finite element computer simulation. Using a form-finding programme, a membrane was stretched across the area in plan and, by adjusting the internal and external pressure, it was shaped until the desired geometry was arrived at. The transverse ribs were made of differently curved laminated timber beams with a cross-section of 10 x 50 cm. The longitudinal ribs are sawn out of three-ply plywood panels in the form of segments of a circle and are hung at intervals of 1.5 m between the transverse ribs. Round steel bracing, and the boarding that is nailed onto it, supports the construction.

The foyer

The roof over the foyer is a ribbed plate. It is made of laminated veneer ribs with a cross-section measuring 57 x 455 mm, that are placed at intervals of 80 cm under a load-bearing roof plate made of three-ply wooden panels. The elements each span as a three-bay beam with a cantilever arm across 7.5 m; they are threaded onto longitudinal beams made of hollow steel tubes 300 mm in diameter. The loads are transferred vertically by means of slender tubular steel columns. Full-height bracing made of round steel bars supports the system.

Location Rheinau-Linx, Germany

Construction period 2000

Client Weberhaus GmbH & Co. KG, Rheinau

Architects Günter Hermann Architekten, Stuttgart

Structural planners Fischer + Friedrich Ingenieure, Stuttgart

Structural design timber Merz + Kaufmann, Planungsbüro für Holzbau GmbH, Dornbirn, Austria

Fire protection Ingenieurbüro Rudolf Drescher, Herbolzheim

Building physics Ingenieurbüro für Bauphysik Hortsmann und Berger, Altensteig

Landscape architect Dipl.-Ing. (FH) Klaus Scheuber, Freiburg, Germany

Event planning Ludwig Morasch Inc., Palm Beach, USA

Black Box, sets Dipl.-Ing. Univ. Johann Kott, Munich

Primary structure Bold GmbH &Co., Achern

Timber construction Kaufmann Holz AG, Reuthe, Austria

Dry construction Schwarzwald-Akustik Decken- und Trennwandbau GmbH, Bad Peterstal

Interior fitting out, exhibition hall Bellprat Associates AG, Winterthur, Switzerland

Joiner Heinrich Hennegriff, Appenweiher

Built volume 55 000 m³

Gross floor area 8 500 m²

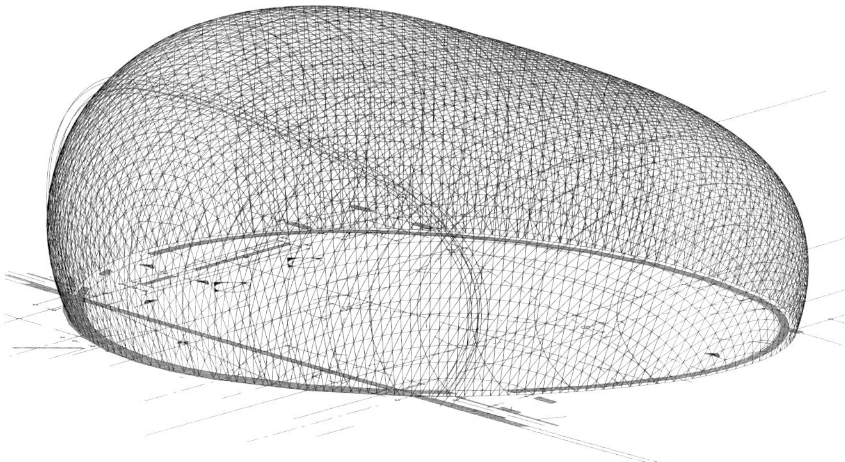

Determining the structure of the hall by means of computer simulation

Trade fair halls in Rimini / Italy

NUOVA FIERA

gmp – von Gerkan, Marg and Partner Architects

In the north of the town of Rimini in Emilia Romagna, a new trade fair complex, the Nuova Fiera di Rimini, has been created with twelve exhibition halls, congress and conference rooms, activity areas, restaurants, shops, administration offices, and the requisite service and storage areas. The trade fair offers a total of 80,000 m^2 of exhibition space and 50,000 m^2 of service and storage space.

The building concept

The architectural concept is derived from the rich traditions of Emilia Romagna, which have helped shape European architectural history since the days of antiquity and the Renaissance. The ensemble as a whole is classically axial and laid out in perspective. The design of the buildings, with their clear geometries, speaks a universally understandable classical language that is formulated through the placing of the buildings while using modern constructions and materials. This classical complex includes a forecourt to the columnar hall of the entrance with tetrapylon light towers that are visible from afar and the trade fair street with its open colonnades on either side, as well as the exhibition halls with the wooden vaults made of rhomboid-shaped elements. The central dome over the rotunda, the columnar hall of the entrance and the covered fountain, as well as

the pools lined by flights of steps, can all be seen as classical quotations.

The materials and the colours of the new trade fair quote from the architectural tradition of the area, while the materials and construction represent the modern technical achievements of our times. The columns, piers, walls and beams are stony, that is, they are made of concrete or prefabricated concrete elements. The roof vaults and the ceilings of the colonnades are wooden, made of wide-spanning timber shell structures in the halls. The floors, made of industrially produced ceramic, are laid using traditional patterns. Filigree facades of steel and glass lend the new trade fair a bright, expansive and transparent atmosphere.

The transport and traffic connections, as well as the extremely long, narrow site, determined the organisational concept, with linear, symmetrical access from east and west and via the main entrance in the south.

The exhibition is conveniently laid out on a single level in a way that is simple and comprehensible for both exhibitors and visitors. For

the flexible organisation of different events, a modular hall system was developed, with the smallest individual module based on the smallest event; modules can be combined for larger events. The halls have no internal columns and span 100 x 60 m (i.e., a floor area of 6,000 m^2). The model for the wooden roofs to the halls was the wooden net-like roof vaults built by Friedrich Zollinger in the 1920s. New timber products, such as glued laminated timber, make possible spans several times greater than in those days, while also allowing far shorter construction periods. In Rimini, a period of about four weeks was required to erect the roof structure of one of the halls. The rotunda, with its filigree construction of rhomoid-shaped lozenges, has a diameter of 30 m, at its highest point it measures 22 m.

The halls

The exhibition halls use two different systems. The lower, load-bearing parts of the walls of the halls (including the foundations) are made from reinforced concrete. This structure provides the vertical bearing for the roof and guarantees the stability of the entire building insofar as external horizontal forces such as wind or earthquakes are concerned. The wooden vault made of glue laminated ribs is fixed by means of steel connectors.

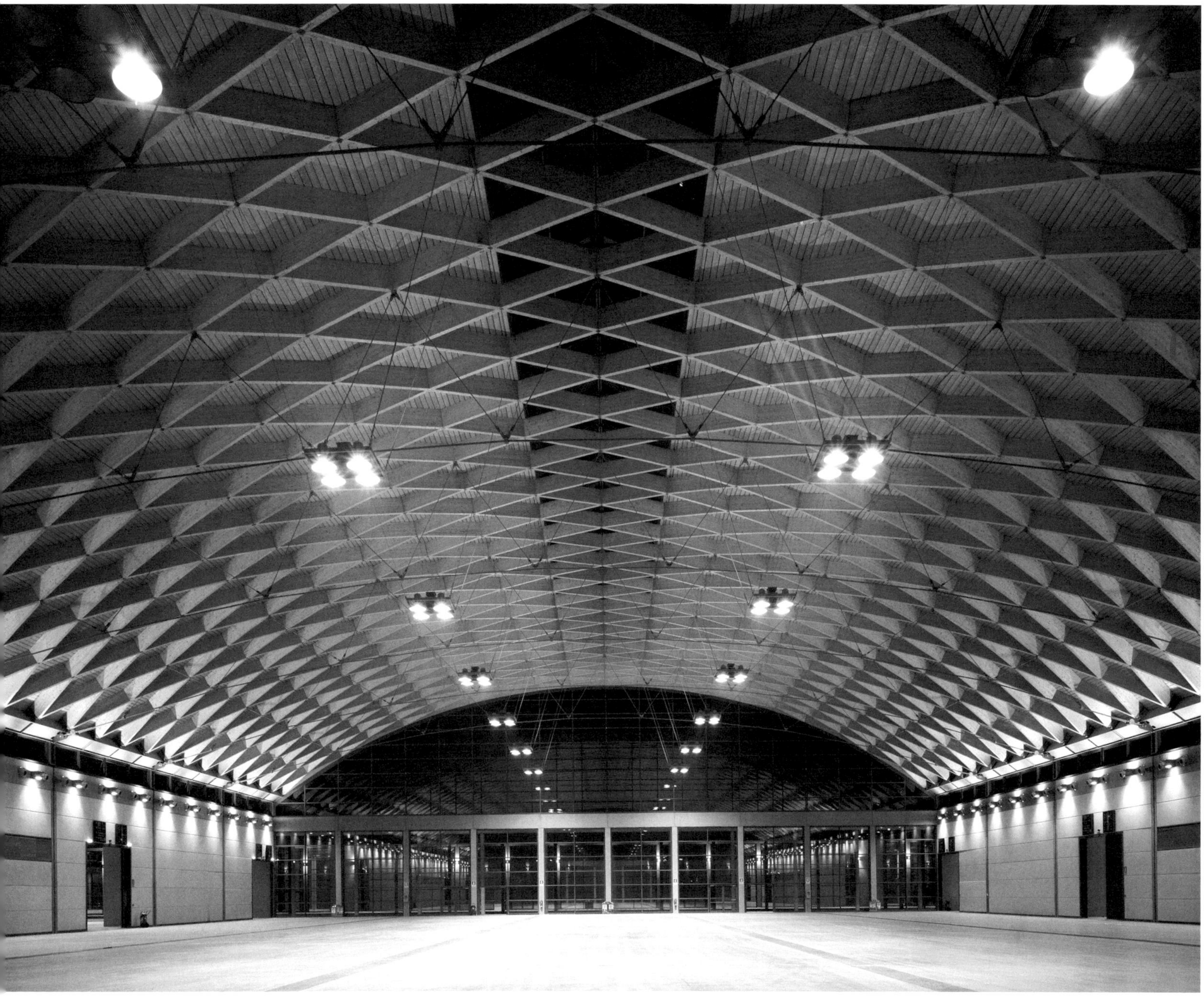

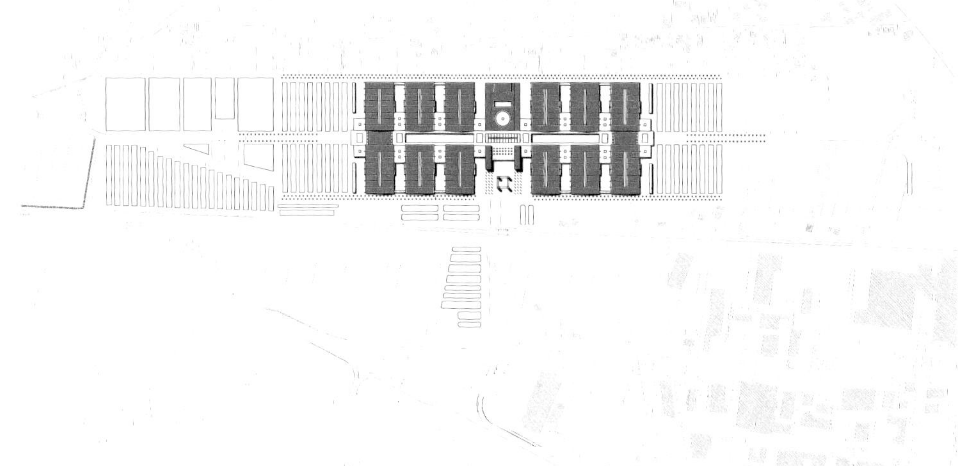

Site plan

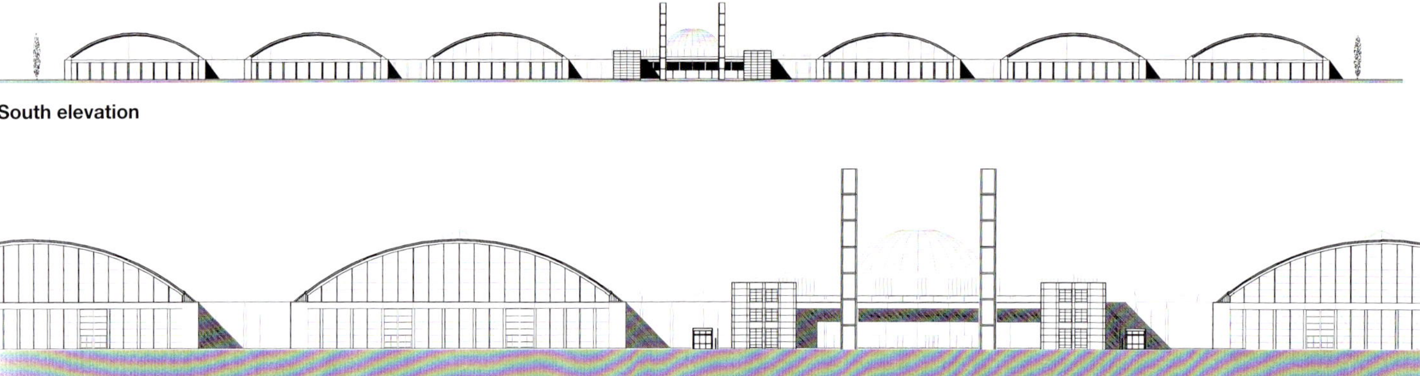

South elevation

View of main entrance

The wooden vaults have a height of 10 m; their crown is 20 m above the ground. All twelve trade fair halls have the same geometry and span 60 m across the concrete substructure. The length of the halls is 96 m.

The structure of rhomboid-shaped elements

The structure of a single hall consists of 1280 glue laminated timber ribs of the same dimensions, assembled using the so-called Zollinger-Bauweise, each with a length of 3.5 m and a cross-section of 160 x 700 mm. The ribs are connected at 693 junctions by steel elements. The intersections of the nodes are 6.25 m apart vertically and 3 m apart horizontally. Thus in a width of 12 m there are four ribs. This is the grid on which the reinforced concrete columns and the bracing are laid out. An edge arch, with a cross-section of 500 x 700 mm, completes the structure at the gable ends.

The connecting of the individual ribs to create a surface structure required tests that were carried out at the University of Udine in Italy. Four wooden ribs meet at each junction. This means that normal and transverse forces, as well as moments, are applied at these junctions. It was important that the assembly should be rapid and simple, and that the connection on site should involve just a few simple work processes.

As a consequence, a special steel-connecting element was developed. Four pairs of metal plates were welded to a tubular section. Each of the ribs has a steel plate that was placed into a slit in the timber section in the workshop and fixed using steel dowels. On the building site, these metal plates were fixed between the pairs of plates welded to the connecting element; the connection was made with just a few bolts as a purely steel-to-steel perforated plate junction. The steel tube was then filled with sealing mortar. The only visible steel elements are the heads of the dowels and the lower cover plate to the steel tube. Thus, the construction achieves the stipulated F 30 rating.

The transmission of forces

The forces from the roof structure are transmitted to the reinforced concrete substructure by means of a hollow steel section. This runs continuously like a beam above all the walls, resting on the wall plate, and forms the bearing for the wooden roof structure. The horizontal forces of the arch are taken up by pre-stressed steel tension bars 60 mm in diameter, placed at intervals of 12 m. The tension bars are attached by diagonal tension rods that are 32 mm in diameter. These rods are then bolted to the nodes of the roof structure and transfer the forces, by means of a steel element, to the glue laminated timber ribs. The roof construction, together with its suspension system, forms a sickle-shaped structure.

The tension band was pre-tensioned to 850 kN using hydraulic presses. The pre-tensioning of the band to this level balances the horizontal forces from the roof resulting from its own weight. In addition, the tension band and the tension diagonals guarantee the stability of the structure in the case of asymmetrical wind or snow loads.

The bracing of the roof in the long direction is achieved by the 50-mm-thick roof decking that was nailed to the lattice. Laminated timber lamellas, joined using wedge-shaped dovetailed joints, were used for the boarding and function as two-bay beams. All the lamellas were shortened to the required length in the workshop after they had been joined together.

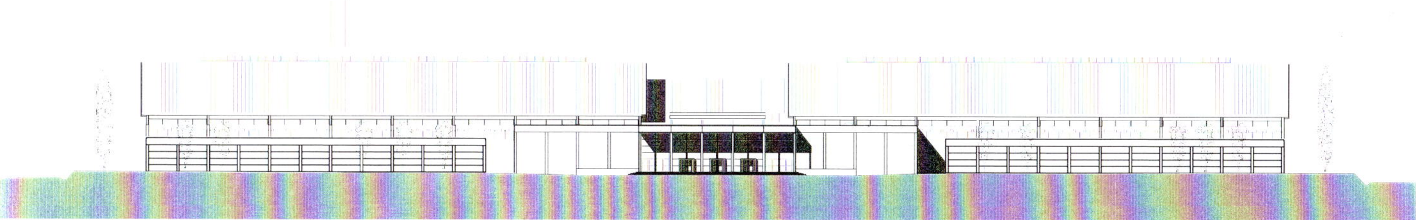

East elevation

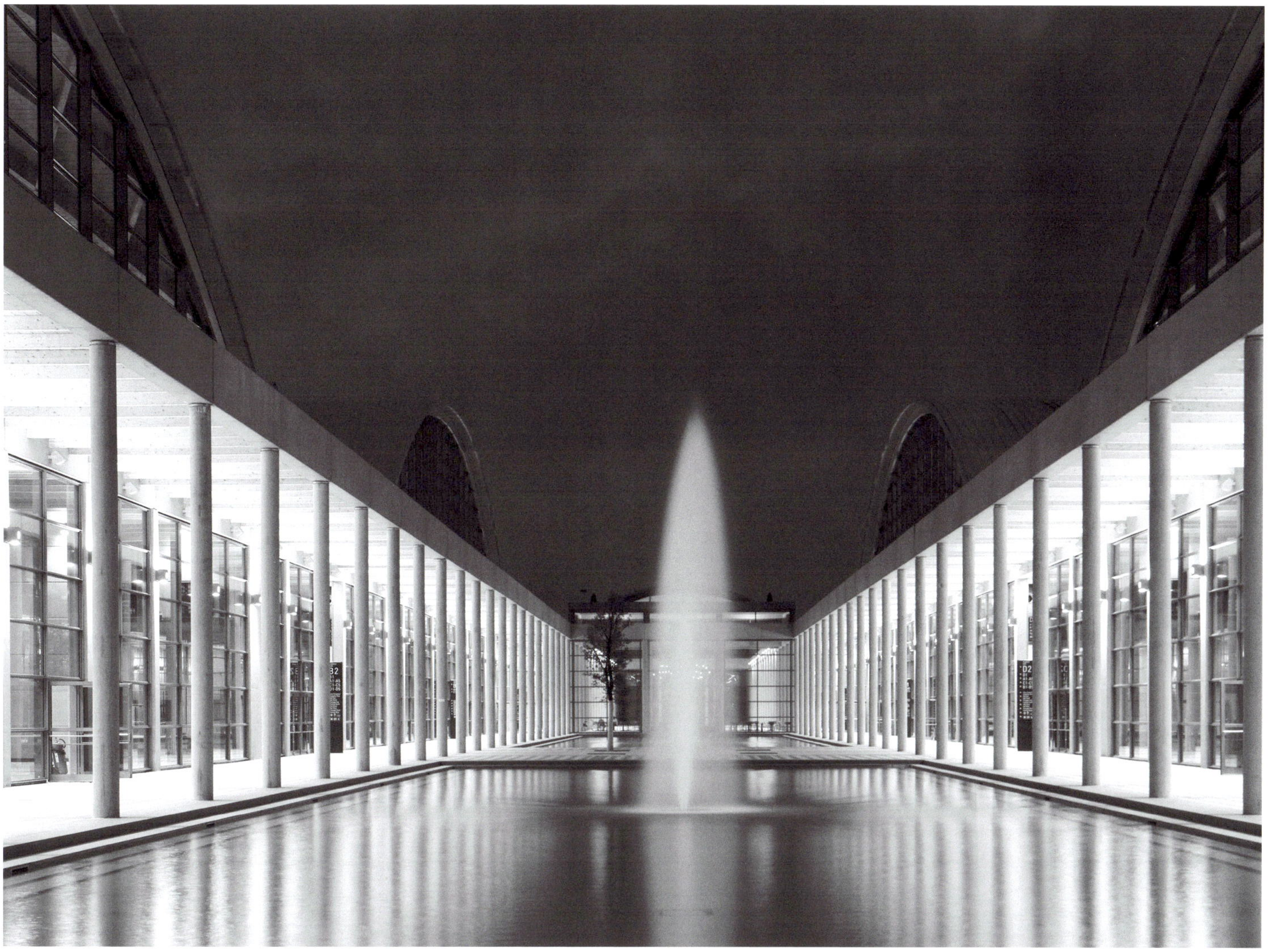

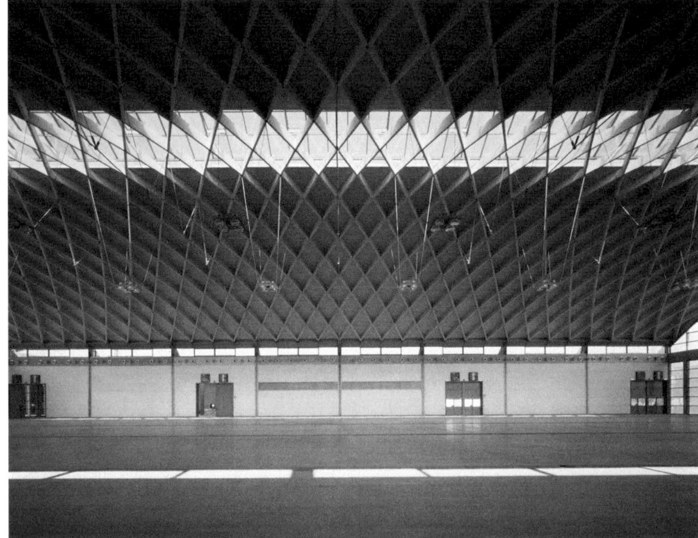
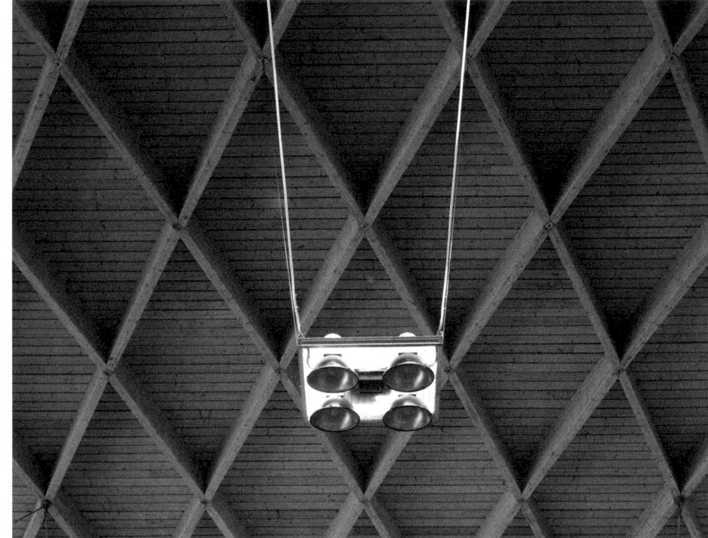
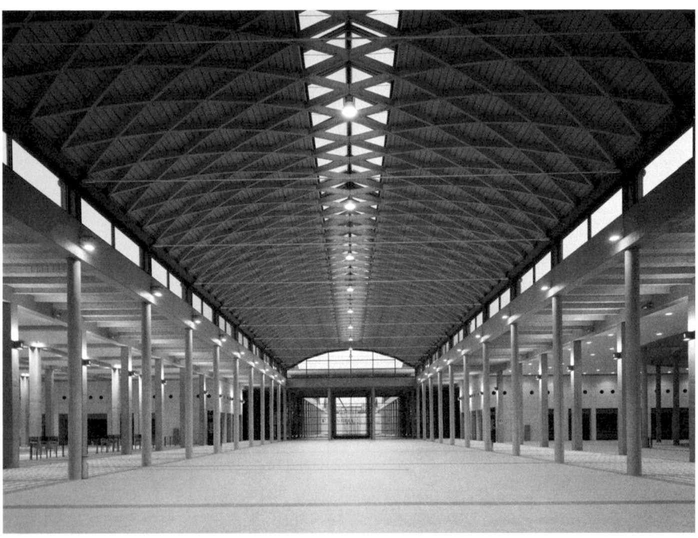
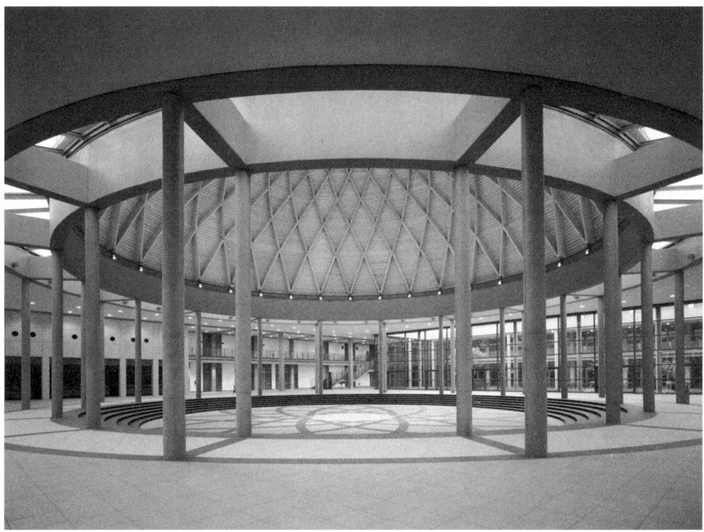

Fitting

The construction was mounted in position with the help of a falsework measuring 12 x 60 m. This was moved from bay to bay in the long direction along three pairs of tracks, allowing the roof to be mounted in sections 12 m wide. The two outer tracks also served as tracks for two assembly cranes; in this way, the crane could reach each point on the falsework. To mount the frame of lozenge-shaped elements the nodes were first placed during the erection process on hydraulic presses that were later lowered. This concept, using the falsework as a working platform and the presses as a support, allowed the centre points of the junctions to be adjusted until all the bolts could be inserted. About four weeks were required for the mounting of the roof construction.

Earthquake safety

The new trade fair complex in Rimini is in an earthquake zone. Therefore, the effects of earthquakes had to be studied by means of a dynamic analysis of the construction. The spectrum of the results served exclusively to limit the strains and the deformation of the construction in case of earthquakes.

After the completion of the halls, static and dynamic tests were carried out on two of the buildings. These allowed the mathematic model used to study the seismic behaviour of the structure to be checked. For the dynamic tests, a machine that produces vibrations, and that can simulate horizontal and vertical forces, was placed at various points on the roof and the resulting movement was measured.

The atrium

Situated between the entrance hall and the dome, the atrium connects the two units of six pavilions. The span of the construction is 18 m, while its length is 72 m. The roof structure is also made of a lattice of rhomboid shapes. A single gluelam rib has a cross-section of 100 x 250 mm. Connecting the elements at the nodes is done much the same way as in the halls. In the atrium, however, two metal plates were let into each rib. On account of this, the fixing bolts had to be dimensioned to take shear and bending forces. Due to the modest spans, it was possible to do without bracing in the form of a truss. Tension rods that connect the two steel sections at the springing points of the arch handle the horizontal shear forces.

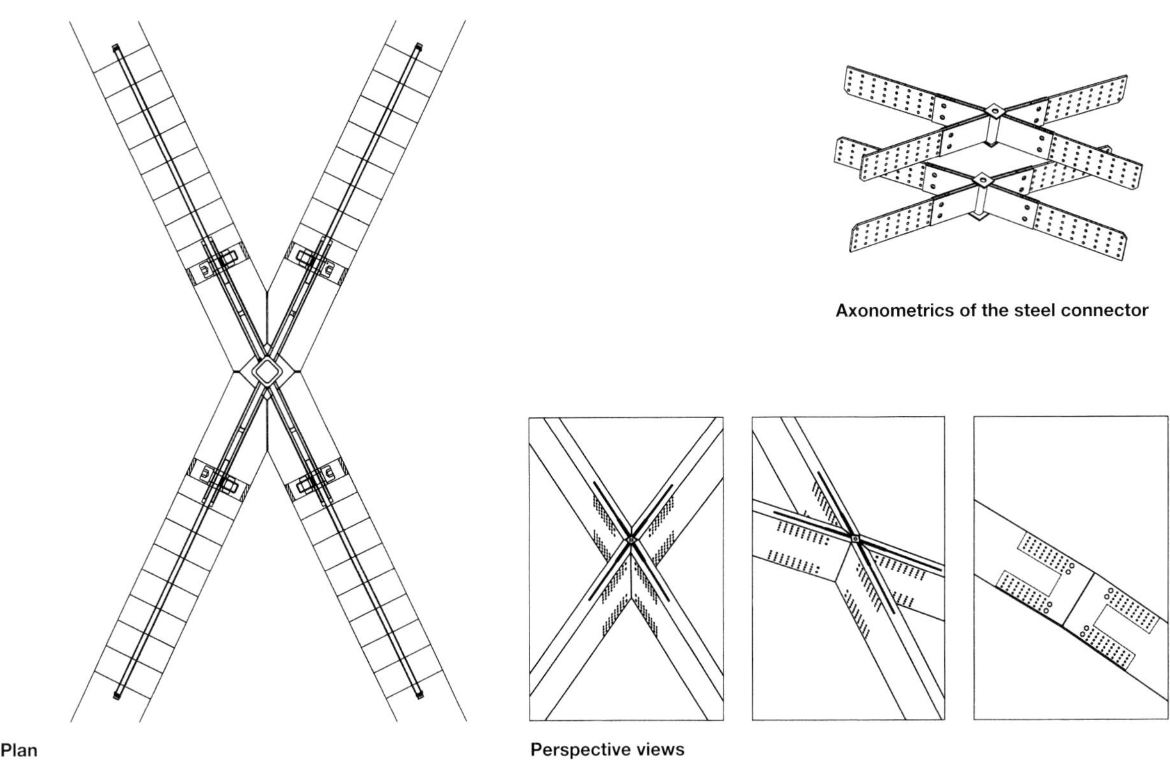

Plan

Perspective views

Axonometrics of the steel connector

Junction of the rhombus-shaped lamella construction with steel connector

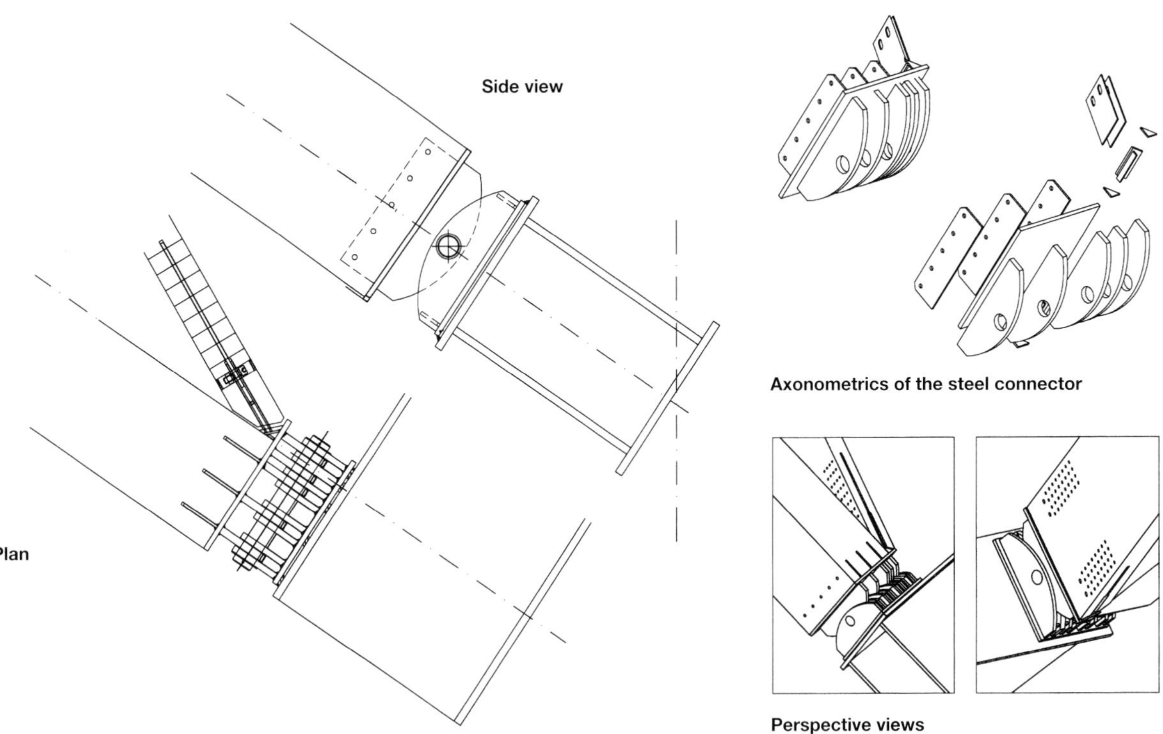

Side view

Plan

Axonometrics of the steel connector

Perspective views

Footing of the final arched beam, showing the connection of the rhomboid lamella construction and steel junction piece

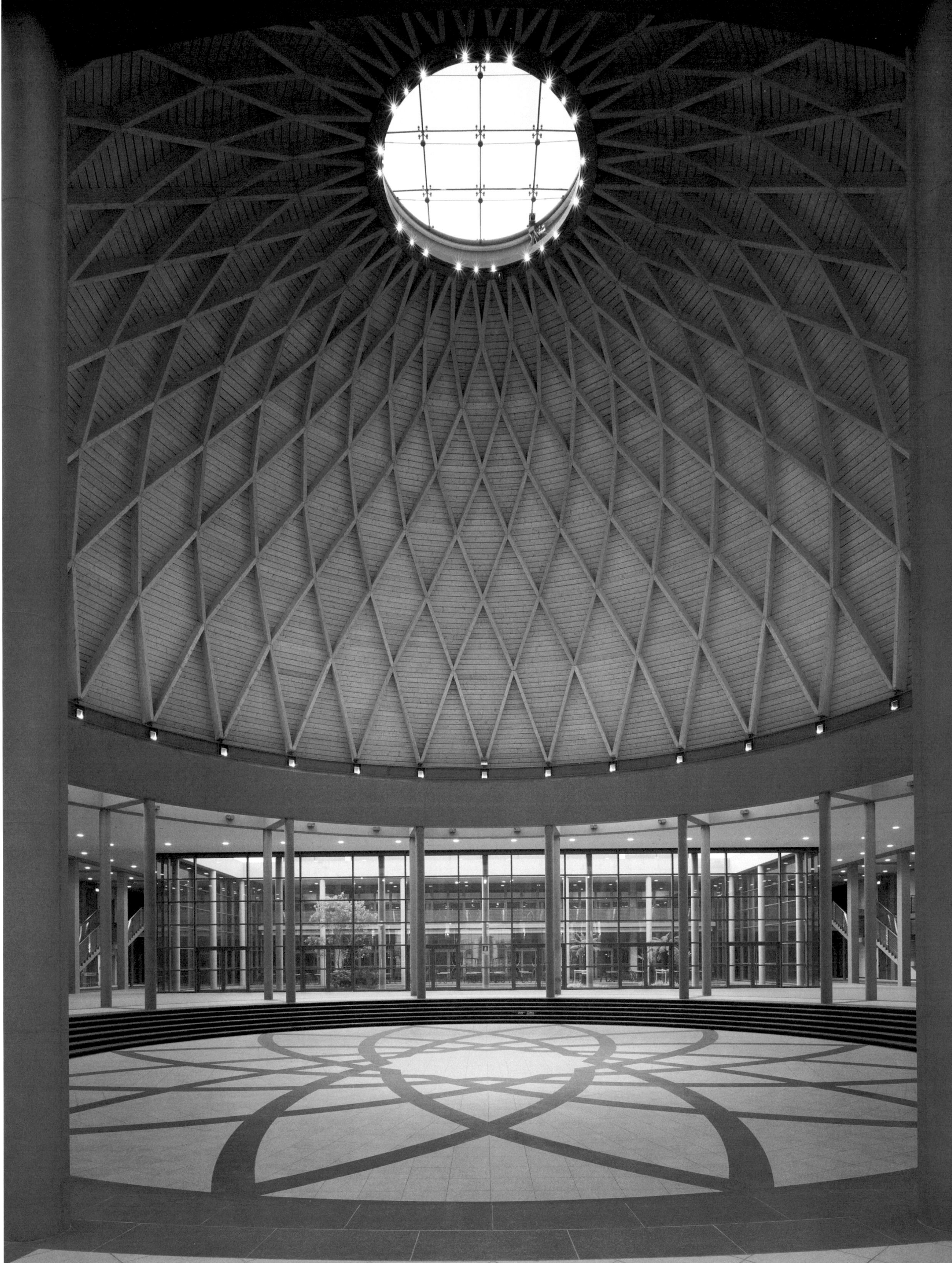

All the building elements, including the slits and boreholes, were prepared in advance in the carpentry shop. The parameters of the machines used were taken into account when designing the nodes. The atrium was assembled in the workshop in individual segments and then transported to the building site. A single segment extends from the threshold to the ridge. To position the pieces during the mounting process, a scaffolding tower was erected at the centre of the atrium.

The dome

A dome that is 30 m in diameter and 22 m high at its highest point spans the central area of the complex. The structure, as in the halls, consists of individual gluelam ribs, combined to create a mesh of rhomboid shaped elements. For the rotunda, the filigree rhomboid constructions of the Italian engineer Pier Luigi Nervi – for example, in the Palazzo dello Sport in Rome – were used as a model. At the lower bearing point, the rhombus ribs are 140 mm wide and 500 mm deep. As they rise towards the roof light, the sections taper conically to a dimension of 300 mm. The upper termination is provided by a 6-m steel compression ring, which supports on skylight.

The complex geometry of the individual elements was worked out with the help of a 3D CAD programme. The edges of the conically cut gluelam ribs meet at a point in each node and form a continuous line. To achieve this, the lower surfaces had to be alternately tilted askew.

The roof decking, made of 40-mm-thick lamellas, takes both the roof load and the ring forces. The boards at the upper area of the dome take low compression loads; those lower down take up the tension. The decking on the lower area of the dome was strengthened at the height of the mesh nodes with a metal band nailed to the upper face, so that the horizontal ring forces are taken up and the transverse strain in the rhombuses is eliminated. Due to the three-dimensional structural effect, the connections between the prefabricated individual segments only had to be dimensioned to deal with relatively low bending moments. There is a metal plate at the node of two rhombuses lying beside each other. So that this plate is not visible from below, the gluelam ribs were rebated to half the thickness of the plate. Two bolts hold the ribs together; for fire safety reasons, the bolts have sunken heads covered with wooden plugs.

The smaller wooden parts could be prepared almost completely in the carpentry shop; the data were transferred directly from the 3D model to the machines. This was not possible with gluelam ribs above a certain cross-sectional size, so the ribs in the lower area of the dome were made by hand. The dimensions were taken from the 3D CAD model, transferred into two dimensions and drawn in the workshop for cutting by hand. In this way, with the help of a few machines, very precise building elements could be made by hand. On the site, the dome was put together in nine shell-shaped segments. In order to ensure the precise assembly of the individual elements, a falsework was built of timber sections that had exactly the same radius of the shell.

The rib construction was fixed on this falsework and the roof decking was fixed afterward. A scaffolding tower was erected at the centre of the dome for the positioning of the compression ring. The tower took up the vertical forces of the load until the dome was fixed in position and could support itself. During the mounting, the wind forces were directed by the prefabricated building parts into the scaffolding tower, which had been suitably anchored. After all the individual prefabricated elements had been mounted, the final missing gluelam ribs were inserted in the bays that were still left open and, finally, the roof decking was completed.

Location Rimini, Italy

Construction period 1999–2001

Client Ente Autonomo Fiera di Rimini, Rimini

Architects gmp – von Gerkan, Marg and Partner, Hamburg

Design Prof. Volkwin Marg

Project management Stephanie Joebsch

Assistants Yasemin Erkan, Hauke Huusmann, Thomas Dammann, Wolfgang Schmidt, Regine Glaser, Helene van gen Hassend, Mariachiara Breda, Susanne Bern, Carsten Plog, Mareo Vivori, Eduard Mijic, Arne Starke, Dieter Rösinger, Olaf Bey, Uschi Köper, Beate Kling, Elisabeth Menne, Dagmar Weber, Ina Hartig

Contact architect Clemens Kusch, Venice

Structural planners Favero Et Milan, Venice

Consultants Schlaich Bergermann and Partner, Stuttgart

Building services Studio T.I., Rimini

Consultant Uli Behr, Munich

Lighting design Conceptlicht, Helmut Angerer, Traunreut

Landscape planning Studio Land, Milan

Control technology Mac Kneißl, Munich

Design 1997

Gross floor area 130 134 m²

Trade fair halls in Friedrichshafen / Germany

RHOMBOID

gmp – von Gerkan, Marg and Partner Architects

The new trade fair complex in Friedrichshafen was erected on a 38-hectare site opposite the airport. In nine halls, a total area of 58,300 m^2 is available for fairs and other events.

The concept of the complex is based on flexibility of use, to cater to the different kinds of events that can, at times, be held simultaneously. Independent of the trade fair business, the large multi-purpose hall can be accessed from outside, so that other events can be held there without in any way disturbing the running of the fair.

A square hall at the centre of the trade fair complex can be linked as required to fair events, to different small events or to the multi-purpose hall for presentations, or it can be used as a foyer. A colonnade in front forms a glazed space around the inner 12,000 m^2 of free exhibition space and allows one to take an attractive tour through all the exhibition halls. A striking office tower for the fair administration offices and a 5,000-space car park for visitors and exhibitors complement the fair halls.

The wooden vaults over the halls are conceived as structural surfaces using rhomboid-shaped elements; they span a 60-m-wide area without the use of internal supports. The result is appealing, thanks to the contemporary nature of the design and the comfortable quality of the environment (despite the huge dimensions), as well as the high level of functionality and the fact that the completion date was met while keeping within the budget.

The roof structures

The needs of the client went beyond the usual major volumes required for trade fair halls. For example, exhibition facilities for large sailing yachts with their masts stepped, as well as openings and parking facilities for aircraft up

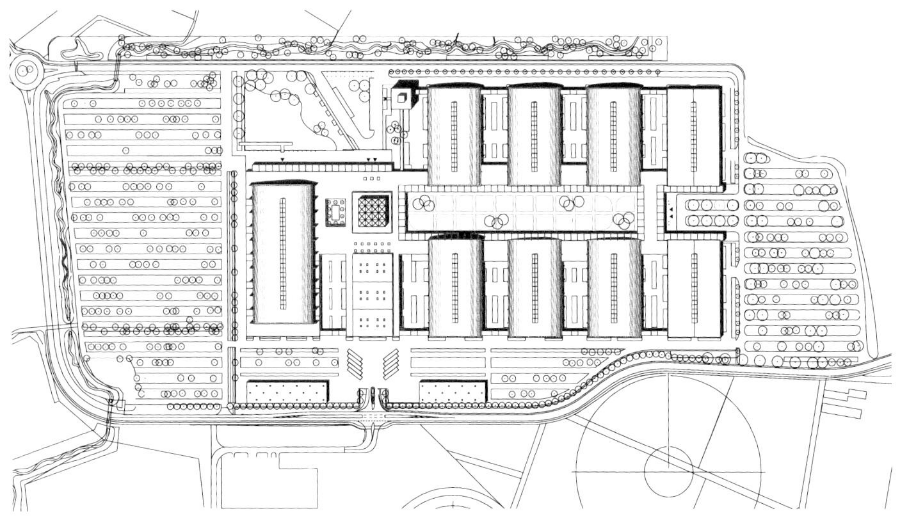

Site plan

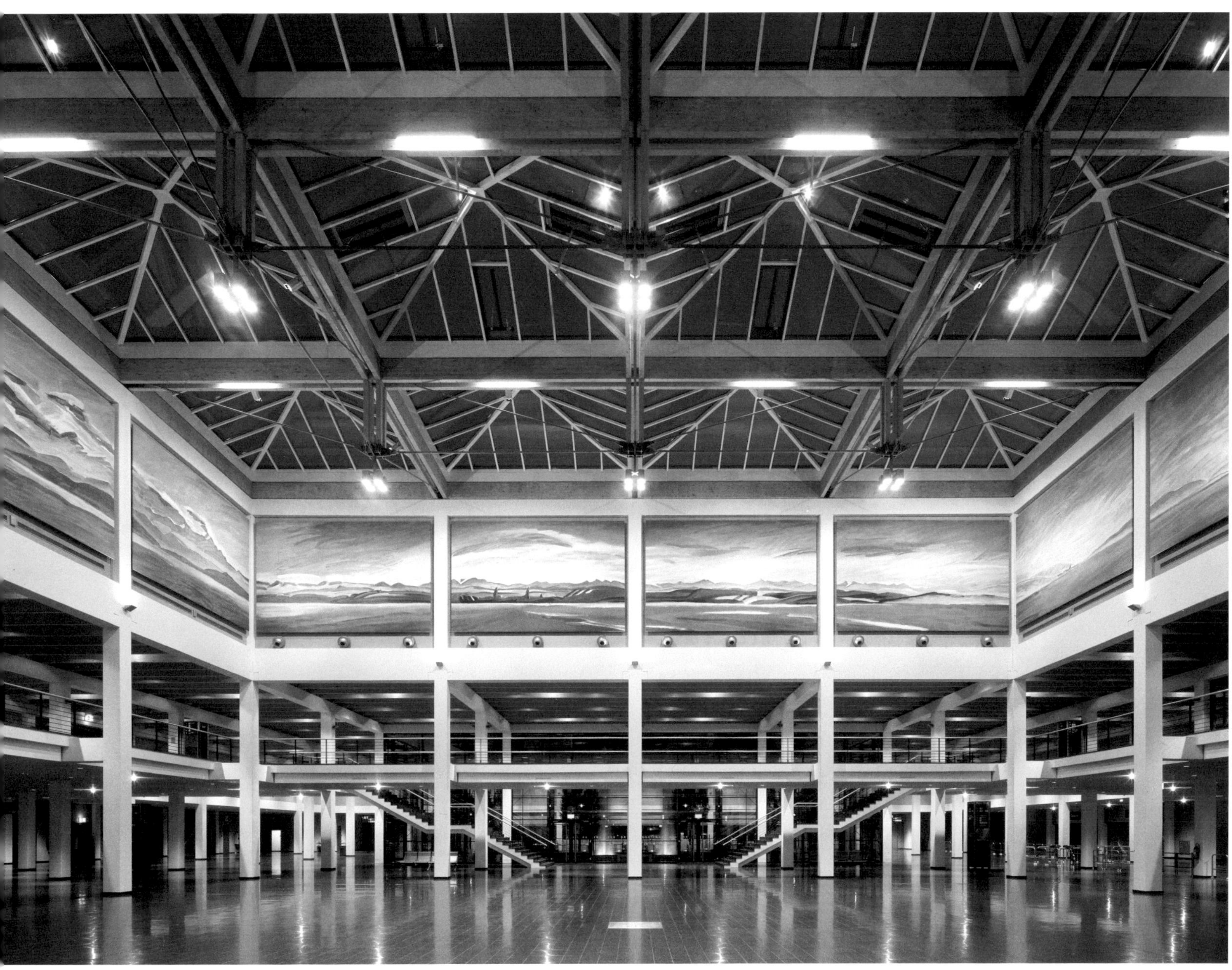

to the size of a Lear jet were required, this in addition to standard halls with the usual cross-sectional shape. It was required that large events, such as concerts, could be held in at least one of the halls and that the multi-purpose hall could be subdivided for a variety of uses. In addition, a large and attractive foyer was required.

The architects' first ideas focused on making the shed roofs in timber. The client had no essential reservations about the technical feasibility or economy of wooden roof structures.

The four different structural concepts that were used for the large roofs of the Neue Messe Friedrichshafen all have one structural characteristic in common: the timber material was used to take compression and bending forces, while steel takes up the tension forces. Essentially, all the beams are trussed. The structural forms used include arches, trusses and a grid of beams (barrel shell).

The six standard halls have roofs made of fourteen glue laminated timber arches that rest on reinforced concrete columns on flat foundations. Concrete block walls were erected between the columns. The roof construction is composed of: aluminium sheeting on the outer skin; mineral fibre insulation 100-mm-thick compressed to 80 mm; a specially made thin and light vapour barrier that can be glued when cold; solid wood boards 28-mm-thick; and rafter purlins with a span of 7.5 m placed at intervals of 1.9 m. Wind and stabilising bracing is introduced at the two end bays.

The main structure consists of laminated timber arches with a cross-section measuring 20 x 107 cm and a steel beam to balance the horizontal forces. The span is 61 m, the eaves height is 15.4 m, or 8.75 m, and the height of the arches above the eaves is 10.1 m. The halls are 105 m long.

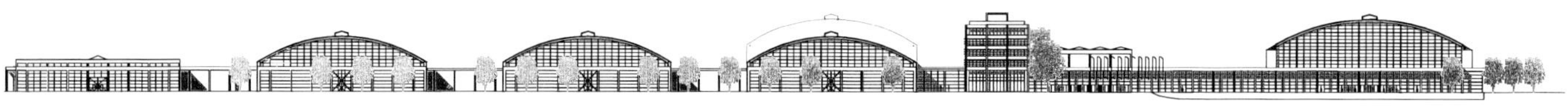

North elevation

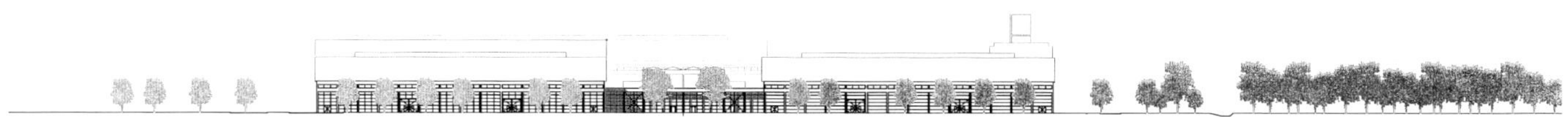

East elevation

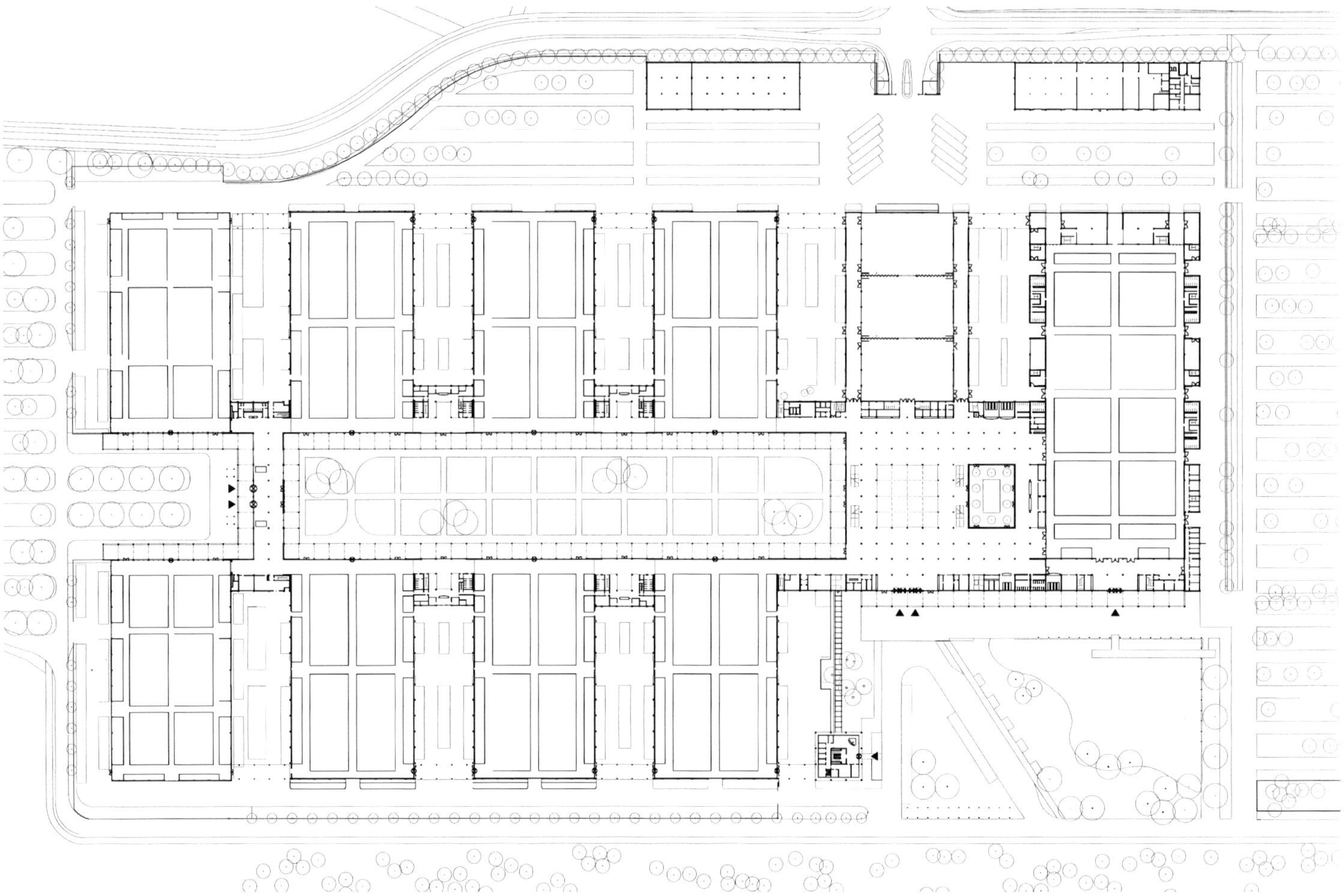

Floor plan of halls

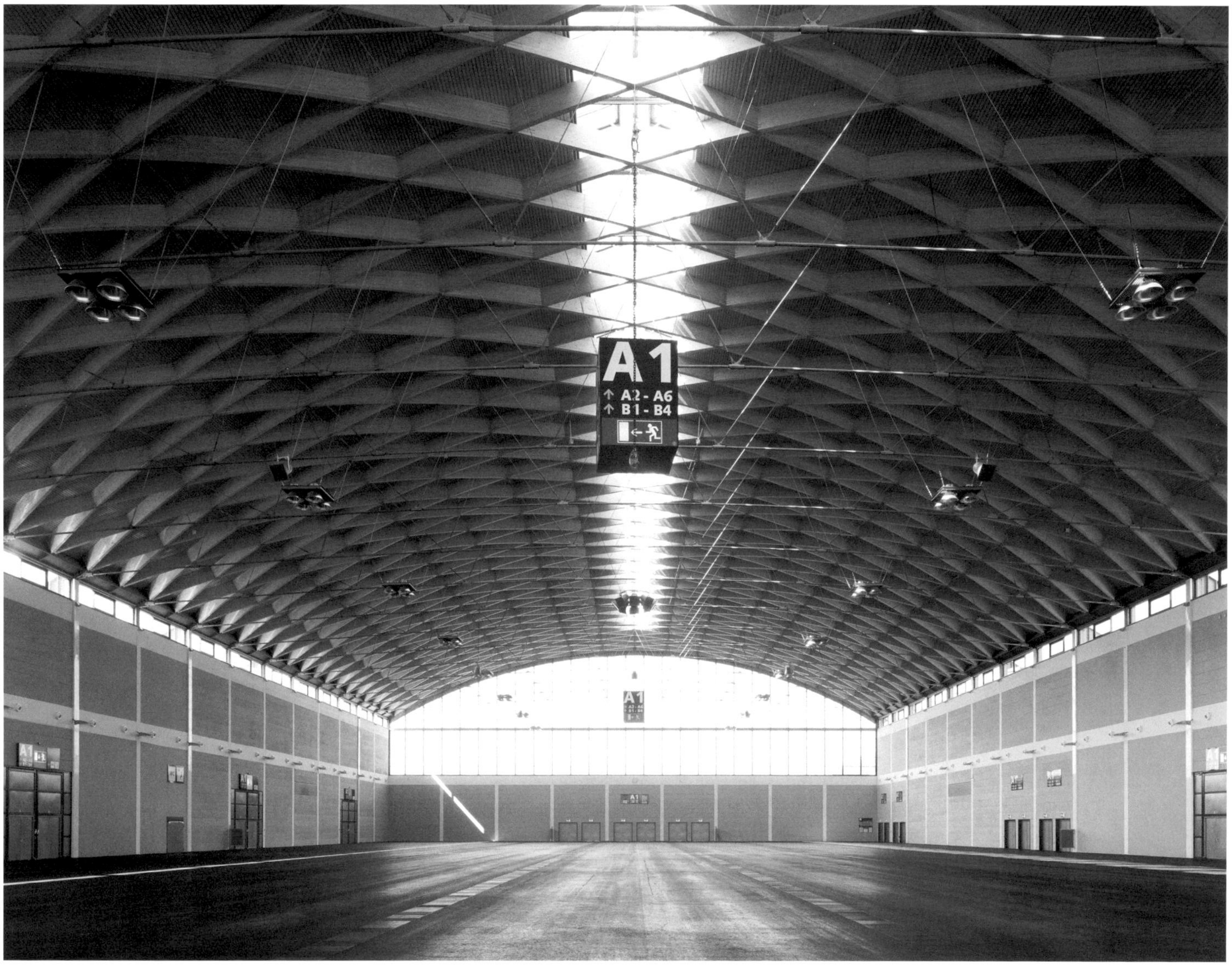

Large multi-purpose hall with timber rhomboid construction

The roof structure of the large multi-purpose hall does not use arched beams; instead, a timber construction was used, made up of lamella rhomboids that rest on point-supported steel beams on reinforced concrete panels. The roof is built up as follows: beneath the outer aluminium sheeting there is an insulation layer made of mineral fibre insulation compressed from 100 to 80 mm on a special vapour barrier. The roof of the hall is lined inside with Lignotrend acoustic elements with a maximum span of 3.75 m. These elements function as a plate that can be used to stabilise and redirect the horizontal forces in the rhomboid lamella roof that are exerted outwards at the gables. The acoustic elements are combined with absorbent insulation and soft-board panels. The layered elements are essentially multi-functional: the acoustic function is included, so to speak. The main structure is a vault using lamella rhomboids made of laminated timber sections measuring 20 x 80 cm in cross-section. The roof has a span of 68 m, an eaves height of 16.6 m and a ridge height of 26.3 m. It also has steel tension chords to balance the horizontal forces. The total length of the hall is 150 m.

Vaults made of lamella rhomboids must be supported on both sides for as much of their length as possible. As a band of glazing was planned between the eaves and the wall in this case, only point supports, placed at intervals of 7.5 m, were possible; above these a steel structure provides continuous anchoring.

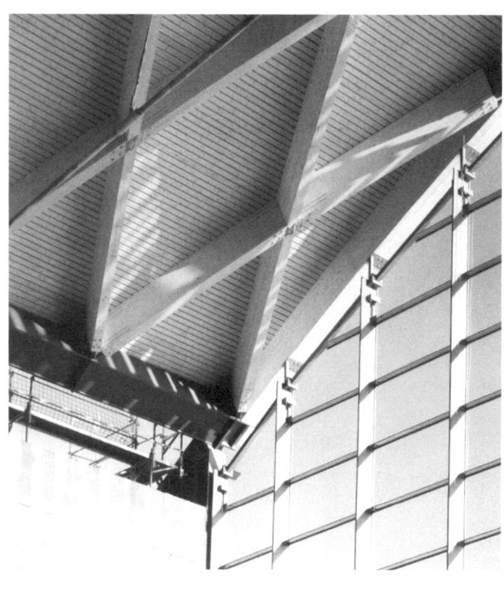

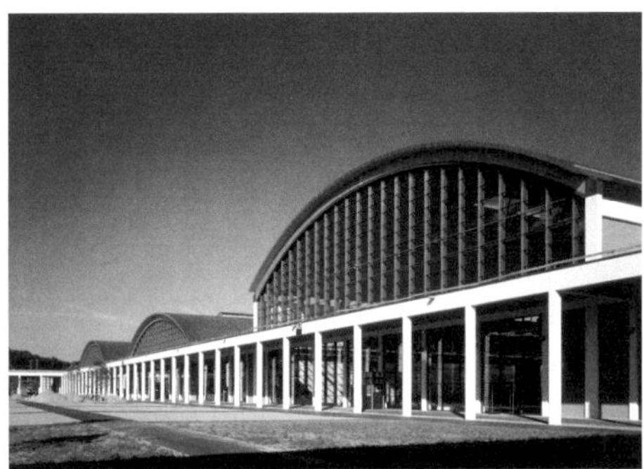

View of hall with colonnades in front (internal courtyard side)

In the three-dimensional frame forming the foyer roof, the square plan, with sides approximately 30 m long, is made up of sixteen square bays with sides measuring 7.5 m. The top surface of the grid of beams, made of diagonal post trusses, lies almost on one plane. Here, too, the upper chords and posts are made of laminated timber, while the lower chords and the diagonals are made of round steel bars. The structural principle is that of a primary and secondary structure. Three continuous beams were prefabricated as planar trusses and placed in position, and the transverse beam elements were hung at right angles between them on site. The result is a structurally dissimilar grid of beams. Pyramid-shaped glass roofs, with a metal structure above the wooden squares, flood the foyer with light.

Fire protection

All the halls must meet the fire resistance class F 30. In large projects such as this one, the cost of a sprinkler system must be compared with the cost of (over) dimensioning the construction to achieve the stipulated fire rating. Timber elements in larger sizes have an advantage compared to other materials because there is no great difference between "warm" dimensioning (i.e., dimensioning to meet a particular fire resistance rating) and "cold" dimensioning (i.e., dimensioning to meet load-bearing requirements only) and, therefore, there are no significant additional costs. In the trade fair halls, wood, concrete and steel were intelligently combined and this effect was considered in the fire protection assessment. Essentially, in such large buildings, not all load-bearing elements must achieve the stipulated fire resistance rating: working in combination they must allow safe escape from the building for the specific length of time stipulated. For reasons of cost, it was therefore decided to dispense with a sprinkler system. Instead, a more economical solution was chosen: increasing the dimensions of the building elements to meet the requirements of the fire protection legislation.

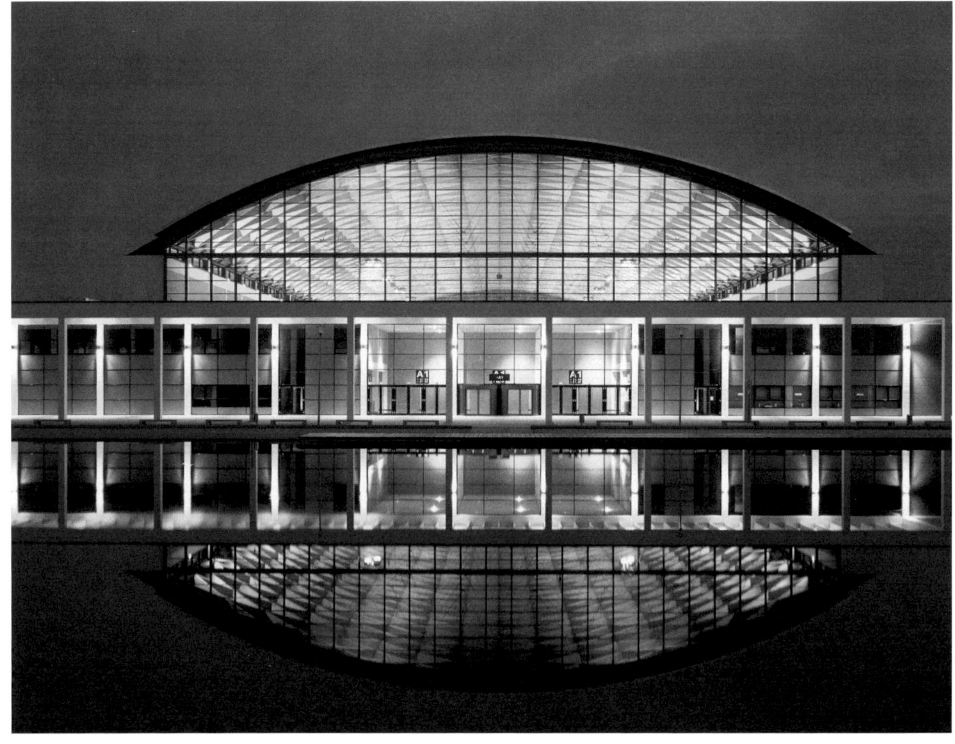

The roof of the large hall is so far away from the floor that a fire at ground level is not expected to have any effect on the roof construction. Thus "warm" dimensioning was only required for the steel elements of the structure. In contrast, the possibility of fire in the roof of the small multi-purpose hall, due to the lower height of the building, had to be taken into account. For this reason, the roof lining had to be made of a material with low flammability. As the wooden roof panels were not classified as F 30-B, the wooden soffit had to be given a fire retardant coating. The insulation in the cavities also had to be of low flammability. The steel tension elements of the beams were dimensioned to withstand the temperatures stipulated. The fire safety assessment assumes that, within the period allowed for escape, a fire occurs only locally and not immediately throughout the entire area of the hall.

The main beams and the rafter purlins were dimensioned to achieve a fire resistance rating of F30-B, which in the case of timber does not require any larger cross-sections than normal (cold) dimensioning. The main steel tension elements were made in a single piece to delay the melting process, while the expansion and the possible collapse of the steel diagonals was taken into account. In calculating the warm dimensioning, it was assumed that, at most, one of the two wind and bracing elements would be affected during the escape period and, therefore, sufficient safety would be assured.

Sound insulation and acoustics

In the trade fair buildings, in addition to the functions of enclosing space and providing thermal insulation, noise insulation and acoustics also had to be calculated. The noise insulation requirement resulted from the close proximity of the airport. It was important that the fair operations and events of other kinds should be disturbed as little as possible by aircraft noise. The acoustic requirements were dictated by the planned multi-purpose use of the halls. Therefore, sound-absorbent roofs with a sound insulation factor of 47 decibels were required. The solution was found by using load-bearing acoustic ceiling elements made of wood (Ligno-Akustik type 90 or type 104) for the roof construction, which, seen from below, resemble wood sections with shadow joints. These layered elements have a high load-bearing capacity and plate stiffening effect. By connecting the elements in a shear resistant way, a surface structure is created with a continuous upper surface, integrated thermal insulation and a soffit that is both sound-absorbent and sound insulating.

Fitting

After fitting the lamella rhomboid construction to the large hall, the acoustic ceilings were prefabricated on the ground in elements measuring 37.5 m^2 and positioned on the structure using a crane. The assembly crew could work safely on the continuous surface of the elements without a safety net or guardrails. The roof elements stabilise the lamella construction and function as tension elements that lead the horizontal forces exerted outwards on the gable arches back into the construction. This solves the problem that usually occurs at the gables of lamella rhomboid roofs. This problem is caused by the fact that each lamella ending carries externally directed horizontal forces with it. Since the edge arches cannot take up this force by deflection, it must be directed back into the vault. The horizontal force amounts to around 30kN/m. Perforated steel plates were nailed over the joints of the elements to redirect the forces.

Location Friedrichshafen, Germany

Construction period 2000–2002

Client Internationale Bodensee-Messe Friedrichshafen GmbH

Architects gmp – von Gerkan, Marg and Partner, Hamburg; Volkwin Marg with Hauke Huusmann

Project partner Wolfgang Haux

Project management Hauke Huusmann

Assistants Katja Beiß, Marina Hoffmann, Petra Kauschus, Martina Klostermann, Knut Maass, Carsten Plog, Peter Radomski, Klaus Reinhardt, Wolfgang Schmidt, Ralph Schmitz, Claudia Schultze, Dirk Tietgen, Petra Wedemann, Gaby Wysocki

Structural designers Hochtief Frankfurt, Abt. Technik

Structural design timber Multi-purpose hall: Merz & Kaufmann Bauingenieure, Dornbirn, Austria; Small events hall, foyer: Ingenieurbüro für Statik, Stefan Schlechter, Albstadt

Electrical services Tessag Rheinelektra Technik GmbH, Aalen

Plumbing/Heating Scholze Ingenieurgesellschaft mbH, Leinfelden

Ventilation HL-Technik, Stuttgart

Outdoor areas Büro Land GbR, Duisburg

Fire prevention reports Hosser, Hass and Partner, Brunswick

Project management Assmann Beraten und Planen, Dortmund

General contractor Bietergemeinschaft Hochtief Building/Tessag Rheinelektra Technik, Stuttgart

Timber construction Arbeitsgemeinschaft Holzbau Amann GmbH, Weilheim/Kaufmann Holzbauwerke AG, Dornbirn, Austria

Acoustic elements Lignotrend, Weilheim

Gross floor area ca. 95 000 m^2

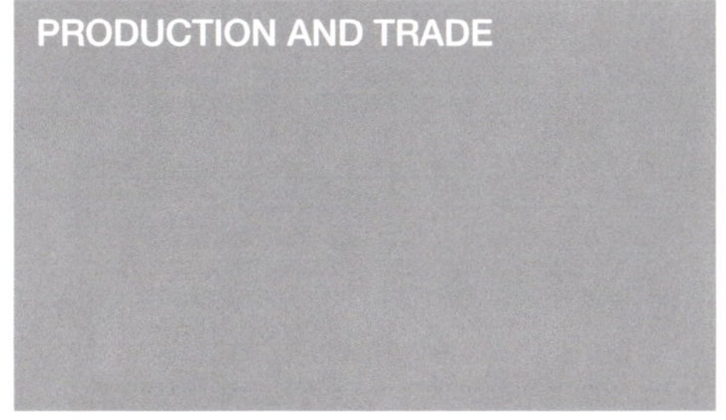

PRODUCTION AND TRADE

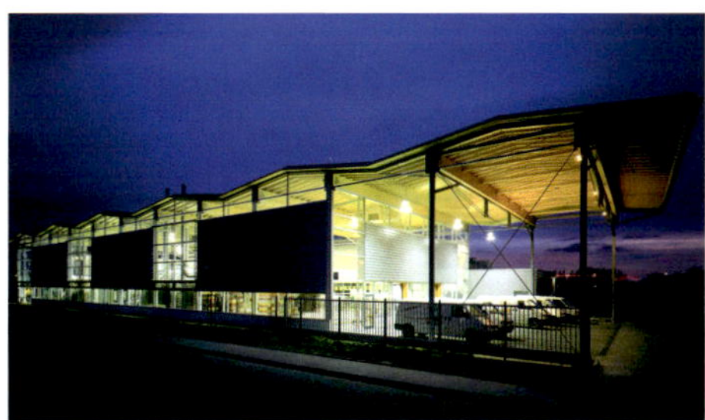

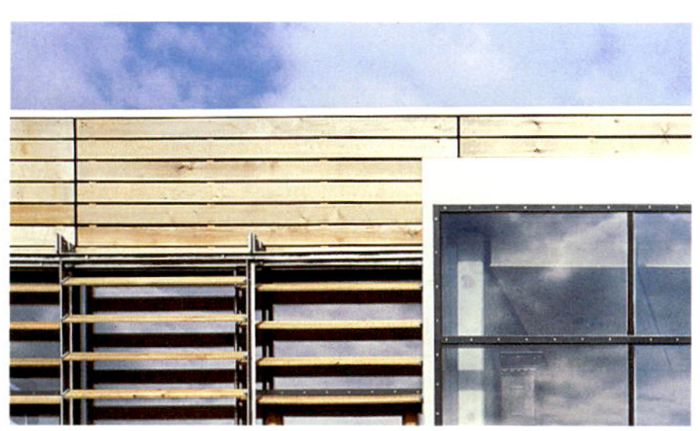

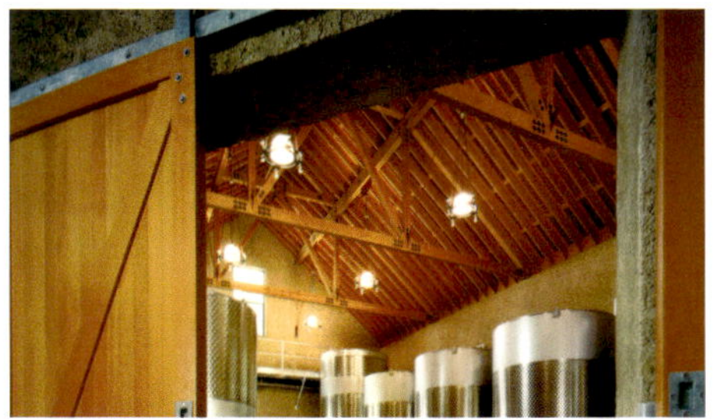

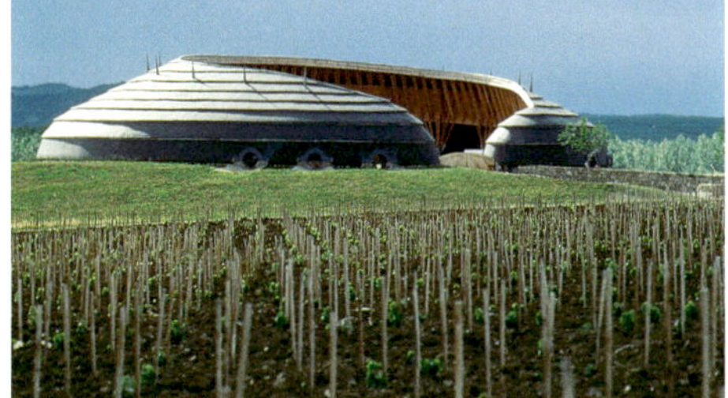

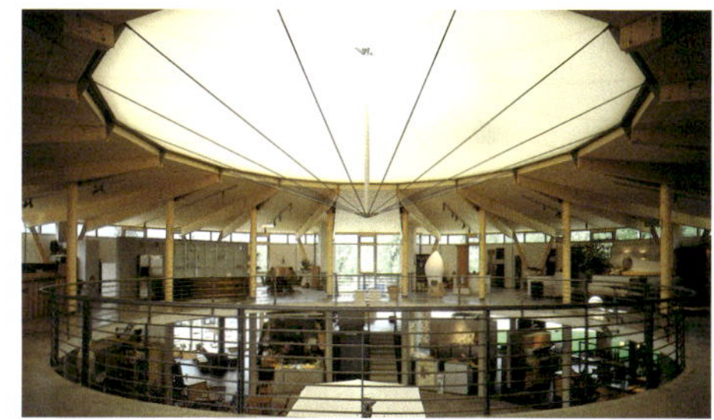

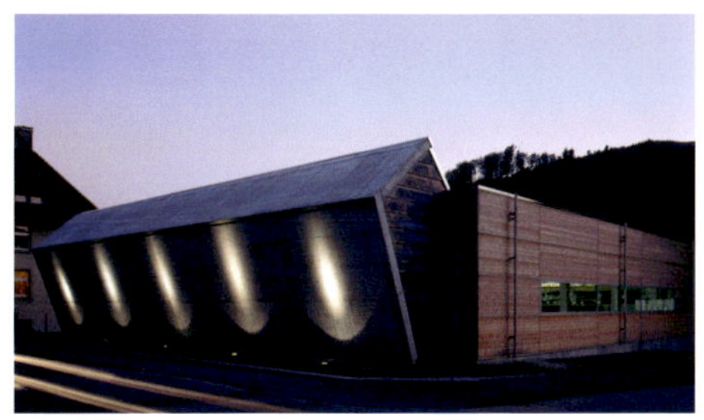

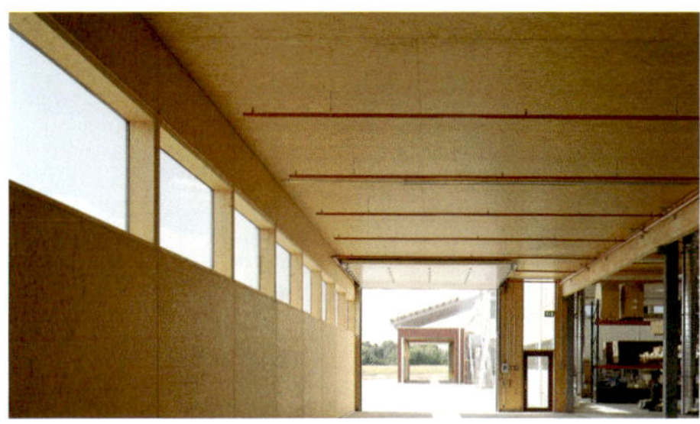

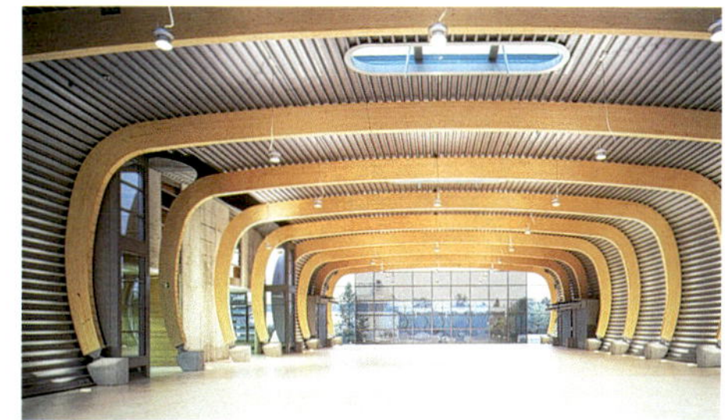

Large bakery in Essen / Germany

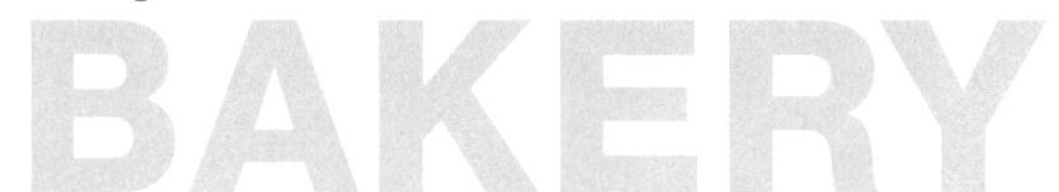

Prof. J. Reichardt Architects

The bakery business is changing rapidly from the model of the "neighbourhood bakery" to industrially operated businesses that – with their highly technical applications for heating and cooling machinery – more closely resemble "baking factories". This transformation creates a number of problems. Previously, in the small bakery, excessive use of energy resulted in high fixed costs as well as harmful environmental influences. Furthermore, the quality of the workplace suffered from uncontrolled room temperatures, unhealthy amounts of flour dust and a lack of visual contact with the outside. The planning of a new building in conjunction with the client offered an opportunity to explore new and innovative approaches. By using integrative 3D simulation techniques for the urban planning, building structure and services,

and manufacturing techniques at the conceptual phase, an attempt was made to find an interactive, ecological and aesthetic synergy between building layout, structure, shell, services, production processes and the quality of the workplace.

Building volume, organisation

The bakery proper has a volume measuring 48 x 21 x 8 m, without internal supports. A canopy roof, measuring 15 x 21 m, is a continuation of the roof structure; it allows the delivery and dispatch of raw materials, etc., to be made, sheltered from the elements, through the use of up-and-over doors with climatic "sluices" behind them. Two slab-like volumes, approximately 9 m deep, are attached to the bakery hall and accommodate additional

functions that form part of the baking process. At the end of the hall, at the ground floor level, there is a foyer, flour silo, workshop, foodstuffs store and service spaces; on the first floor level, there are office spaces as well as a lounge with changing rooms and lavatories that is used during breaks. The offices are glazed towards each other. The completely glazed corridor wall and the open gallery allow workers to have continuous contact with the hall. This is an important symbol of communication, since it was hoped that the traditional familiar relationships between staff members would be preserved.

Running parallel to the various stages of the baking processes are the service functions: refrigeration rooms, pastry making, snack area,

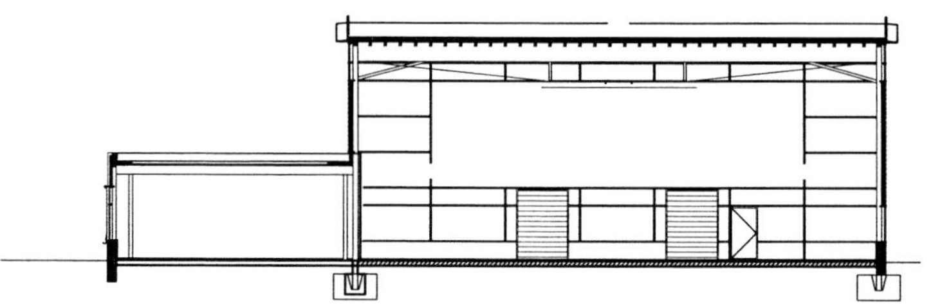

Cross-section

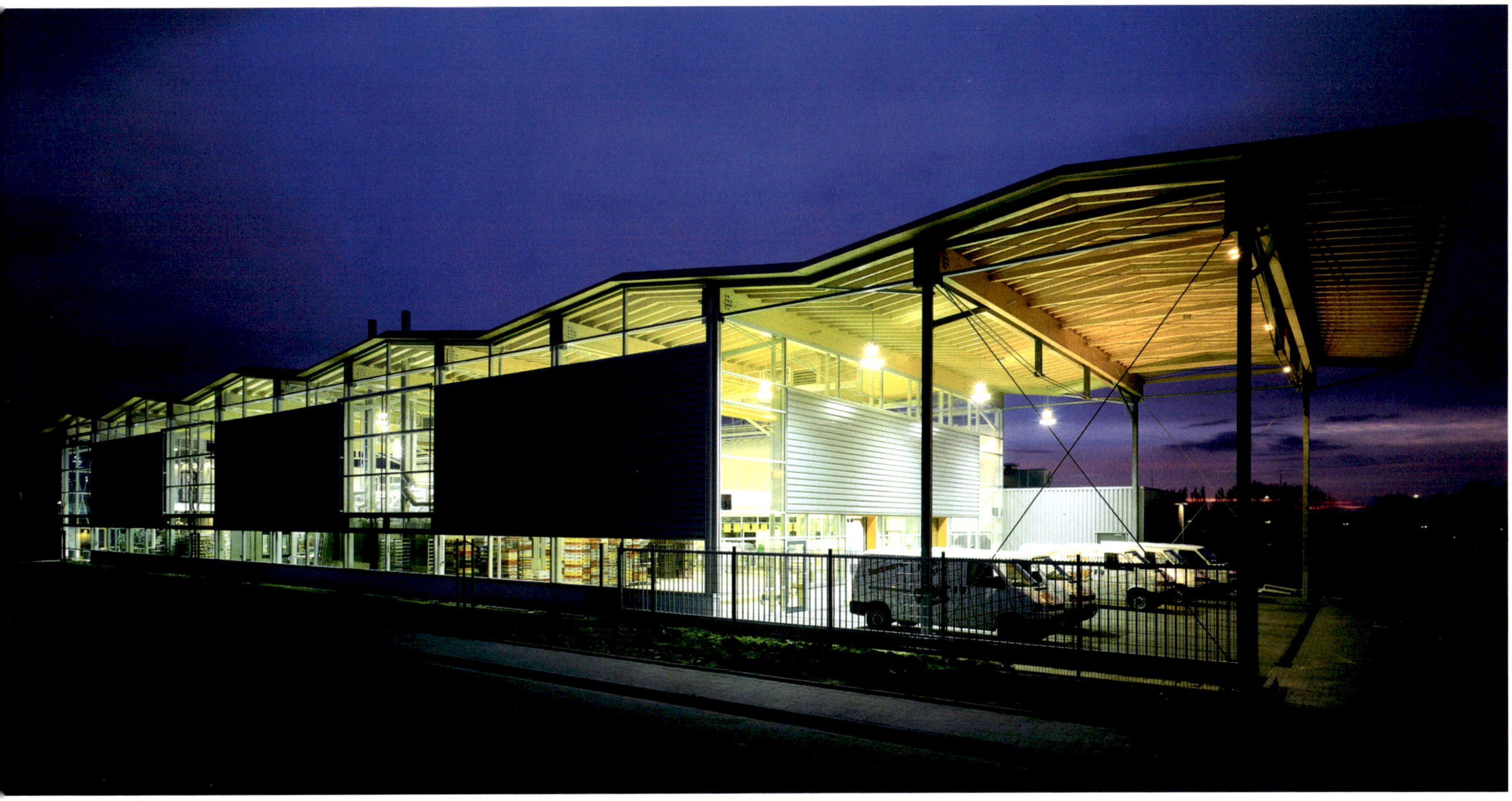

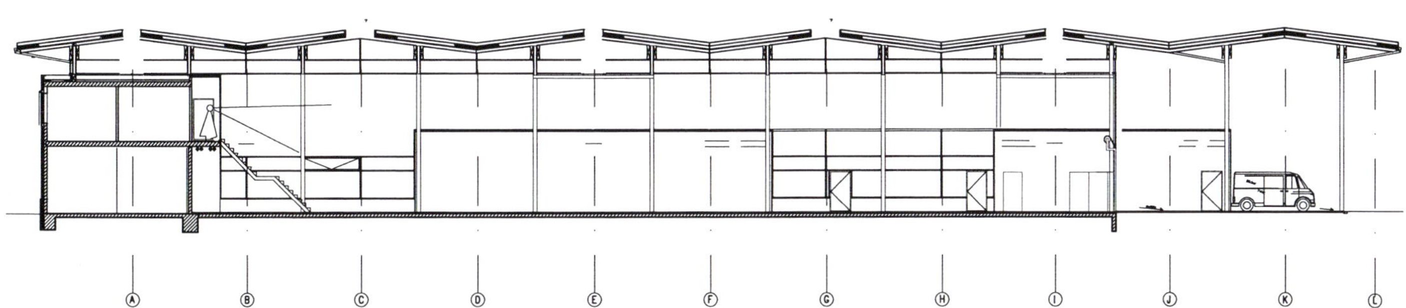

scullery and returns were all organised in a single-storey wing on the long axis of the hall. Between the offices and the service wing there is a sheltered area for the delivery of foodstuffs. In the layout of the building volumes, care was taken so that the service wing and baking hall could be accessed independently of each other.

Structure, building materials

A combination of different materials seemed to offer special advantages in terms of construction. The load-bearing frame of the baking hall is made up of steel columns with trussed glue laminated timber beams; for the roof, a folded construction of laminated veneer timber strengthened with wooden ribs was chosen.

The steel columns are MSH 200 sections and are laid out on a 6 x 21 m grid. Together with double M36 / St 52 trussed gluelam ties, measuring 20 x 60 cm, they form a fixed-end beam with corners made rigid by an MSH 120/180 angle brace. The gently pitched gable roof over the delivery area and the office wing consists of a 30-mm-thick laminated veneer decking; wedge-jointed gluelam purlins, 20 x 18 cm, are screwed to the soffit work as continuous beams. The hall is stabilised in the long direction by bracing in the roof plane as well as vertical bracing at right angles to the frames.

The ancillary buildings (office area and services block) are partly built as two-storey elements in massive construction style (reinforced concrete, blockwork) and partly as a single-storey skeletal frame with an envelope of metal sheeting.

The choice of the folded timber construction system for the bakery hall was influenced by the energy and climatic simulations carried out parallel to the design process. The selected height of the hall, combined with the slight fold of the roof, enables the warm air from the ovens to be bled off quickly, helping to cool the working area. The wooden surfaces of the beams and roof absorb and release moisture and help stabilise the internal climate. By suitable detailing of the structure – particularly

Longitudinal section

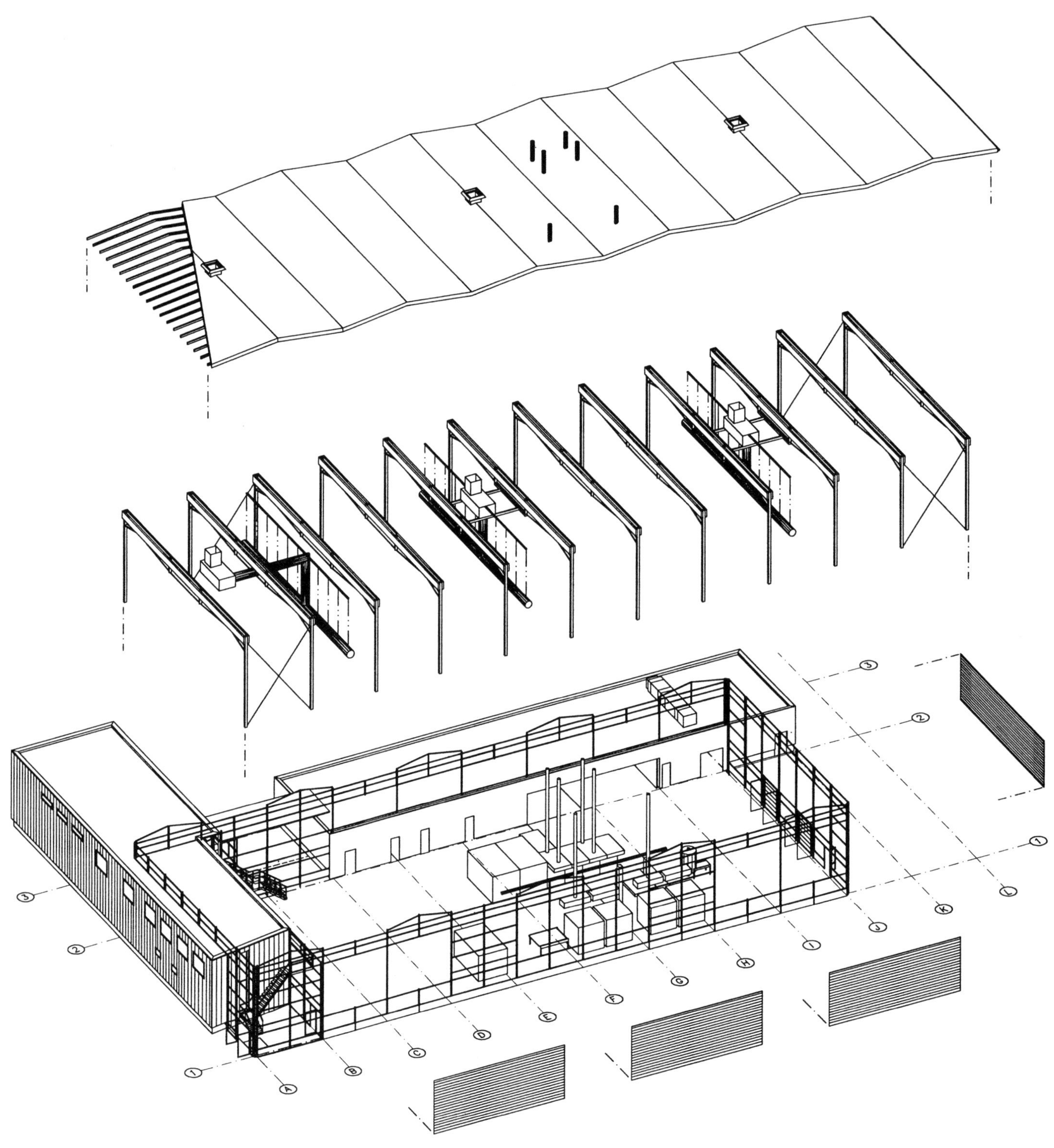

Building structure

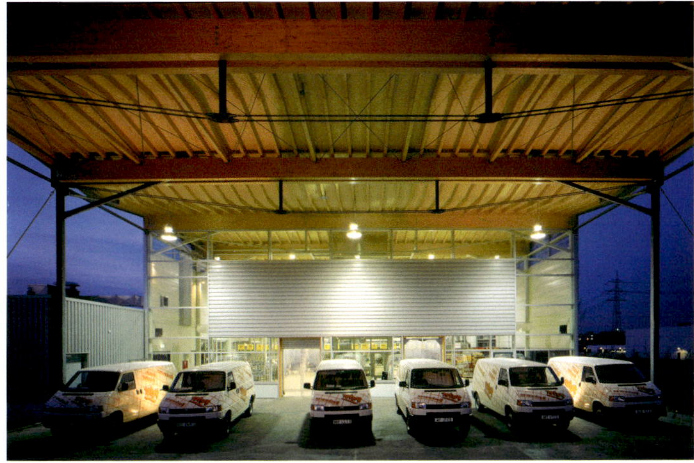

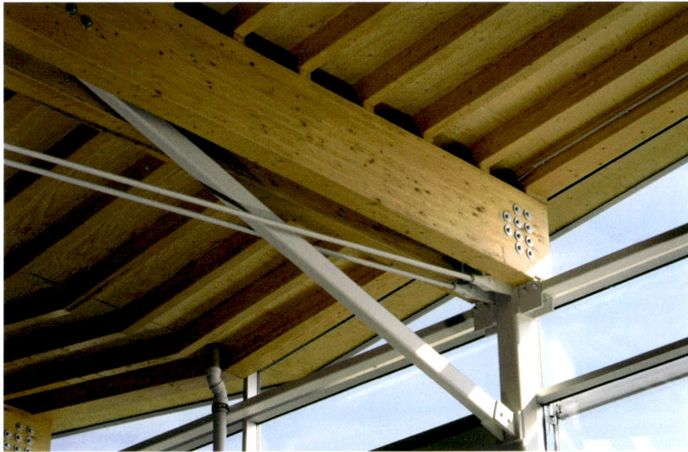

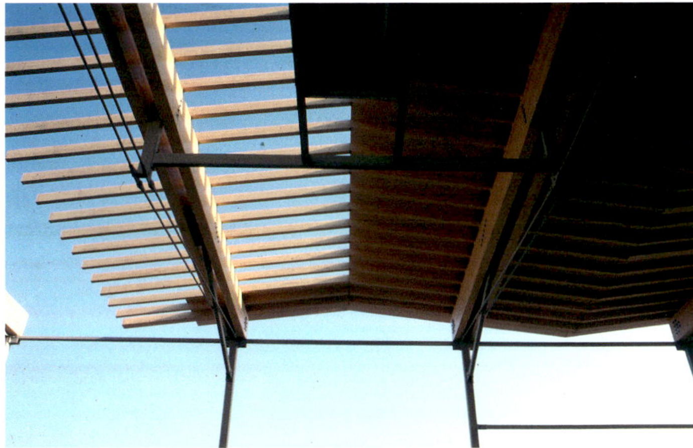

the choice of tie rods instead of profiles for the lower chord – the problem of flour settling on surfaces was reduced.

To cater to future demands, the building structure is made, for the most part, of a recyclable skeletal frame. Throughout the entire building, the use of PVC coverings, composite sandwich materials and nitro-bound paints was avoided.

Architectural envelope

A particular concern of the client was to create a bright attractive workplace with a view outside and a view into the "bakery" to show off the exemplary baking methods. Roof lights, in the form of shed lights or domes, were considered at the design phase but, in the end, they were not used because the energy simulation studies done during the design phase showed that they would result in overheating and uncontrolled thermals during summer. Instead, vertical glazing directly beneath the projecting roof was used on all four sides.

This basic lighting – which allows atmospheric light temperatures that vary according to the position of the sun to enter the hall – is augmented by east-facing bands of glazing, which run the entire length of the hall, as well as large areas of full-height glazing. Vertical blinds in front of the window walls allow the sunlight to be filtered and the amount of glare to be reduced when required. In the baking hall, a total area of approximately 600 m^2 of glazing (k = 1.3) was used, supported by a thermally separated post-and-beam structure.

Energy simulation (TAS)

To optimise the energy performance of the building volumes and manufacturing processes, a detailed analysis and recording of the production processes was required. Detailed plans with the positions of the machines and equipment were examined over a specific length of time, taking into account several simultaneous factors, to realistically calculate the need for warmth and cooling in the bakery. On the basis of the data collected, the room air temperatures and ventilation variations needed to achieve a comfortable working environment in a building of this volume could be simulated and calculated. Thermodynamic air currents in the building, materials and surfaces were taken into account in the process. To calculate the warming and cooling loads, a dynamic thermal building complex simulation programme, known as TAS, was used. The simulation also revealed that there was no need for the usual insulation of the floor slab, as it would have unfavourably raised the room temperature by about 2 to 3 °C.

Energy supply

The energy supply for the machines was extensively examined in the initial planning phase of the bakery. The primary energy sources, gas and oil, as well as electricity – as a secondary energy source – were compared and evaluated in terms of costs. Investment costs, including all the important ensuing costs, were taken into account. The results showed that, due to special rates offered by the supplier, electricity was the most economic option. The advantages lie in electricity's enormous 99 percent efficiency rate as well as the 30 percent reduction in the electrical connection value due to the planned microprocessor-controlled load management system.

Each of the baking sections in the individual ovens can be used without the need for preheating. This means a reduced loss of heat to the hall and minimal overheating. A further consequence is that the ventilation system can also be reduced to a minimum.

In the production hall, an electrical cable track system was used to achieve maximum flexibility in the use of the space. The amount of cabling required to the individual ovens could be reduced and the cable runs kept short. The danger of fire in the hall was therefore reduced to such an extent that the building authorities did not insist upon an automatic fire alarm system.

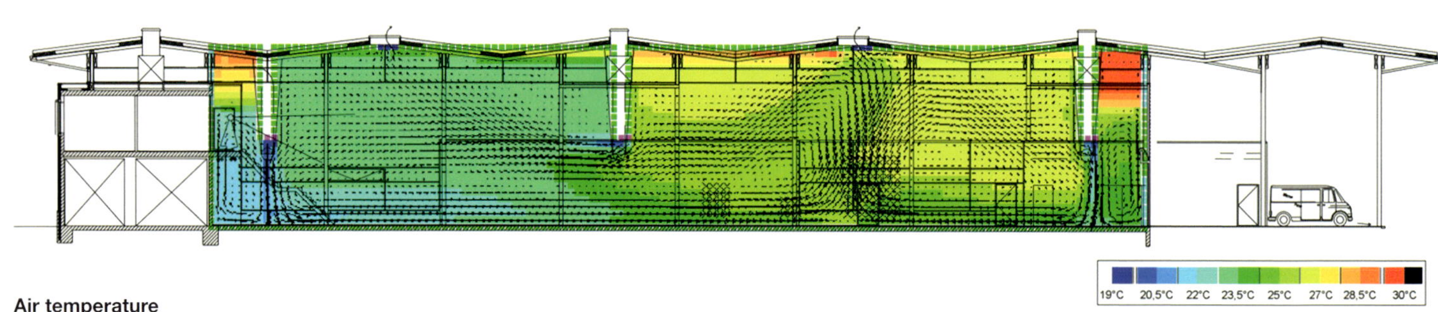

Air temperature

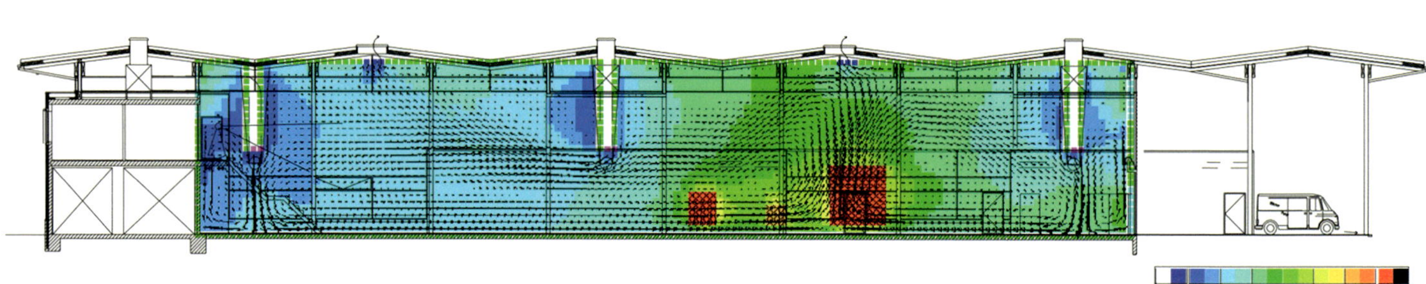

Radiant temperature

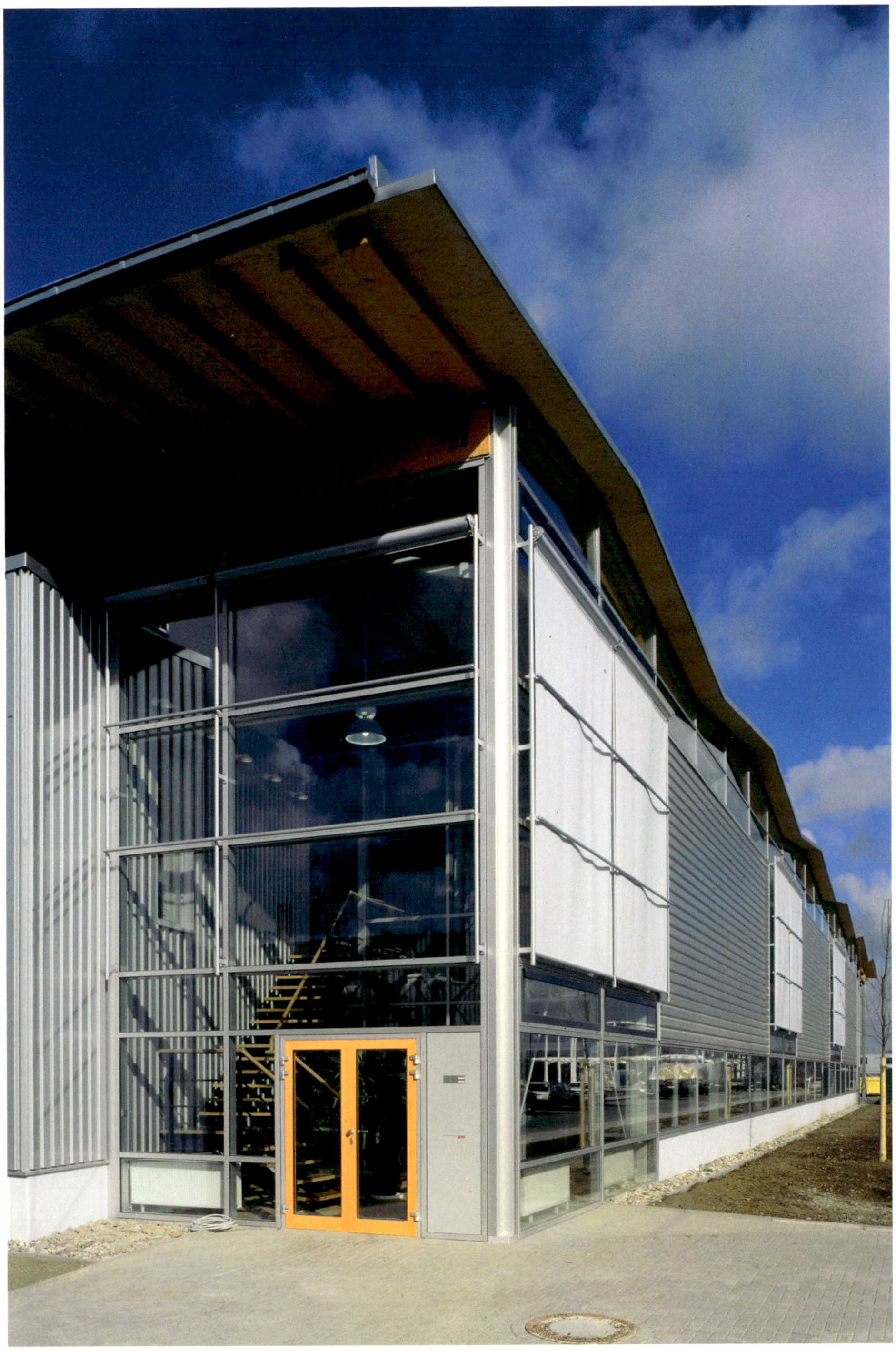

Bakeries use more energy than other types of industrial businesses. In the course of the integral planning optimisation process, a reduction of the annual heating requirements in the bakery of up to 62 percent and a reduction of the cooling load of up to 39 percent were achieved. At the workplaces near the ovens, temperatures were kept between 22 °C to 27 °C. The energy requirement value of 80 kilowatts per hour of electricity to bake 100 kilograms of flour, a standard value for bakeries, thus sinks to around 60 kilowatts per hour per 100 kilograms of flour.

A thermal solar energy system supplies hot water for the lavatories and the scullery. The amount of energy used in these areas represents 60 percent of the annual energy consumption; the overall efficiency factor is 0.28. The ten highly selective absorbers are each 2.3 m^2 in area. They are combined with a warm water cylinder with a capacity of 2,000 litres. This system represents an equivalent reduction of carbon dioxide of around 1,700 kilograms of CO_2 per year.

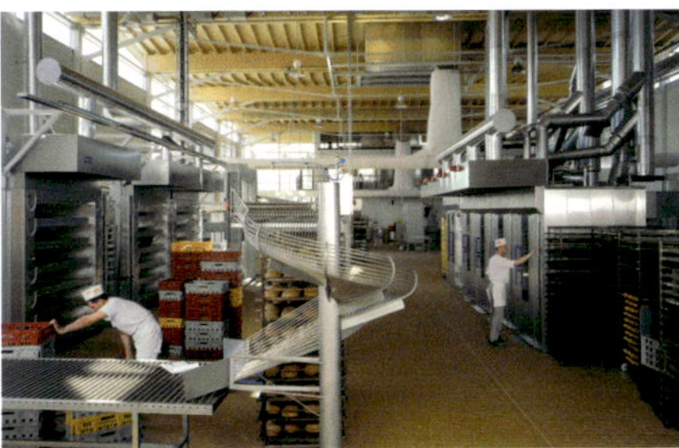

Section through hall, along axes G – L

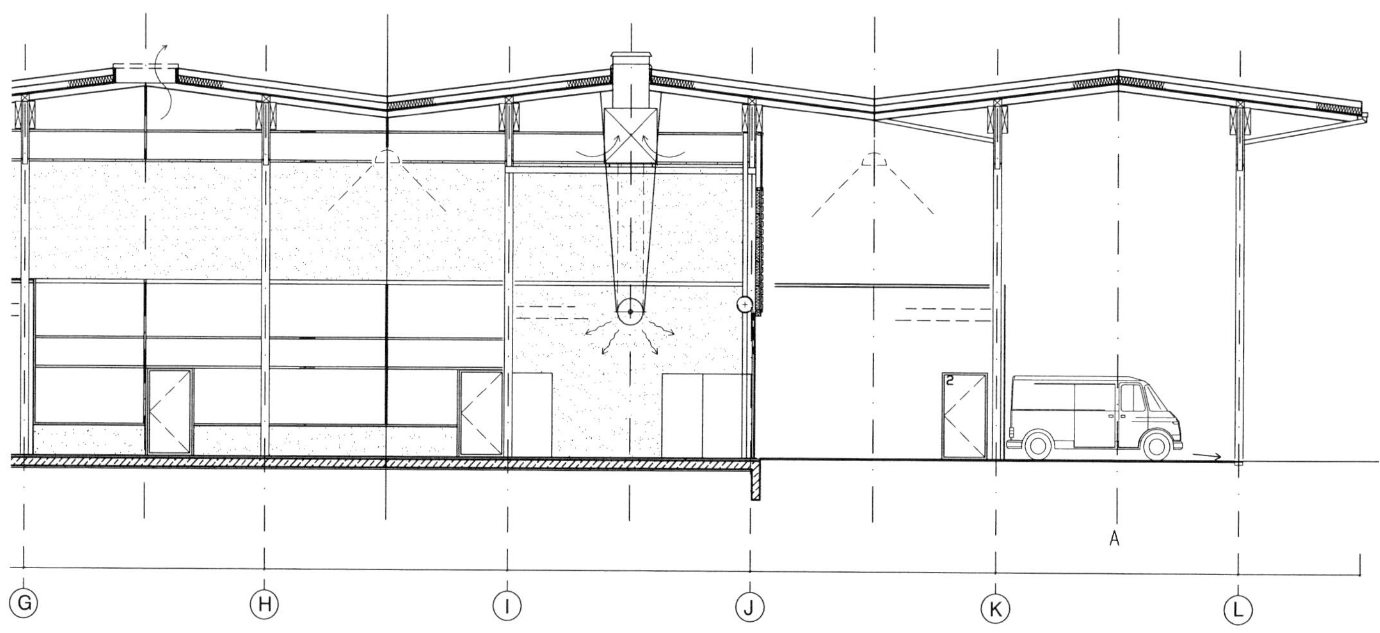

Lighting technology

In planning the new bakery building, particular emphasis was placed on environmental factors and the quality of the workplace. This is revealed not only in the structure of the building but also in the choice of lighting.

The bakery hall is lit using prism lights that are particularly suitable for use in industrial areas. Their prism reflectors are made of borosilicate glass that is resistant to changes in temperature, and the external prisms are protected against dust and mechanical damage by an aluminium sleeve. The inner glass surface is absolutely smooth and thus needs practically no maintenance. The light can be directed with such precision that the number of lighting points can be reduced to an absolute minimum. For a bakery hall measuring 24 x 54 m, only twenty-four light fittings were required. Fixed at a height of 5.5 m, they produce a lighting intensity of 500 lux on the work surface. Thus, the installation, maintenance and natural energy costs could be substantially reduced. After precise calculations had been made, a light distribution system was chosen for the bakery in which the light fittings are staggered to achieve the most even distribution of light, while using the lowest possible number of light fittings. A further advantage of this particular light fitting is a certain self-cleansing effect. When the reflector is open at the top and the bottom, the heat of the lamp and the resultant temperature difference causes a constant circulation of air that moves dust and dirt away from the reflector.

Ventilation technology

In view of the rapidly growing number of asthma cases and other allergies among bakers in recent years, ventilation systems have acquired added importance in bakeries. In the Essen bakery, it was decided to use a specially developed system designed to handle the specific air-quality requirements of bakeries.

The system provides ventilation and heating for the hall and the ancillary spaces and, in addition, meets all the requirements of the building codes in terms of fire prevention. The ventilation system for the bakery consists of three mechanical fresh air supply systems with textile nozzles through which large volumes of air – every hour a volume of air up to ten times the volume of the hall is circulated – are introduced into the space without creating draughts. The continuous filtering of the circulated air reduces the dust content. The system is equipped with recirculation chambers, a two-phase filter system, and a heat exchanger, as well as a pole-changing ventilator. The controls are made of corrosion-resistant aluminium. The lighter weight of this metal meant that the system could be mounted below the roof of the hall, which saves floor space. This layout leads to short vertical air ducts in which no dust can gather.

The heat load in the bakery is used by the system to heat the intake air. This represents a further energy-saving measure, since additional heating of the intake air is only necessary when the external air temperature is extremely low. The stale air is conducted to multi-purpose roof ventilators by natural, energy-free, upward ventilation. The air supply system has no heat exchanger, as this system also uses the excess warmth in the bakery hall. A computer-controlled regulating system permanently monitors the most important data, enabling the temperature, humidity and dust content of the air can be kept within the prescribed limits.

Location Essen, Germany

Construction period 1996–1998

Client Christa Peter, Essen

Architects Prof. J. Reichardt Architekten BDA, Essen; Assistants: A. Schöpe, S. Czech

Building site supervision agiplan, Mülheim; Assistant: B. Fürst

Production logistics Gideon Auerbach, St. Augustin

Structural planners Baum and Weiher, Bergisch Gladbach

Building services Planungsgesellschaft Karnasch mbH, Essen;

Project management K. Drüke

Energy simulation TAS G. Hoffmann, Frechen

Gross building volume 16 500 m³

Floor area 2 600 m²

Manufacturer of pharmaceuticals in Essen/Germany
FRAGRANT BOX

Prof. J. Reichardt Architects

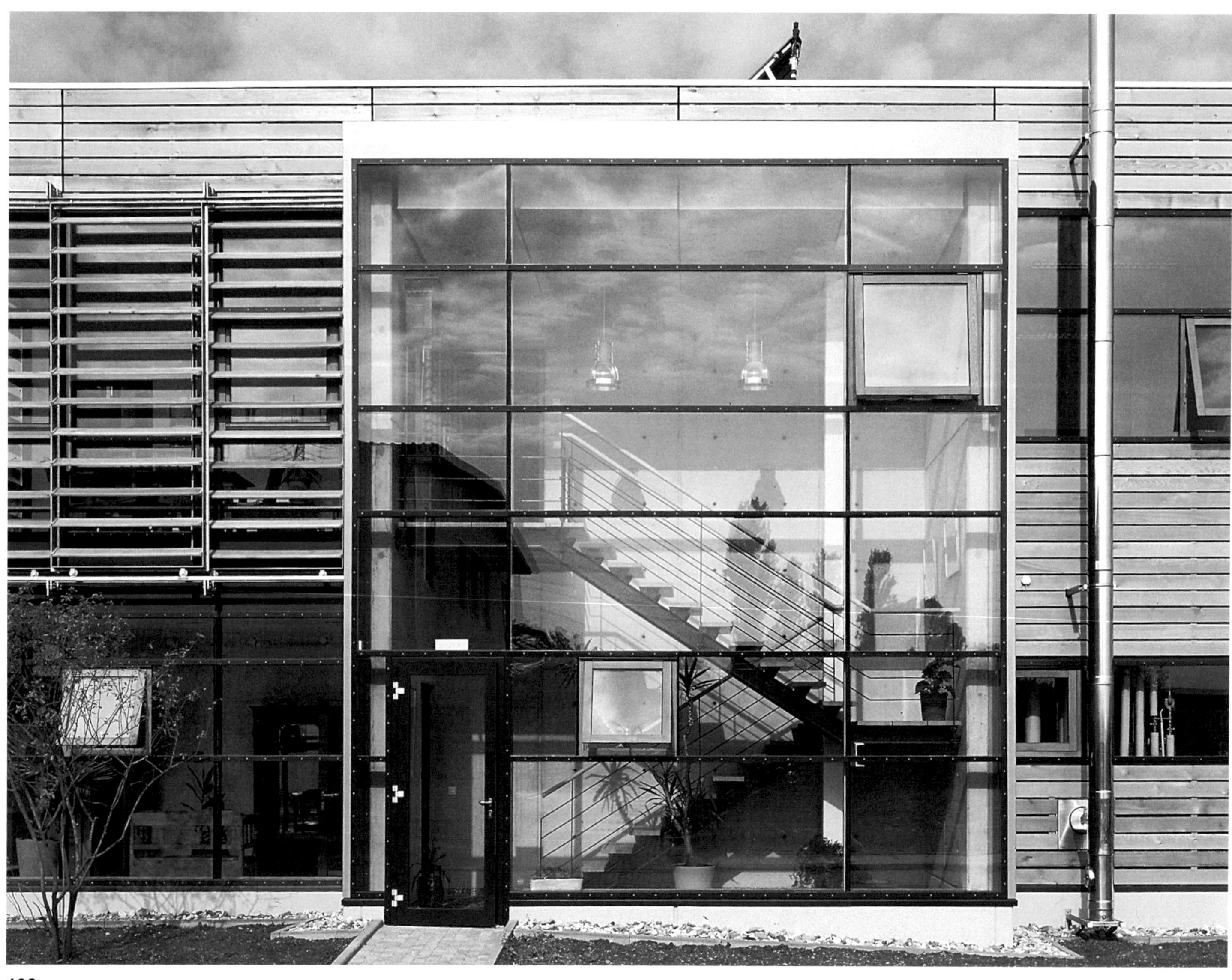

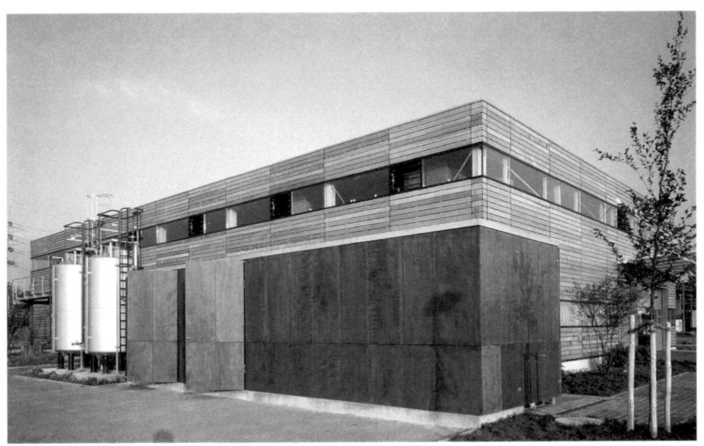

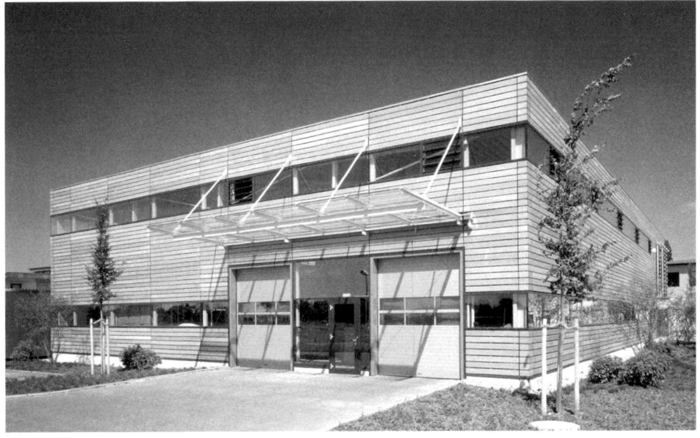

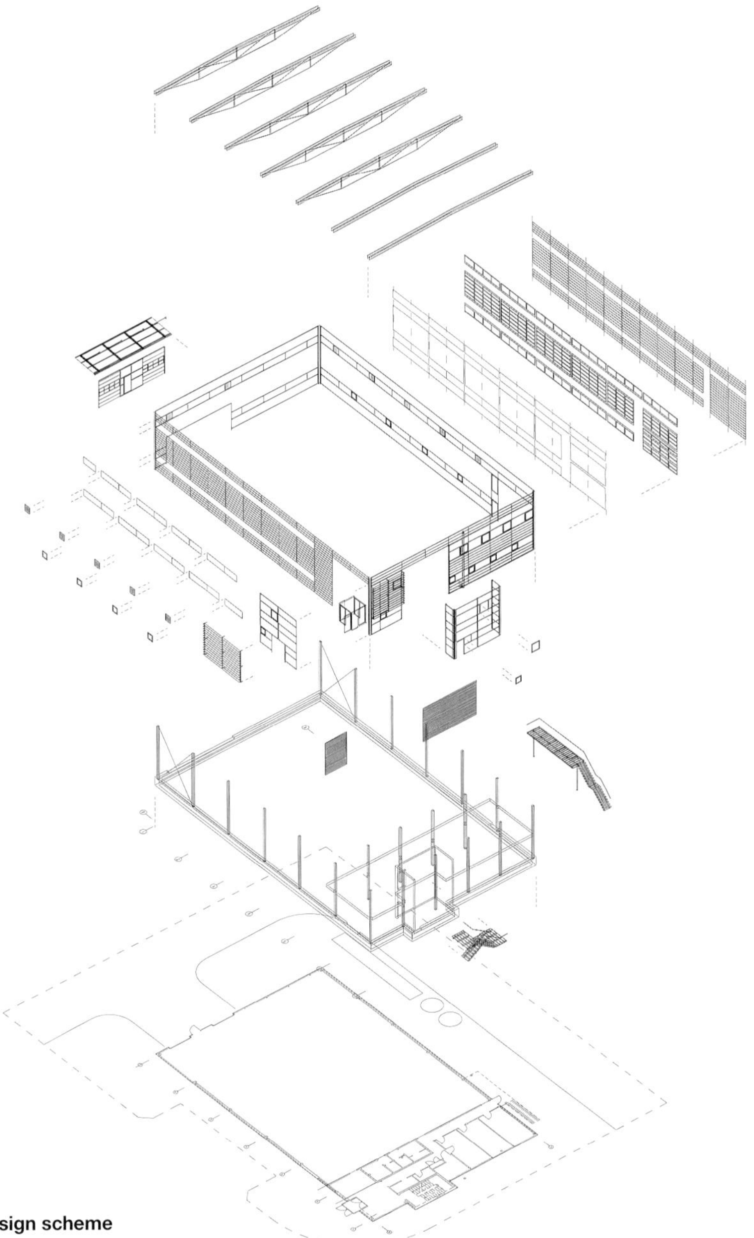

Design scheme

In this new building – for a manufacturer of equestrian cosmetic and pharmaceutical products based on natural ingredients – the planner and the client jointly reached the decision to combine the production area, warehouse and offices in a single building. The client wanted to create a visible symbol of the basic idea behind his pharmaceutical products, using an ecological building system. This wish was answered by the widespread use of wood and renewable sources.

The shell of untreated western red cedar that encloses the building volume is interrupted only at the southeast corner by the entrance foyer and staircase. On this side, the offices and service spaces are located on two floors adjoined by the production hall measuring 675 m² in area that has no internal supports. Six gluelam beams with tension cables rest on steel columns on which the prefabricated wall elements are mounted. The latter have a structure of solid wood that is sheeted with wood-based panels. Cedar boarding (back ventilated) is fixed to these panels. Bands of glazing run around the building between the areas of wood. The great care taken in designing the facade gives this hall a special elegance. The areas of glazing are set flush in the facade; the cedar boarding is continued to the upper edge of the roof parapet, where it is terminated with a narrow metal flashing. A high degree of

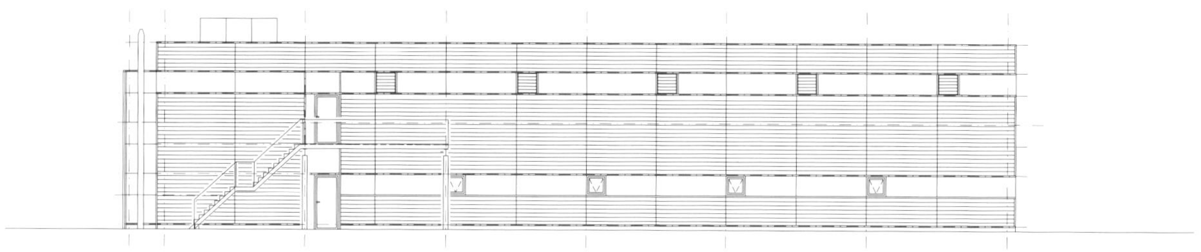

North elevation

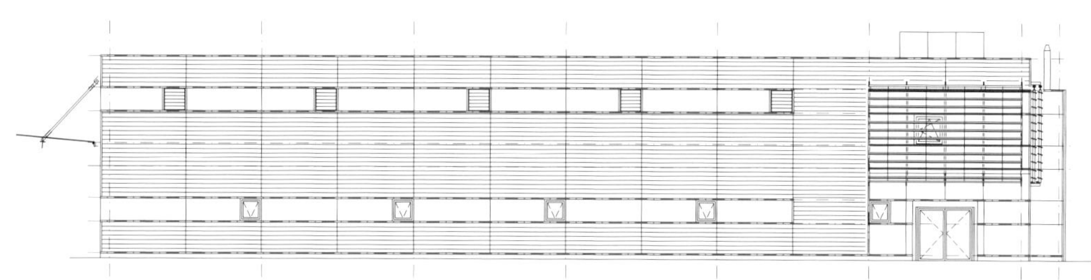

South elevation

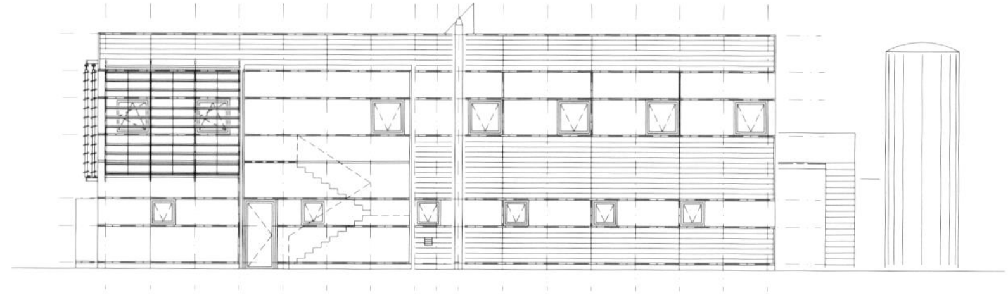

East elevation

precision was employed at the corners to ensure that there, as throughout the bands of glazing, framing sections were not needed at the vertical joints.

Building volume, organisation

The production hall has a volume measuring 22.5 x 30 x 6 m and has no internal supports. A block attached to one end of the hall contains the foyer, changing rooms and common rooms at ground floor level and a meeting room and offices on the upper floor. Externally the different levels and uses are contained in a uniform appearance but the differentiation of the facade allows the attentive visitor to read the various different functions. Two oil tanks, as well as storage space for tins and palettes, had to be provided outdoors. They are located in a special zone and attached in the form of a wooden-clad "cupboard".

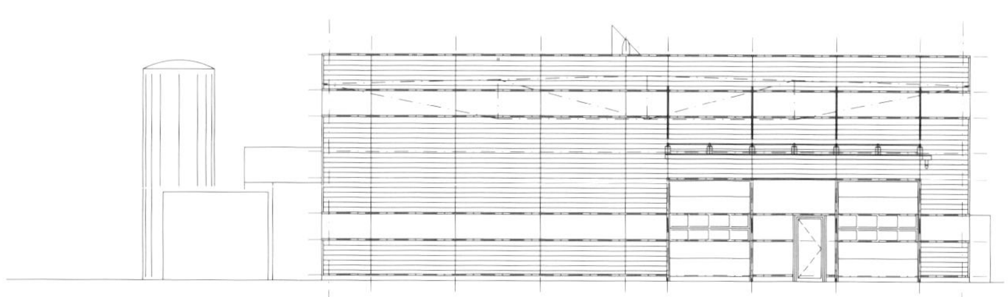

West elevation

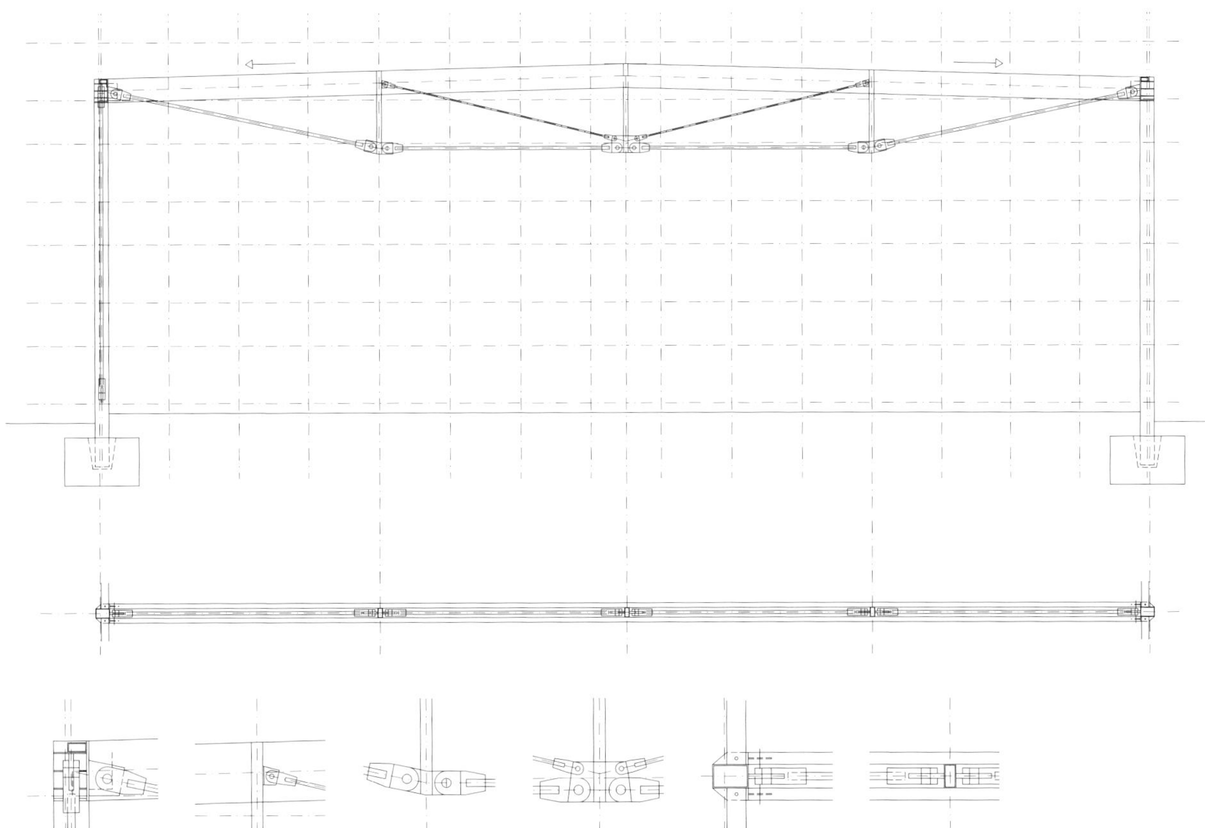

Detail of the structure

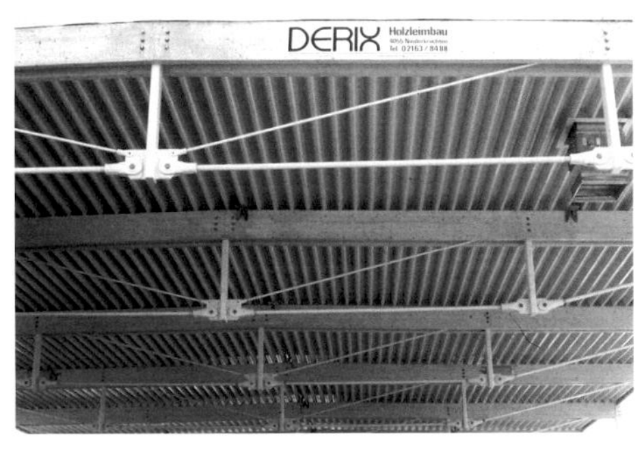

Structure

The structure of the hall (built to allow for future expansion) is formed by six gluelam beams with tension cables that rest on MSH 200 steel columns. The building at the end of the hall, which contains offices and various service spaces, is made of in situ concrete with circular columns and flat floor slabs. The roof construction consists of profiled metal sheeting that continues past the edge of the building and, together with the diagonal bracing in the long facades, contributes to stabilising the hall.

Envelope

The model for the architectural approach used here is the "box", a form frequently found in industrial zones and often justifiably criticised. Here, it is a careful composition of fixed and flexible areas of wood and glass (understood as a "skin") that results in a graceful cube and surprises the senses.

Lugs were attached to the steel columns for fixing the bays of prefabricated self-supporting lattices made of horizontal and vertical structural timbers. These wall elements are planked on both sides with wood-based sheeting and the cavity is filled with mineral wool insulation. The external layer of the building envelope is made of untreated cedar boards with gaps between them. Cedar's natural resistance to pests meant that no additional protection of the wood was necessary. The continuous bands of glazing between the areas of wood have integrated glass louvers as well as top-hung windows with glazed larch frames. No framing sections were required at the vertical joints of the glazing.

In the entrance area, the severe volume is broken up by the projecting draught lobby, the staircase and the adjustable wooden louvers of the conference corner on the upper level. The ends of the draught lobby, staircase and the outside "cupboard" are clad in glazed, sealed marine plywood panels with an Okoumé cover veneer.

This building illustrates how to make a contribution to appropriate design in industrial areas: not by spatially complicating simple manufacturing processes or by concentrating on unusual details at prominent positions, but instead by making the simplicity deliberate – carefully designing the details and harmonising them with the function and the content. And an element of surprise remains: the cedar emits a pleasant fragrance, particularly after a rain shower. It is an appropriate way of advertising one's presence, especially for a company that makes its money by selling cosmetics.

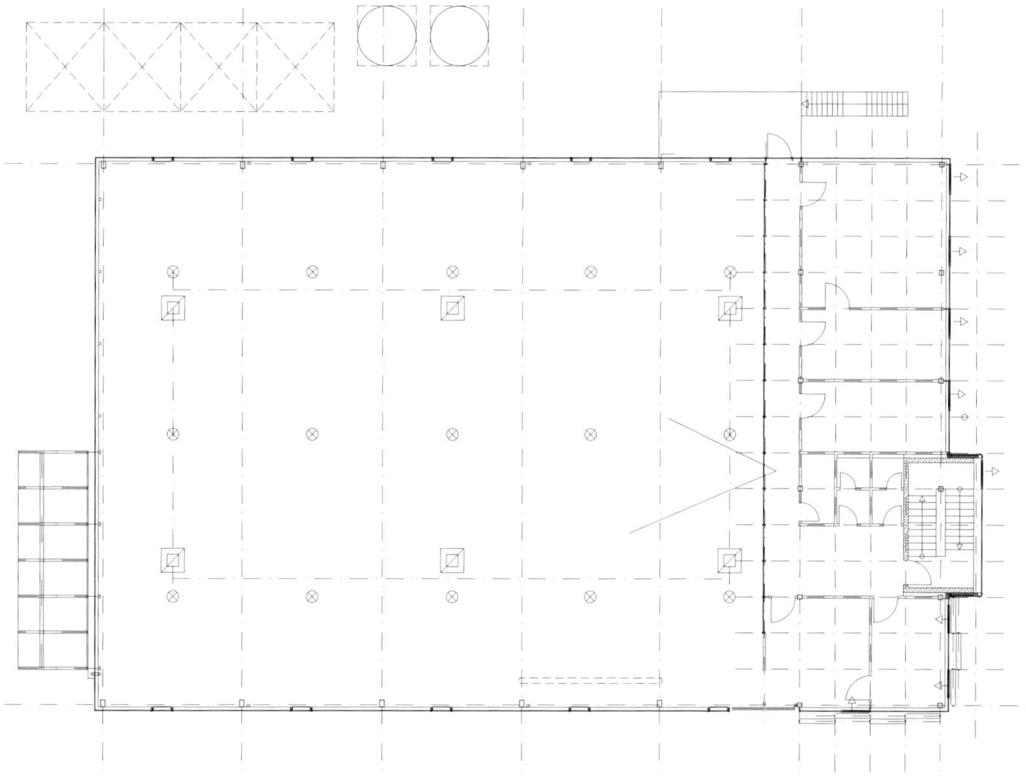

Upper floor

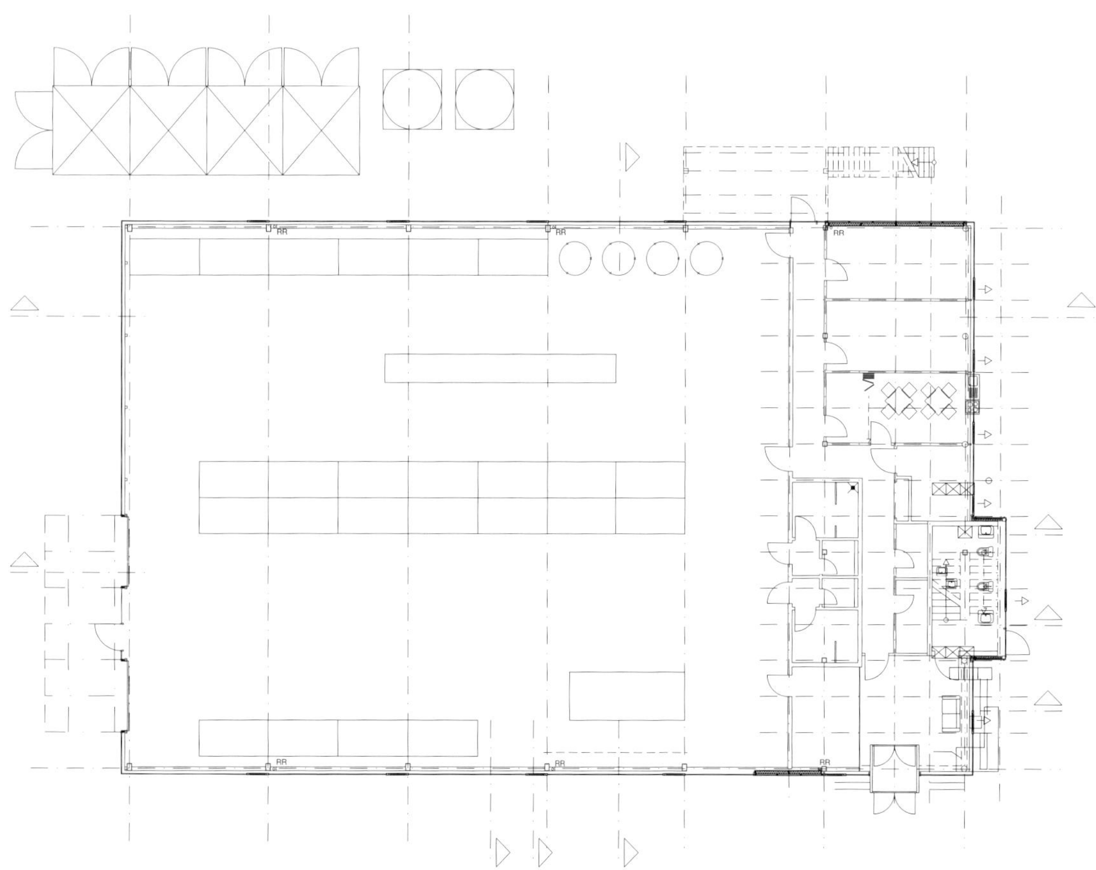

Ground floor

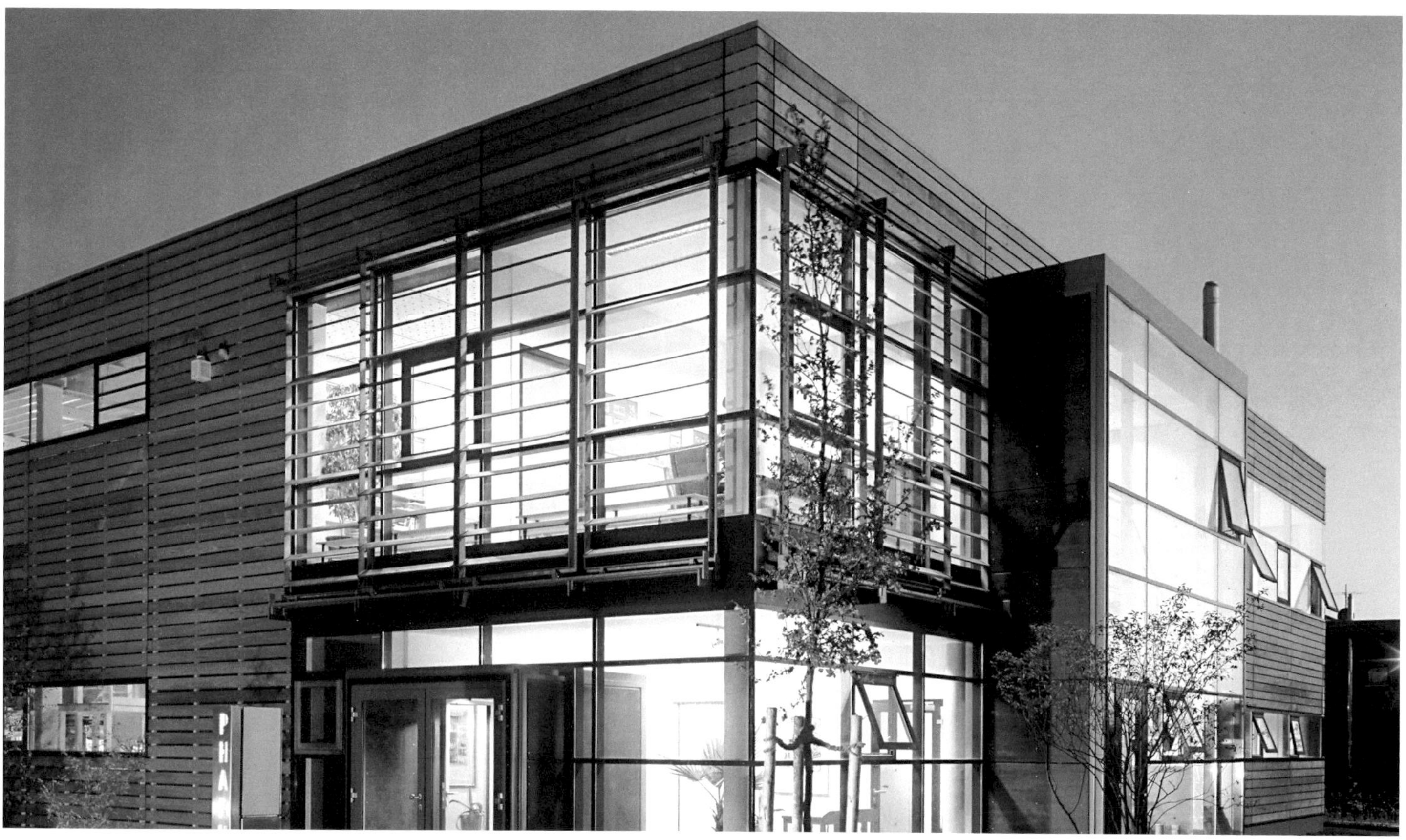

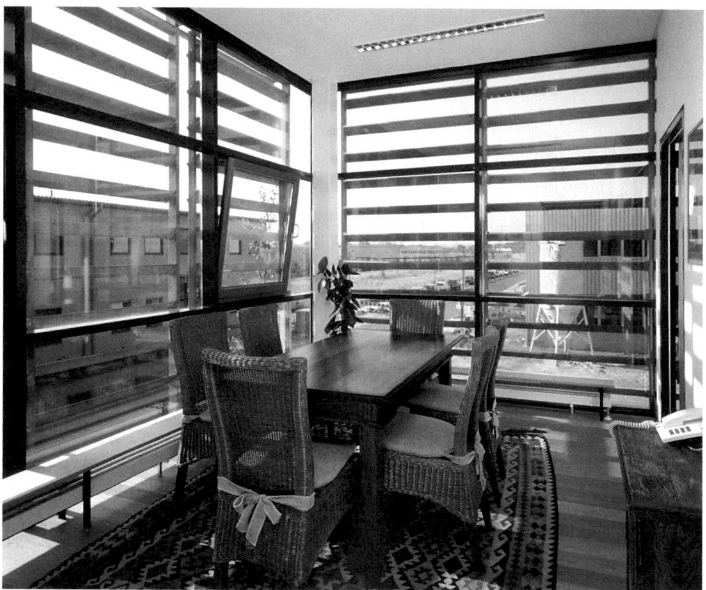

Location Essen, Germany

Construction period 8/1998–2/1999

Client PHARMAKA, Essen

Architects Prof. J. Reichardt Architekten BDA, Essen;
Assistants: J. Conrad, S. Czech, O. Sönmez

Project management agiplan, Mülheim/R;
Assistant: B. Fürst

Structural planners Baum and Weiher,
Bergisch Gladbach

Heating, ventilation H. Rüschenschmidt, Werne

Electrical services Planungsgesellschaft Karnasch
mbH, Essen; Projektleitung: K. Drüke

General contractor Fa. Becker, Essen

Carpentry Fa. Pieper, Datteln

Joinery Fa. Alofs, Witten

Built volume 6500 m^3

Floor area 860 m^2

Olive press and winery in the Napa Valley, California / USA

PRESS

Turnbull Griffin & Haesloop Architects

The olive oil processing plant and the winery are part of a small family business whose cosy farm lies in the hills above the Napa valley. The challenge for the architects lay in using the spaces to give architectural expression to the spirit of wine and olives.

The sequence of spaces starts with the production areas at ground floor level and in the vaulted cellars and extends to the study, conference room and office on the upper floor. The concrete floors and the galvanised steel elements on the ground floor, where forklift trucks drive around, are replaced by wood in the spaces upstairs. This is first revealed at the staircase. The walls are a timber-frame construction with loam rendering. The building structures, including the loam walls and the timber roof, have been left exposed, as have the services running along the walls. The plywood panels between the rafters of the exposed timber roof structure are given a colour that matches the red of the wine. The office spaces and the conference room are panelled in wood.

The furniture and the lamps were developed on the site in order to produce continuity in the design that related to the work environment. The study on the floor above the olive oil press has stainless steel elements that correspond visually with the protective screen around the oil press. Despite the contemporary nature of the fittings, the character of a traditional ranch has been created.

Location St. Helena, California, USA

Client Long Meadow Ranch, St. Helena, CA

Architects Turnbull Griffin & Haesloop, Architects, Berkeley, CA

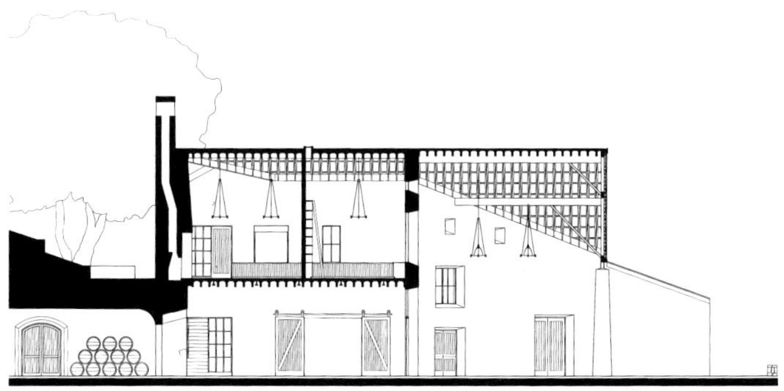

Cross-section

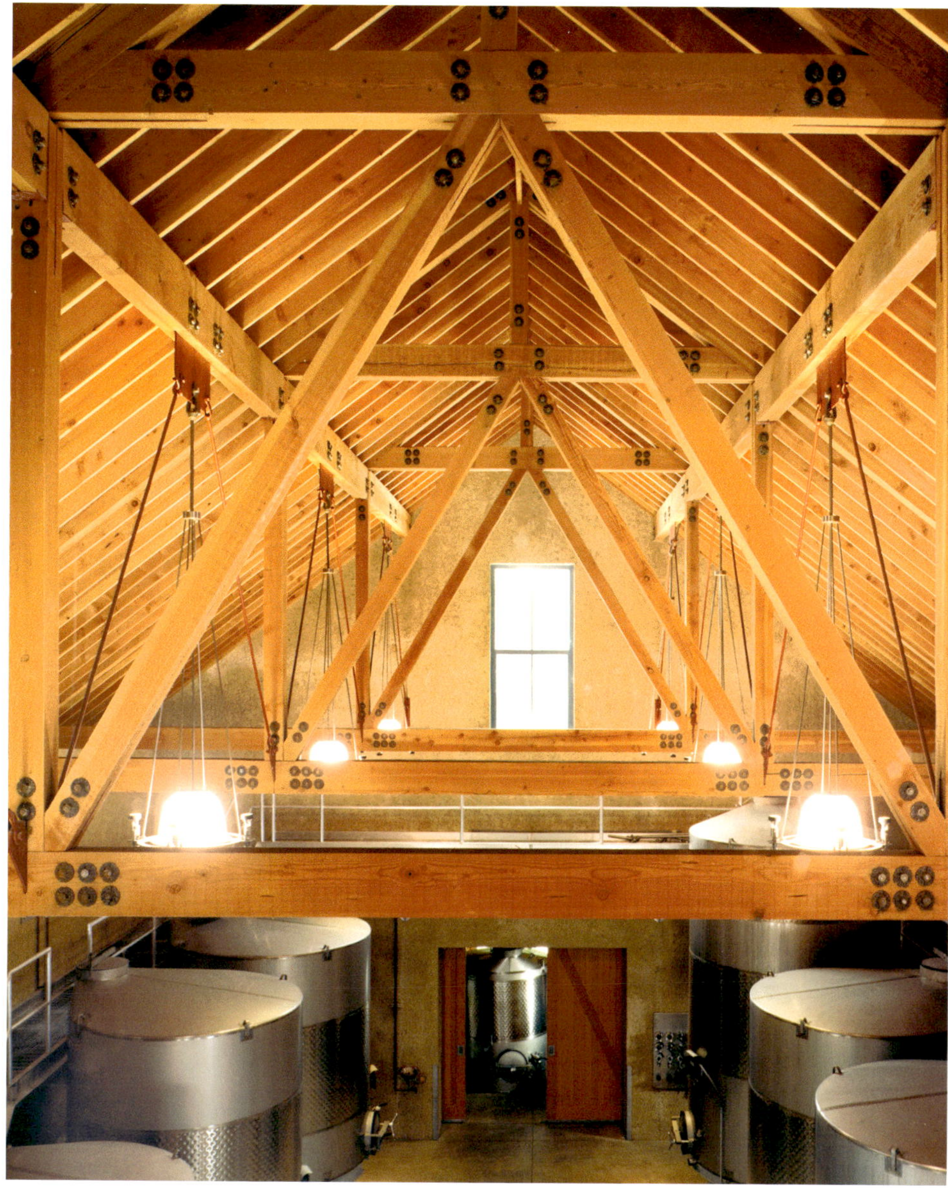

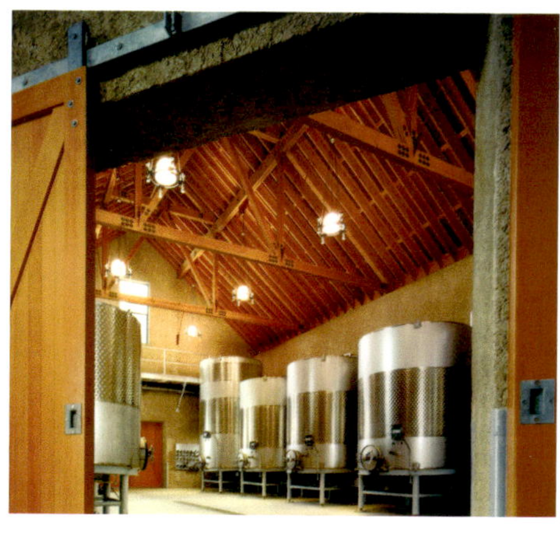

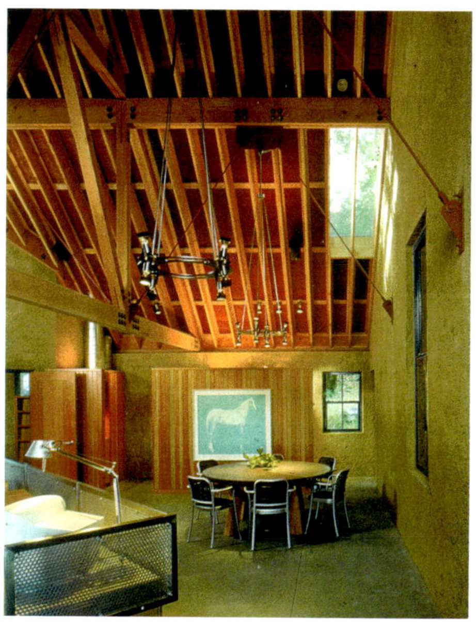

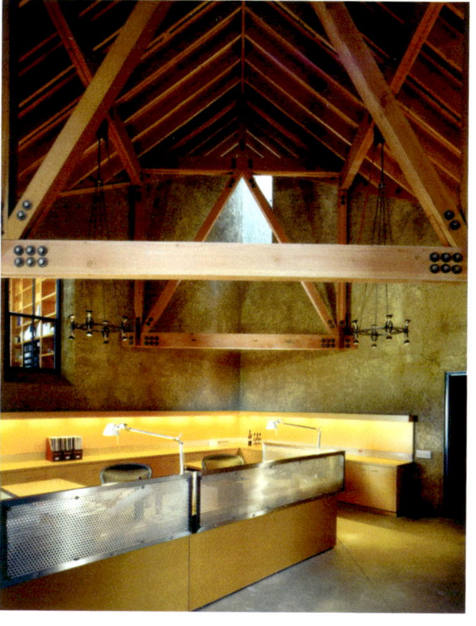

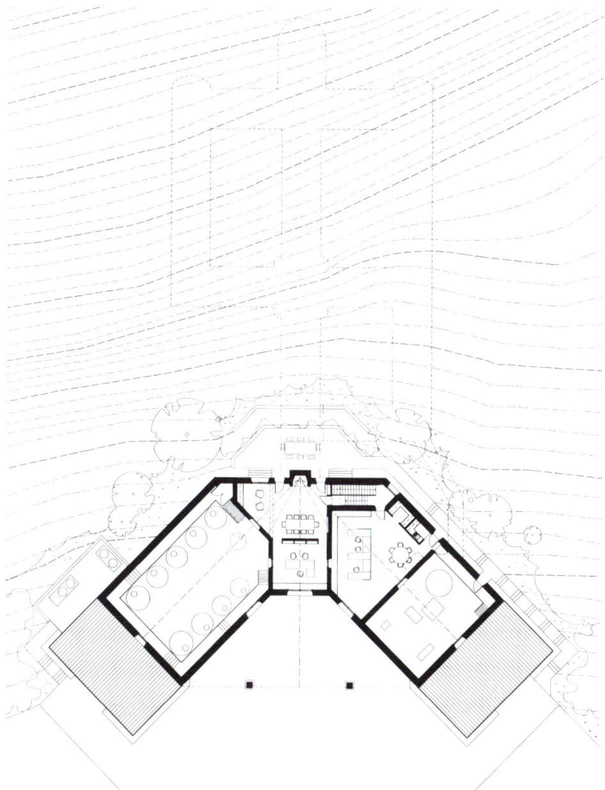

Site plan

Winery in Mezözombor / Hungary
ORGANIC

Architect: Prof. Dezsö Ekler

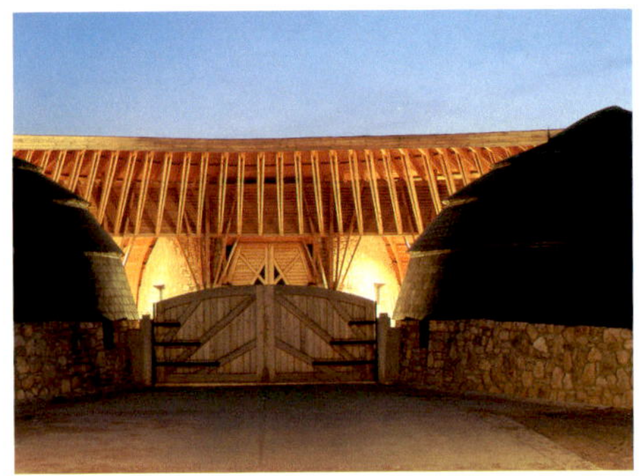 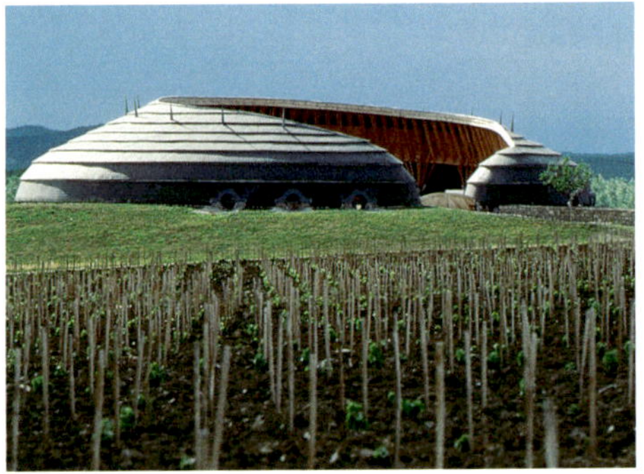

"Dezsö Ekler's works are the abode of an endless serenity. Time flows slowly, spaces widen, opening to the heavens and moving us with them. His buildings are spiritual gifts of the experience of space, where we can be at one with ourselves, outside of space and time." So writes architecture critic Cecília Lovas about the work of the Hungarian architect Dezsö Ekler.

But in addition to the sensual use of materials and the artistic forms of his architecture, Ekler's buildings are also characterised by the functional organisation of spaces. In its structure, and its internal and external appearance, his winery in Mezözombor revives the

archetype of the Hungarian Tokai wine cellar. The gentle central curve is penetrated by three buildings that are influenced by the traditional cellars of the Tokai-Hegyalja region. As such cellars are usually embedded deep in mossy hillsides, only their doors remain visible.

The three main buildings of the winery repeatedly surprise the visitor with changing perspectives. Responding to the phases of winemaking in detailing, plan and equipment, the complex of buildings meets all the functional requirements while at the same time reflecting the character of the Tokai landscape. During the day, the radiating composition of the

differently proportioned wings of the main building leads to a play of light and shadow: the movement of the shadows across the light yellow walls constantly changes the visual effect of the colouring.

The round building for the tractors is a typical example of Hungarian "organic" architecture. Its structural methods and formal characteristics are derived from the school of the architect Imre Makovec, manifested in this project using Ekler's own poetic architectural language. The almost entirely closed circular building that opens towards the site is reminiscent of a snail shell. Its closed back, clad in grey slate, is

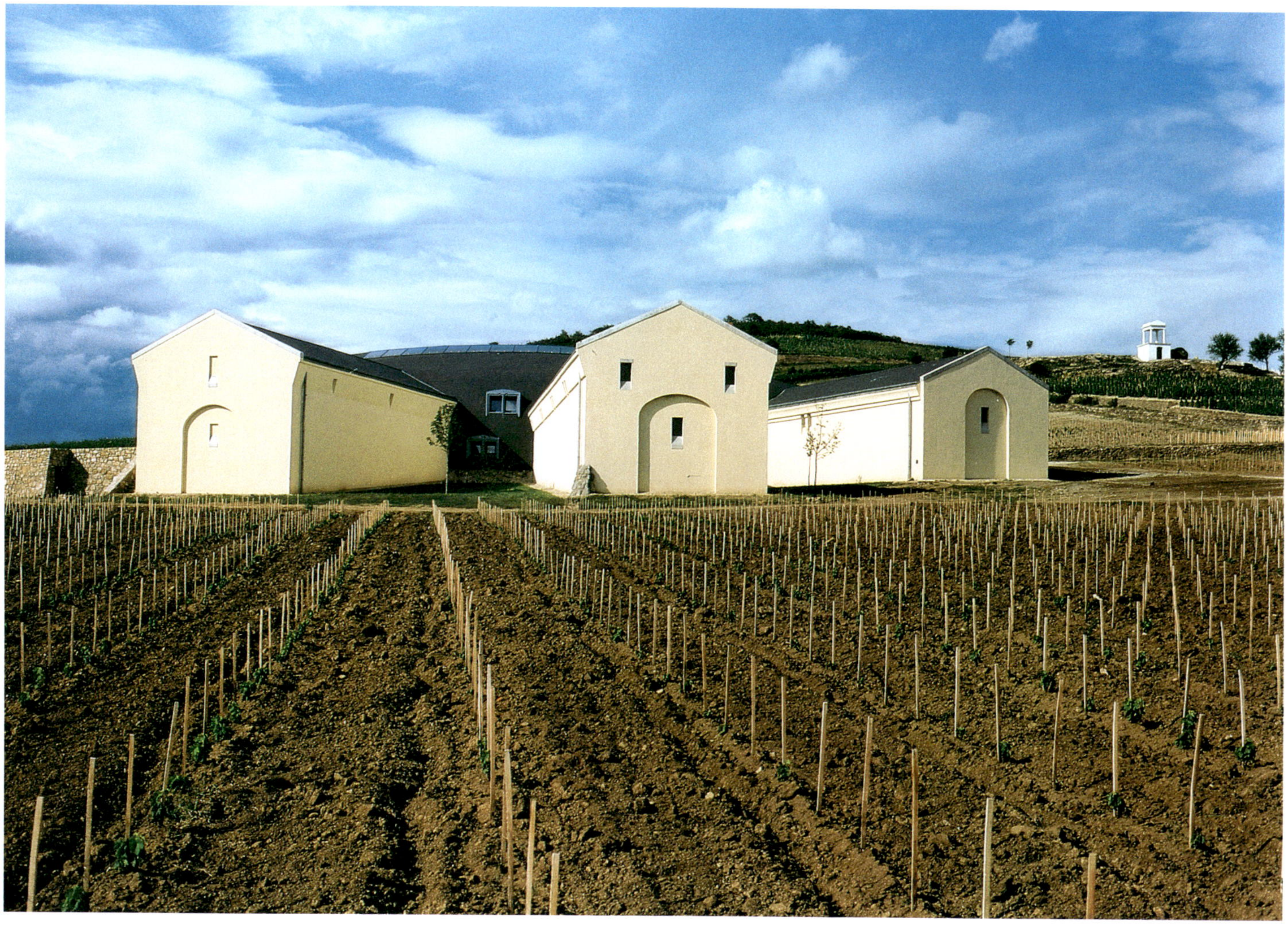

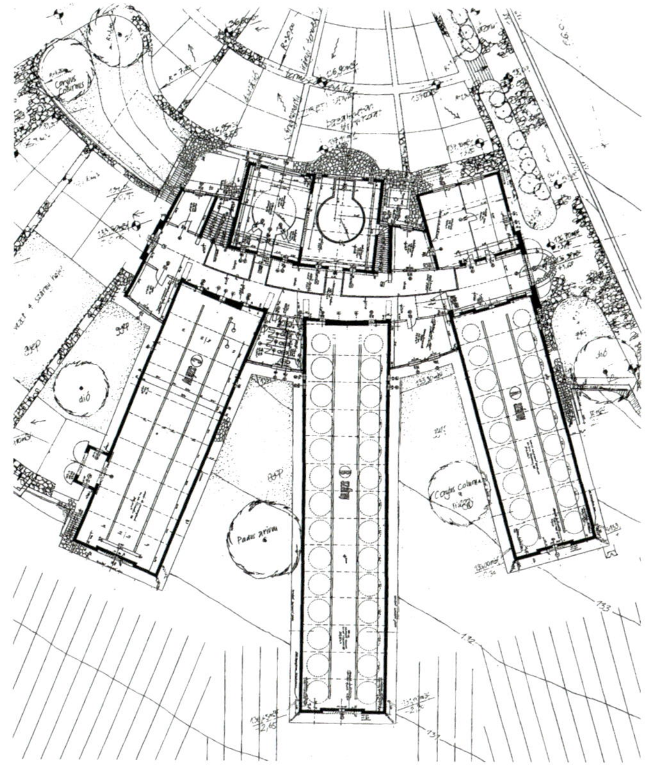

Site plan

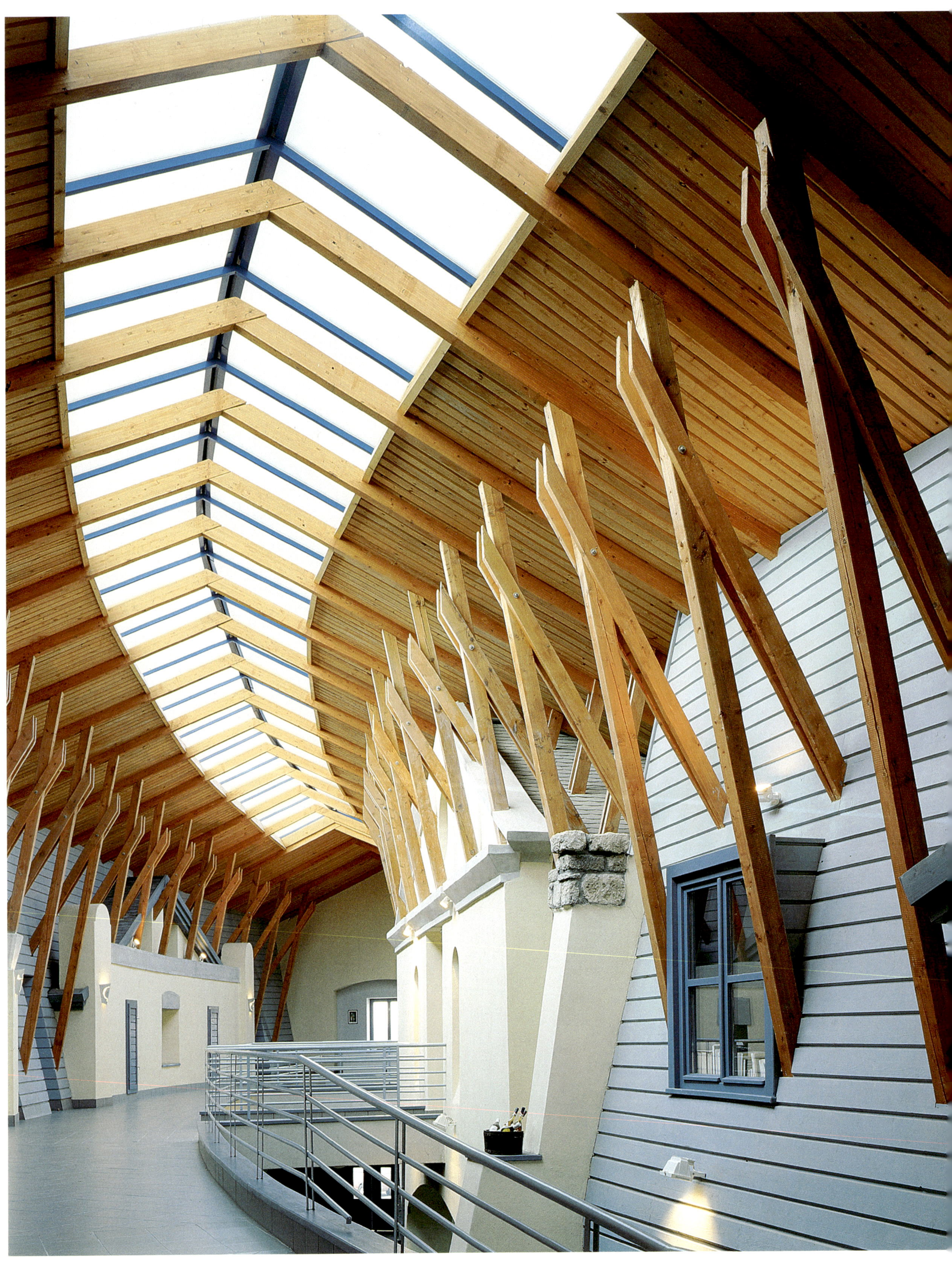

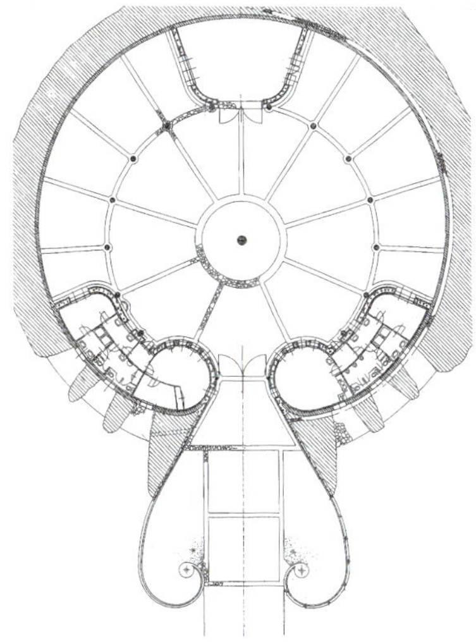

Plan of Garage yard

Location Mezözombor, Hungary

Construction period 1993–1995

Client Disznóko Rt., Mezözombor

Architect Prof. Dezsö Ekler, Budapest

turned to the nearby highway. Using a slightly asymmetrical floor plan, the complex curves around the inner courtyard. The end elements, spiral shaped domes on either side of the entrance gateway, use the motif of grapevine seedlings that branch in the middle, growing to the left and the right. The tractor garage has a differentiated wooden structure and is a lyrical composition by the architect, whereas the winery building is in Ekler's neoclassical style, which refers to the existing buildings from 1830, representing a more epic form.

The complex as a whole – with its loosely arranged, unmistakeable buildings – is inter-preted using building materials that come from the surrounding landscape and therefore establish a relationship with it: rubble stone walls and wood combined with painted and rendered surfaces.

The density of this architecture is what Lovas means above by "endless serenity". There can be no doubt that the winery in Mezözombor is an excellent work by a representative of the Hungarian school of organic architecture; its spirit is intended to express coexistence, the symbiosis of humanity, architecture and nature.

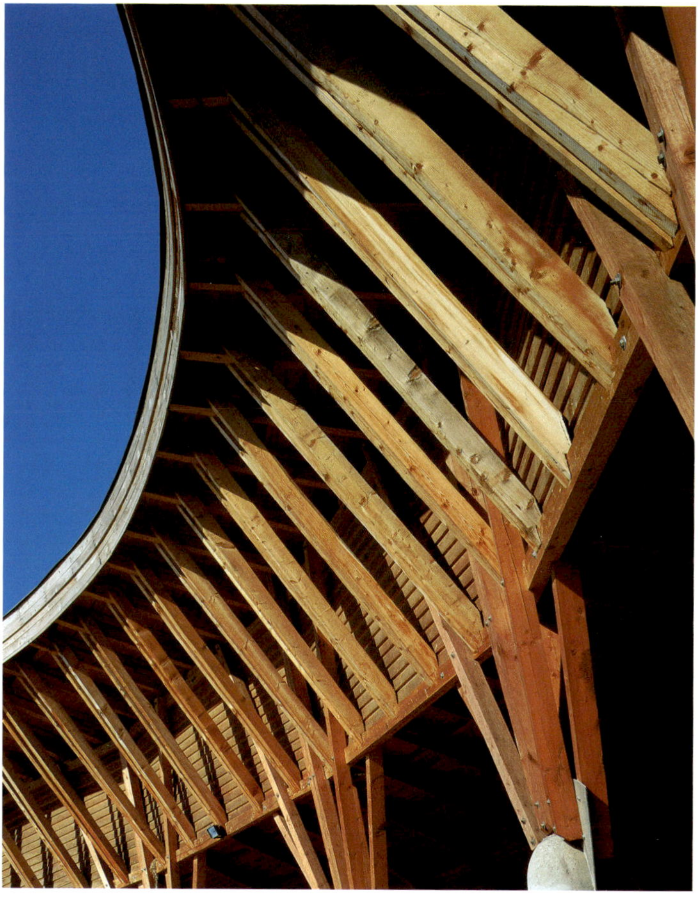

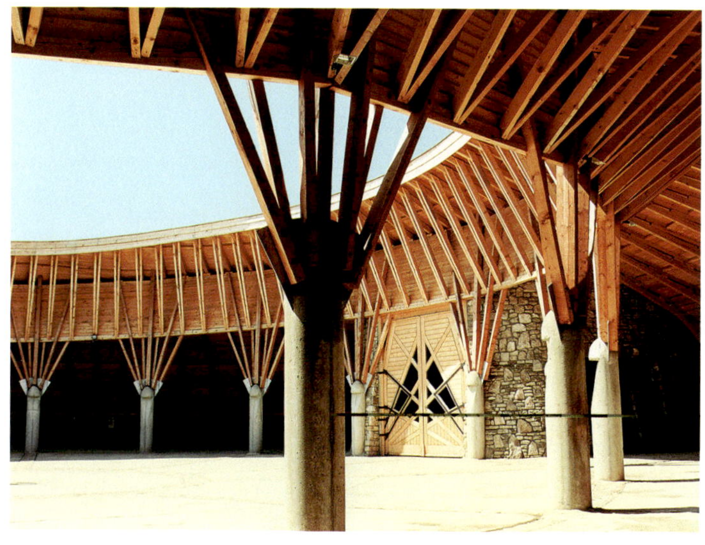

Buchecker Architects

WERKHAUS

Centre for building trades and house outfitters in Raubling / Germany

The Werkhaus represents the realisation of a vision the client had of establishing a platform for various building trades where the products from well-known companies in the areas of building and fitting-out could be presented. Inside this exhibition building, tile- and stone-layers, interior decorators, plumbing and heating technicians, interior designers, and kitchen and lighting specialists, all present their professional services and high-quality products.

The idea was to offer the customer the collaboration and coordination of the various trades – which designers, clients and investors need for the completion of their building projects – along with all the necessary information, products and services under a single roof. The participating firms would also profit from the synergistic effects. The client for the Werkhaus building is also represented there through his special furniture department. In the view of the client and project developer, the building should, on the one hand, have a striking presence but, on the other hand, should avoid trying to attract attention with aggressive design features.

Building concept

A dual sense of transparency was achieved with this building: first, in the way the range of products is presented, including advice,

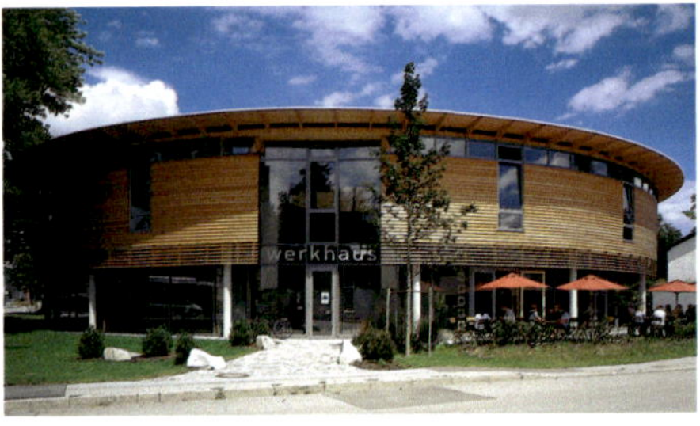

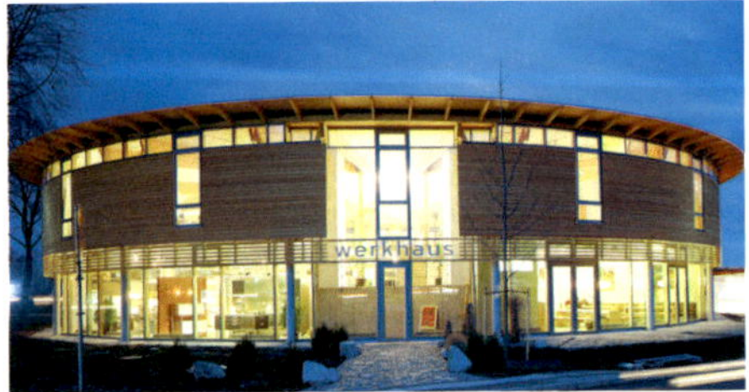

lectures and training, and second, in the architecture itself. The architects conceived a two-storey circular building with 2400 m² of exhibition space in an open hall at ground level, a continuous gallery on the first floor and 1000 m² of storage area in the basement. Around the open centre of the building, which serves as a space for lectures, exhibitions and cultural events, the individual companies are organised as at a trade fair. Separating walls were deliberately dispensed with in order to offer an optimal overview in the interior. A translucent membrane roof, measuring 15 m

in diameter, spans the open centre and supplies both levels with additional daylight. The entire facade of the ground floor is glazed.

Like a trade fair hall, the aim was to be able to carry out minor rebuilding and adaptations quickly and simply. The building was linked to a specific function but the momentary use influenced the concept only as far as was necessary. Thanks to its flexibility, the circular building can be remodelled at any time. Even an entirely different kind of use should be possible without the need for expensive interventions in the building substance. The architects succeeded in designing a building that is flexible in various ways: its structural flexibility results from the regular column grid, the absence of load-bearing internal walls and the ceilings slabs without downstand beams. In terms of the building services, flexibility is achieved through the use of standard details for the service runs. Provision was also made for separate access from the outside into the individual segments.

Construction

Due to the high level of the ground water (about –1.50 m), the basement was built as a continuous waterproof trough. The ground floor, originally planned in timber construction, had

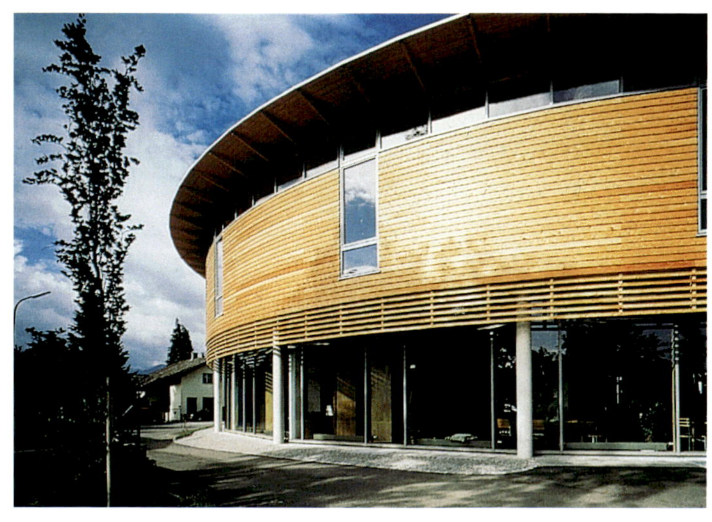

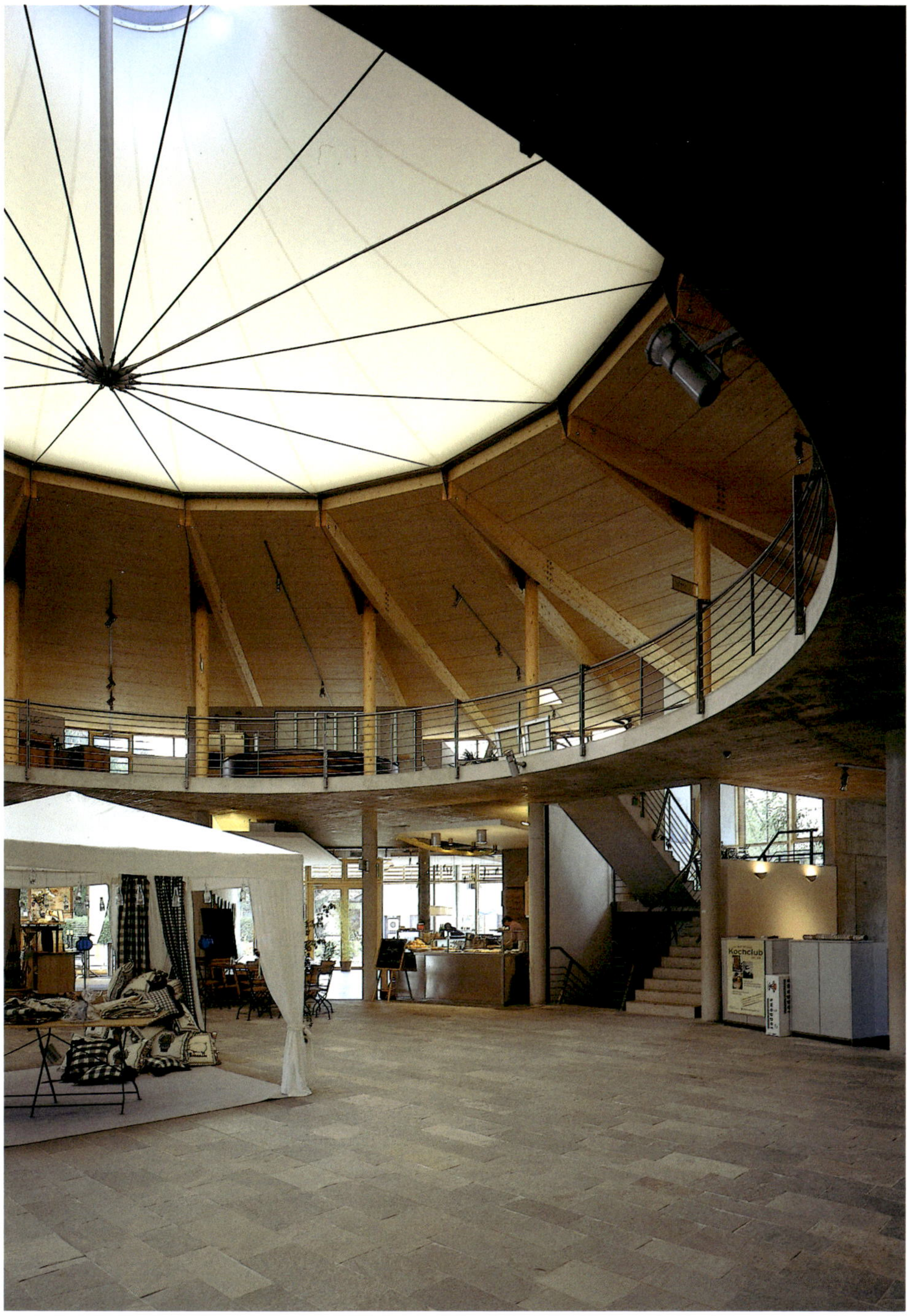

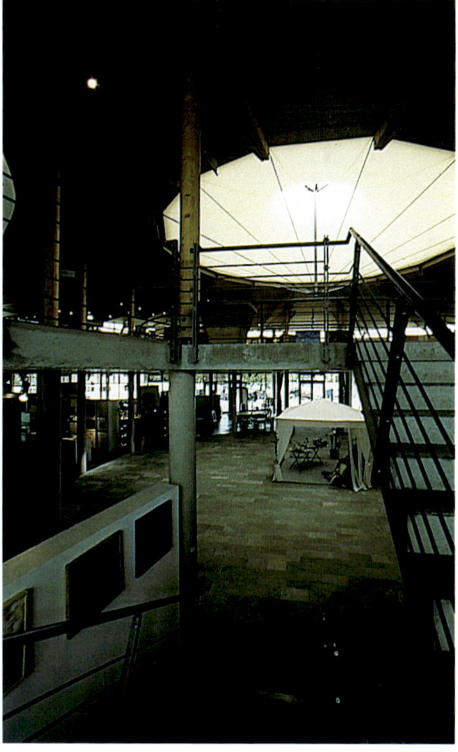

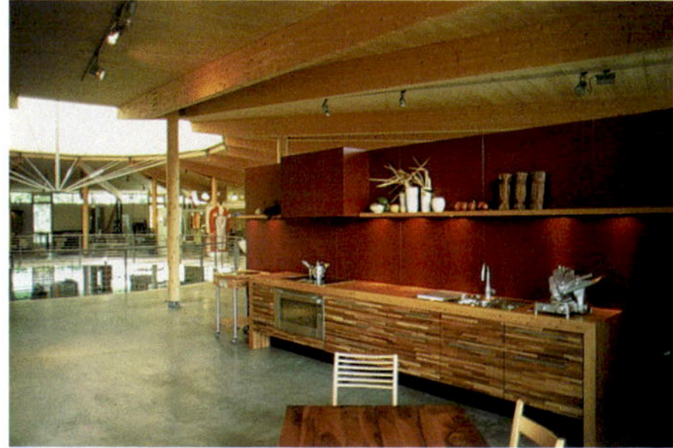

to be made of reinforced concrete to provide sufficient resistance to the upward forces. The grid of columns chosen is relatively tight due to the water pressure and to allow economical use of reinforcement steel. The wall bracing on the ground floor is assured by the end-fixed columns and the staircase slabs.

The first (upper) floor was prefabricated as a completely timber structure. The V-shaped external columns, on the one hand, reduce the spans of the wooden ceiling elements, while, on the other, they provide wind-bracing because they are tied at either side. The ceiling beams – made of glue laminated timber held by a pin-jointed column with a circular cross-section – span over the V-shape supports and meet at the centre. The ceiling elements complete the structural system.

A specialist shop in the basement can be reached from outside via a ramp. The ceiling of the basement level is cut back there to allow the entry of light and to provide a view outside. The larger part of the basement is used for storage purposes. The machinery for the goods lift is below ground floor to avoid having those elements at ground level where they could interfere with the planning.

Facades

The external wall of the first floor is in timber frame construction. The choice of small segments allowed straight building elements to be used for the uprights, cross beams, etc. The only truly curved building elements are the back-ventilated larch wood cladding on the outside and the plasterboard shell on the inside. The facade uprights, mounted in front of the end of the ceiling, project down towards the

ground floor and carry a small screen of wooden louvers that shade the large windows on the ground floor from direct sunlight. A band of high-level glazing makes the roof appear to hover over the building: this effect is particularly impressive at night when the projecting roof is lit from below.

On the ground floor, the facade is made entirely of glass that runs around the entire building behind the uprights. The way the facade is broken up into bays allows a shop door to be built for each unit. The ground floor facade does not appear round but, through the use of large-scale elements, it traces the polygon drawn by the columns. The fact that the concrete columns on the ground floor are free-standing gives the building an impression of extreme lightness.

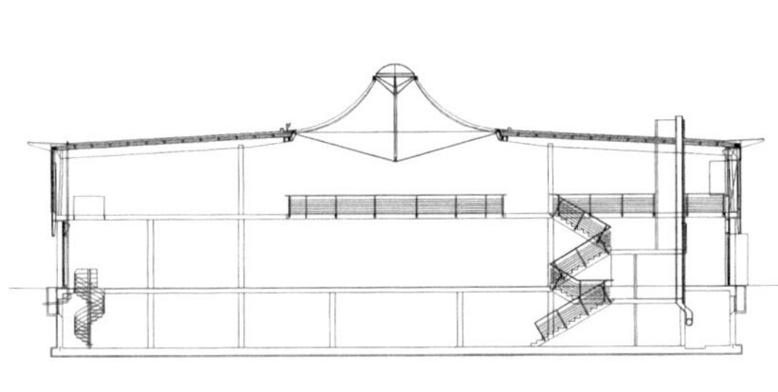

Section

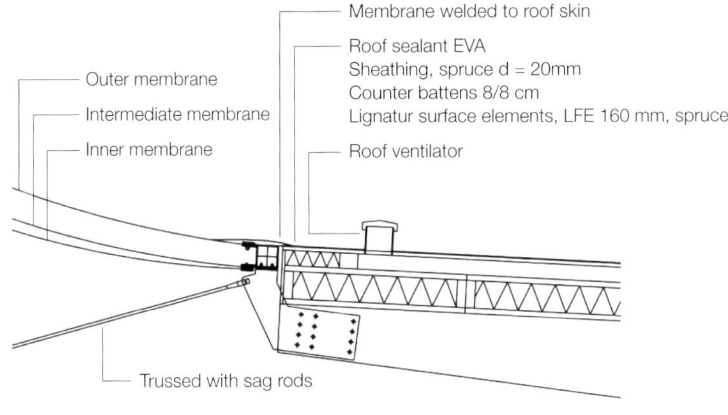

Connection of solid roof and membrane

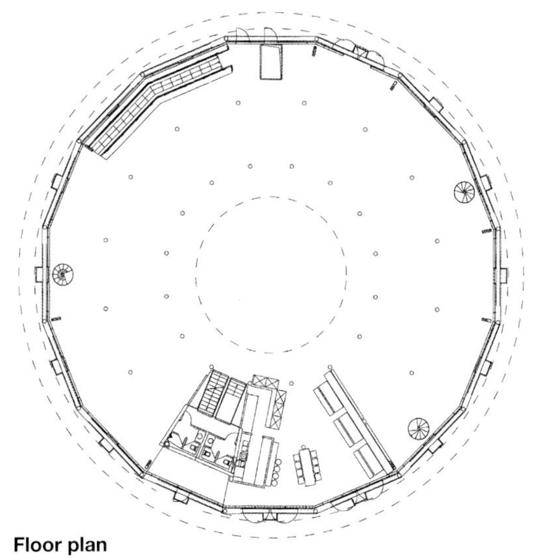

Floor plan

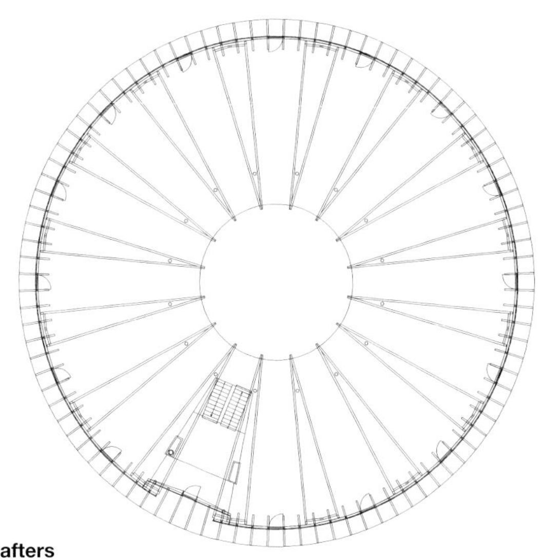

Rafters

Roof structure

The roof consists of prefabricated timber box elements; the ease with which they could be fixed enabled the building to be roofed quickly. The use of roofing foil on the wooden roof allowed the projecting part of the roof to be made so that it slopes in the opposite direction to the main part of the roof (i.e., towards the centre), which means that no gutters or down pipes had be attached to the facade. The roofing foil is welded to the roof membrane without overlaps. The ventilating of the roof is ensured by the use of individual ventilators below the edge of the membrane roof. The roof construction consists of three layers with two air cavities in order to achieve sufficient insulation. A steel compression ring takes up the tension forces that occur due to the pre-tensioning of the membrane. The suspended column at the centre carries a central transparent roof light (skylight) that can be opened to provide ventilation.

Building services

Fixed radiators heat the ground floor and basement. The first floor is an open gallery that receives enough warmth from below; therefore, there are no radiators. Standard details for the service runs (heating, electricity, plumbing) are provided in every second facade column, allowing each segment to be individually serviced. High-level glazing at ground and first floor level provides good natural ventilation. The stale air is efficiently drawn off at the highest point of the roof light, which has a 2 m diameter.

Economy and effect

Thanks to the prefabrication of the building elements, the Werkhaus was completed in only five months. Its economy is based on the use of prefabricated construction elements, simple building technology and – with the future in mind –a flexible concept. Despite all its plainness, it has proved that it is possible to make a kind of architecture that, particularly in the evening, magically attracts visitors; it is an illuminated commercial building, without garishly illuminated advertising.

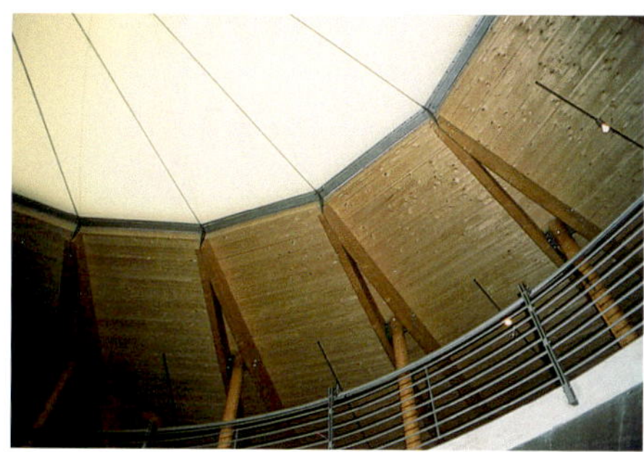

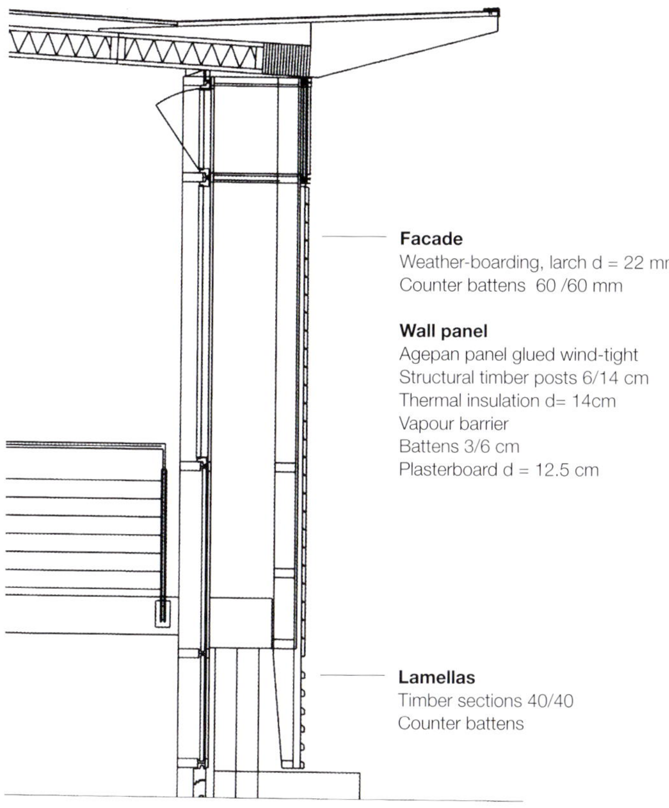

Roof
Roof sealing layer EVA 2mm
Combined with separating mat
Roof sheeting, spruce d = 20 mm
Counter battens 8/8 cm
Lignatur surface element,
LFE 160 mm, spruce
Main beam: glulam

Facade
Weather-boarding, larch d = 22 mm
Counter battens 60 /60 mm

Wall panel
Agepan panel glued wind-tight
Structural timber posts 6/14 cm
Thermal insulation d= 14cm
Vapour barrier
Battens 3/6 cm
Plasterboard d = 12.5 cm

Lamellas
Timber sections 40/40
Counter battens

Section through facade

Location Raubling, Germany

Construction period 6/2000–10/2000

Client and project developer Willi Bruckbauer, Raubling

Architects/Structural designers Buchecker Architekten, Munich

Structural calculations: concrete Ing.-Büro Augustin GmbH, Regensburg

Structural calculations: timber construction Ing.-Büro Mitter-Mang, Waldkraiburg

Structural planning: membrane Ing.-Büro Wakefield, Bath, England

Timber construction Ing. Wolfgang Ritzer GmbH, Kufstein, Austria

Ceiling elements Lignatur AG, Waldstatt, Switzerland

Flagpole factory in Arnsberg / Germany

SHOWCASE

Banz + Riecks Architects

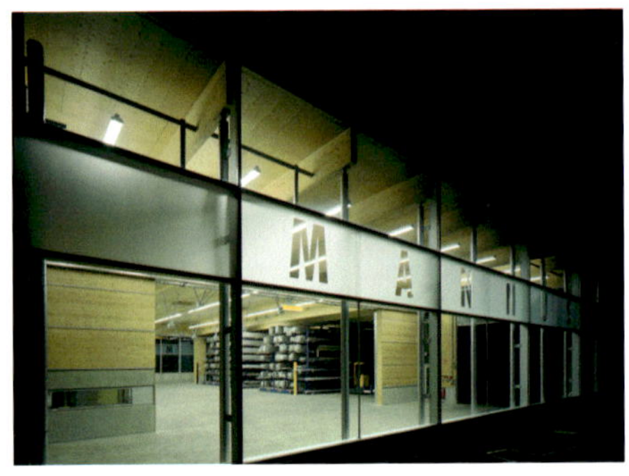

The starting point for the design of this building was the complex layout of a manufacturing process that had been jointly developed by the business planner and the architects. The specific architectural solution was found through an interdependent planning process involving various specialised disciplines. The client sees the innovative approach of the project as fitting into the framework of his own corporate identity.

Concept

The transportation possibilities and the manufacturing technology of the flagpoles, which are up to 12 m long, determined the floor plan. The manufacturing building is a wide-spanning timber frame structure using a low-energy system. The front of the building is moved against the road embankment with a difference in height of 3 m. An inclined wall projects into the road space and forms a striking, outward-oriented feature of the building. The tilted block is both a highly practical and a functional element. Inside the building, thanks to its skylight, it acts as a highly effective "light shovel" and is a kind of third facade. The simple building is augmented with two blocks, one on either side of the main volume, that provide optimal thermal insulation. In these areas materials can be delivered and the flagpoles dispatched, protected from the weather.

The delivery blocks

The units attached to either side of the building allow the loading and unloading of the trucks to be carried out inside the building, independent of weather conditions. This improves the quality of the workplaces in the delivery and dispatching areas. The quickly opening sectional doors are thermally insulated and are only opened briefly to allow trucks drive in and out.

Intensive natural lighting was required in the truck entrance areas. For this reason, the side facades of the timber frame walls have large areas of glazing using uprights in a linear layout measuring 20 x 7.5 m. The structure in this area is made of glue laminated beams with a cross section of 14 x 62.5 cm. The glazing consists of panes measuring 2.5 m high by 5 m wide over the entire length of 20 m. The technical precision, as well as the transparency and the gleam of the glass bays in the surrounding timber facade, makes them seem like precious stones set in wood. In order to incorporate a portal crane for loading and unloading the long pieces of material, the thickness (height) of the load-bearing structure had to be kept to a minimum. The columns that stand at the same intervals as the beams were produced by the client himself; they are made of aluminium tubes with a diameter of 150 mm and a material thickness of 10 mm.

Determining the structure

The dictates of fire protection, the organisation of the technology and the logistics of the manufacturing process all had to be considered in designing the structure for the manufacturing hall.

Further considerations involved the nature of the existing building ground and its foundations. Economic and ecological elements – for example, the primary energy content of the building materials – were taken into account in the search for the best possible structural solution. The constraints of energy optimisation in the direction of low energy standards were an additional factor and ultimately led to the use of timber as the primary building material.

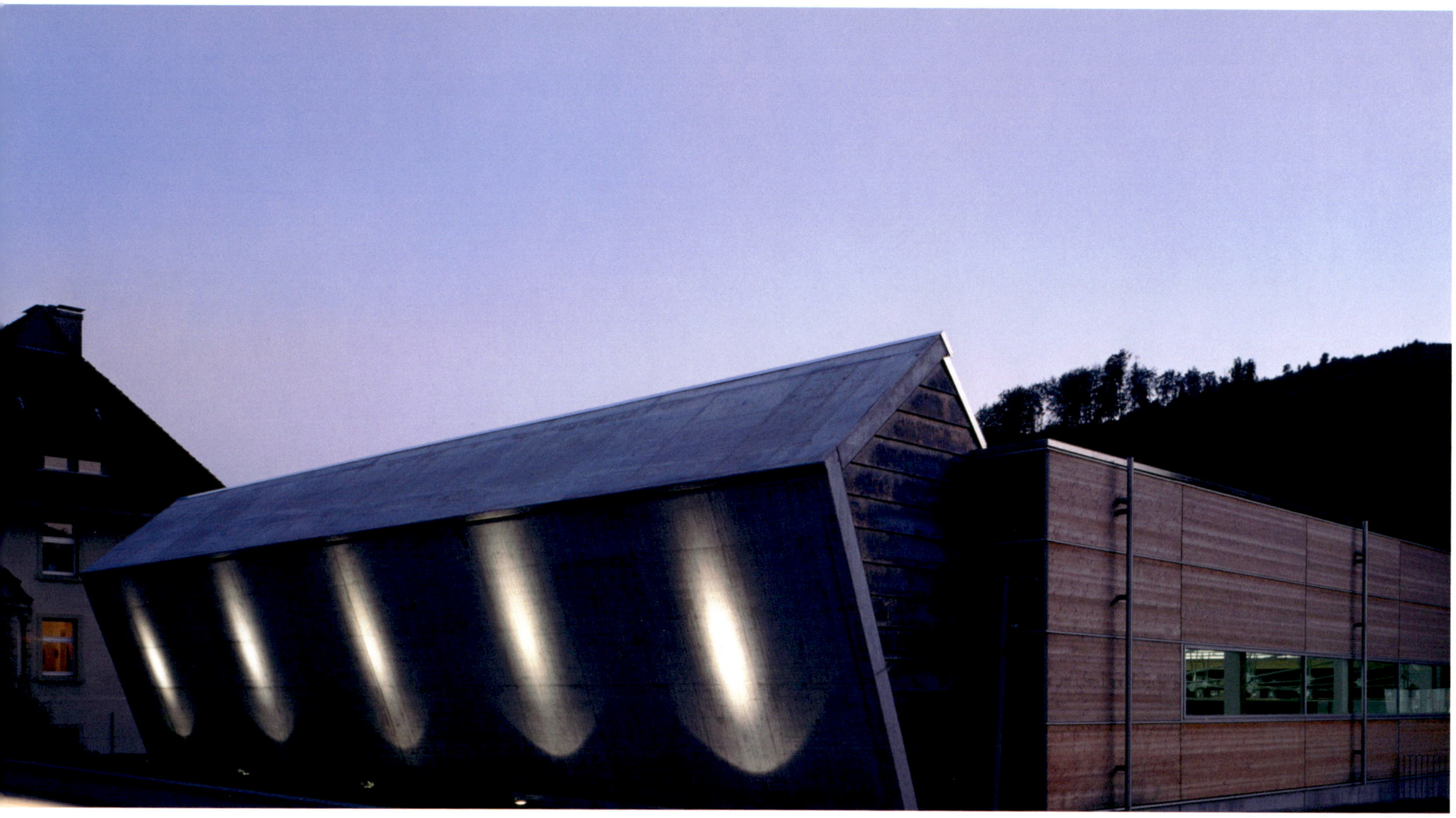

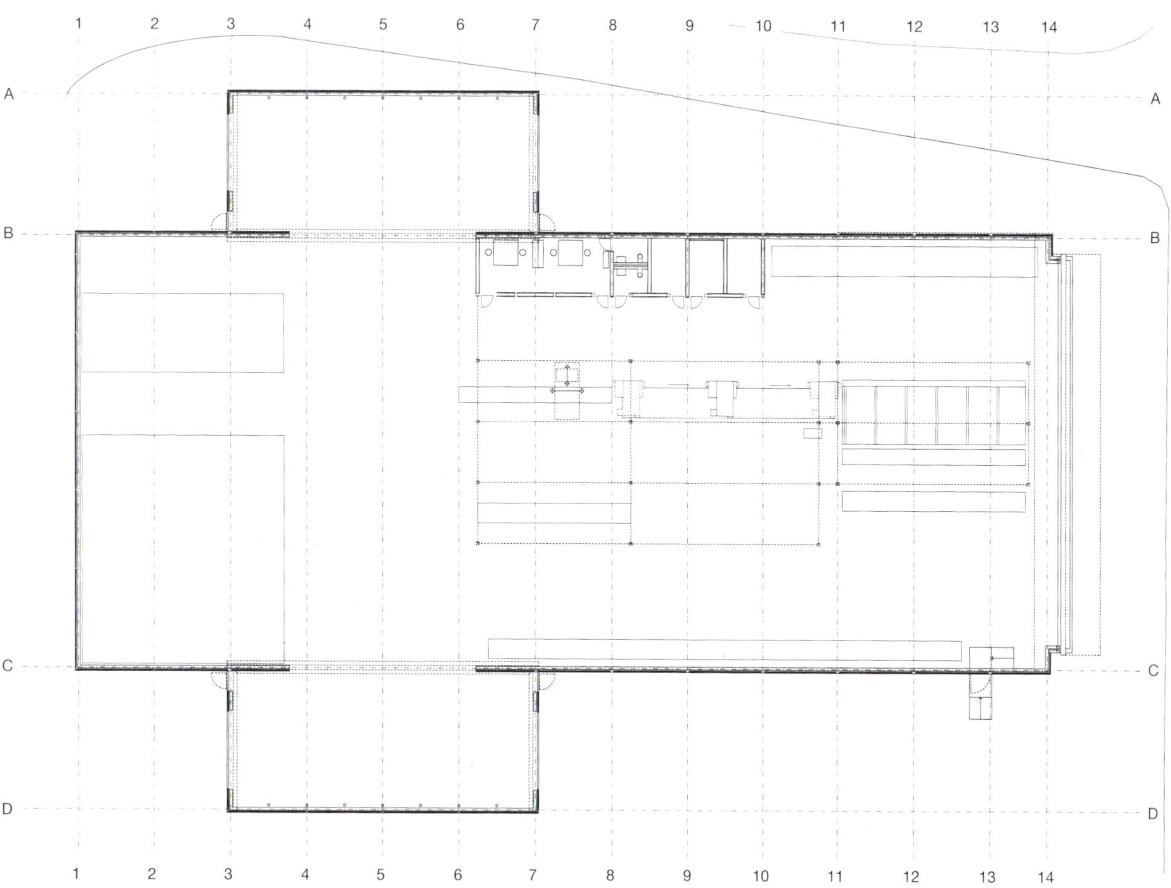

Floor plan

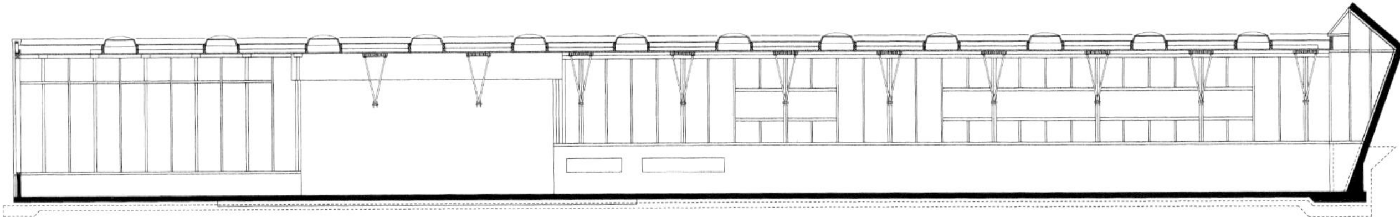

Longitudinal section – looking towards axis B

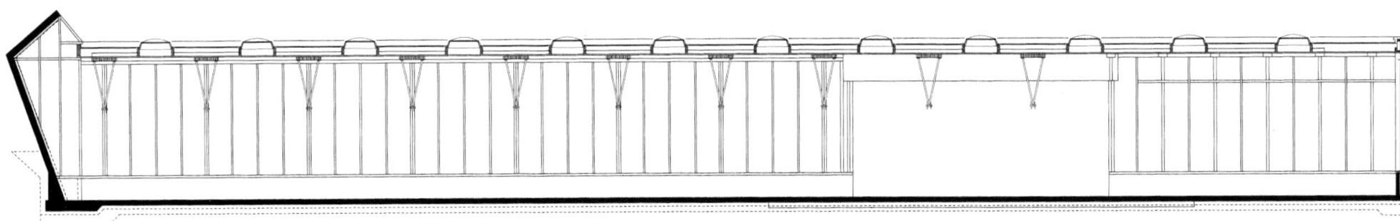

Longitudinal section – looking towards axis C

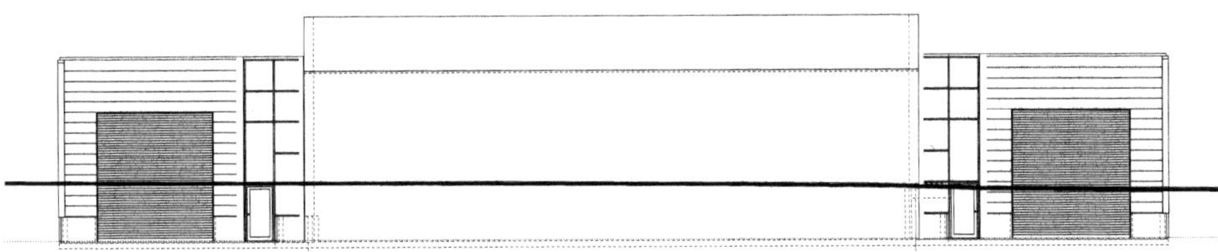

East elevation

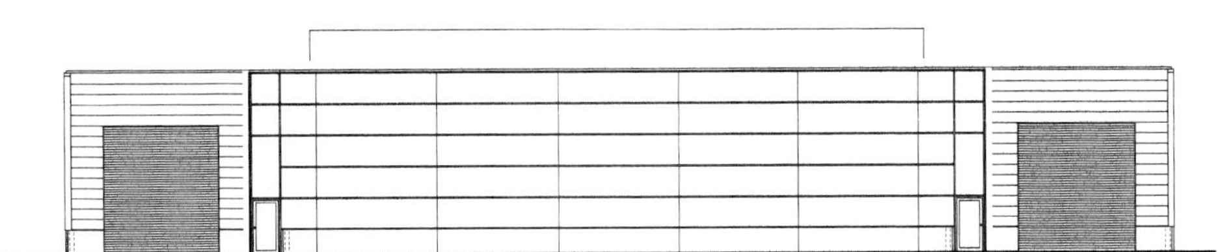

West elevation

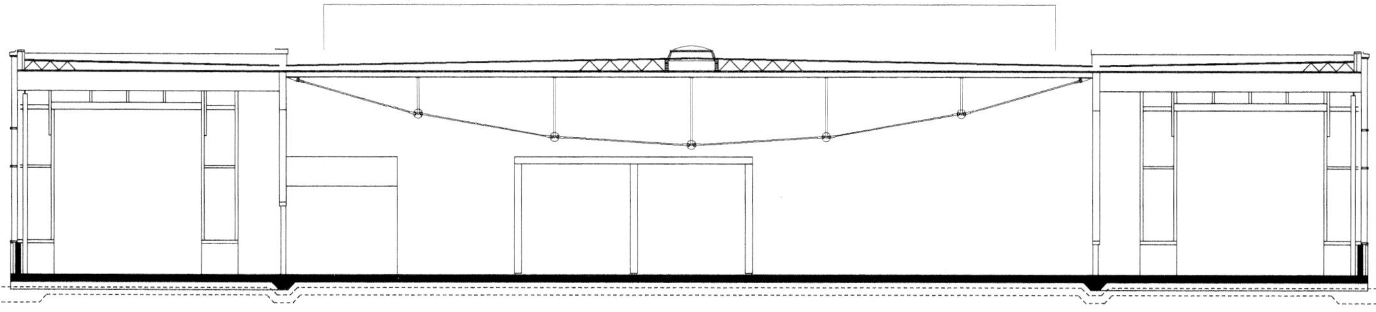

Cross-section

Wall construction elements

The floor slab, the lower areas of the rising walls and the inclined wall towards the road were all cast in reinforced concrete. The plinth provides resistance against loads of materials knocking against the building.

A timber frame construction system, well known in the area of house building, was used for the load-bearing walls carrying the wide spanning structure of the manufacturing hall. The wall elements are insulated on the plane of the posts with 24 cm of mineral wool. In this system, the load-bearing plane becomes a thermally insulated shell and no valuable internal space is lost due to internal supports behind the facade plane. Positioning the thermally insulated, space-enclosing layer in the plane of the vertical and horizontal transfer of loads contributes to the economic optimisation of the structure. The cladding of 22-mm OSB-3 panels in the wall plane makes the structure airtight.

Optimised cross-sectional shape

The greatest clear cross-sectional area was required between axes 1 and 4 of the building (see floor plan page 123). With the use of squat, T-shaped glue laminated beams at intervals of 2.5 m, the height of the load-bearing structural elements in this area was reduced and the required clear cross-sectional area achieved.

In other areas of the hall, the transport and handling of the tubular flagpoles is conducted directly at floor level using the appropriate means of moving the material, which means that the height of the space does not play an important role. The clear height was therefore reduced to 4.2 m, which means that the hall construction is based on two different primary structures.

Roof plane

In the storage area for long materials (axes 1 to 4) the structure consists of 1.25-m-high T-shaped beams at intervals of 2.5 m. In the area of the delivery buildings (axes 4 to 7) it consists of 0.625-m-high beams at intervals of 2.5 m. Between axes 4 and 14, trussed beams were used at intervals of 5 m consisting of V-shaped hollow sections as compression rods and a flat glue laminated timber section 1.2 m wide as a horizontal top chord. The steel trussed beams with the flat glue laminated top chord measuring 16 cm x 150 cm were designed as an element of the roof plane that

defines the space. The top chord fulfils various different functions in the context of the structure as a whole: it handles the compression forces of the primary structure and at the same time, through the flat glue laminated beams, it reduces the span between the beam axes of the uppermost roof plane (made of 51-mm-thick laminated veneer panels) from 5 m to 3.5 m. The laminated veneer panels serve in one plane as both purlins and sheeting. The structural connection of the roof plane with the horizontally laid gluelam beams creates a spatial structure that braces the entire hall in the roof plane through 65 m. The junctions are screwed together in much the same way as the fixed corner of a frame.

The entire roof system was calculated as a three-dimensional structure, taking into account the precise degree of stiffness of the revolving fields of the screws. This kind of structural calculation meant that no additional wind or tilting bracing was required in the roof plane. The span of the roof plate in the transverse direction of the hall is 63.7 m. At axis 1, the loads are transferred to the timber walls; at axis 14 they are transferred by a flat steel truss to the inclined reinforced concrete wall.

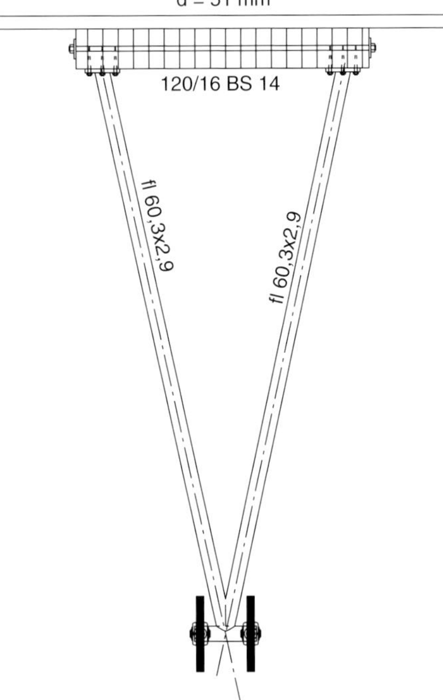

Section through beam in production area

Media scaffold

The task of minimising the traffic loads on the roof construction inevitably conflicted with the demands for a flexible production system. This led to the concept of a so-called "media scaffold". This classic steel structure takes the loads of the crane and transport equipment used in the manufacturing process as well as those of all installations relating to manufacturing. This construction can be demounted and adjustible for changes in the sequences of the manufacturing process. The primary structure consists of two steel angle columns 240 x 240 mm, the load-carrying members; along which the various media (or machinery) run, are IPE 240 rolled sections, adapted to take the machinery. The corner connections are resistant to bending, thanks to the use of special elements.

Energy concept

For the manufacturing hall, the goal of the energy concept was to meet the requirements for internal climate control and daylight while at the same time achieving a high level of energy efficiency, using the simplest possible means. With the aid of computer-supported simulations, calculations were made in order to examine the performance of the building.

With a required temperature of 17 °C in winter and a greater general tolerance (compared to office buildings) of fluctuations in the internal climate in summer, the demands made on the climate in the production hall are not extreme. Nevertheless, an attempt was made to achieve optimal conditions. Two points in particular should be mentioned here. First, the building shell is extremely airtight in order to prevent draughts and the loss of heat during winter. The doors to the hall were an important feature in this respect. To minimise the loss of heat when the doors are opened, a kind of airlock situation was worked out. The doors are opened only to let trucks drive in and out. During the process of unloading and loading, the doors are kept closed, and the trucks remain standing inside the hall. The doors

themselves are thermally insulated and open and close relatively quickly to keep heat loss to an absolute minimum.

The second requirement was to reduce the amount of glazing to the area in order to prevent overheating in summer. From the first sketch design onwards, windows were provided in the hall only where light was needed for assembly work. Thus it was possible to reduce solar heating to an acceptable minimum. However, a light simulation showed that in the area where traditional assembly methods are used at the centre of the hall, roof lights were needed to provide adequate light. For the southwestern truck area, a type of solar protection glass was used to avoid overheating in summer. In general, these measures produce a pleasant internal climate. The maximum summer temperature in the production area is about 27 °C. In winter, the temperature during working hours falls below 17 °C only briefly, when the doors are opened. During the night and over the weekend, the temperature in the hall is, naturally, somewhat lower.

Thermal insulation

In the manufacturing hall, a high level of thermal insulation was emphasised. According to the simulation, the heating energy value is 3.5 kilowatts per hour per m^2 in relation to the total volume of the building. This is about 80 percent less than the borderline value in the thermal energy regulations. The average U-value of the building envelope is 0.280 W/m^2K.

The original idea of using warmth produced by the manufacturing process to heat the building had to be abandoned due to the small amount of heat produced by the machinery. Instead, a central ventilation plant with a heat recovery system was planned. Heating is done by means of heating coils with an air supply system. This limits the number of service runs and also the costs.

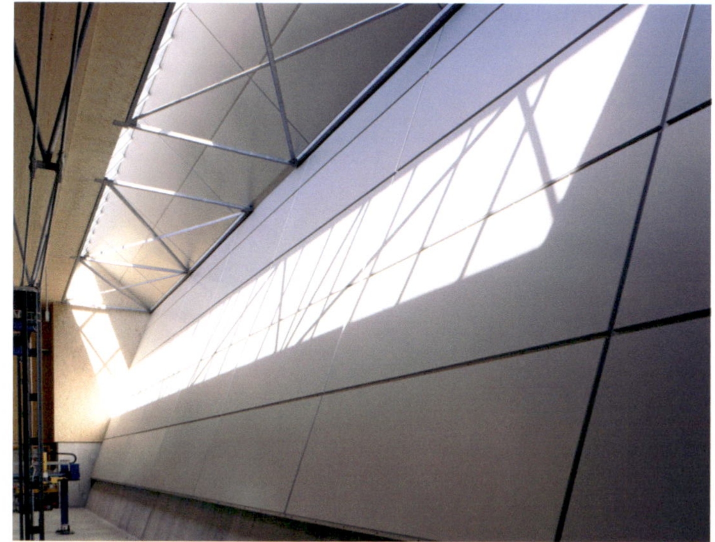

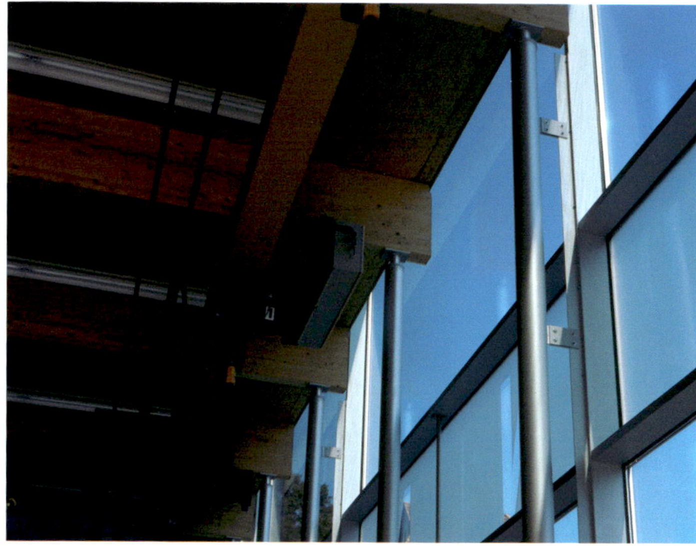

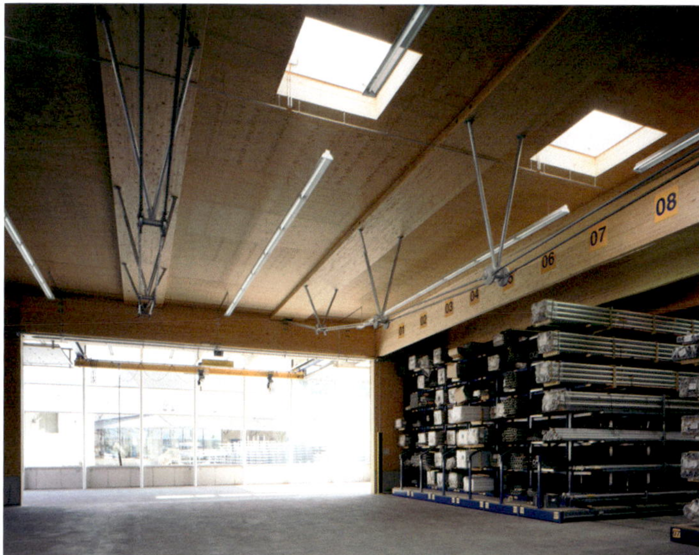

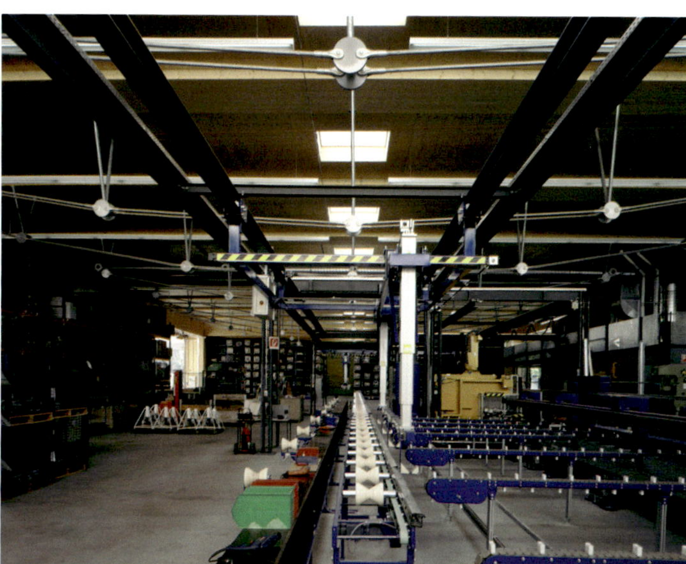

Location Arnsberg, Germany

Construction period 2000–2001

Client Julius Cronenberg oH, Arnsberg

Architects Banz + Riecks, Architects, Bochum
Dipl.-Ing. Elke Banz, Dipl.-Ing. Dietmar Riecks

Assistant Julia Hoch

Production logisticsk Gideon Auerbach, St. Augustin

Structural planner Ingenieurbüro für Bauwesen,
Dipl.-Ing. Burkhard Walter, Aachen

Building services Ingenieurbüro Gerhard Riedel,
Holzwickede

Energy and daylight simulation solares bauen
gmbh, Dipl.-Ing. Martin Ufheil, Freiburg

Solar energy system manufacturer in Brunswick / Germany

ZERO EMISSION FACTORY

Banz + Riecks Architects

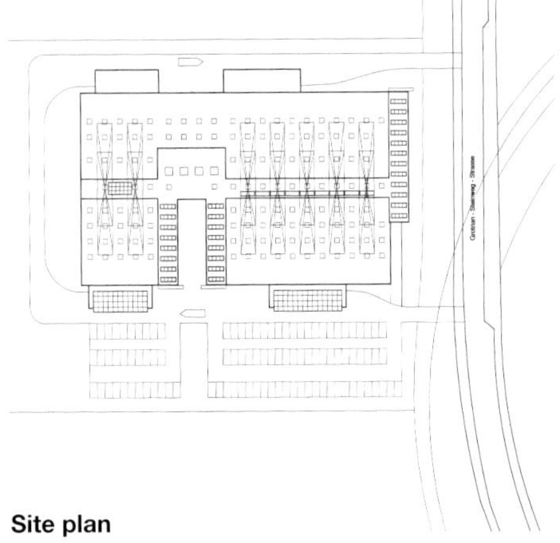

Site plan

The path to an optimal use of energy

The initial concept for this production building for a manufacturer of solar energy systems was developed during the client's weekly, staff-led "happy hour" meetings with the architects and all the manufacturing company's employees. These meetings helped in the rapid development of all the necessary building specifications, as workers were encouraged to contribute their ideas during the design process. In a plan that was defined by tight scheduling, developing the concept, planning and construction took a total of only eighteen months.

Planning process

The building's concept is derived from the company's requirements in the areas of production logistics and optimisation in the manufacturing process. The result is chains of production processes that stretch at right angles to the building axis. The administration areas were not centrally positioned, but are arranged in two-storey spaces, always directly beside the production processes to which they refer. The direct collaboration of "head and hand" throughout this business is a fundamental company principle.

Placing the administration close to the manufacturing area created a unique entrance to the main building as well as a courtyard of considerable quality within the volume of the building.

The company axis

Longitudinal circulation is at right angles to the production chains, along the central axis of the building. This is where internal staff movements meet the production lines. The long axis of the building thus becomes the central focus of the building. This axis, along with the associated areas, was built in reinforced concrete in order to utilise the thermal storage mass, the night-time cooling effect and the fire protection advantages that this material offers.

On the ground floor, all the necessary functional service spaces, including sanitary facilities, are arranged along the work axis. All mechanical services for the building are placed on the first-floor level, where they are clearly visible. This axis, described by the company as the "Solvis-route", gives the development concept its specific identity. As a space where the building services are coordinated and organised, it becomes an identity-forming central area for this manufacturer of building services, appliances and systems.

The timber structure

The production and storage areas are timber structures, each spanning 27.5 m, and are positioned on either side of the primary reinforced concrete structure of the "Solvis-route".

Spanning broad halls without centre supports is not a problem in timber construction. The first designs envisaged a 1.9-m-high glue laminated beam or, as an alternative, a 2.4 m truss. As the usable volume of the hall extended only up to the underside of the beams, the volume between them would have been a useless (but heated) space. The reinforced concrete walls of the "Solvis-route" are elements that can carry heavy loads. As a result, it was decided to hang the roof structure by cables from A-frames standing on the concrete walls.

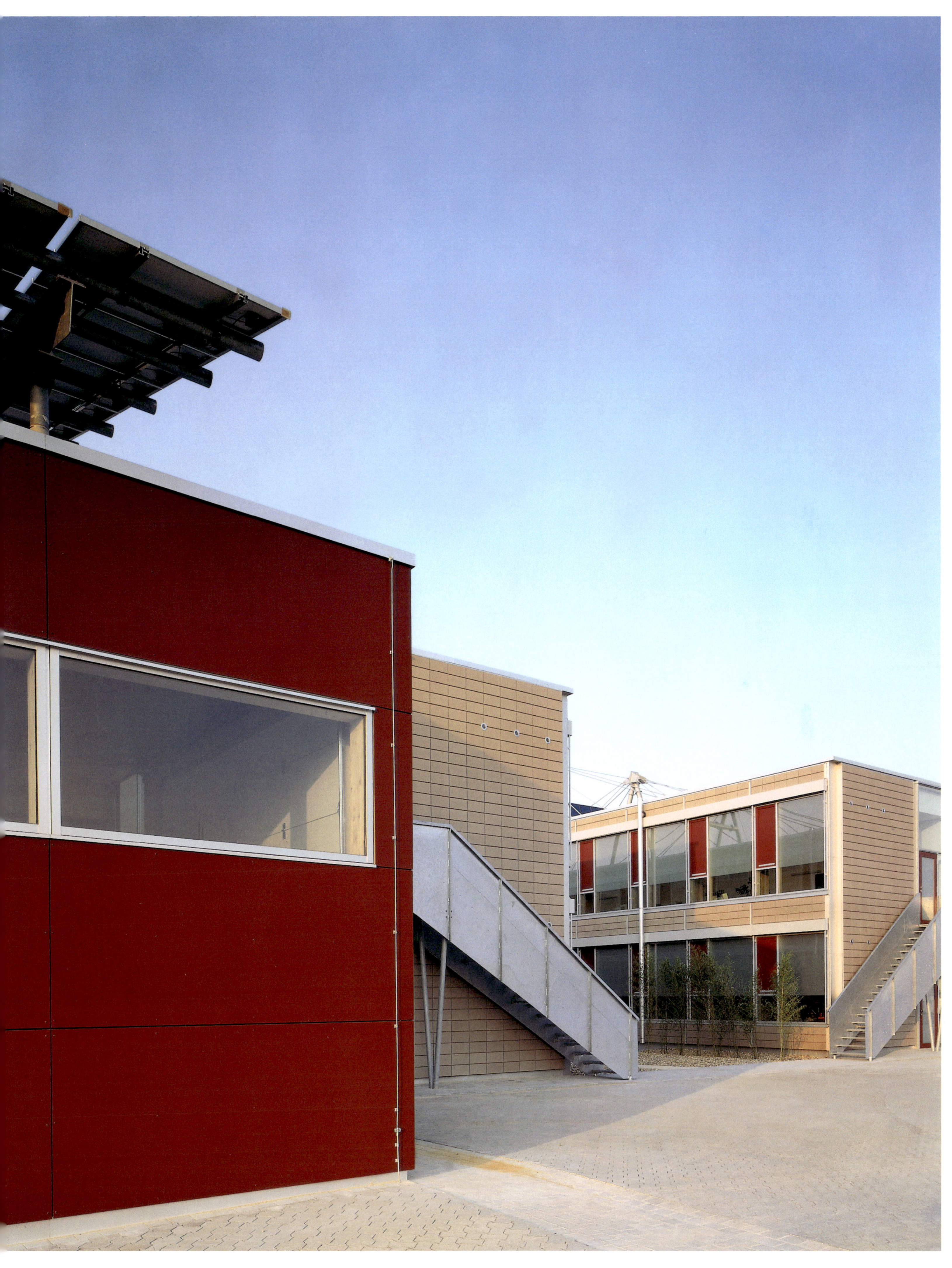

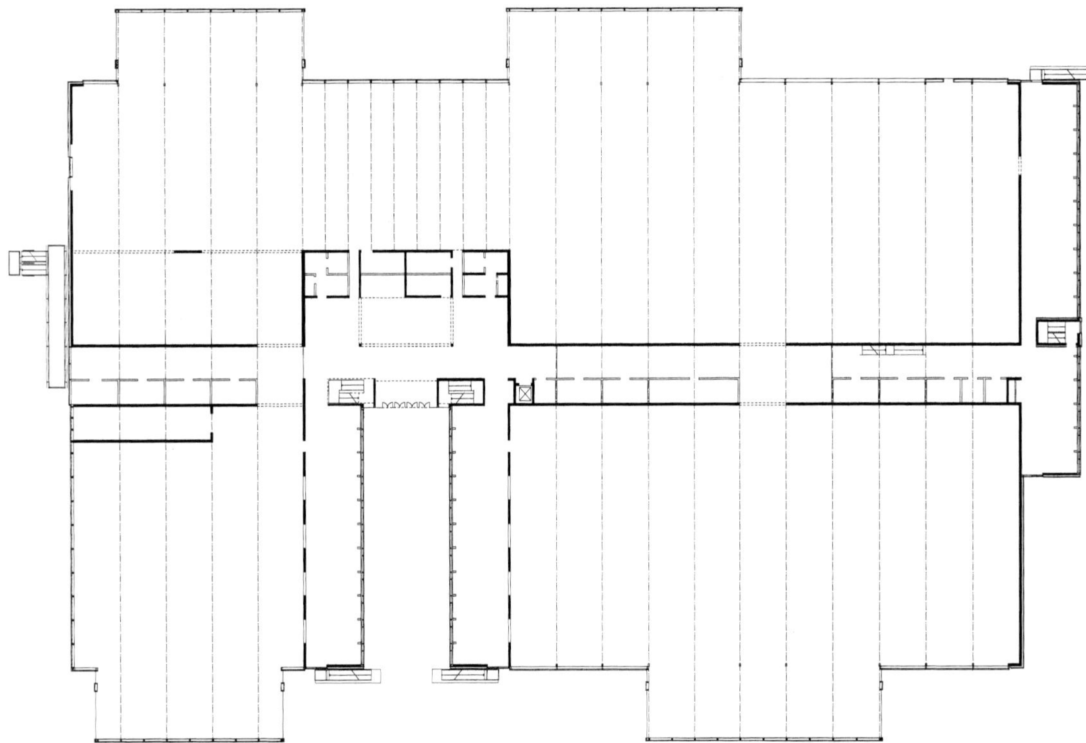

Ground floor

Thus, two-thirds of the weight of the roof could be transferred to the reinforced concrete core. The depth of the beams could also be reduced to 62 cm, thereby saving a volume of approximately 9,450 m^3 (over the version using a 1.9-m-high glue laminated beam).

Two gluelam beams were hung at a distance of 5 m from all of the A-frames on either side of the hall. The hanging points of the beam were selected in a way that optimised the cross-sections and created the same vertical deformation for the hanging points. The visual attractiveness of the pylon structure was then exploited by fixing supports for solar energy systems between the pylons of the A-frames.

The initial design envisaged directly connecting the tension rods to the gluelam beams. These rods would have transferred considerable compression forces to the beams, which would have caused them to buckle unless their cross-sectional size was increased. By introducing a steel frame that hovers horizontally above the roof surface, this problem was solved. The wooden beams are hung from these compression frames by means of 30-mm thin rods, which means that the insulation layer of the roof was to be penetrated to only a minimal extent.

Individual roof elements, measuring 5 m by 2.5 m, were easily prefabricated and were spanned 5 m apart between the wooden beams. This design led to minimal wastage of the OSB-3 sheeting, which was produced in these dimensions. This sheeting was also used

for the horizontal bracing of the larger hall roofs, making additional horizontal bracing unnecessary. The choice of prefabricated roof elements enabled the large roof surface to be covered rapidly.

On the two long outer sides of the hall, the gluelam beams of the pylon structure rest on timber columns. Since forklifts drive around the halls, these columns had to be dimensioned to withstand knocks from these vehicles. Dimensioning a timber column to cope with such forces would have required uneconomical sizes that, in turn, would have meant the loss of valuable space in the halls. Instead, the idea of hanging the transverse beams at right angles from the gluelam beams, which run along the

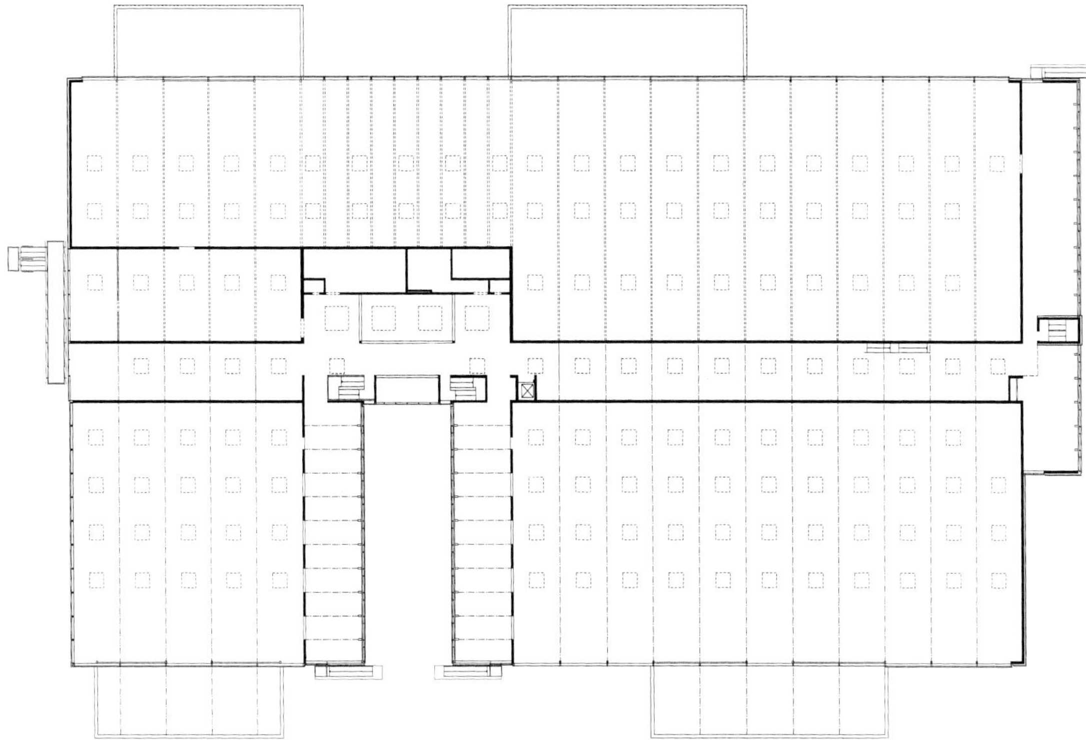

Upper floor

line of the columns, was arrived at. If one column is damaged, these beams transfer the load that had been carried by the damaged column to the neighbouring columns. The larger spans in the delivery areas meant that this system could not be used there; instead, rectangular structural steel columns, dimensioned to withstand knocks by the forklifts, were used. To reduce the deformation of these columns in the case of such an accident, the rectangular hollow section columns were filled with concrete to a height of 2 m.

Fire and corrosion protection

In the administration area, a fire resistance rating of F60 (i.e. sixty minutes of resistance to fire) was required. This requirement was met by the reinforced concrete walls and floor slabs. On the facade walls, gluelam columns carry the loads from the concrete floor slabs. The timber cross-sectional area, was necessary to ensure that the columns can support the load even after sixty minutes of fire. A combustion rate of 0.8 mm per minute was used for these calculations. The result is columns that are structurally over-dimensioned for their normal function, but which provide the necessary sixty minutes of resistance to fire.

The steel construction above the roof surface is intended to remain maintenance-free for a considerable period. As normal galvanisation wears away, rust can form after a certain period. Also, in the case of localised damage to the galvanising, an electro-chemical process leads to deterioration of adjoining, undamaged areas. As a result, a duplex process was used, with a primer and a top sealing coat. This coat prevents the galvanising from wearing thin and, if the sealing coat is damaged, the galvanising prevents the rusting of the primer coat. The additional protection provided by this system is 1.5 to 2.5 times that of single coat systems.

Following discussions with the building authorities as well as the fire brigade, it was possible, for the most part, to dispense with the fire compartments that were initially planned for, by installing a sprinkler system. Thus, it was possible to realize the concept of an open production hall that is divided into different areas only in terms of temperature. The entire floor area of the wide-spanning hall structure is 8,120 m^2 was granted planning permission as a single fire compartment without fire protection requirements.

Optimising the building through the use of simulation

The reinforced concrete walls along the centre axis offered building elements that could support considerable loads. The beams of the roof structure were hung from steel A-frames resting on the concrete walls. The structural depth of these beams could be reduced to only 1.2 m, which meant a reduction of the building volume (and, consequently, of heating and ventilating costs) of around 9 450 m² (approximately 15 percent) as well as a reduction of the facade area by 1.2 m on all sides, while keeping the same cross-sectional height clearance of 5.6 m in the halls. The reduction of building parameters resulted in an economy of the structural concept chosen that was confirmed by later tests.

The steel frames stand on the roof, so to speak, and provide a landmark or symbol for the building. The way the construction penetrates the roof skin was simulated, taking into account heat transmission and long-term behaviour in terms of building physics. The hanging points were designed to take purely vertical loads; horizontal compression frames, which form part of the steel construction mounted outside the roof plane, take up the horizontal loads resulting from the structure.

An important element in the energy optimisation of the entire system is the layout of the areas dealing with the movement of goods within the thermal building shell. The logistics of these areas allow delivery and dispatching of goods to be carried out in warm conditions. Rapid-opening doors keep the length of time that the envelope as a whole is open to a minimum, while special controls mean that only one door in the entire building is ever open at once, preventing the loss of heat in winter that would result from rapid air change.

A simulation of daylight conditions produced the layout for the necessary transparent areas in the facades and the roof. This allowed the use of electric lighting to be reduced to a minimum.

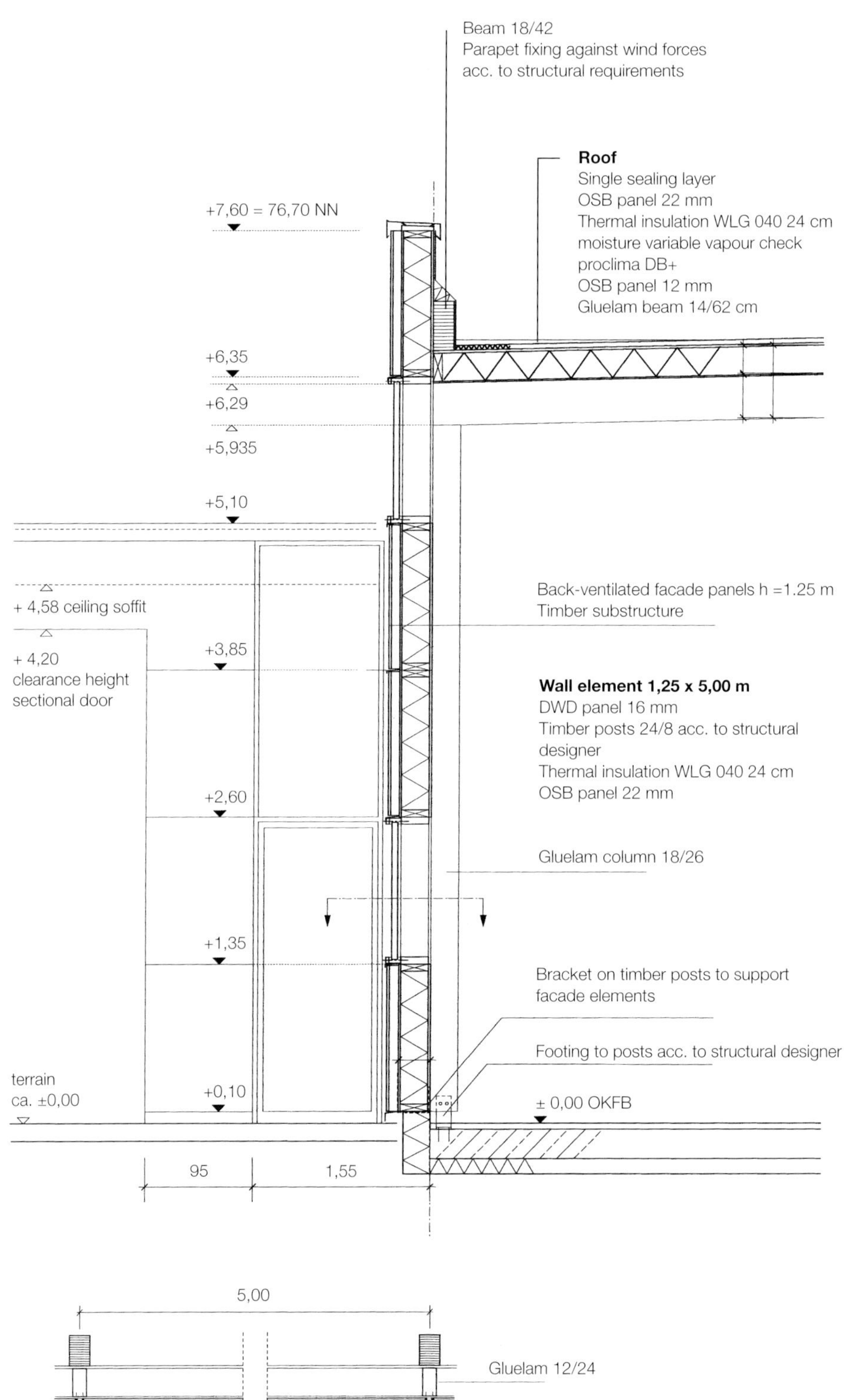

Section through production hall

Delivery zone

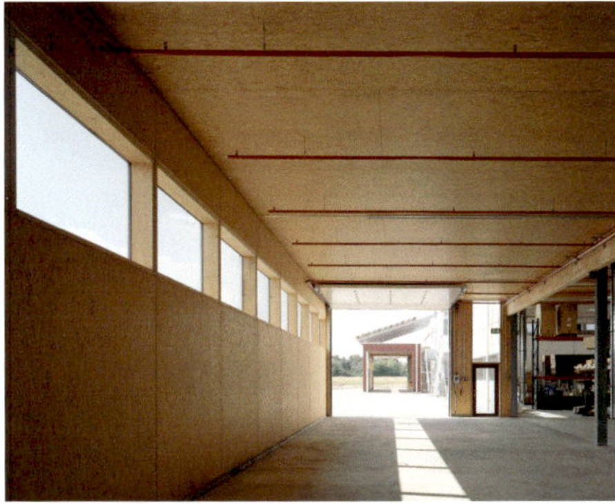

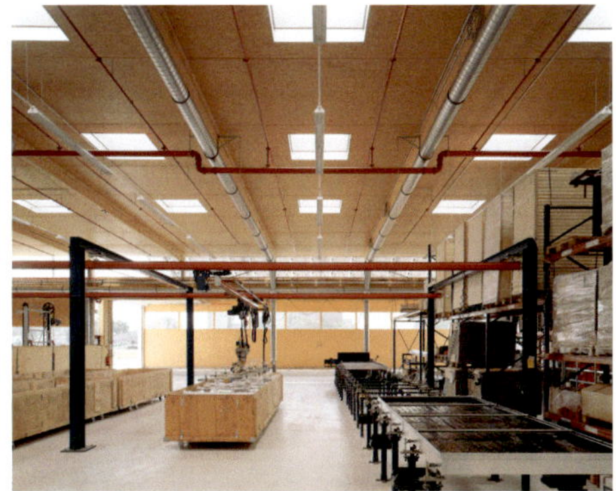

Production

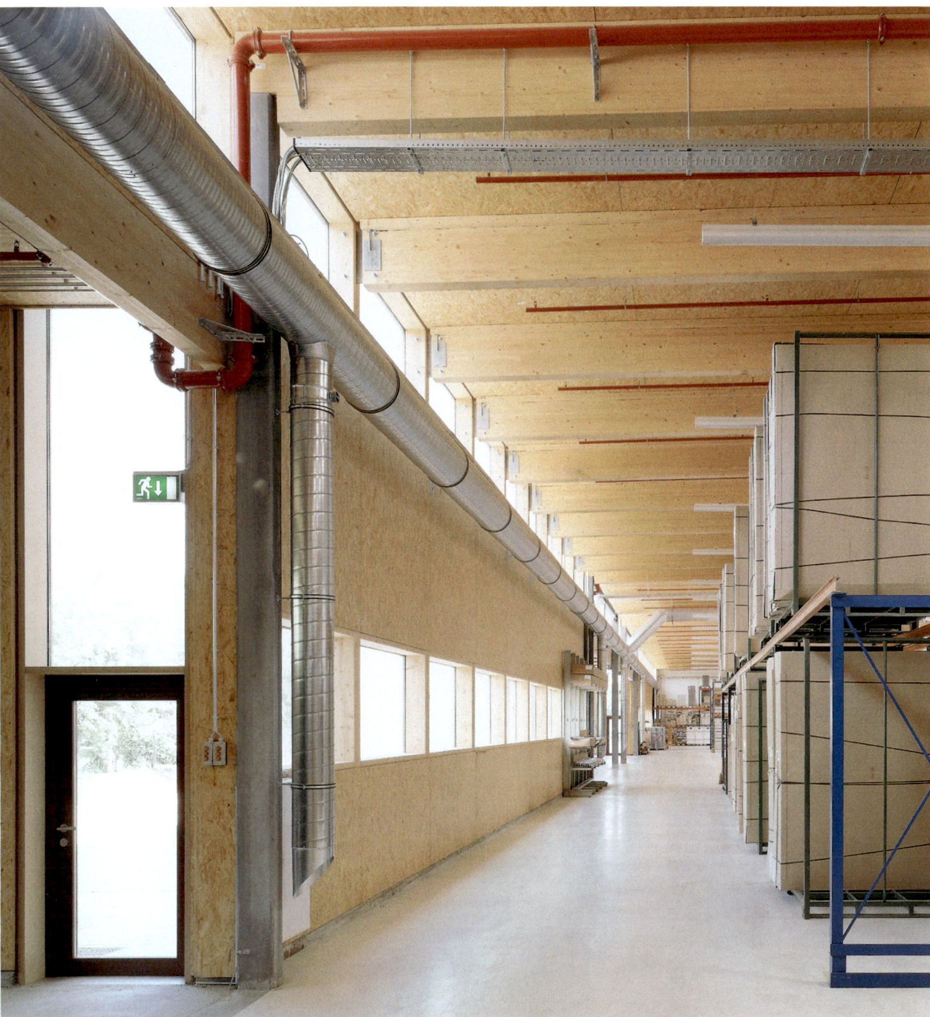

Warehouse hall

The facade design as a didactic element

The two outer long axes of the timber structure were built as columnar structures with a curtain facade made of wood elements or as a highly insulated timber frame construction. The construction elements were prefabricated with 24 cm of thermal insulation as well as the internal and external weather-resistant cladding.

Three measures determine the technical, comprehensible design of the administration area facades. The timber post and rail structure has areas of glazing 2.5 m high that extend between the parapet elements and the upper solid top edge of the building. Particularly where facade areas lie opposite each other (e.g., in the internal courtyard), the third glass layer of these tall areas of glazing was sandblasted from a height of 1.65 m upwards.

This creates a horizontal "viewing slit" at eye level when one is working. These sandblasted areas of glazing produce a diffused light in the depths of the space that gives the open plan offices a special quality. To reduce solar heat gain in summer, the opening elements in the facades are solid and coloured.

The opening elements in the facades have vacuum insulation panels with relatively low construction thicknesses and high insulation values. The intake of fresh air is by means of ventilation elements in the parapets. The air is led into the interior through these elements (in winter in conjunction with a low temperature convection heater). The parapet elements also use the service runs in the long facade axes for heating, electricity and data transfer.

In the design of the facades, the partially matte glass areas and the closed (i.e., not glazed but colour-coded) opening sections, as well as the front ventilation boxes, have been deliberately employed by the architects in a didactic way to encourage the users to employ these building components in a more conscious way.

Energy concept

Three important constraints defined the goals of the energy concept: high quality work areas intended to produce high productivity levels, work areas with short communication routes that were uniform in terms of quality and, finally, production without the emission of climatically harmful gases, a requirement that results from the company's ecological self-image. Due to the nature of the production processes, emissions from generating the energy required

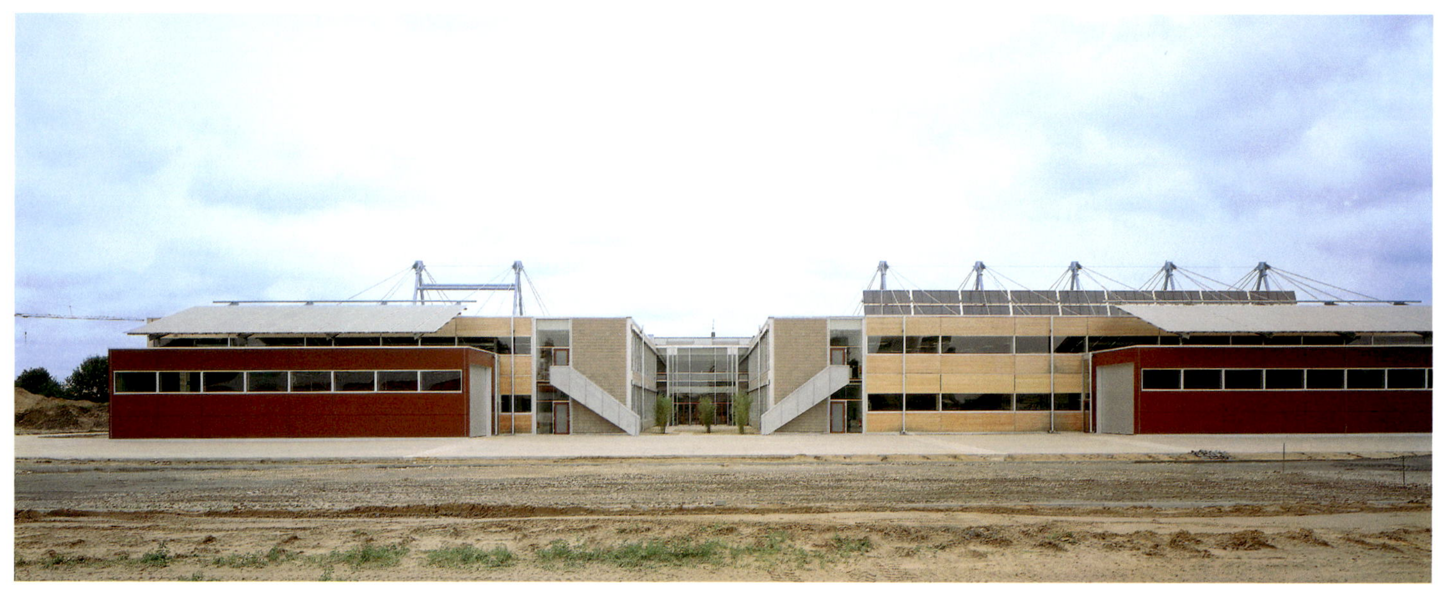

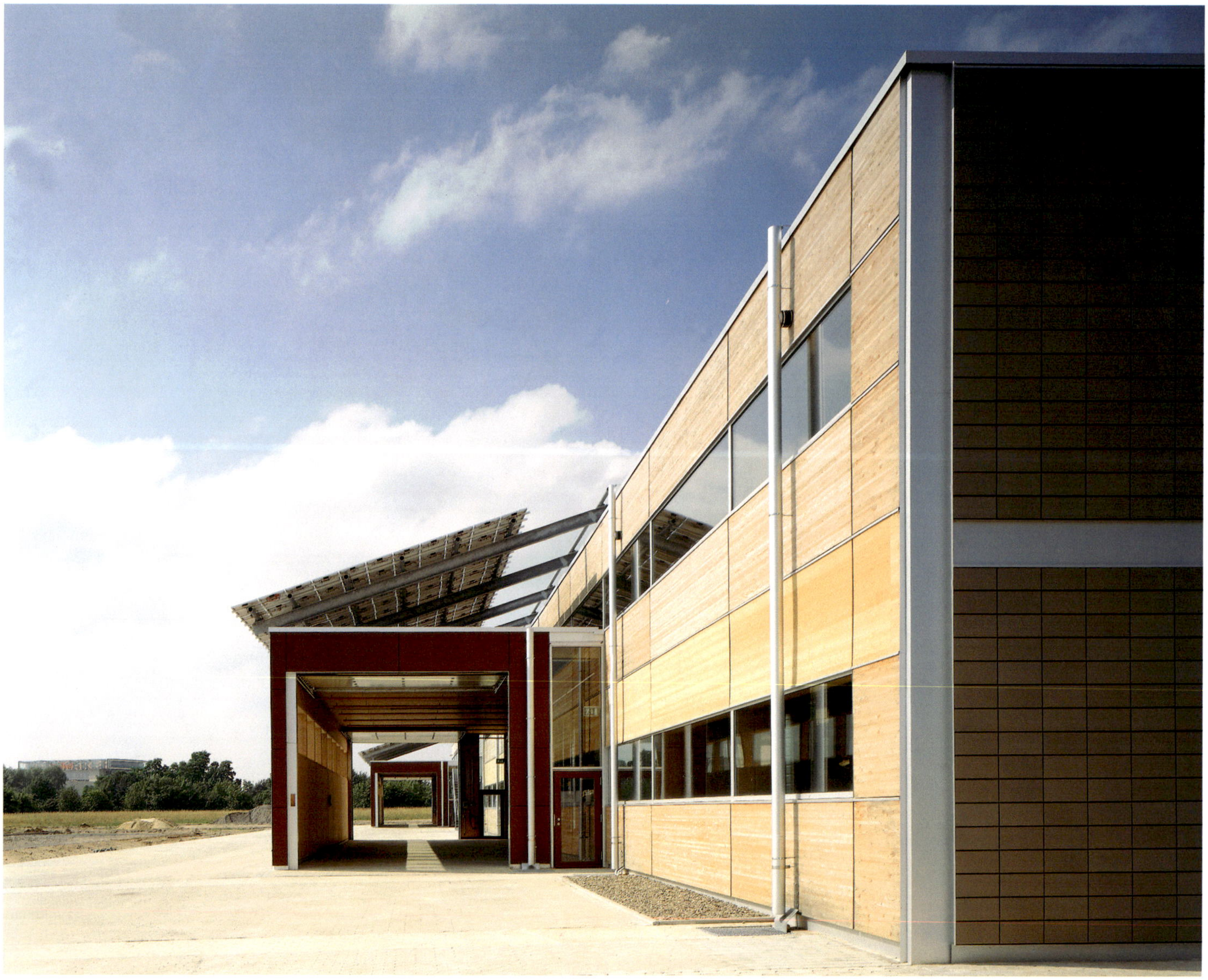

for electricity and heat are the only potential emission sources. The concept of a zero emission factory is therefore primarily a concept that aims at reducing the electricity and heating requirements as well as at providing a CO_2-neutral energy supply.

The high level of thermal insulation, combined with the compact volume of the production hall and the offices, results in a heating energy requirement of under 30 kWh/m^2 a.

A zero emission factory

Energy sources that provide energy without CO_2 equivalent emissions sources are generally regenerative (renewable) sources, such as solar energy (photovoltaic systems and collectors), wind and water. At this location, water and wind energy were not available, so recourse had to be made to other regenerative energy sources, such as wood pellets or cold-pressed rapeseed (canda) oil. To the requirement for additional heat and electricity, a rapeseed oil-fired combined heat and power plant was used. Conventional methods of producing rapeseed oil do cause CO_2 emissions, but CO_2 neutrality can be achieved by using ecological methods in which the energy used in the production of rapeseed oil is also provided by rapeseed oil. By feeding inexcess energy from the photo-voltaic generator, and thus substituting electricity produced by conventional methods, a CO_2-neutral energy supply can be achieved using self-produced energy from a combined heating and power plant, even if it is fired with conventionally produced rapeseed oil.

The goals for heating energy of 40 kWh/m^2 a and for electricity use for building services of 20 kWh/m^2 a are derived from the values in the German government programme to encourage solar-optimised building. In addition, the goal of a CO_2-neutral energy supply and the maximum available area for the installation of photo-voltaic modules of 600 m^2 resulted in limits of 20 kWh/m^2 a heat and 12.5 kWh/m^2 a electricity for both building services and operation. The targets show that, in addition to a low heating energy requirement, the amount of electricity to be used for the building services was intended to be very low. The focus, therefore, lay on energy-efficient ventilation,

exploitation of daylight and a suitably adapted artificial lighting system, as well as integration of the solar energy supply.

Room climate and protection from summer heat

Protection from summer overheating in the offices is provided by an external two-part solar protection system: the use of triple solar pro-tection glazing reduces the g-values (solar energy transmittance), in addition, the opening elements in the windows are wooden panels with vacuum insulation so that the heat gain in summer can be reduced without increasing the loss of energy during the heating period. By consistently controlling the internal energy loads (e.g., proper management of electronic data processing usage) and the lighting according to actual requirements, these loads can be considerably reduced. Due to the dense occupancy, it is necessary during summer to extract heat at night by night-time ventilation (air change rate 3/h). To provide protection against break-ins, this is carried out by a mechanical ventilation system. The number of working hours when the temperature exceeds 25 °C is 245, less than 9 percent of the total number of working hours in a year.

Heating energy needs

The low requirement for heating energy is a result, first, of the high levels of thermal insula-tion and, second, of the efficient ventilation system in the hall, with its incorporated heat

recovery system. The precondition for achieving a thermal provision factor > 75 percent is an airtight building envelope. This building achieves a very low air change rate of 0.22 1/h at 50 Pa negative or positive pressure. This value is measured by means of a blower door measurement. The results (according to dynamic building simulations) for this building are a heating requirement of 220 MWh/a, that is 27 kWh/m^2 a in relation to the net floor area with internal heating loads (produced by machines, computers, lamps, people, etc.) of 150 Wh/m^2 a.

Use of daylight and artificial lighting

Thanks to the roof lights, the production hall achieves a daylight quotient of 3 percent, so that the daylight supply is suitably adapted to the requirements. The artificial lighting is automatically dimmed in accordance with the amount of daylight by means of an external brightness monitor. On the one hand, this reduces costs in comparison to a decentralised control, while on the other, it avoids having the sensors depend on the reflection qualities of the surfaces in the interior. The offices are well supplied with daylight; the daylight quotient in the work areas is, on average, 4.5 percent, daylight autonomy is 77 percent at a depth of 0.75 m in the space (i.e., 75 cm from the out-side wall) and 47 percent at a depth of 2.75 m. As in the production hall, the artificial lighting in the administration areas was combined with daylight-sensitive controls.

Wall construction

	Office	Hall
External wall	Timber frame with 24 cm insulation U=0.20 W/qm K	Timber frame with 24 cm insulation U=0.20 W/qm K
Roof	Timber frame with 30 cm insulation U=0.16 W/qm K	Concrete with 22 cm insulation U=0.17 W/qm K
Floor	Screed, concrete 20 cm, 12 cm thermal insulation U=0.27 W/qm K	Concrete 20 cm, 12 cm thermal insulation U=0.30 W/qm K
Window	Triple solar protection glazing U=1.1 W/qm K, g=46%	Double solar protection glazing U=1.4 W/qm K, g=58%
Roof lights		U-value 1.8 W/qm K, g=50%
Doors to hall		U-value 0.9 W/qm K

Electricity requirement

A major part of the electrical energy (around 55 percent) is used for lighting and data processing/ communication. Therefore, conventional energy-saving measures were employed in the area of electricity energy supply. These include the control of artificial lighting, TL5 fluorescent tubes, flat-screen monitors, and energy-saving motors for pumps and ventilators, as well as energy-saving operation of the data processing system. The use of vacuum drainage reduced the water requirements by 80 percent over conventional drainage. The remaining wastewater flows into the town drainage system; the sewage sludge is processed in the company's heating and power plant.

List of electricity users

User	Energy requirement [MWh/a]
Ventilation	23
Other	12
Lighting	70
Building services	**105**
Production: basic load	15
Production: operation	25
Office: operation	15
Use	**55**
Total	**160**

Solar energy supply

Heat is supplied by means of a rapeseed oil-fired central heating plant (180 MWh/a), a collector system (20 MWh/a) as well as the heat given off by the development department (20 MWh). The electricity requirement is met by a 60 kWp photovoltaic system (45 MWh/a) and the rapeseed oil-fired heating plant (115 MWh). Thus the energy requirements are met by the use of regenerative energy sources. The amount of primary energy required for heat and electricity is 700 MWh/a, that is 90 kWh/m^2 a. By means of the collector system and the photovoltaic generator, a solar energy contribution of 22 per cent is achieved.

The sprinkler tanks placed in the building are not insulated and so they serve as buffer storage for the 150 m^2 collector system and as low temperature radiant heating. The waste heat given off by the burners in the development area is fed by a collector line to a buffer storage element in the rapeseed oil-fired heating plant. The waste heat from the data processing system helps to heat the storage hall in winter, while an air circulation cooler is used in summer.

Heating and ventilation

The function of mechanical services in a building is to provide a pleasant level of warmth and high air quality. In addition, there are various other intake and extract functions. In planning these services, a primary concern was always that the objectives should be achieved in as energy-efficient a manner as possible and, with the economical use of resources, by avoiding an excessive use of technology. It was also desired that the client's own products should be used wherever it made sense. After extensive preliminary studies in the field of energy economy, a highly efficient overall system was developed and installed that combines numerous innovative elements.

In heating and ventilation, a distinction had to be drawn between the production halls and warehouses on the one side, and the offices with the adjoining service spaces on the other. These zones have very different requirements in terms of the air changes and temperatures required. Various demands were made on the ventilation system in the production and storage halls: emissions from the production process, as well from trucks making deliveries, had to be discharged safely. The production and storage hall had to be heated to at least 17 °C and a heat recovery system with a dry heat recovery value of ≥ 75 percent was required.

The planning resulted in a system with an independent ventilation appliance for each of the three hall areas that has a dry heat recovery value of about 80 percent.

To ensure adequate air quality, an air change rate of 2.0 1/h, up to a height of 2 m in the hall, is necessary in areas where people stay. In the halls, this meant a very low overall air change rate of 0.35 1/h. Nevertheless, thanks to the high level of thermal insulation, it is possible to heat the hall completely by using the ventilation system; the use of wide-discharge nozzles achieves a suitable air mix. The ventilation appliances themselves, as well as the entire duct network, are generously dimensioned in order to reduce loss of pressure and to keep the electrical energy requirement of the ventilators to a minimum. The specific requirement of the appliances is only 0.45 Wh/m^2. It is not planned to ventilate the halls at night thanks to the relatively unproblematic temperature performance of the appliances in summer. However, the hall areas can be ventilated at any time by opening the doors and the roof lights from a central control. Two different types of appliance were deliberately chosen for the ventilation plant so comparisons could be made in the subsequent performance monitoring. They are visibly mounted and form a striking feature on the first floor level of the "Solvis route".

The demands made on heating and ventilation in the office spaces differ from those in the production halls: here an air temperature of at least 20 °C is required, as well as night-time cooling. In the offices, a supply/extract air-conditioning system with an integrated heat recovery system, like in the halls, was not used because the amount of energy required to operate the ventilators would be very high due to the more complicated network of ducting and the night-time ventilation. This would dramatically reduce the saving in primary energy consumption provided by the ventilation heat recovery system. Comparisons showed that a simple extract system with heat recovery by an exhaust heat pump would provide approximately the same primary energy saving for considerably lower investment costs.

Stale air is extracted from the offices through three central roof ventilators. Fresh air intake flows over the air supply elements in the parapet area of the facade. These fresh-air elements have an electrical drive and can be controlled from a central control board. With the help of heat pumps, heat is extracted from the stale air and fed into buffer storage units. By means of mixed gas sensors and flow rate control, a means of regulating the air quality is provided that lowers the flow rate when there are less people in the building. This further minimises ventilation losses.

One of the decisive advantages of the air exhaust system is that the night-time ventilation needed to achieve a pleasant room climate can – with little additional expenditure – be carried out using the same system: only the ventilators and ductwork had to be dimensioned some-what larger. In night-time ventilation, the ventilators are operated at higher speeds, thus increasing the flow rate. The higher negative pressure compared to daytime ventilation is not a disturbing factor at night. In this way the building mass can be cooled down using relatively little energy. The office spaces are heated using radiators.

A basic prerequisite for the correct functioning of the ventilation systems is the airtightness of the building envelope, which was tested using a blower door measurement and achieved an excellent value of nL50=0,22 1/h.

Plumbing and water

Wastewater is removed entirely by a vacuum system. In the planning process it was revealed that, when compared with a conventional system, this system was cost-neutral and that, as it eliminated the need for underground piping, the construction process could be speeded up. The vacuum system reduces the amount of water required to flush a toilet from 6 to 1.5 litres. Urinals that do not use water were employed in the building. The number of warm water outlets was reduced to a minimum. All rainwater runs off into the site. The sprinkler system has a closed circuit, so that if it is regularly serviced and tested no loss of water occurs.

Conclusion

This project, its size and its technical achievements, are the result of an integral planning process involving architects, specialist planners and the client and, in this sense, it is an exemplary demonstration of an industrial and commercial building that is holistically planned and organised in ecological, economic and production terms, and with respect to the well-being of the people who work in it.

Location Brunswick, Germany

Construction period 6/2001–5/2002; timber construction erected: 10/2001–12/2001

Client SOLVIS Energiesysteme GmbH & Co. KG, Brunswick

Architects: Banz + Riecks, Architekten, Bochum; Dipl.-Ing. Elke Banz, Dipl.-Ing. Dietmar Riecks

Production planning and logistics Vollmer & Scheffczyk GmbH, Hannover; Dr.-Ing. Lars Vollmer

Production logistics Gideon Auerbach, St. Augustin

Structural designer Ingenieurbüro für Bauwesen, Aachen

Energy and daylight planning Fraunhofer Institut für Solare Energiesysteme ISE, Freiburg; Dipl.-Ing. Sebastian Herkel

Building physics Büro für Bauphysik, Aachen; Robert Borsch-Laaks

Mechanical services Solares Bauen GmbH, Freiburg Dipl.-Ing. (FH) Martin Ufheil; together with Dipl.-Ing. Olaf Seiter

Fire protection Neumann Krex & Partner, Schmallenberg; Dipl.-Ing. Peter Neumann

Examining engineer Ingenieurbüro kgs, Hildesheim; Prof. Dr.-Ing. Martin H. Kessel

Blower door measurement Ingenieurgesellschaft Bauen+Energie+Umwelt, Springe; Dipl.-Ing. Paul Simons

Timber construction Gumpp AG, Binswangen; Kaufmann Holz AG, Reuthe/Austria; Holzbau Seufert-Niklaus GmbH, Bastheim

Wood treatment AURO Pflanzenchemie, Brunswick

Gross building volume 54,736 m³

Built area 7,092 m²

Building length 108.75 m

Building width 76.25 m

Overall building height 7.60 m

Total height with structure 16.10 m

Bothe Richter Teherani, Architects

LIGHT TUBES

Light-fitting manufacturer in Rellingen/Germany

The commission was to build a new company building for a manufacturer of light-fittings in Rellingen with a staff of thirty. The brief included a prefabricated parts storehouse with a final assembly zone, and a deliveries and dispatch area, as well as an office section with a design department. The goal was to create quality architecture using the simplest means possible, such as gluelam timber. Three years after completion, the building was extended in a second building phase, which had been taken into account in the planning of the first phase in terms of design, the technical processes involved and costs.

Design and construction
The architects produced a completely new building concept. The first building stage consists of an elongated oval volume. An identical form was built as the extension and was connected to the first building by a two-storey, almost square block.

The structure is made up of gluelam trusses placed at intervals of 5 m that span over 20 m and support the external aluminium skin. An inserted concrete "table" in the first building creates a two-storey structure and also serves as bracing. On the upper floor, the structure is completed by socketed wooden columns.

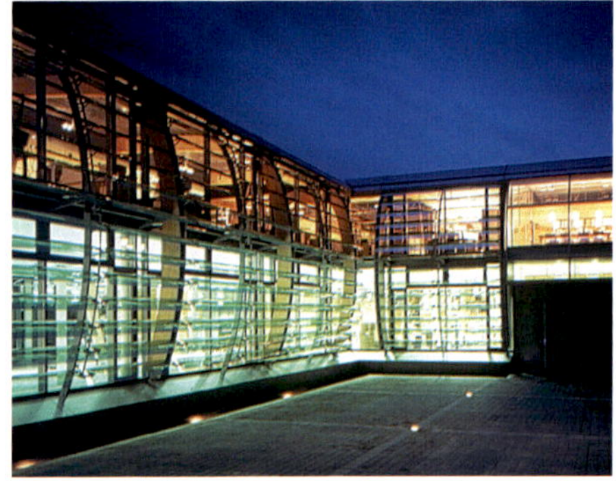

The extension is a large hall without internal supports, built using appropriately dimensioned laminated timber beams. It is both conceivable and technically possible to extend the building further by adding more such extensions.

Statement and presence
The building emanates transparency, openness and the common goal of all the different company areas. This is manifested in the uncomplicated relationship between staff and management and the high mutual respect that exists between staff members. Floor plans based on the "short route", as aimed at here, led to uncomplicated communicative teamwork.

Starting from a basic design, the architecture, fittings, services, interior and the furnishings were developed in the context of an entrepreneurial culture. That is to say, for a building made up of simple but functional parts, the appropriate elements were either selected from the range available on the market or were specially designed for the building.

Lighting and light fittings
The client, a producer of light fittings (fixtures), was here presented with the opportunity to design the light fittings for his own building. As a consequence, almost all the lights designed for the conference room, the sanitary facilities, the staircase, and the cafeteria down to the lighting at individual workplaces, have been drawn from the company's industrial product range.

The architecture of the company building thus furnished ideas for the development of individual products and ranges of fittings. Furthermore, the building offers a stylish background for photographs of light fittings in the company catalogue. The architecture has become, in every sense, an inseparable part of the corporate culture.

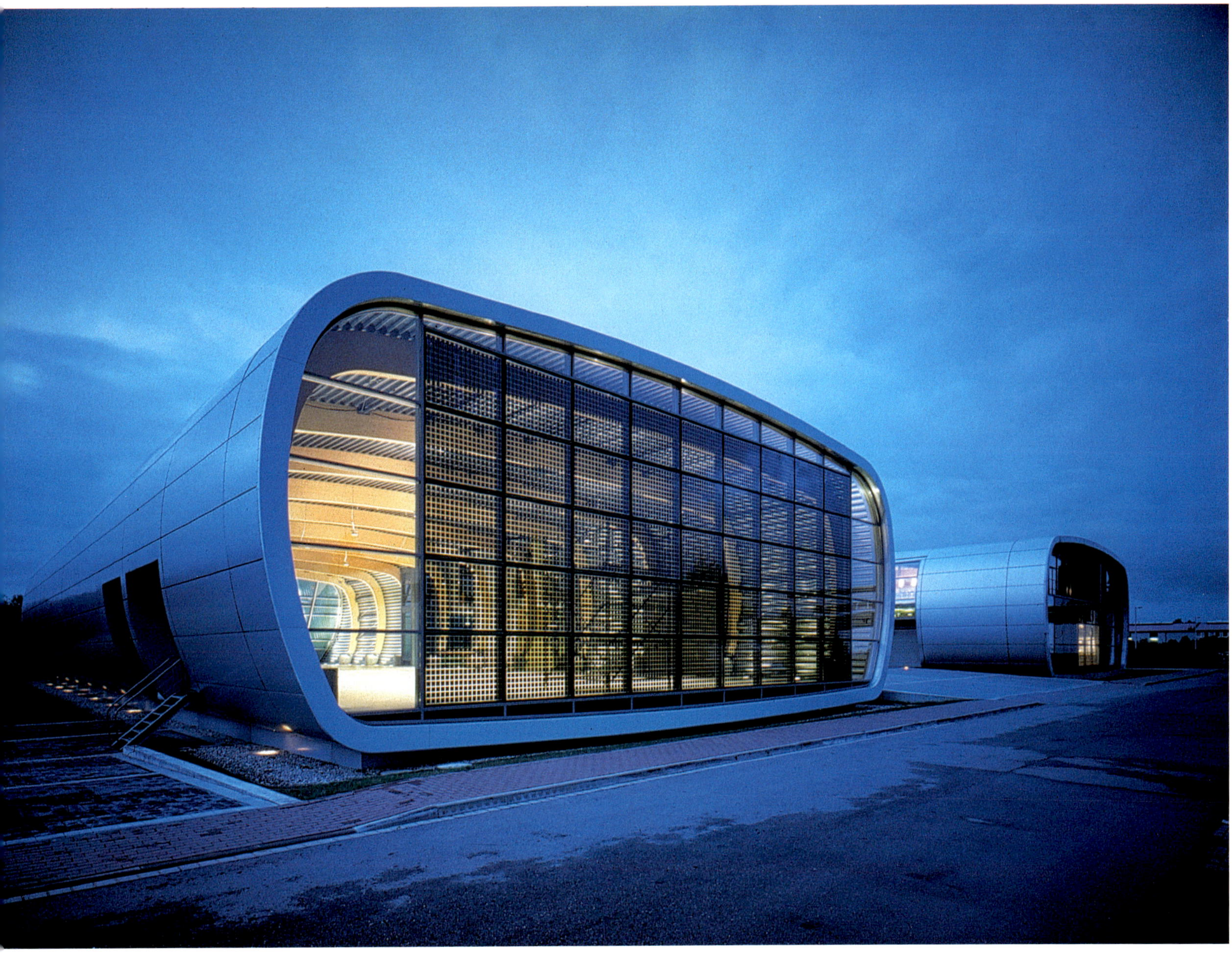

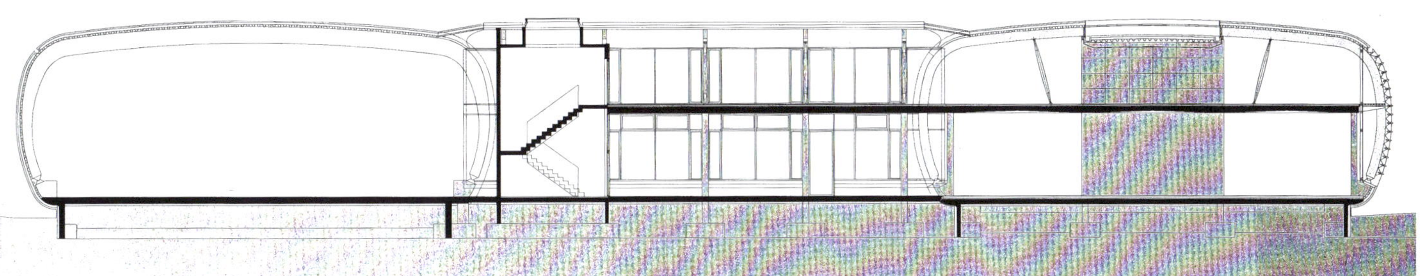

Section

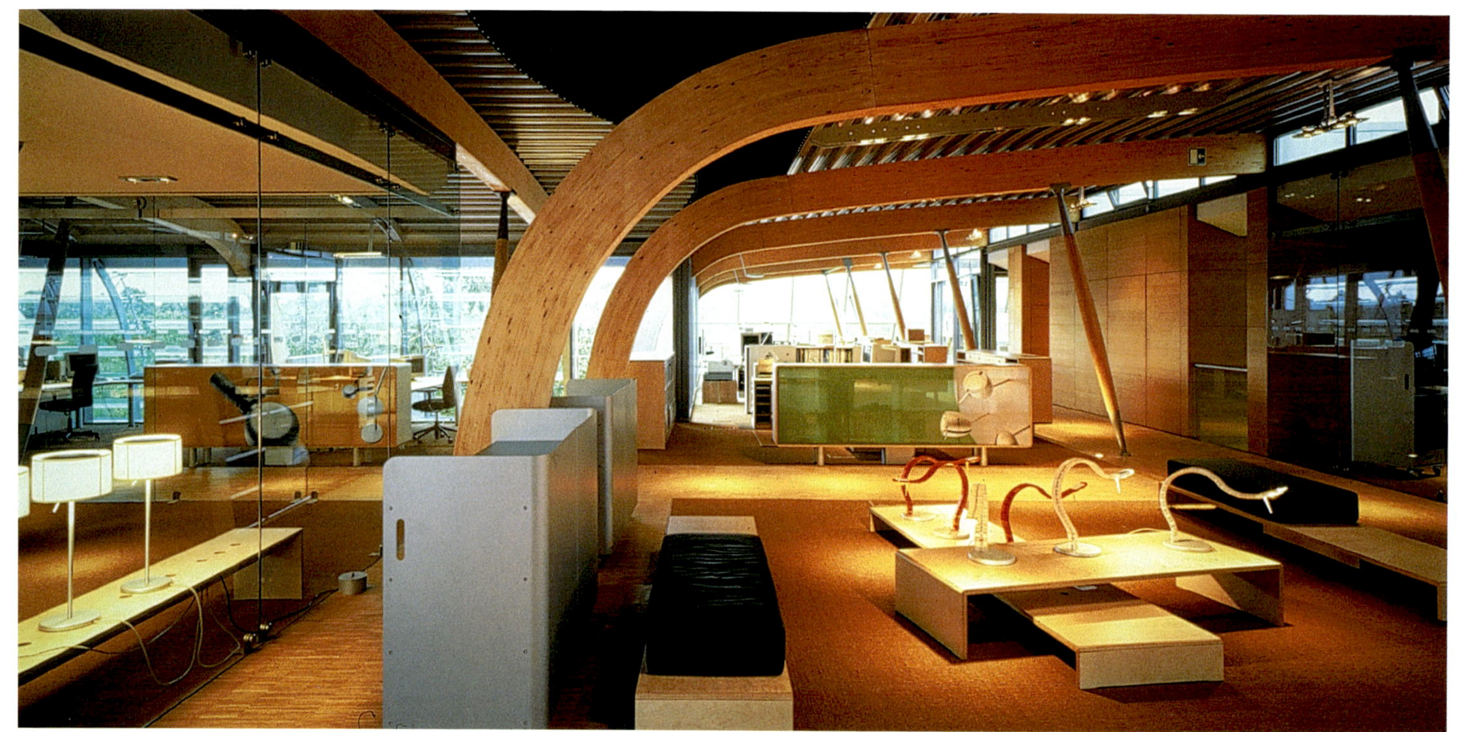

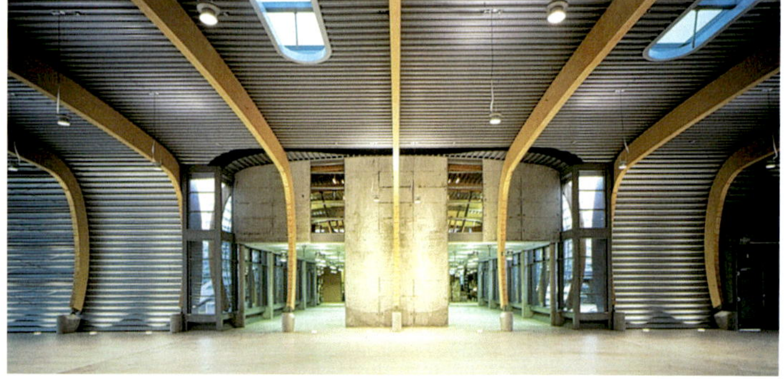

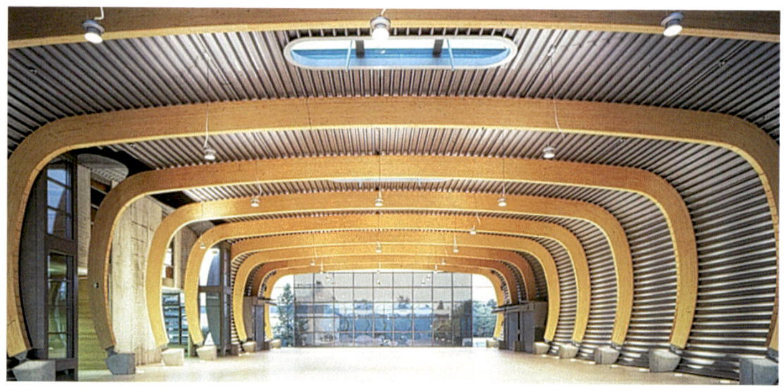

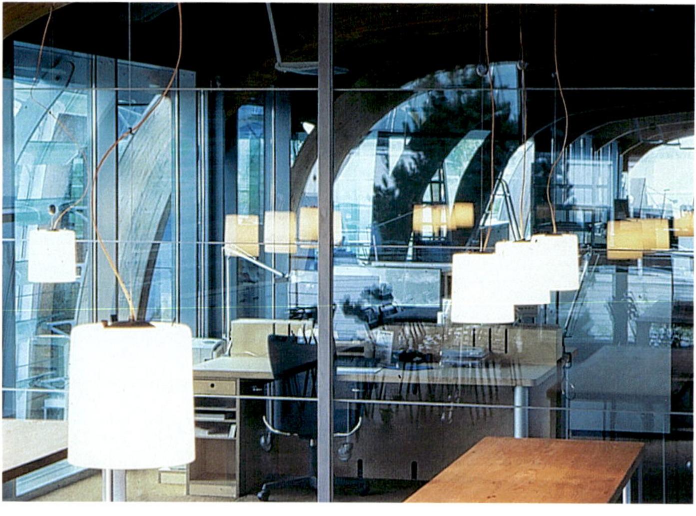

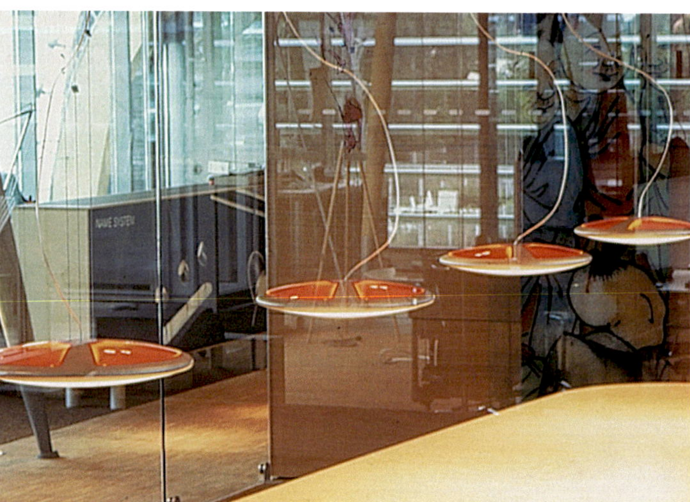

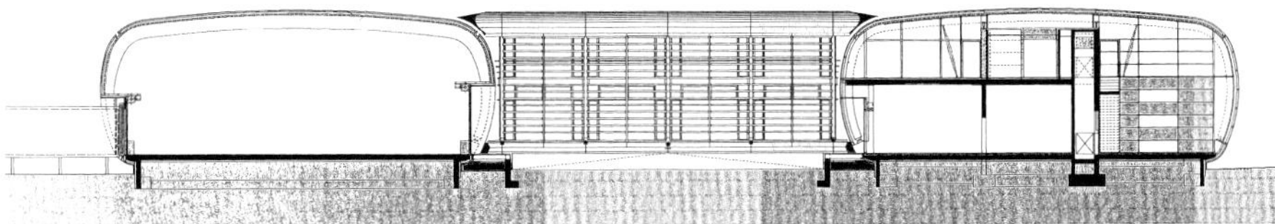

Section

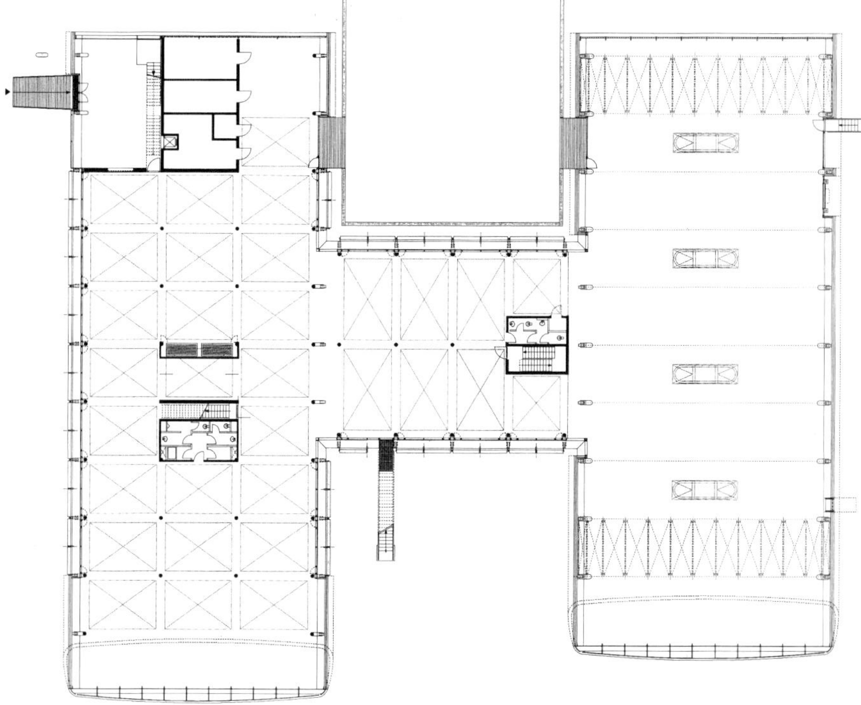

Upper floor

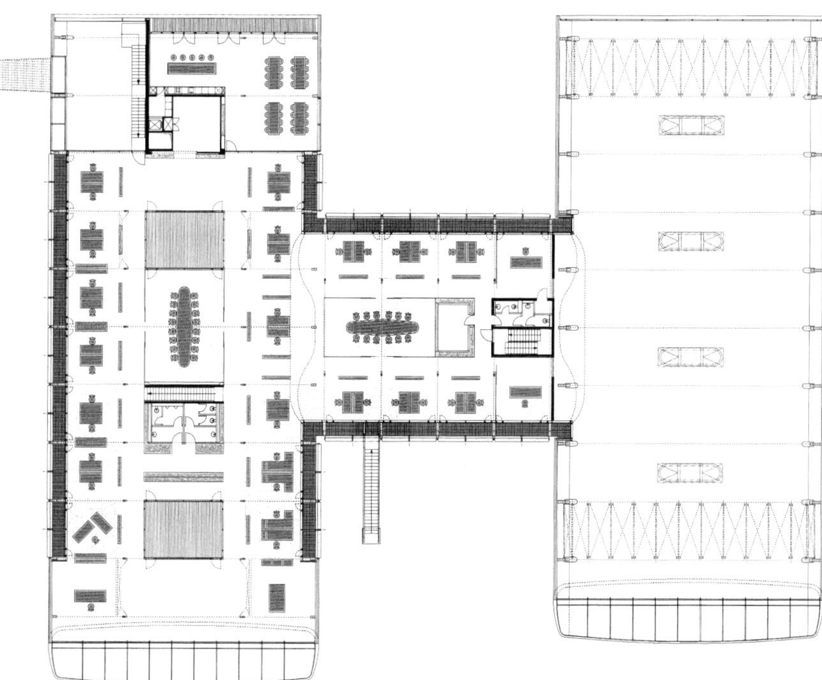

Ground floor

Office landscape and office furniture

Despite the building's unusual form, it was registered and accepted without difficulty. One reason for this lies in the clear architectural language that is continued in the interior by a warm-feeling open office space. The office furniture, which was designed by the client especially for this building, is deliberately low-key to fit in with the architecture.

At some of the work stations a window allows a view outside. The counter bordering the corridor is a storage and communication piece and one to three desks are placed between the counter and the outside wall. Shelving, half the height of the space, replaces walls between the different offices. Glazed conference rooms, as well as the sanitary facilities, separate the individual offices. Office and communication appliances are installed at different strategic points. Despite the conventional office layout, with the simple storage systems and circulation systems, the situation is more like a flexible

Location Rellingen near Hamburg, Germany

Construction period First building phase, 1998; Second building phase, 2001

Client Franziska and Tobias Grau, Rellingen

Architects Bothe Richter Teherani, Hamburg

Design: Hadi Teherani

Structural planners Ridder, Meyn + Partner, Hamburg

Furnishing and Lightning Tobias Grau, Hamburg

Furnishings and lighting First building phase: 2300 m²; Second building phase: 2000 m²

OFFICES AND ADMINISTRATION

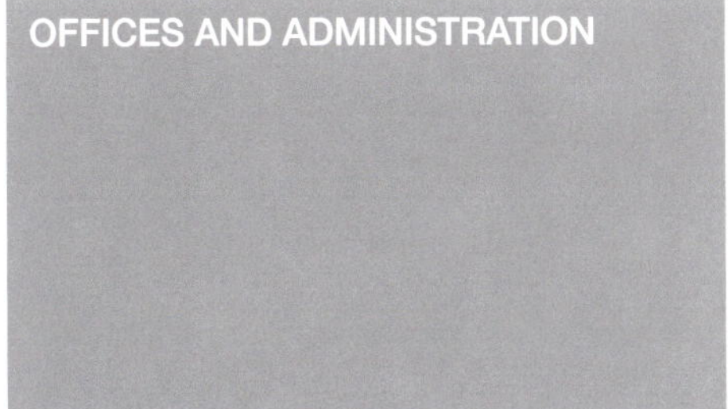
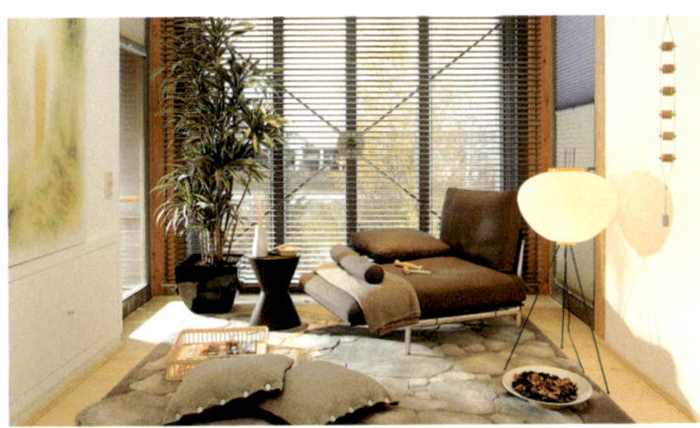
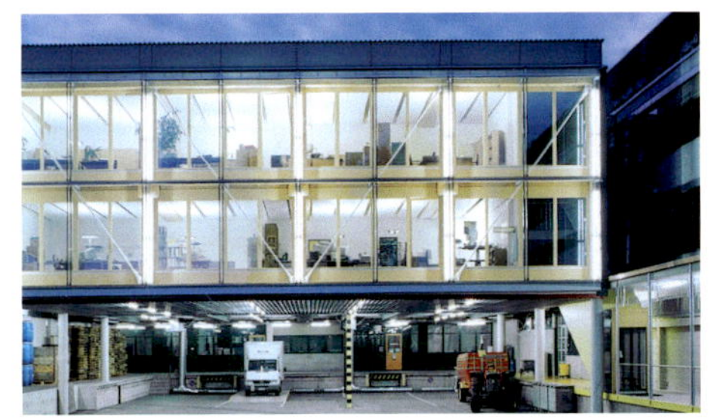
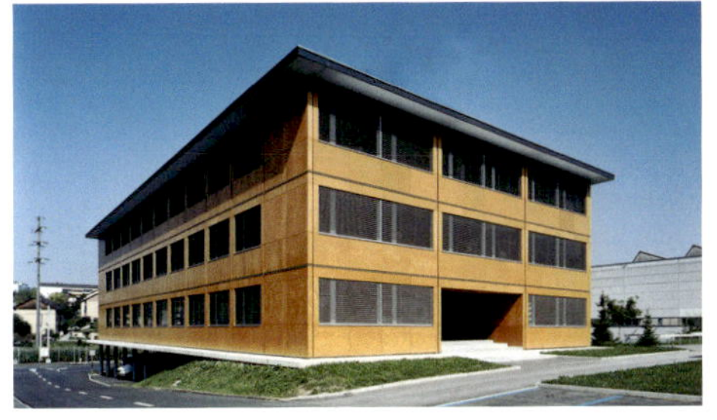
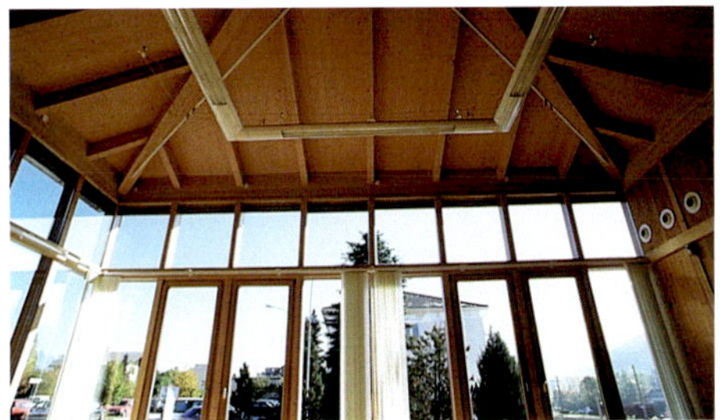
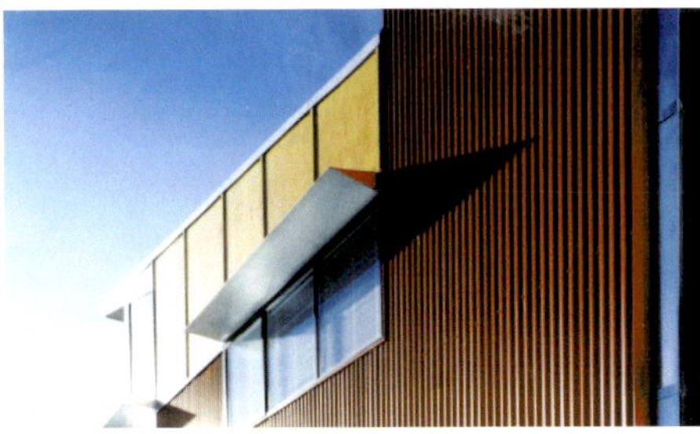

Architect: Andreas Weber

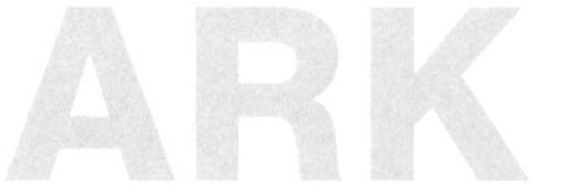

Office building in Erkheim/Germany

The concept of a humane office

With this project, the client wanted to define a holistic and humane office environment of the future and apply this concept to his business. The first step in realising this vision was to make a critical assessment of the existing situation, so the client met with the planners and outfitters to discuss his concerns. Taking into account all architectural, ecological, technical, ergonomic, sociological, psychological and energy issues, an overall concept was developed that favoured timber as a building material because it is regarded as a humane building material and allows alterations to made to a building without great difficulty.

The existing situation

In an office building, a human being becomes a machine. Due to the spatial situation, it is often not possible to arrange the workplace in a way that is suited to the individual personalities of the staff members. Frequently, the supply of light, air and colour – the stimuli of life – is not adequate, despite all the standards and knowledge available from work psychologists. Staff members are expected to store their personalities in tiny containers under their desktops. Only rarely are materials and their ecological, biological and tactile qualities taken into account. Excessive noise levels are common and areas for staff members to retire to seldom exist, although the working day often requires undisturbed reflection about particular problems. Communication spaces and areas that allow exchange between staff members – which can lead to positive group formation – are generally neglected. There is no room in such an environment for motivated, creative and efficient work by individuals.

Approach to a solution

On the basis of an ecological, biological and health-oriented approach, the project team prepared a building framework and determined the criteria for a holistic, humane office. The well-being of the workers – on all levels – was the focal point. This concept began with the subdivision of space and the optimal positioning of the workplaces and developed through to a consideration of the effects of colour, light, form and materials, and the incorporation of nature or natural elements into the world of work. Aspects of Oriental Feng Shui theory were included as well as the establishment of rest and relaxation spaces for the staff, including elements that would encourage playful creativity. Thus, the staff members were no longer viewed as means of achieving certain aims, or as simply a business factor, but were directed in the workplace towards an individual and social way of behaviour that was suited to each of them personally.

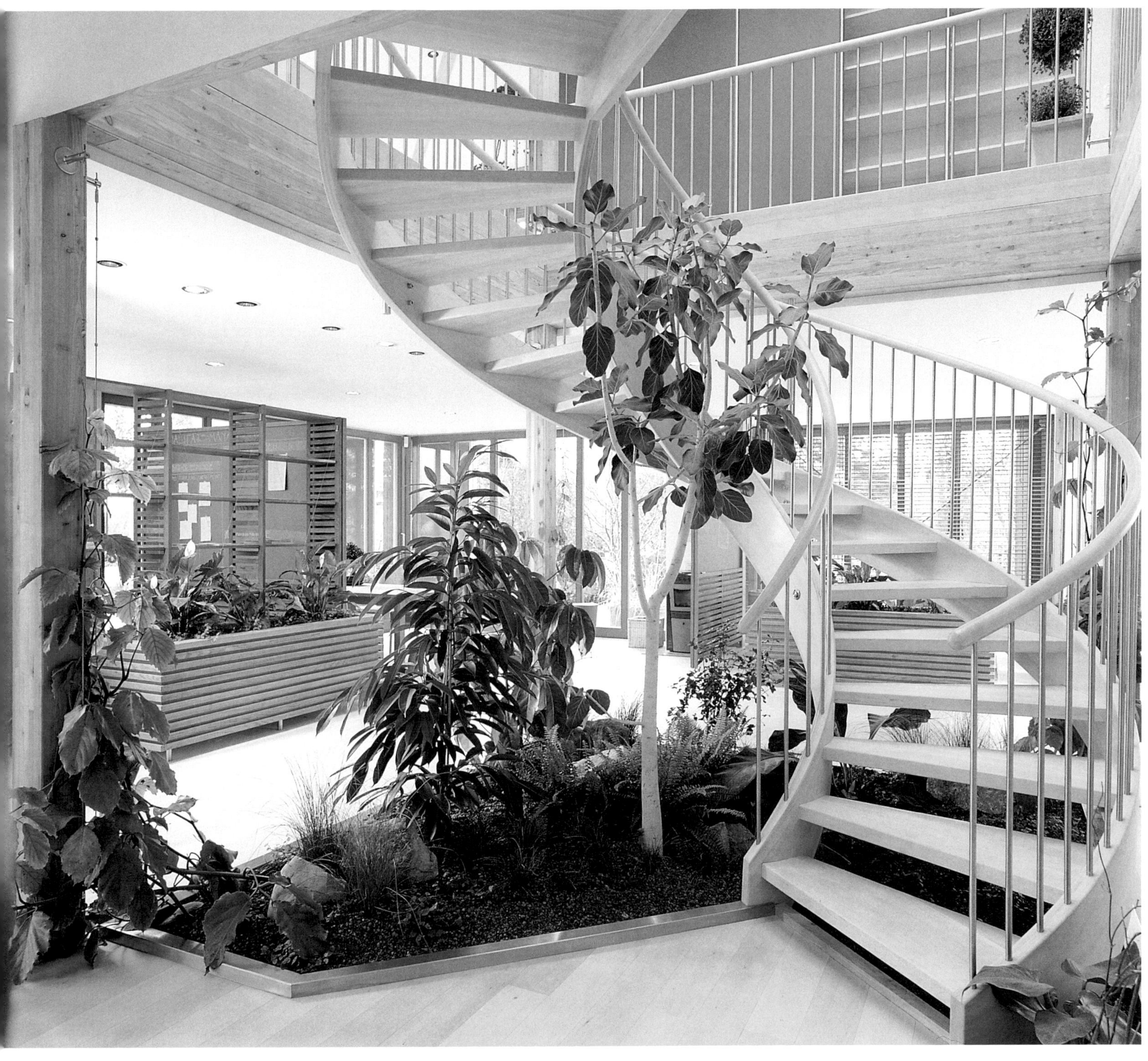

The project

The building concept was developed at the company headquarters of the client, a producer of houses in Erkheim (southern Germany), as a new space for customer reception and sales. The name of the office is, in a sense, the brief word for the project. It is called "Arche", meaning "ark"; the building is meant as a symbol of preserving what is valuable, or what should be reintroduced into the public consciousness of work. The basic needs of human beings, which are at times perceived as "archaic" in the business world, are integrated into the work environment without neglecting the high-tech requirements.

The architecture

Built in the form of a square (with sides measuring 15.3 m), the architecture was extended and enlivened with four small rectangular bays. The wooden skeleton frame structure, as well as ceilings and roof, are made of larch wood; the facades of the two-storey building are also glazed. The building is roofed by a flat, light, metal pyramid roof, with a pyramidal glass skylight that floods the two-storey centre of the building with light. The windows and doors of the buildng are made of wood, painted medium grey, which contributes to the building's quality of lightness and transparency.

Sliding shutters have been mounted in front of the facade to provide shade. They are spanned with light grey fabric and are an eminently suitable advertising medium that presents a visual image of the company. At first glance, this enhances the company's image, although (or indeed, perhaps, because) classic prestige-oriented claddings, such as marble facades, are not to be found here; a perfect example of how to convey corporate identity by means of a building's exterior.

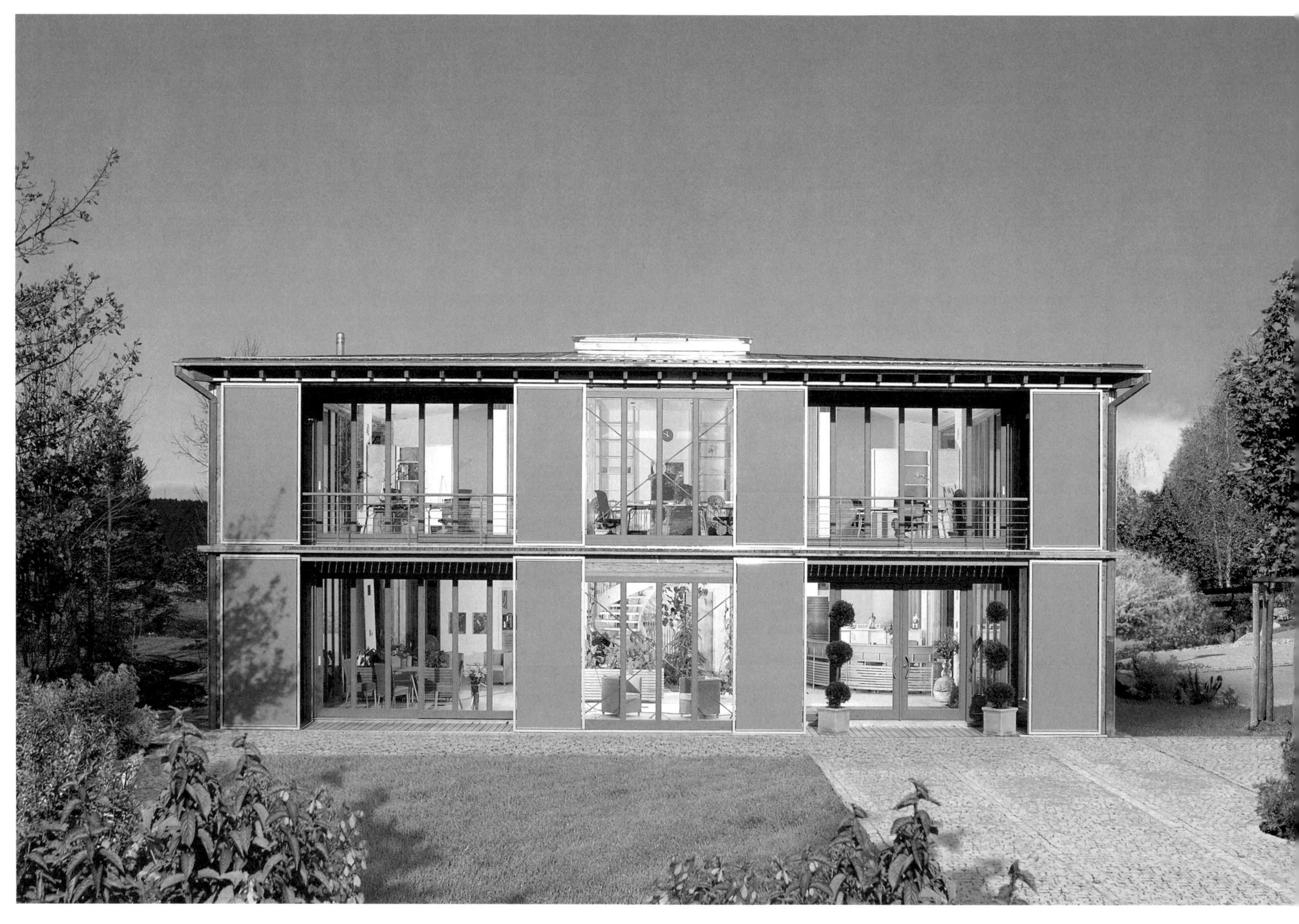

One important requirement was to integrate flexibility and variability into the architecture in order to meet the varied requirements of the company. Thus, thanks to its flexible, open facades, the building can be extended at any time: for example, if the company grows and a need for additional space develops. This flexibility is also found inside the building, because there are no internal load-bearing walls. On the upper floor, a division of space is created using sliding walls, while on the ground floor, divisions are created using plants.

The building is surrounded on all sides by a terrace that is also made of larch wood. The transition between outside and inside is harmonious; it is developed in the interior by continuing the lines of the wooden flooring to the terrace in the beech parquet of the interior.

All fittings, colours, plants, materials, light and sound reflect the most recent discoveries in health, psychology, sociology and Feng Shui. Numerous impulses in the building emphasise the sensual aspect of humanity, encourage creativity and playfulness, and also promote the good humour and cheerfulness of the staff. The company assumes that the staff notices the attention paid to their needs and that this improves both their motivation and their willingness to achieve.

Staff members and visitors are led along a curved path, lined by plants, towards the building. When they arrive at the building, a protected entrance area – enlivened internally by the use of plants – receives them. The entrance is the mouth of the building, according to Feng Shui, and this one leads to a very unique office interior. The gaze initially encounters the transparent reception desk with

an adjoining advertising column. The two areas around the reception and the desk are in shades of blue and grey; behind the desk is a lively and energetic yellow-orange workstation for technical appliances.

A second look takes in the centrally positioned spiral staircase, surrounded by large planters. Tall climbing plants visually accompany the route upwards to the next level and introduce a natural element into the office building. To the left of the entrance area, the visitor can find a "mediathek" a waiting area with information about the company, where they can browse through specialist journals and brochures. Waiting, which is usually a negative experience, is made into a positive experience here. The cool functional blue colour scheme indicates that the waiting area is a place where

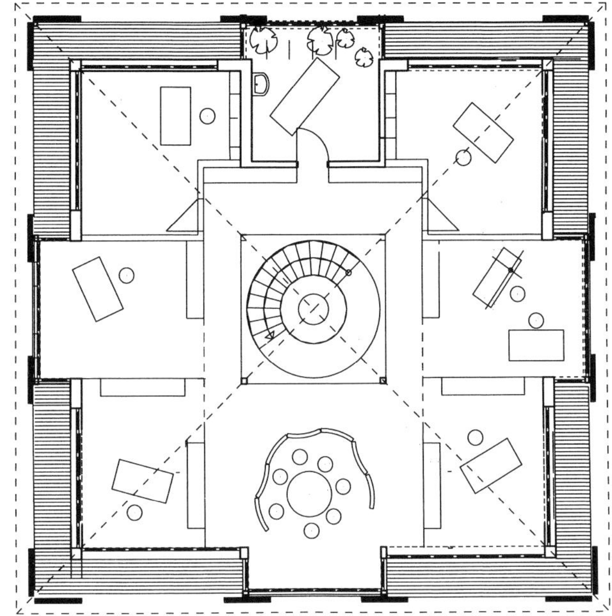

Upper floor

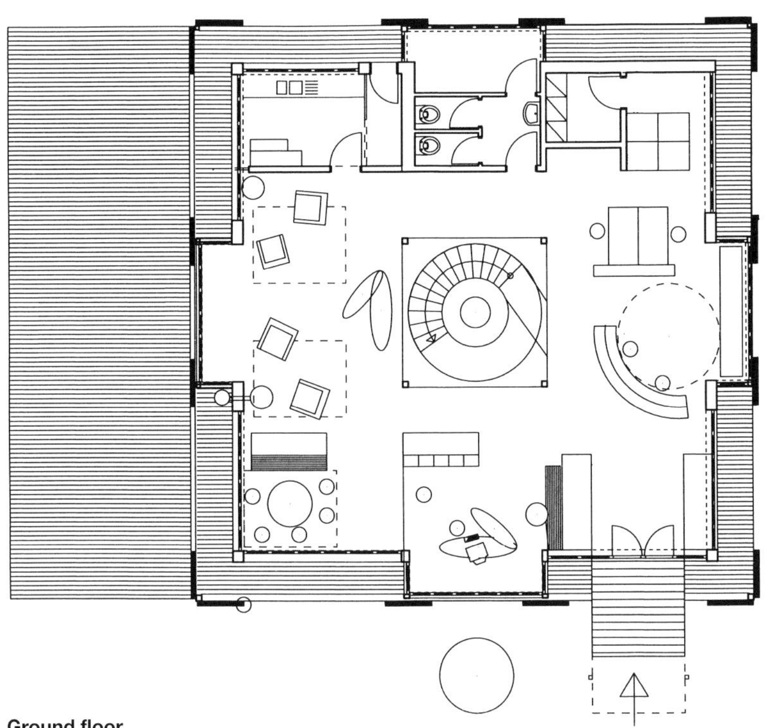

Ground floor

information is conveyed. A room divider, made of wood and plant containers, defines the boundary between the mediathek and the main space.

On the lefthand of the building's entrance, there is a small area for discussions between staff members and customers. A counter with a cafeteria and a separate kitchen meets the needs for refreshments This area is designed more like a living room with loom chairs and tactile felt carpeting and has additional accents such as an open wood-burning stove and a fountain sculpture, whith splashing water that not only helps improve the quality of the air and the atmosphere but, as a Feng Shui element, also symbolizes "wealth". The colour scheme in this area is warm and sensual; at the rear of the reception hall, green accents are added to the yellow-orange shades.

The entire ground floor is arranged in an open plan around the central staircase and its planting. Throughout this level, the impression is

cheerful, natural, enthusiastic, domestic, comfortable and sensual.

The spiral staircase directs the positive flow of energy on the ground floor toward the upstairs. On the upper level, offices between 10 and 13 m² in floor area provide space for eleven staff members. Only two offices are separated by fixed walls; the other six can be opened up or separated off by the use of sliding walls and mobile storage elements. In front of the fixed walls is a central library for work documents and materials, where each staff member has a personal section. The sliding walls are clad with slate – staff members can write notes or present an image on the slate surface. The client encourages his staff to introduce personal elements into the individual work areas in order to create a more relaxed atmosphere and to establish a sense of identity.

The flexible and open design, as well as the flexible furnishings of the workplaces, allows the upper floor to be transformed into a large

meeting room if and when required. The desks can be put together for the duration of a meeting or presentation to form a single large conference table.

Each staff member can retire at any time to a motivation and meditation space to think, calm down, relax or even get a massage – a local masseuse comes by when required. This space has a particularly meditative and calming character. At the centre is a wool carpet that imitates a Zen stone garden. A daybed and a chair invite one to relax. The reductionist grey of the furnishings is contrasted with a large picture whose gentle, calming green colour reflects the theories of colour psychology. For exhausted staff members, this picture suggests the calm and serenity needed for themselves and their work. Each staff member can choose, from a wide-range of objects, whatever they need to enhance their personal sense of well-being, including: plants, music, sounds, fragrances from the aura-soma, changeable light effects, and blinds of different colours.

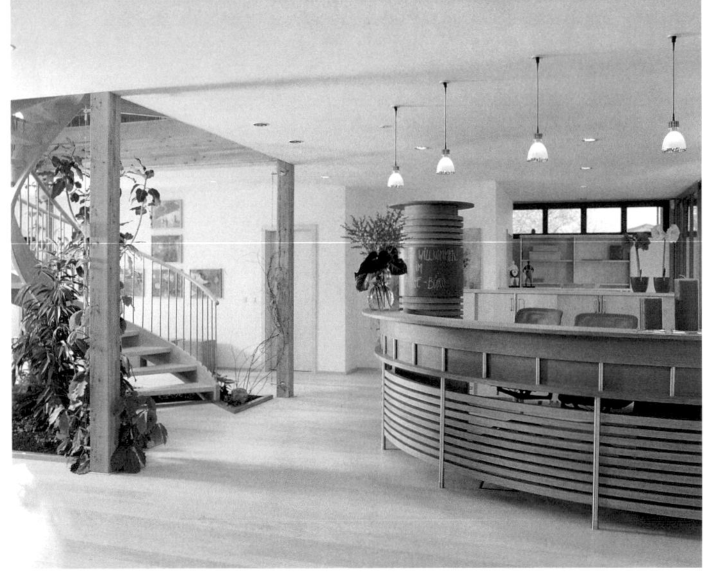
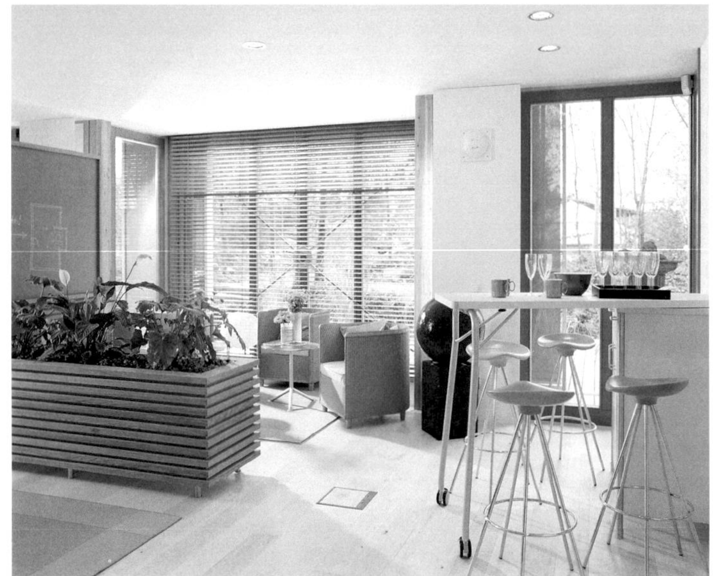

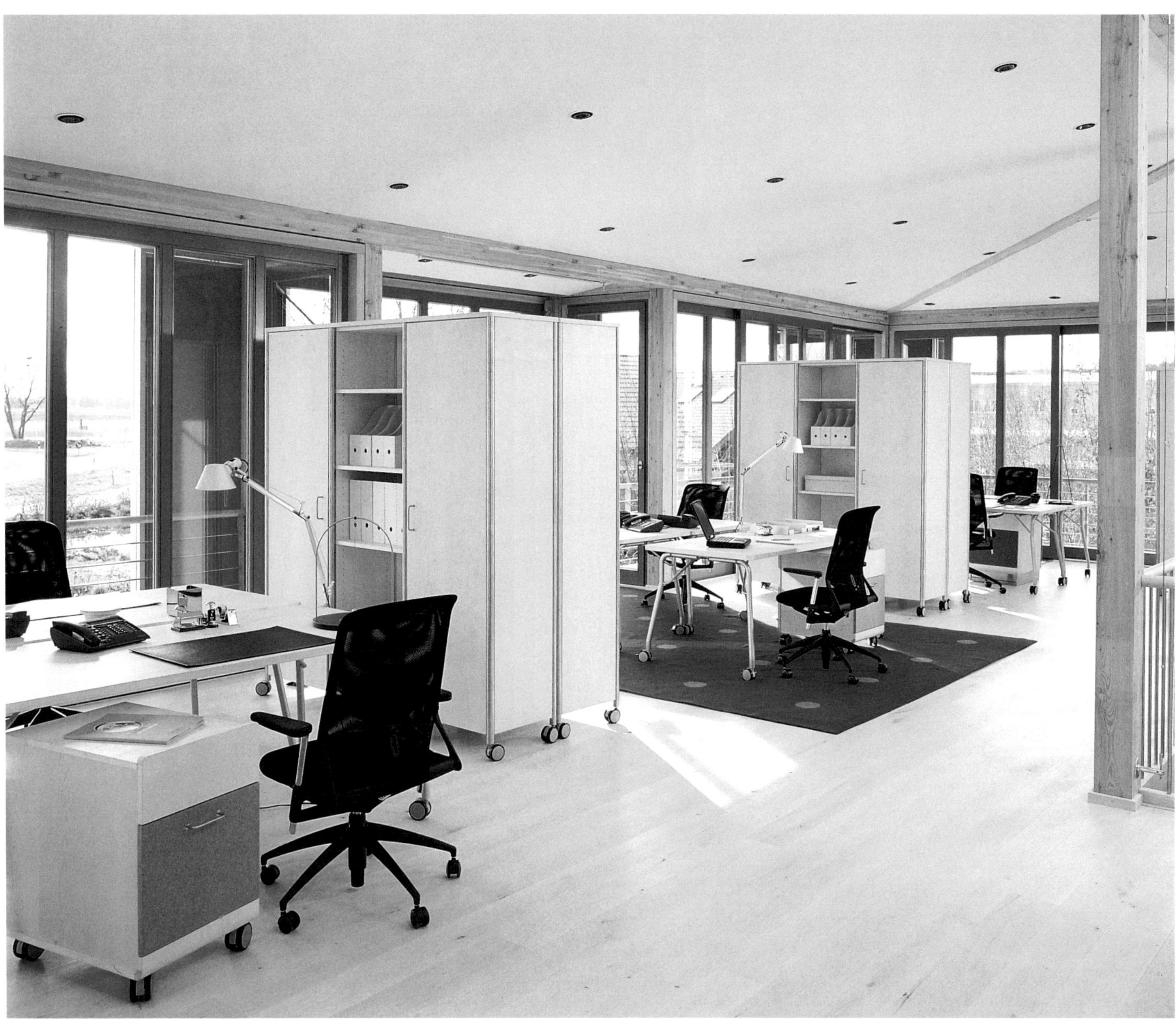

Building services

The internal room climate is an important factor in a building that seeks to influence the well-being of its inhabitants. The environment is created by the building's mechanical services; the heating, ventilation and lighting are all intelligently controlled by means of a bus-installation.

An excellent level of thermal insulation in the external envelope, coupled with the energy-saving ventilation and heat recovery concept, completely obviates the need to use energy from fossil fuels to heat the building. Energy is provided in an environmentally friendly way by using a water-water heat pump. The heat pump can be used in summer to cool the building.

Heat is distributed by means of a modern underfloor heating system. Due to its relatively low flow temperatures, underfloor heating is the ideal distribution method for an energy system based on heat pumps. The heating system is integrated into the building's control technology system – LONworks bus technology – and can therefore react to the individual needs of the users as well as the objective conditions of the office environment. Extensive simulation calculations examined the suitability of the concept in advance.

A broad range of technical office equipment is standard nowadays in almost all office spaces. Their effect on the quality of the air is considerable and they indirectly influence the need for a fresh air supply. Worker efficiency and a sense of well-being are ensured only when a

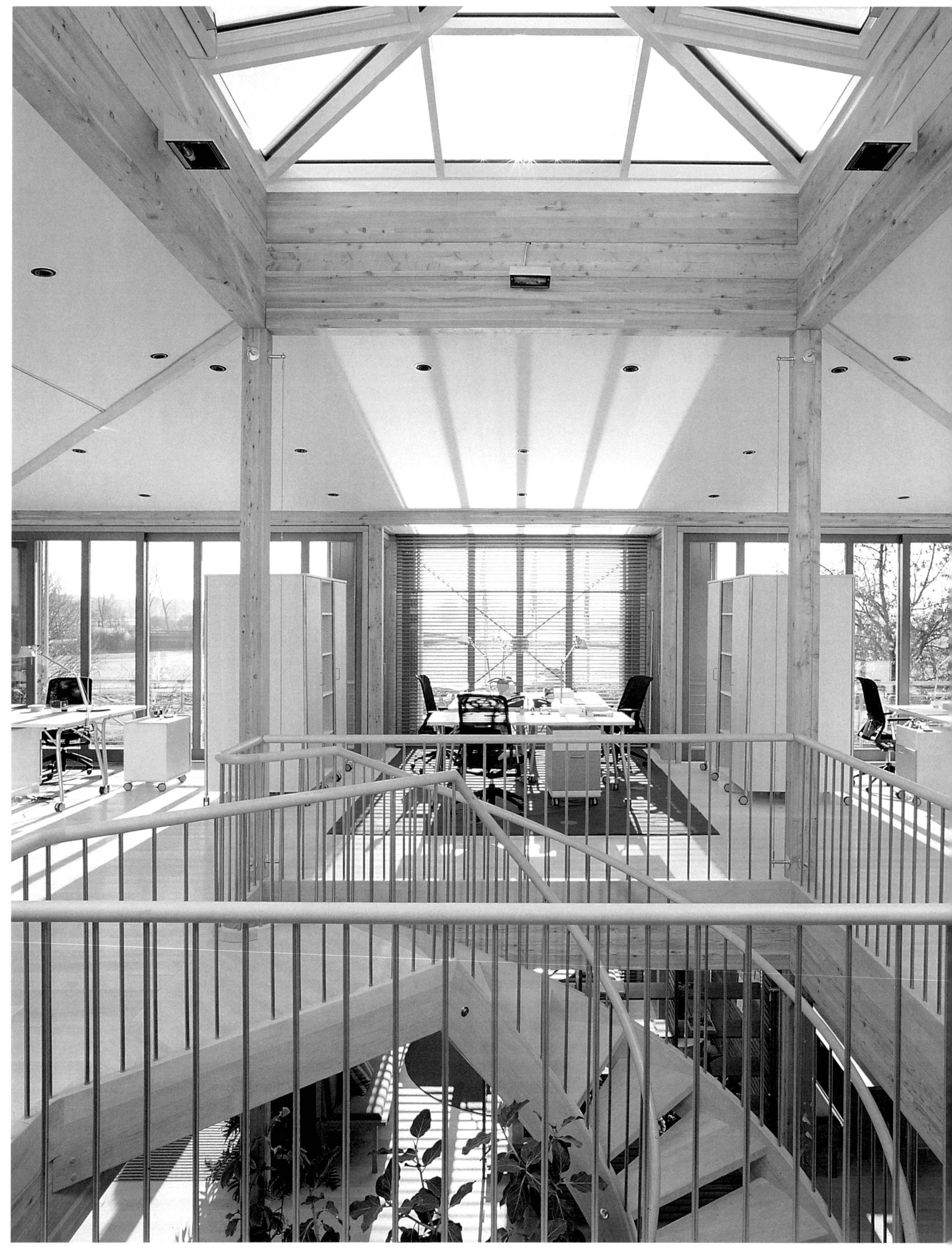

hygienic supply of high quality air, without draughts, can be assured. In this project, the decentralised ventilation system meets these requirements in an ideal manner. An extremely quiet and energy-saving air-blower carries stale air outside for a period of eighty seconds. The warmth contained in this stale air is stored in a heat accumulator. After eighty seconds, the motor of the ventilator automatically reverses and cold air from outside is introduced through the heat accumulator and enters the rooms as warm air.

The fact that the air intake is decentralised and does not take place through ducts, guarantees hygienic fresh air. Filter systems prevent the entry of insects or pollen. The system has a heat recovery value of 90 percent for a minimal energy consumption of 5 watts, thus making a considerable contribution to energy saving.

Lighting and illumination

Daylight is introduced into the office building as much as possible. An aluminium blind with a controlled light deflection system is fitted on the inside of the windows. In the upper third of this blind, daylight is cast onto the ceiling and reflected from there into the space. The louvers are electronically controlled and react to different light conditions, allowing the motivating and encouraging effect of daylight to be exploited. Through a light dome, which can be shaded if required with the use of sailcloth, additional daylight enters the building.

This modern system of directing daylight provides effective protection against glare and makes optimum use of the available daylight. The controlled use of daylight not only improves the quality of light in the rooms but also reduces the use of artificial light, which, in an office building, makes a serious contribution to energy savings. The effective deflection of daylight is conducted by means of two separately controlled areas of the internal blinds. The upper area deflects the daylight, while the lower area provides protection from glare.

The mechanisms are controlled from the LON works network. The light intensity, position of the sun, wind strength and an interval timer are entered as variables. The controls and regulating devices ensure that the system fulfils the functions of daylight deflection, and protection from glare and heat in an optimal manner, independent of the users. In addition, the users can adapt the automatic system by means of individual controls to suit their personal preferences and requirements.

When planning the building, it was decided that no low-voltage lighting would be used, in order to avoid the negative effects of electrical-smog. Instead, full-spectrum light fittings, which produce a white-yellow light similar to daylight, were used. These are also connected to a system that allows individuals to select their personal lighting from three colour variations.

The entire lighting system is regulated by the building's services control system. This integration means that the use of artificial light can be coordinated, depending on the direction of daylight, and the glare control can be provided by the shade system. It also allows different light effects to be produced for different office situations (working at a computer screen, at a desk, conducting presentations, interviews, etc.). The programmed light games form a special attraction; they are cleverly integrated into the garden, colonnade areas and the glass dome. Halogen technology (50 Hz) was employed for environmental health reasons.

Building control technology
(LON bus technology)

The building services as a whole can only make a suitable contribution to the holistic humane office environment if all technical functions are intelligently connected with each other. In the "Ark" office building, the important services, such as heating, ventilation, shade and lighting, are linked to each other by means of the LON-works technology.

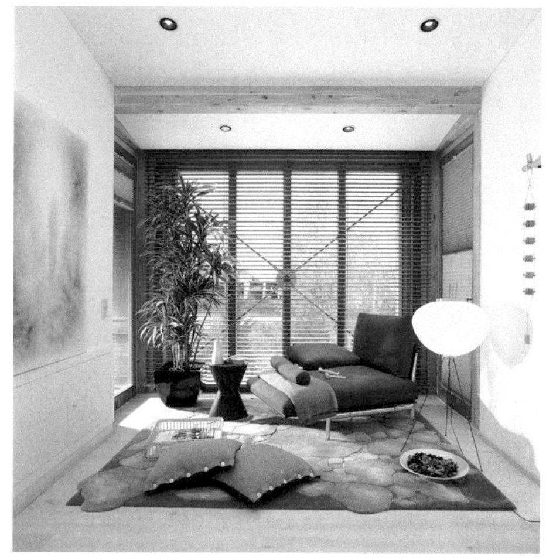

Relaxing during office hours in the meditation room

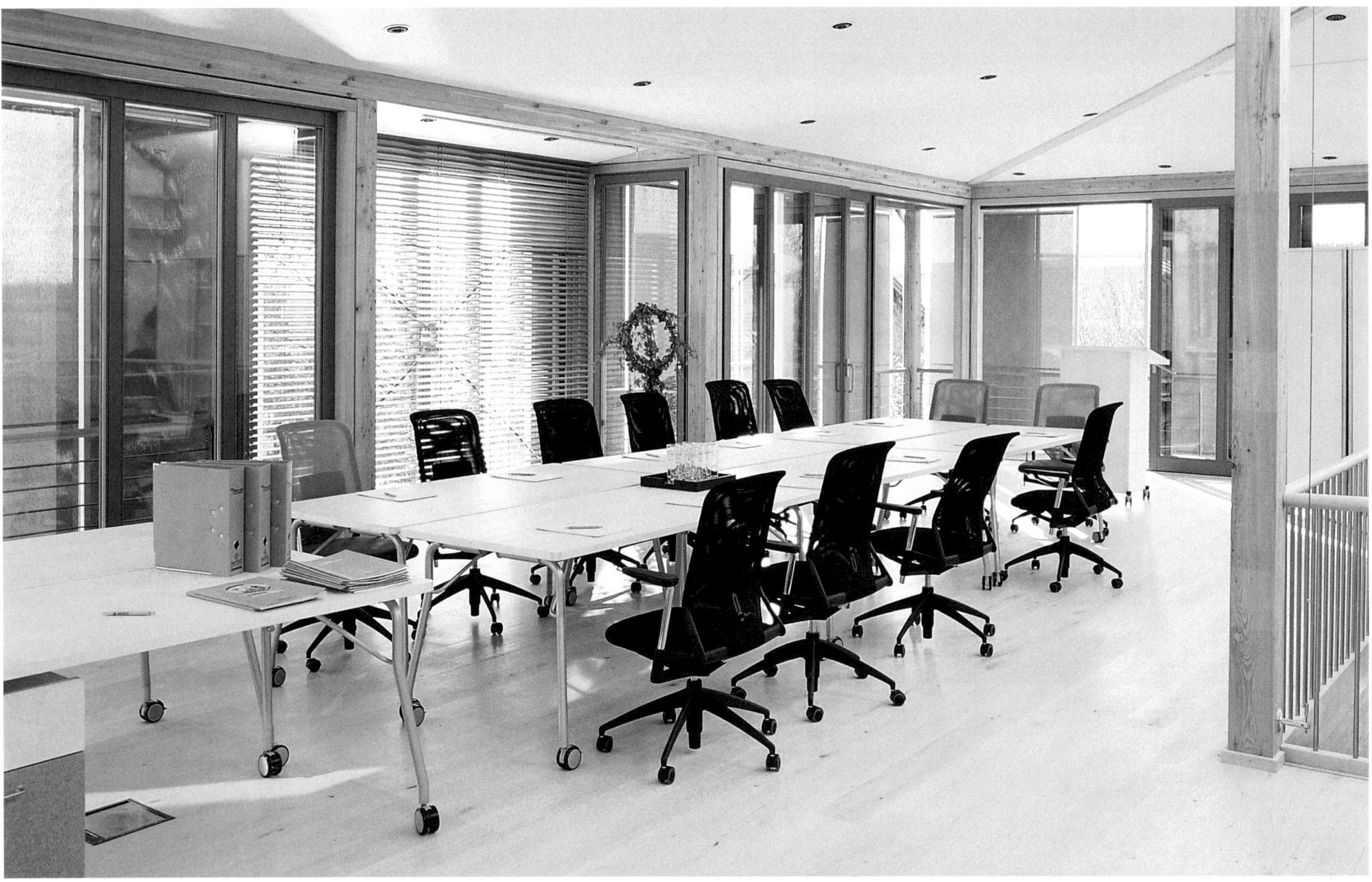

Sliding storage units and mobile tables allow a large conference area to be made out of the office units in just a short time.

Contacts report whether the windows are open or closed and therefore exert a direct influence on the regulation of the heating and ventilation. The entrance door contact allows the status of the main door to be entered as a variable in the system. In combination with the window contacts and movement detectors, this creates an efficient alarm system that is automatically activated. The LON system allows entry control at the entrance door. It is opened automatically by a passive transponder system and checks the authorisation of the person entering.

The individual room controls link shade, artificial light and heating with each other. The heating reacts immediately to heat gains produced by the use of artificial light and daylight warming.

The system is informed in the opposite way when protection from heat (shades closed) or an energy increase (blinds open) is necessary.

If the fire alarm system is activated, various processes are set in motion. The ventilation system is switched off, the exits are unlocked and a report of the fire is sent to the telecommunications system.

By means of a multi-functional communications box, it is possible to communicate with the building control systems from outside the building, via (radio) phone or external computer. Thus, the state of the building, including heating, lighting, etc., can always be monitored and controlled. Services such as external security companies, the reading of energy meters, energy management, etc., are all made simple and convenient.

The computers are in sound-insulated, nearly airtight wooden containers earthed (grounded) against electrical smog. One such container houses an air-water heat exchanger that transforms the ventilation warmth (exhaust air) given off by computers into heating energy by means of a heat exchanger. Using a control system, the heat exchanger conducts the warmth produced to a water storage cylinder that heats the utility water for the entire building; the power produced amounts to 1 kW from seven computers. The exhaust air from the computers does not enter the workspaces but is directly led off into the containers. This also helps to prevent overheating in the workspaces. The air in the rooms remains free of harmful substances, which in turn leads to a better internal climate.

The advantages of this office concept for the company

This office building can grow or be altered at any time. It is therefore suitable for growth businesses with a steadily increasing need for space and also for medium-sized industrial businesses, since both can alter their built environment in an uncomplicated way. Various different needs in the workplace can be taken into account. Multiple uses of the spaces are also possible, which substantially reduces the financial input for the company.

At first glance, one notices that this office building is different and that the company is characterised by concern for its staff and an interest in innovation, and possesses an incomparably personal management style. To the visitor, small hospitable oases convey the feeling that they are welcome. Visitors to the company who feel welcome are generally more cooperative, and an emotional tie between business and guest is established more quickly and directly. Staff members do not have to establish a "safe distance" because they are more prepared to identify with the company; as a result, there is a reduction in staff turnover.

The fact that human beings are the focal point of all considerations means that the staff members find themselves in a humane environment and therefore behave in a more humane manner, which means, in turn, that factors such as mobbing are reduced from the very start. The working person is not seen as a means of fulfilling certain tasks but as a complete person who has needs, in part archaic, that must be met in both private and working life. The workers respond to this esteem on the part of the employer and feel both accepted and respected. The consequence is an increase in motivation and a greater desire to make a productive contribution.

Ecological and biological aspects maintain health and encourage a positive, healthy room climate. The interior fittings, including the furniture, are designed according to ecological and biological criteria. All facilities, colour schemes, plants, materials, light, sound and scent reflect the latest discoveries in the areas of health, psycholog, and sociology. On both the conscious and subconscious level, people's needs are respected in this building. There is an unconscious resonance experienced by both staff and visitors, not only through its motivating work environment but also pragmatically, through healthier work conditions; staff members feel well and stay in good health. A considerable reduction in the number of sick days is the result.

The Ark office also has its own relationship to nature: sliding glass facades and easy transitions between inside and outside mean that desks can be moved onto the terrace. Work is combined with the enjoyment of nature and sunshine. Workers who are positively stimulated show more emotional intelligence, are more creative and cooperative, and they perform better and make decisions more easily. These are precisely the attributes that are regarded by modern psychologists as necessary and desirable for the success of a business.

Feng Shui, the "energy acupuncture" of space, is a Chinese science that is more than a thousand years old. Taking its discoveries and wisdom into account ensures a harmonious flow of the energy ("chi") between the building and the people using it. According to this ancient theory, this energy not only stimulates personal well-being, but also positively influences important business areas, such as prosperity and creativity.

Location Erkheim, Germany

Construction period 2000

Client BAUFRITZ, Erkheim

Development of the general concept Architektur und Design Andreas Weber, Weßling; BAUFRITZ, Erkheim

Project group technology ERCO Leuchten, Lüdenscheid; NETWORK Consulting, Herrenberg; Prof. Dr. Schönemann, Winden; VISSMANN WERKE, Allendorf; ZAE Bayern, München; WINI BÜROMÖBEL, Coppenbrügge; Irene Fromberger PR, Germering; Hauptverband der Deutschen Holzindustrie, Bad Honnef; REKO Electronic, Marktheidenfeld; SPEGA GmbH, Duisburg; Winkler Kommunikationssysteme, Oberkochen

Floor area 15,55 x 15,55 m

Built site area 242 m^2

Usable floor area 380 m^2

Timber skeleton frame system
Glued laminated larch wood

Column grid 477,5 cm

Insulation Wood shavings HOIZ

Electrical smog protection panel XUND-E

k-value wall 0,23

k-value glazing 0,9

k-value roof 0,21

Roof pitch 8°

BRIDGE

Office wing in Roggwil / Switzerland

Architects: Inauen & Partner

The restructuring of a company that produces high-quality herbal remedies into three cleanliness zones – required by regulations – necessitated a reorganisation of the flow of materials and staff. Monitoring staff movement from one zone to a cleaner one was only possible by introducing a new functional unit. This solution blocked off the centrally located handling yard, which is enclosed on three sides and could not be relocated. Therefore, the only possible solution was to utilise the air space above the yard. This unusual "site" is thus surrounded by three buildings. The soffit of the new building had to be a minimum of 4.5 m above ground level to keep from obstructing trucks and lorries. The required floor area was 700 m², the span across the yard was about 20 m. The constraints imposed by the location demanded a special solution. The idea of a bridge building was quickly found and the architectural design had to incorporate this structural solution.

A bridge as a connection

A bridge as a connecting element satisfied the functional requirements (i.e., the connection between the administration, production and warehousing areas). In design terms, it mediates between the buildings dating from various periods and also creates a connection between the "head" (administration) and the "hand" (production and storage) of the company.

The basic form resulted almost automatically from the delineations of the available space combined with the required floor area: a two-storey cube about 7 m high, 20 m wide and 16 m deep. The structure is the main theme of the architectural statement. Three 7-m-high trusses, visible internally and externally, span the courtyard. The clearly defined building volume is a sharp-edged cube standing on six columns. Recessed mirrored transitional areas connect it functionally with the surrounding company units. The trusses connect the two upper floors of the new building, unifying the new element in height and giving it a scale that differentiates it clearly from the surrounding buildings and documents its independent

quality. A curtain wall of glass further strengthens this effect. This open quality relates directly to the openness of the business and its relationship to the public and to nature. The company philosophy (the founder placed nature and natural ingredients at the centre of his activities) is applied in an exemplary way through the use of natural materials and is developed consistently. Following this logic, all the structural elements are of wood and, as far as possible, they are exposed internally and externally, thus allowing them to be visually experienced.

Solution in wood

The involvement of a timber construction engineer at an early stage in the planning, and the clear definition of the constraints, provided an ideal basis for a close and fruitful collaboration. The solution of the three large trusses, 7.5 m high with spans of 20 m, emerged from a feasibility study of the various options. Wooden beams and hollow box elements connect the trusses and form the floors, ceiling slabs and walls. Protections from the weather, thermal and acoustic insulation and fire protection are

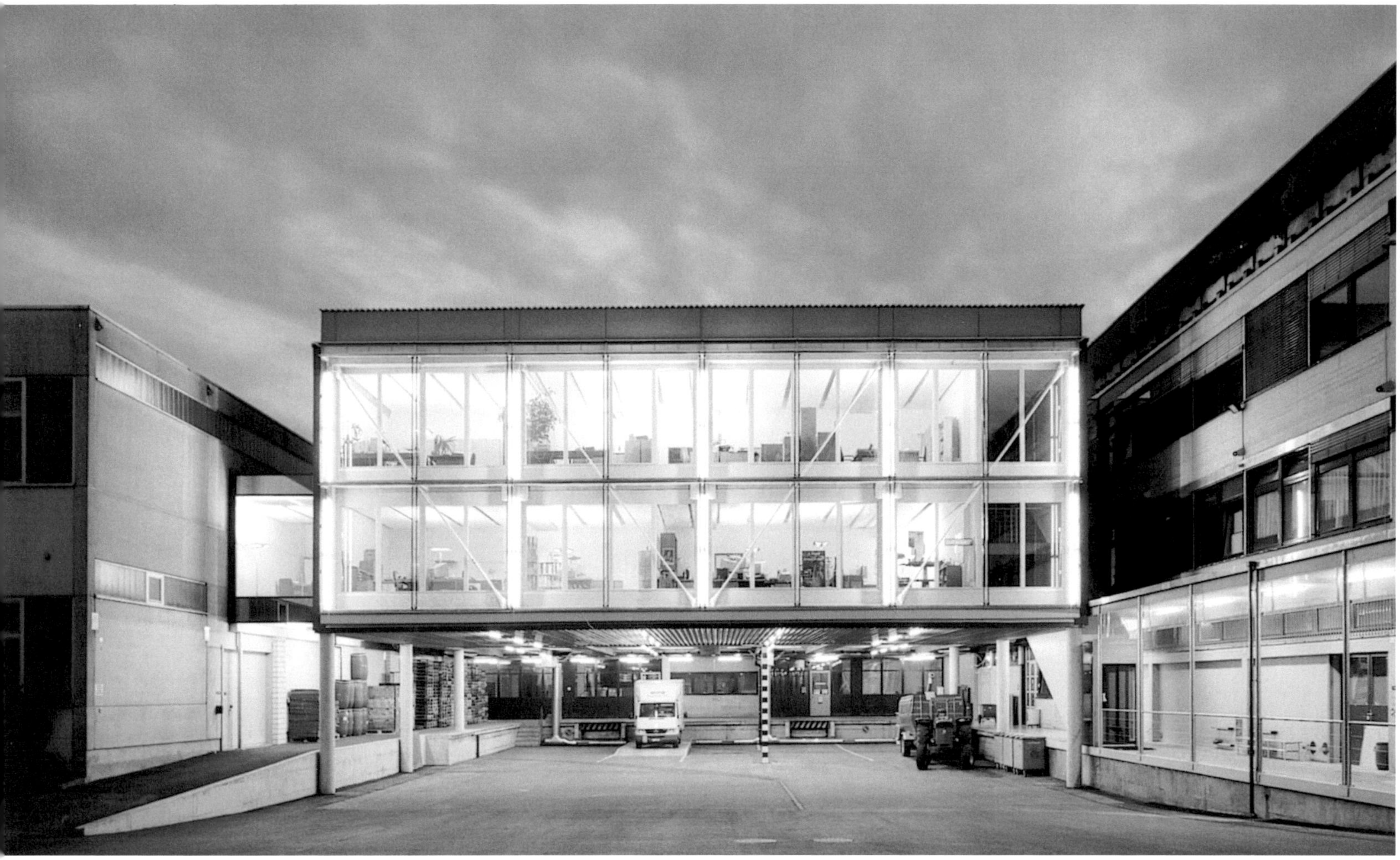

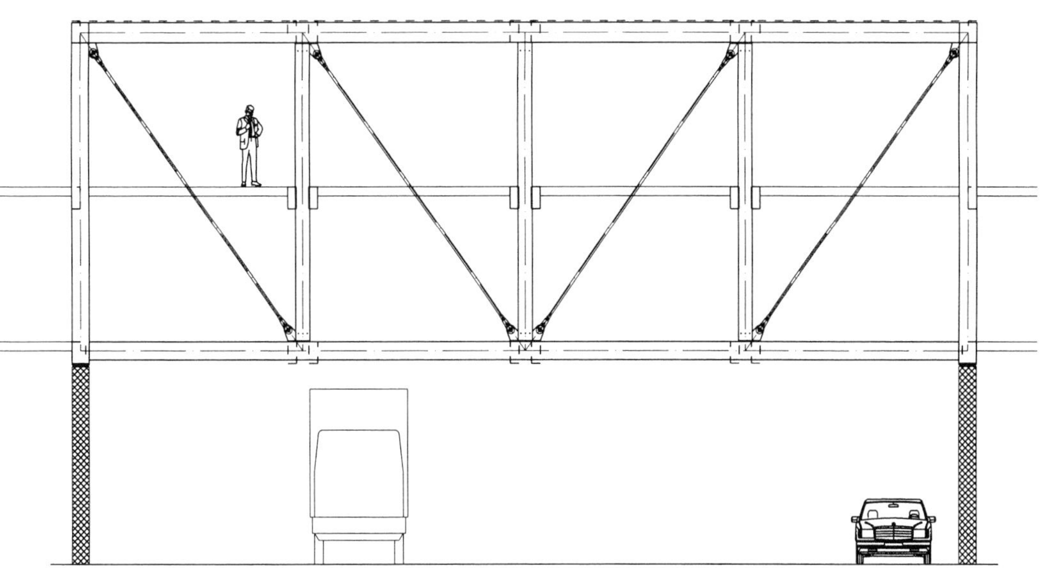

Section through structure

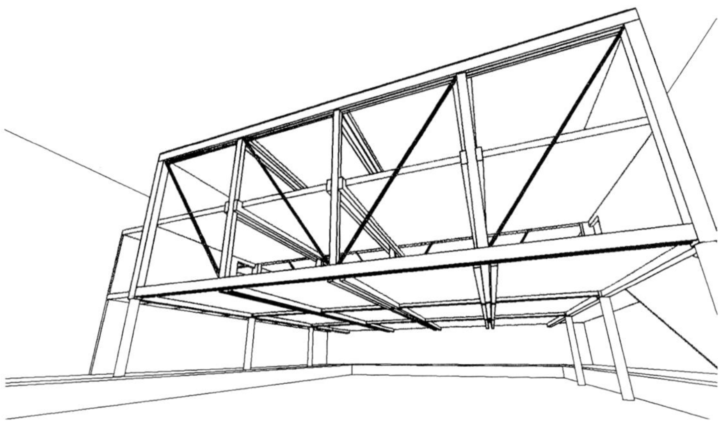

Computer simulation: overall view of the structure

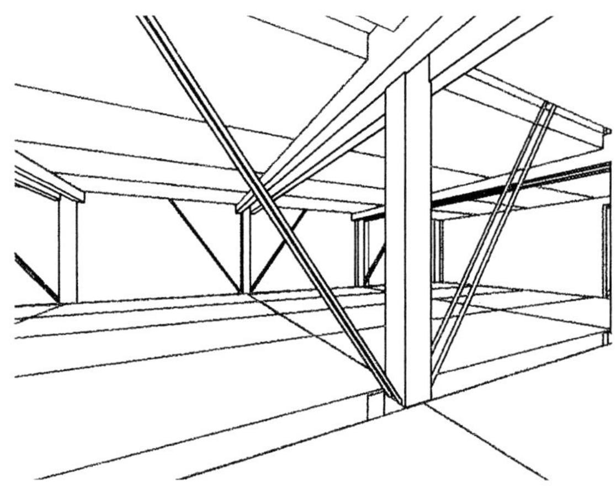

Computer simulation: detail of the structure

important aspects of timber buildings. In this case, the entire wooden structure is enclosed by a shell of glass. The glass wall set in front of the structure offers protection from the elements and from noise. The well-thought-out floor construction protects against structure-borne and airborne noise.

Forces of up to 200 tonnes are exerted on the most highly stressed wooden elements. In contemporary engineered timber building, efficient wood-based materials are available to deal with such forces. Thus, the linear load-bearing elements such as posts, beams and chords are made of gluelam of different kinds and strengths. The floors are composite elements consisting of 200-mm-high solid wood ribs planked on both sides with 27-mm-thick three-ply laminated panels. These so-called hollow wooden box elements are not only highly efficient as a floor slab system but, combined with the appropriate wall system, they also help to brace the entire building. Due to the bridge design used, particular attention had to be paid to the oscillation of the floors and of the structure as a whole. The most up-to-date research results formed the basis of the structural calculations and dimensioning. The low dead weight, the predictable behaviour in the case of fire, and the possibility of building thermally and acoustically well-insulated structures, here confirmed the choice of wood as the building material. An additional factor was the economic advantage offered by the shorter construction period: despite poor weather conditions the basic structure was completed in only four days.

Planning for the addition of a further storey

It proved possible to satisfy the sound insulation requirements in combination with the thermal insulation measures. The floor over the driveway is subject to noise emitted by the trucks; the centre floor must provide insulation against the transfer of both structure- and airborne noise between the various work areas. The roof had to provide thermal insulation and also allow for the easy addition of another storey at some time in the future. The roof was planned in such a way that adding a third storey will be no problem; in terms of structural design the entire building was calculated to take three storeys. The roof consists of hollow box elements, 120-mm thermal insulation and, standing on this, a light wooden structure covered with a gently sloping, self-supporting roof of metal sheeting.

The "office bridge" offers about 320 m² of floor area per storey. The connections between the old buildings and the new building are made by two corridors outside the cube on the lower level and by a two-storey staircase, half integrated in the new building, half in the existing building. Visually these connections recede behind the main building so that it seems like a freestanding form. Inside, it has an open plan that is divided on both floors only by a corridor on the long axis.

Due to the considerable depth of the spaces, it was necessary to allow as much light as possible enter the interior of the building, while at the same time shutting out the noise of the trucks and loading activities. The sides most subject to noise are nevertheless completely glazed. On the street side, the facade glazing and the windows are staggered in depth. Towards the rear yard, there is a completely glazed corridor in front of the offices at the first floor level, whereas the upper floor is lit entirely by windows. Achieving the fire rating of F30 for the structure was not a problem, as wooden building elements achieve this rating without any need for additional measures (see Basics / Fire!).

As this example from Switzerland illustrates, building above a courtyard without obstructing the flow of traffic is easily possible with the use of wood. The project also leads us to reflect on how existing sites, even where they consist only of "air space", could be sensibly utilised.

Location Roggwil , Switzerland

Construction period 1/2001 – 9/2001

Client Bioforce AG, Roggwil

Architects Inauen & Partner AG, St. Gallen

Structural designer Josef Kolb AG, Kesswil

Timber construction Kaufmann Holzbau AG, Roggwil

Floor area 640 m²

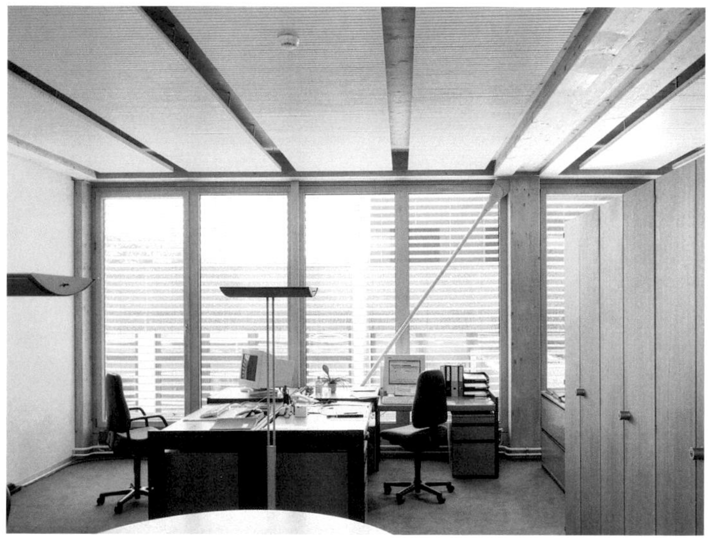

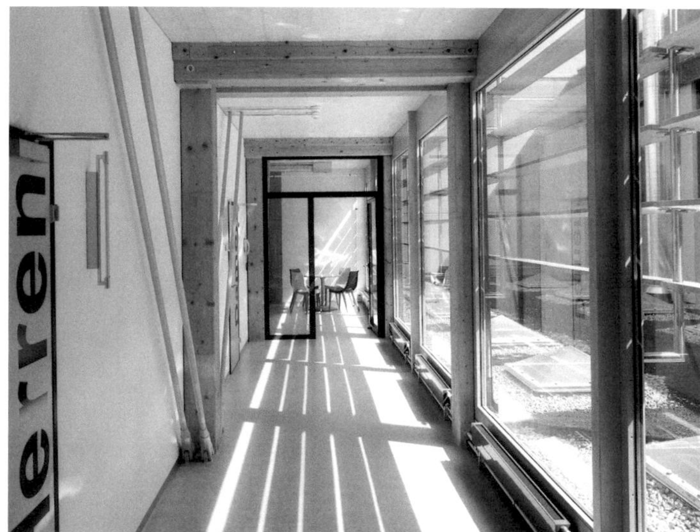

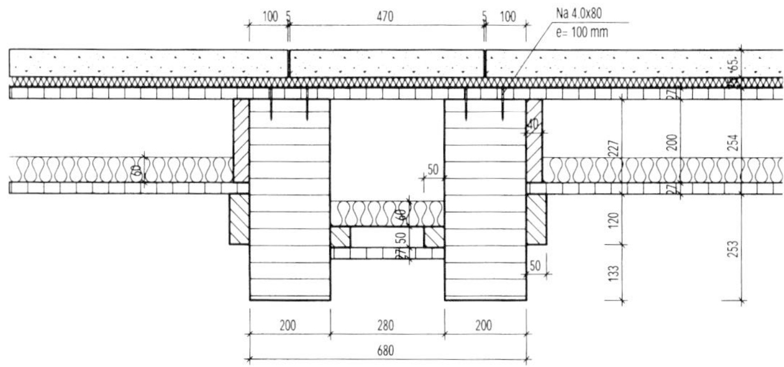

Floor construction above the first floor level

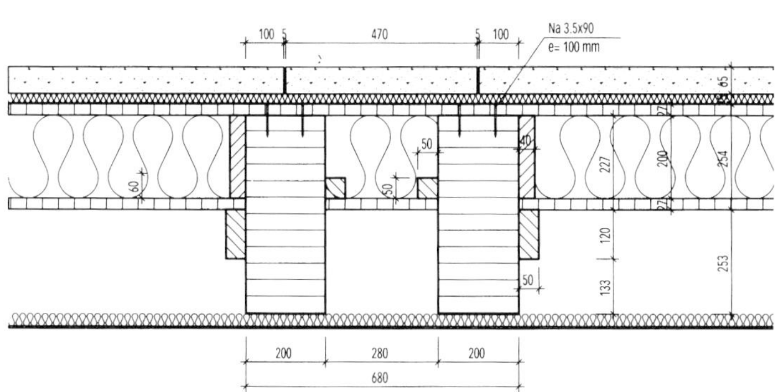

Detail of floor construction (floor over the driveway)

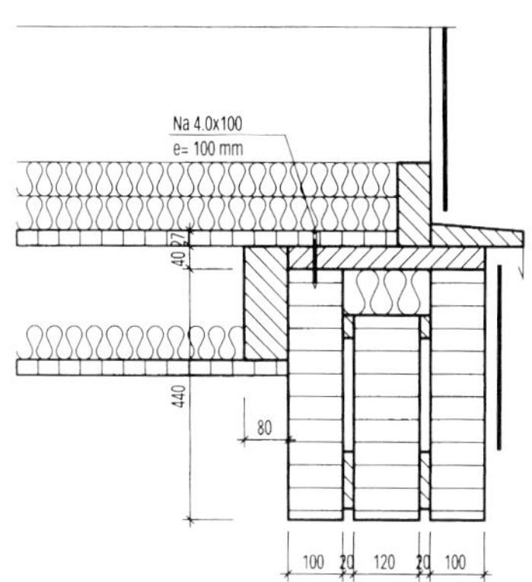

**Verge detail – roof construction,
planned for the addition of a further floor**

Lift manufacturer in Ebikon / Switzerland

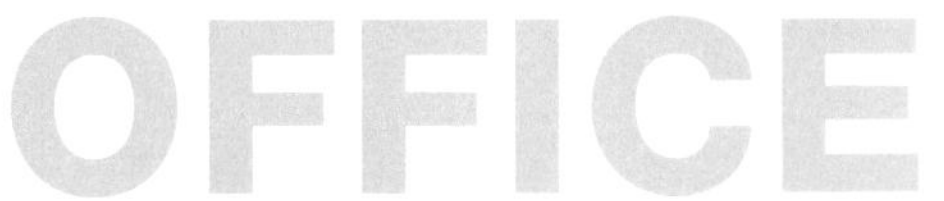

Kündig. Bickel Architects

This office building – for the research and development department of a company specialising in lift construction – offered the first opportunity to realise the planners' theoretical reflections about the construction of multi-storey buildings using a prefabricated modular timber system. The advantages of the client's innovative lift system, specially suited to buildings with a lightweight structure, were to be demonstrated in a direct fashion in this industrially produced three-storey modular timber building.

Design planning

Through collaboration between the architects, the timber construction company, and the specialist planners at the preliminary planning phase – and as a result of the designer's years of experience in modular construction systems – it was possible to design the building to the construction stage in a very short period. In contrast to conventional building processes, almost all the planning work had to be completed by the start of the production of the cellular units.

The traditional handcraft methods of continual building – in which the planning and project management process continues throughout the entire construction phase – was, in this

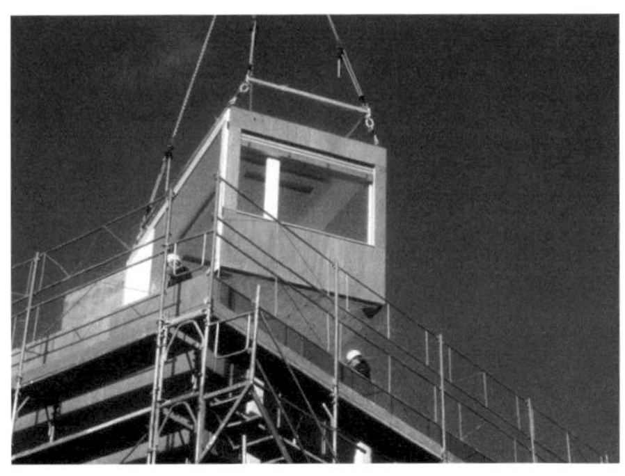

case, replaced by a composition of industrially produced standardised building construction components. The lift and air-conditioning plant were used in the same way as the wood modules, which eliminated the conceptual differences between these different building parts. Series and an additive system are the outcome of this method.

The decisive questions in this design were, first, how architectural means could be used to adapt the primarily serial character of such a building to create a new unity and, second, how a standardised modular system with its own constructive and geometrical laws could be adapted to the specific demands of this commission.

Architecture and programme

The most important element in this project is the three-storey central well, which structurally organises the large building by means of vertical penetration. Light is the architectural means of presenting the space, which becomes a demonstration podium for the business and its product. On the centre axis, the lift defines the light well on one side and is flanked by the rising services ducts for this company product. The circulation zone for the 200 m^2 of office space is organised around the light well. The office area originally opened onto the light well and was designed as an open plan office, but later it was divided into smaller units using a mobile partition wall system.

For reasons of fire safety, the staircases are modular steel constructions. All the other spatial cells are built in timber construction with an integrated sprinkler system as a fire prevention precaution.

Structure and typology

The building rests on a concrete slab that is a mediating element, forming a link to the sloping site. The tripartite complex erected on it is made of spatial cells along both long sides. Wood panels hung from the modules span the

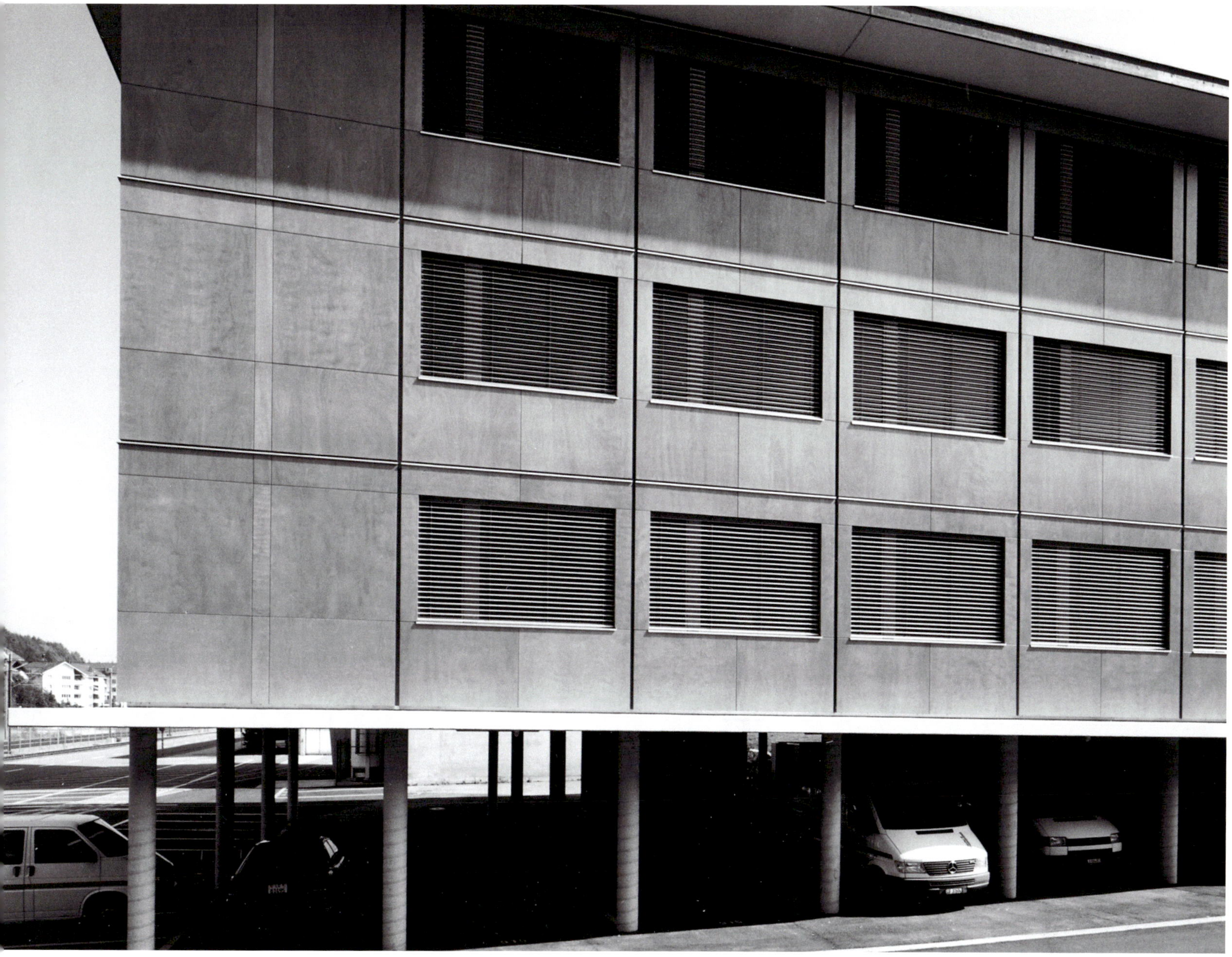

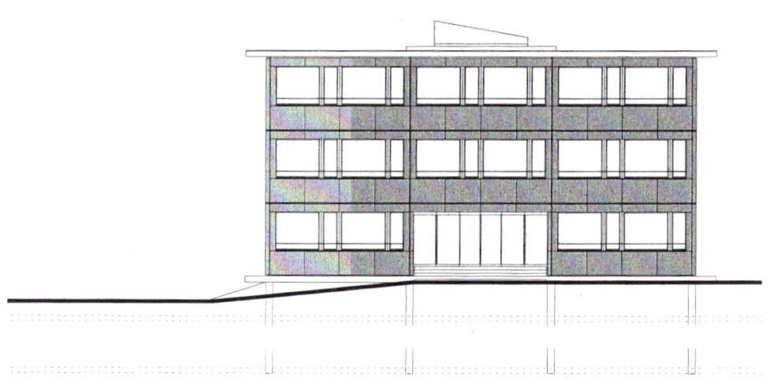

View of south facade

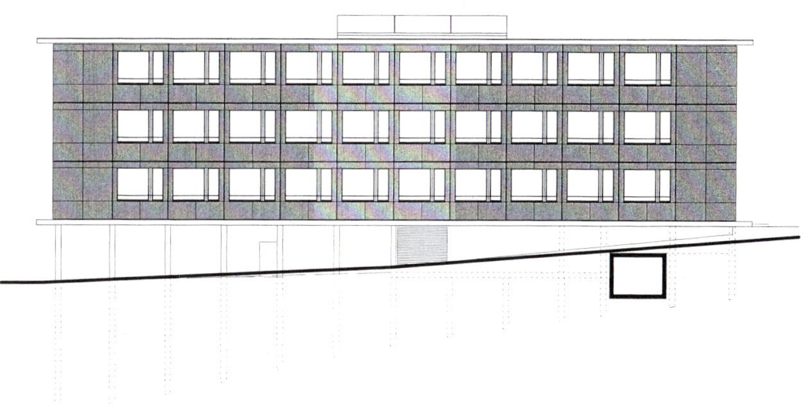

View of west facade

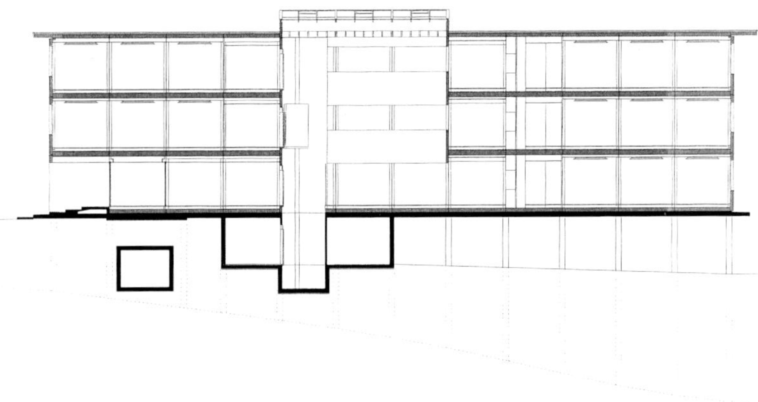

Longitudinal section

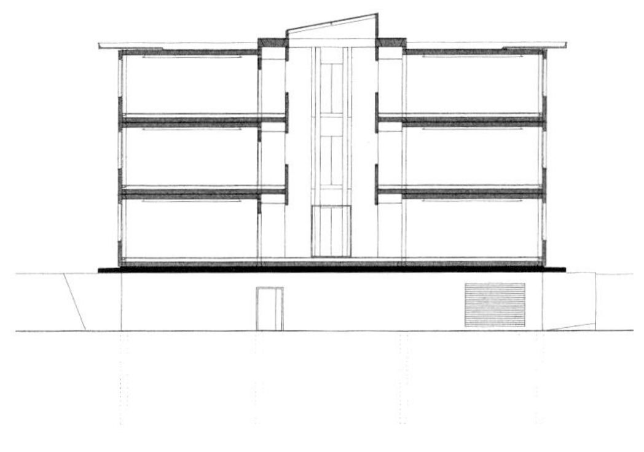

Cross-section

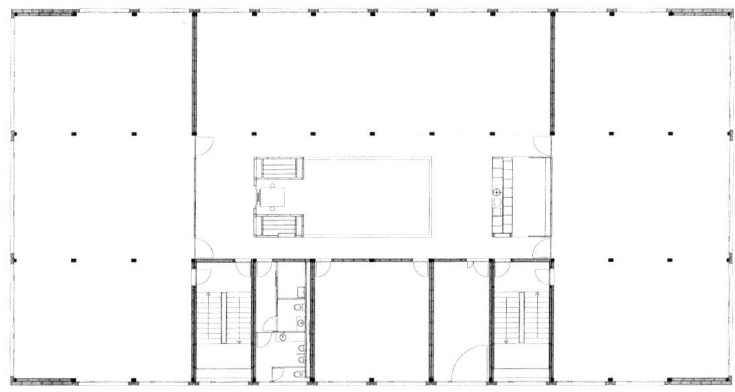

First and second floor

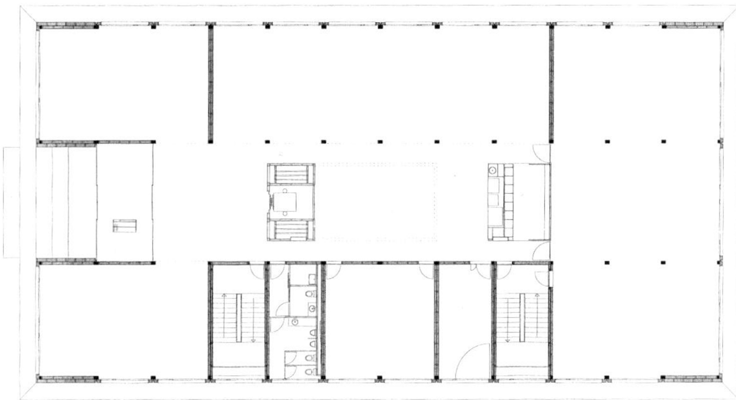

Ground floor

interior. By omitting the floor slabs at the centre, the conventional building is transformed into a building with an internal courtyard. The light well is the architectural, constructional and circulation centre of the entire building.

The modules bordering the internal courtyard have a projecting floor slab that forms a circulation zone. The space below this projecting slab is used for the horizontal distribution of the sprinkler pipe work and for the runs leading to the various services and from the cellular units. The entire structure of the building is made with untreated wooden columns and beams. Weatherproof Okoumé plywood was used for the facade cladding, which is not back-ventilated.

Connections

Specially developed steel parts were used to join the modules together precisely and create structurally effective connections. These steel parts connect the floor and ceiling elements of each spatial cell with the wooden columns so that tension forces are transferred within the module. The same connecting parts were also used to hang the modules from the assembly crane, to fix them to the concrete slab and to fix the roof. Thanks to this simple connection technology, the modules can be easily separated from each other, entirely dismantled and re-erected at another location.

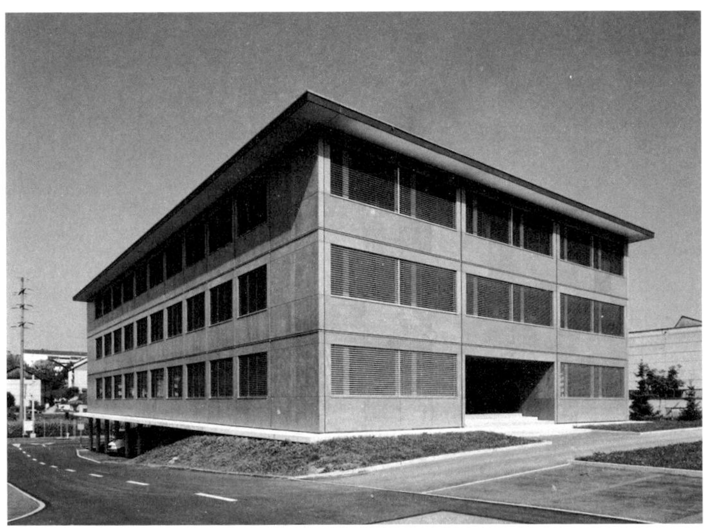

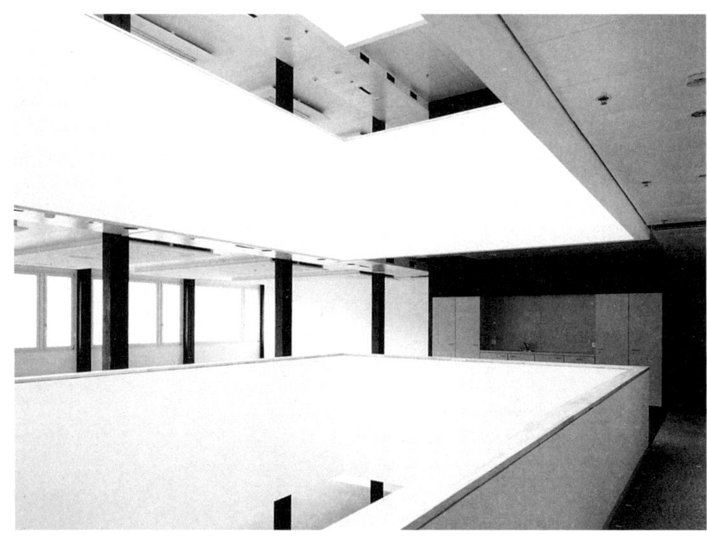

Prefabrication

Spatial cells have the advantage of being almost completely fitted out before they are mounted on site. In this project, for example, the individual modules were delivered to the site with the electrical services, including controls, ceiling lighting, sprinkler system and fixed partition walls, already fitted and finished.

Fire protection is provided by a sprinkler system as well as a fire alarm system. The core of the building services system is a suspended floor that, on the one hand, serves as a pressure chamber for the distribution of fresh air and, on the other hand, allows great flexibility in laying ducts and services to the various workstations. This suspended floor and the various media services were built into the almost entirely prefabricated spatial cells directly on site.

Location Ebikon, Switzerland

Construction period 7/1998 – 1/1999

Client Schindler Aufzüge AG, Ebikon

Architects Kündig. Bickel Architekten ETH SIA BSA, Zürich

Project manager Markus Kummer

Assistants Lukas Walpen, Guido Schnegg

Structural planner, timber Merz + Kaufmann, Lutzenberg. Gordian Kley, Bruno Ludescher

Structural planner, reinforced concrete Mühlemann & Partner, Ebikon. Richard Nufer

Planning of heating, ventilation, air conditioning Gallusser + Partner, St. Gallen

Electrical planning Elektro Wey, Luzern, Xaver Husmann

Planning of plumbing services Anton Wyss, Luzern

Acoustics and building physics Wichser AG, Dübendorf, Michael Herrmann

General contractor Bauengineering AG, Altenrhein. Peter Mettler, Stefan Rausch

Timber construction Erne AG Holzbau, Laufenburg

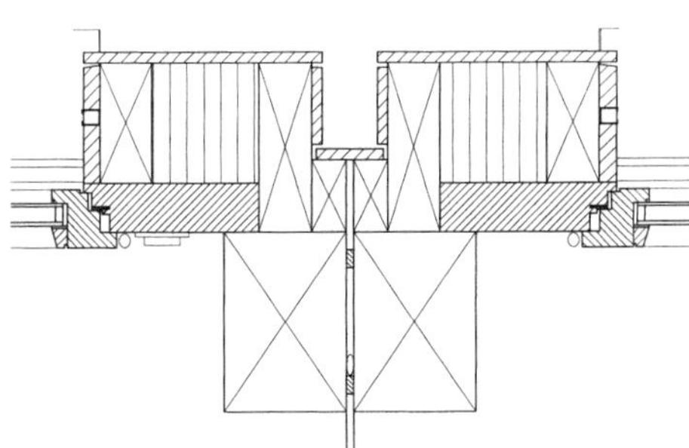

Junction between two spatial cells with connection to a wooden column

Office building in Stainach/Austria AGRICULTURAL COOPERATIVE

Architects: Herwig und Andrea Ronacher

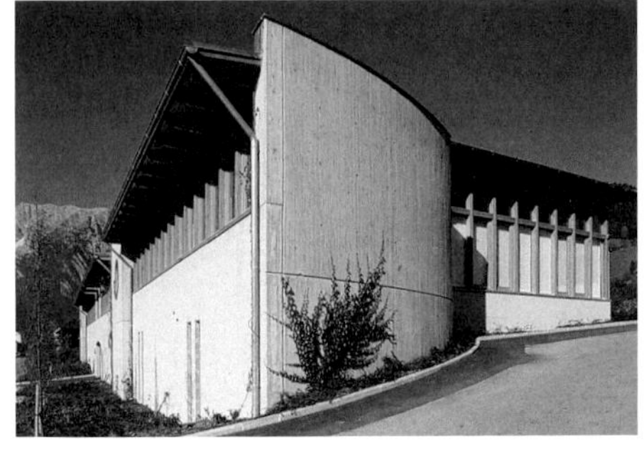

The clients' wish to erect a new timber-built administration building provided the architects with an interesting and delightful task, but at the same time the call for a single-storey office building in existing urban surroundings consisting, for the most part, of buildings two or more storeys high and built using traditional solid construction methods seemed initially to present almost insoluble problems.

Urban situation

The solution finally lay in building a garage beneath the entire office area, which, through the natural difference in height of about one storey between the street level and the level of the site at the main front of the building in the south, plays a visually decisive role in the appearance of the building. Additionally, the area of the window parapet on the south side of the office floor, together with the plinth formed by the underground garage, were built using reinforced concrete.

These construction measures mean that, from the south, the main elevation of the building appears to be two-storey. There were thus no further difficulties in meeting the requirement to place all the offices at ground floor level and to use purely timber construction. Only the core, containing the sanitary facilities and the staircase, and the eastern end wall to the office wing made of reinforced concrete were intended to distinguish themselves externally from the timber frame construction.

Functional solution

The agricultural cooperative provided a space and usage brief, on the basis of which the concept for an overall solution consisting of two building phases – that is, two building parts with a centrally situated entrance area – was developed.

The two office wings are separately accessed but can be also connected to each other by one of the corridors. In the double-loaded office wing, the office spaces face outwards; while communally used spaces, which are adequately lit from courtyards, face inwards. For instance: the secretarial areas are open or half-open towards the entrance and, thanks to their central position, can be quickly reached from all the offices. Meeting rooms are located opposite them at the end of the central area. Between the four core areas, with their pyramid roofs over the secretarial areas and the meeting rooms, there are three light wells, the central one of which forms the entrance area.

Determining the building form

The form of the building as a whole follows the internal spatial concept. The building consists of simple outward sloping mono-pitch roofs over the office areas and pyramid roofs on top of the core area, above the secretarial zone and the meeting rooms.

This design of the building made it possible to leave the differentiated and characteristic outlines of the interior spaces, such as the pyramid roof and the primary timber structure, exposed and to incorporate these features in the design of the interior. Thus a roofscape is created that uses the principle of roof drainage directed outwards to avoid problematic construction points.

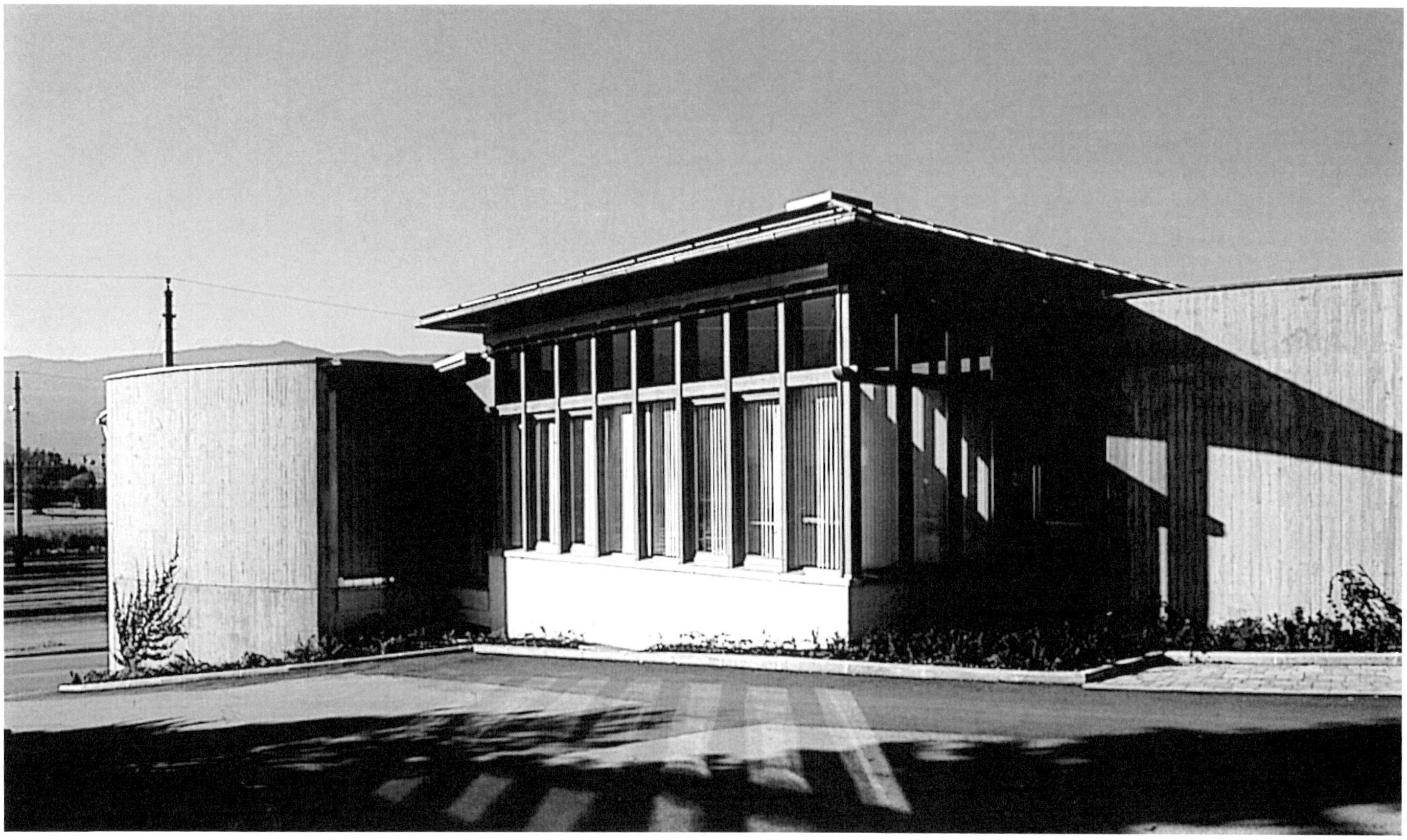

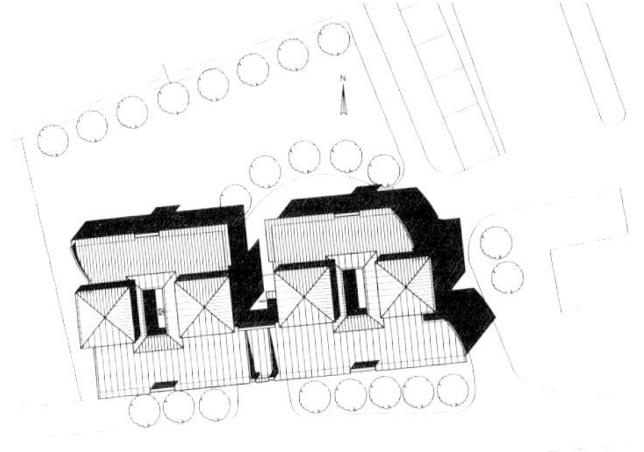

Top view

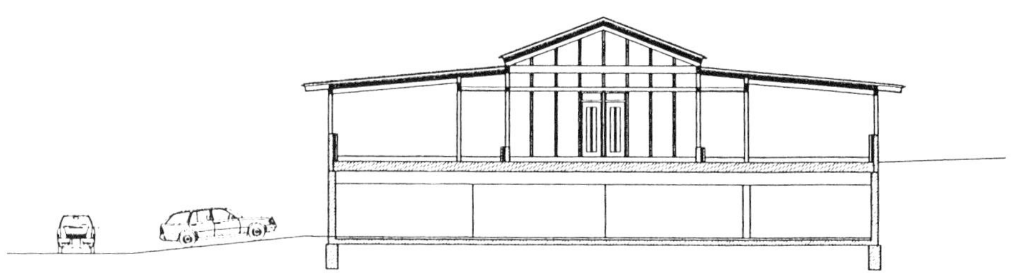

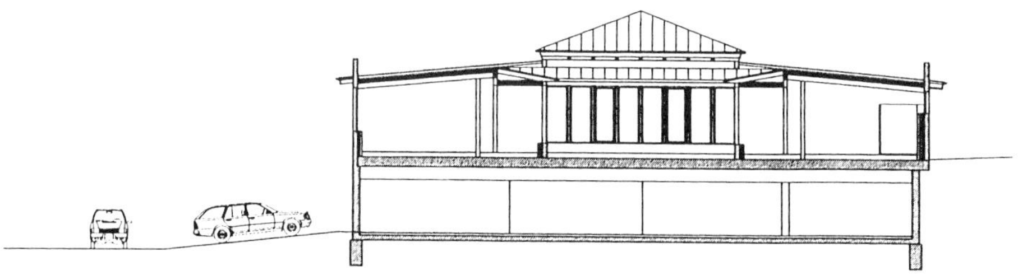

Sections

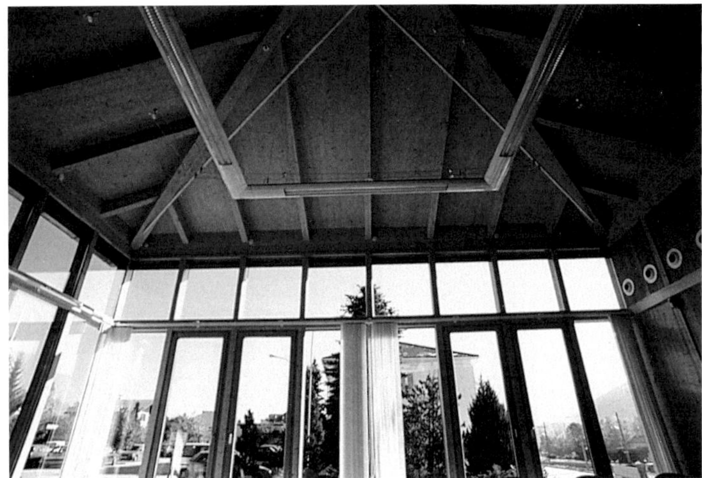
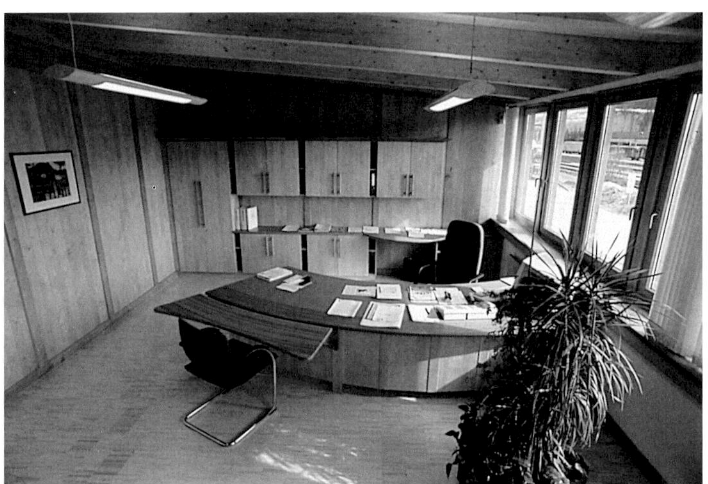

Construction

With the exception of the underground garage and individual parts of the ground floor, such as the eastern end walls and the wet-room areas that were built in reinforced concrete or brickwork, the entire building consists of a wooden frame structure on a column grid of 1 m. All wooden building elements, such as columns, purlins and rafters, are made of glued laminated timber and are left visible in the spaces. The entire roof structure was built using a double layer of rafters to provide a continuous thermal insulation layer, whereby the construction could be left exposed in the interior. The upper layer of rafters, which is visible only in the area of the canopy roofs, was made of solid timber sections.

Fitting out

In fitting out, interior three-ply, laminated wooden sheeting with a polished surface was used for both the walls and the roof soffit. Large fir panels were used in the corridors, the reception hall and the offices. The large meeting room was lined completely in larch wood. The major office spaces were panelled using other native hardwoods, such as beech, maple, birch and elder. Strip parquet floors were used, mostly of elder, but in places matching the wall panelling of beech or maple. The furniture is made of fir but, in places, it matches the wall panels and is also made of beech, maple, alder or birch. It was individually designed to harmonise with the grid of the primary structure.

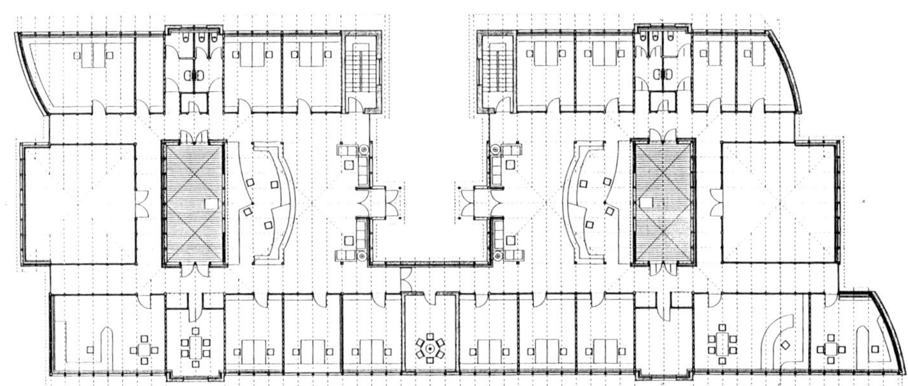

Floor plan of the entire building

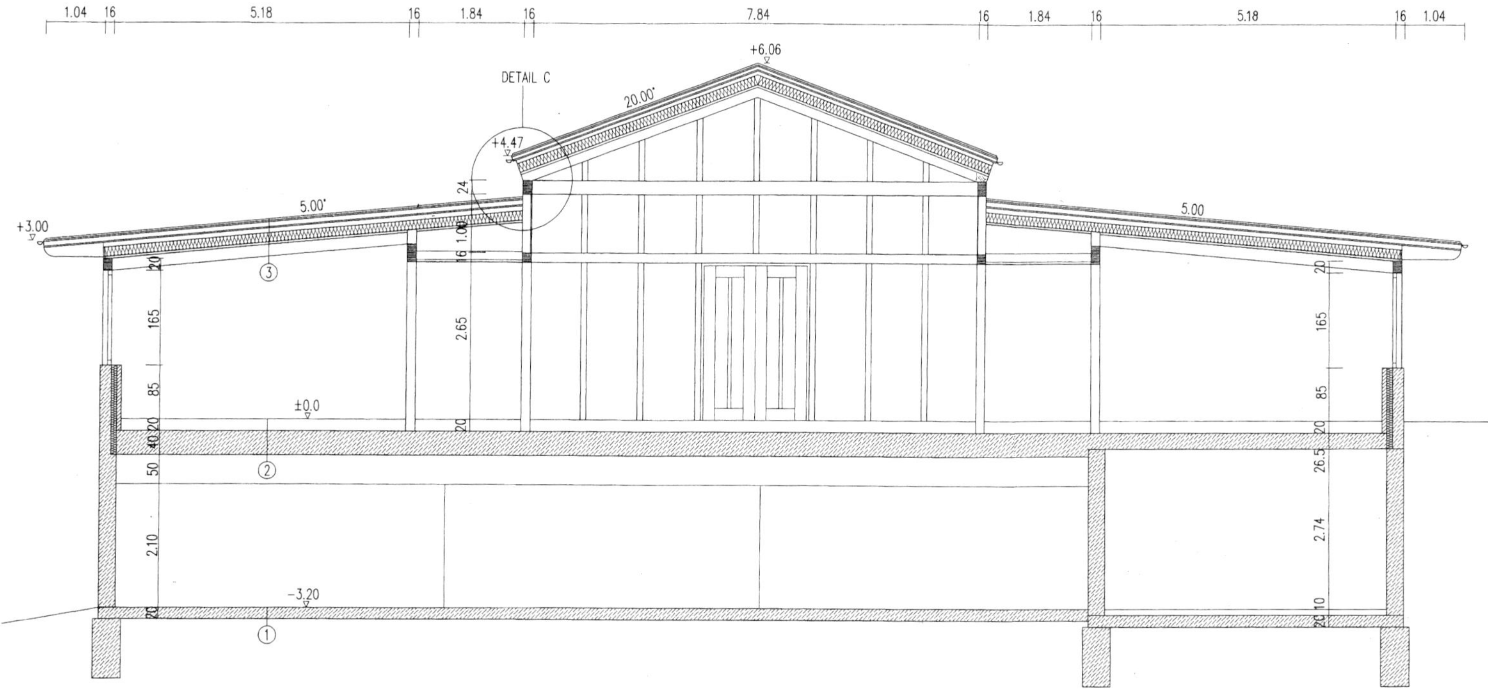

Cross-section

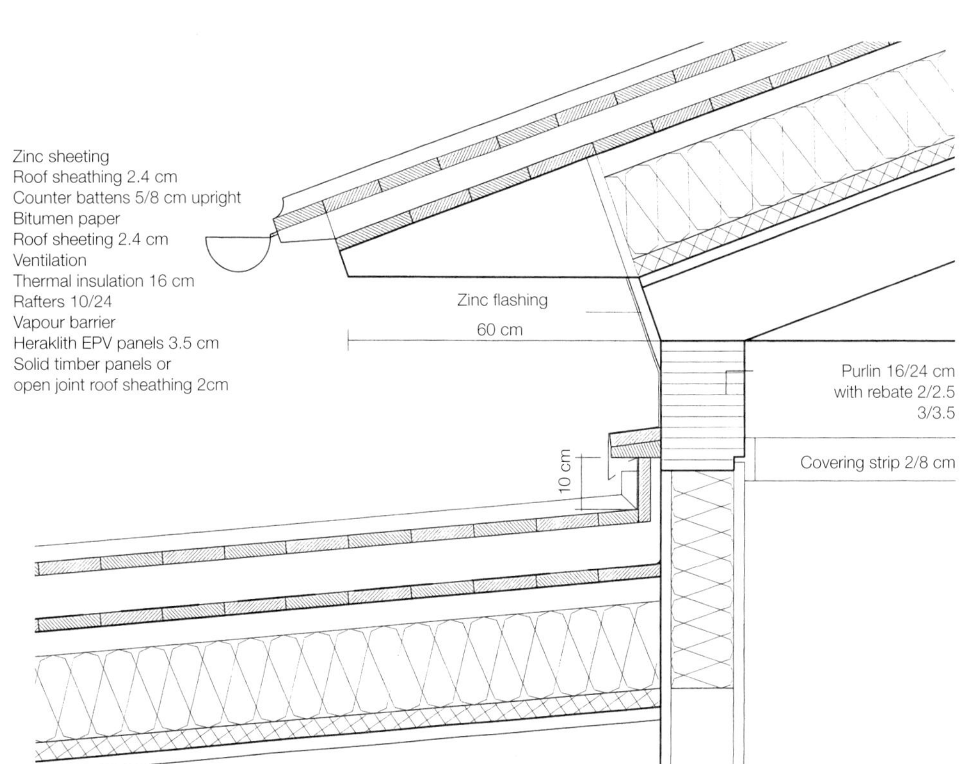

Zinc sheeting
Roof sheathing 2.4 cm
Counter battens 5/8 cm upright
Bitumen paper
Roof sheeting 2.4 cm
Ventilation
Thermal insulation 16 cm
Rafters 10/24
Vapour barrier
Heraklith EPV panels 3.5 cm
Solid timber panels or
open joint roof sheathing 2cm

Zinc flashing
60 cm

Purlin 16/24 cm
with rebate 2/2.5
3/3.5

Covering strip 2/8 cm

Detail C

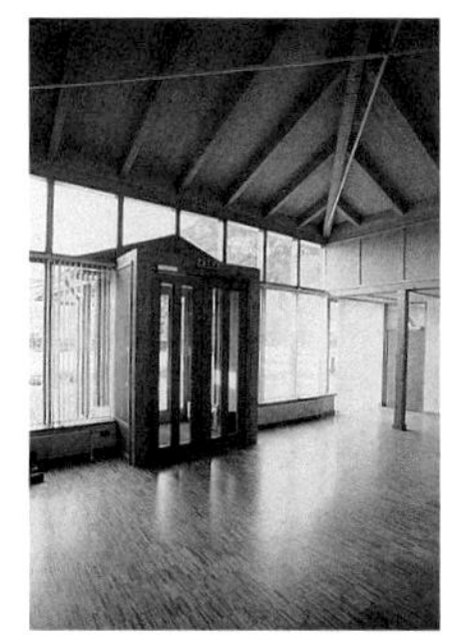

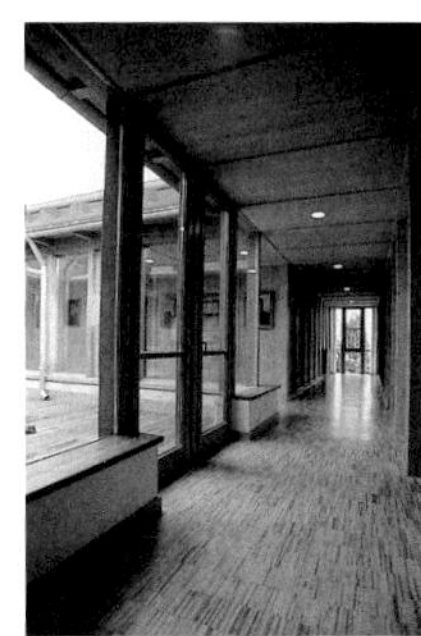

Location Stainach, Austria

Construction period 1994–1995

Client Landgenossenschaft Ennstal

Architects and structural designers Dipl.-Ing. Dr. Herwig Ronacher and Dipl.-Ing. Andrea Ronacher, Hermagor

Enclosed volume: 2720 m³

Total floor area 690 m²

Office floor area 560 m²

Acton Johnson Ostry Architects

DOCKED ON

Steel spring factory in Surrey / Canada

Due to shortage of space, a producer of heavy steel springs had to move his business from the inner city core of Vancouver, British Columbia to an existing building in neighbouring Surrey. To ensure optimum production conditions, it was also necessary to add a two-storey wing. The client wanted the architects to design this building as an expression of corporate identity with a maximum budget of CAD 250,000 (Canadian dollars).

To complete the two-storey office wing within the allotted budget, the architects decided upon a timber frame building. As a consequence, they were even able to reduce the costs below this limit; the actual construction sum finally amounted to CAD 200,000. Thus, the extension is an example of good value architecture that can nevertheless be seen as the basis for a corporate design specific to the company. The rectangular block that is

attached to the existing development faces the street, presenting itself like the visiting card of the business. The sloping roof and a projecting staircase serve to reduce the severity of the two-storey building, as does the use of different facade materials, such as black and yellow plywood and red corrugated metal. The main entrance is marked by a plywood canopy.

The steel staircase inside the building, connecting the two storeys of the administration area, is an immediate eye-catcher. It is built to display the company's own products: it hangs from a spring and rests on compression springs. The railings are also made of steel springs. The walls of the staircase hall are lined with maple veneered, transparently glazed plywood. The floors are covered with green tiling and the walls are painted white: in some areas, colour accents of red and gold are used.

Location Surrey, British Columbia, Canada

Construction period 1996

Client Dendoff Springs Ltd., Surrey

Architects Acton Johnson Ostry Architects Inc., Vancouver, British Columbia

Structural designers Fast+Epp, Vancouver, British Columbia

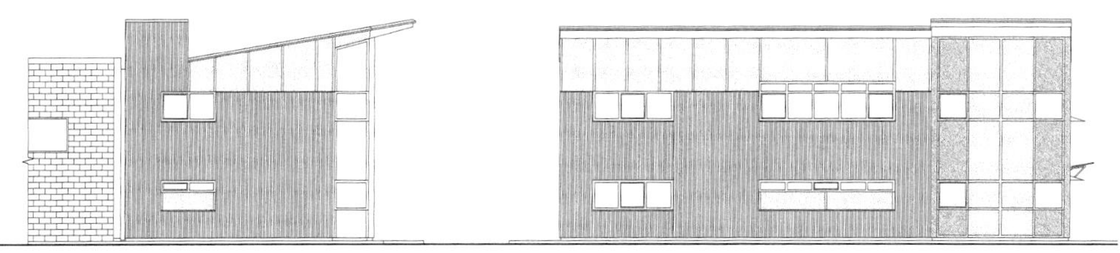

Northwest elevation

Southwest elevation

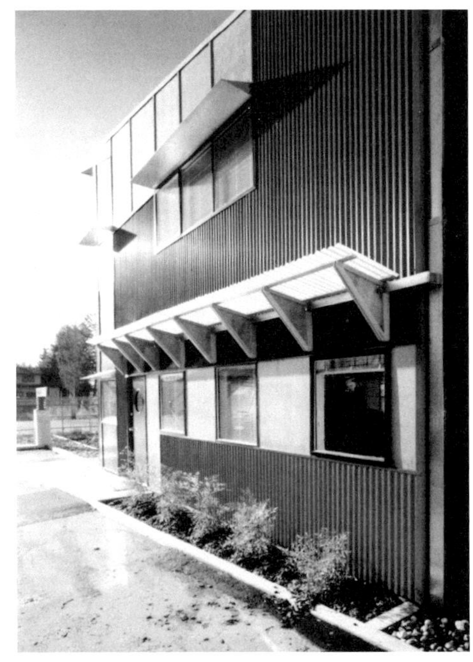

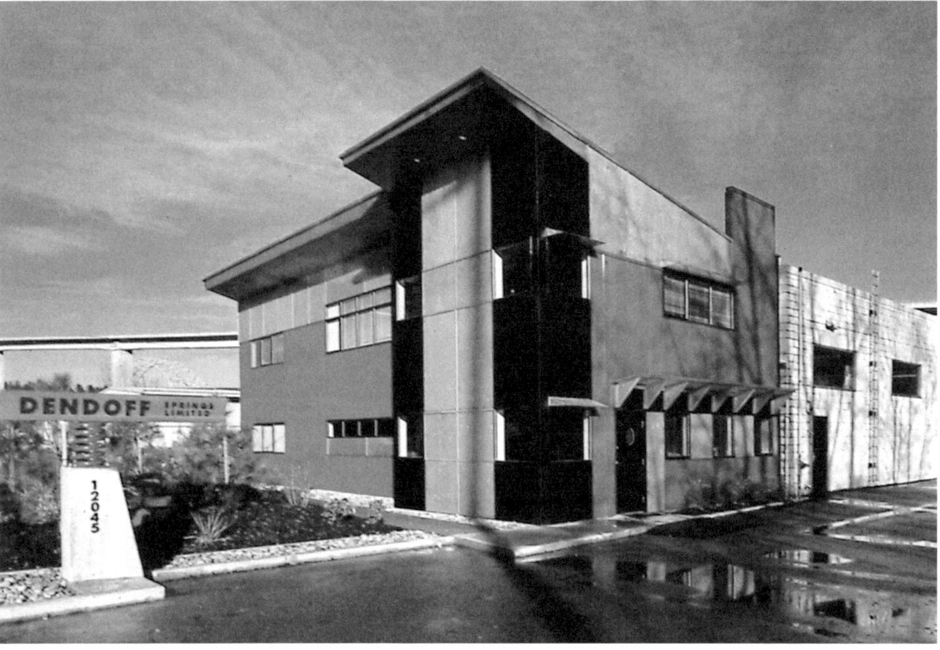

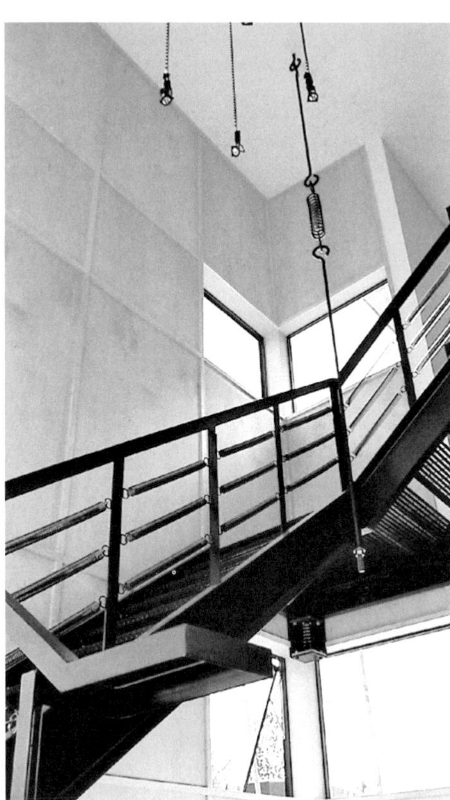

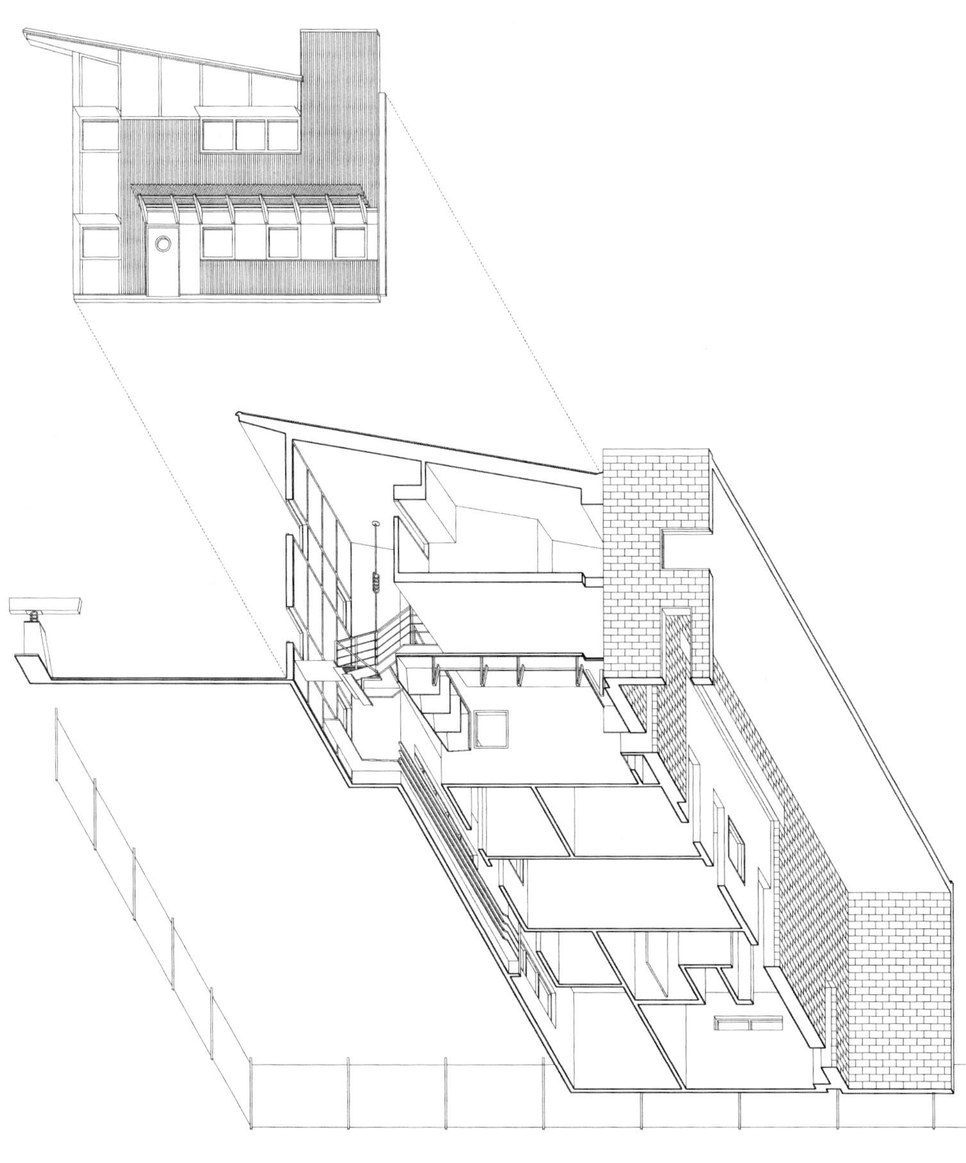

Index

Bibliography

Ackermann, Kurt, *Industriebau*, Stuttgart 1984

Arbeitsgemeinschaft Holz e.V. (Ed.), *Wirtschaftsbauten aus Holz*,
Düsseldorf 1987
Entwurfsüberlegungen bei Holzbauten, Düsseldorf 1979
Industrie- und Lagerhallen aus Holz, Düsseldorf 1979
Industrie- und Gewerbebauten – Planungsgrundlagen,
Düsseldorf 1993
Feuerhemmende Holzbauteile, Düsseldorf 1994
Grundlagen des Brandschutzes, Düsseldorf 1996
Holzbauten bei chemisch-aggressiver Beanspruchung,
Düsseldorf 1996
Brandschutz im Holzbau – gebaute Beispiele, Düsseldorf 2001
Industrie- und Gewerbebauten, Düsseldorf 2001

Arbeitsgemeinschaft Industriebau (Ed.), *Stahl, Glas und Membranen im Industriebau*, München 2003

Banz, Riecks (Ed.), *Solvis - Auf dem Weg zur Nullemissionsfabrik*,
Leinfelden 2002

Bund Deutscher Zimmermeister (Ed.),
Holzrahmenbau mehrgeschossig, Karlsruhe 1996

Bundesministerium für Verkehr, Bau- und Wohnungswesen (Ed.),
Leitfaden Nachhaltiges Bauen, Berlin 2001

Erhorn/Kluttig, *Energiesparpotentiale im Verwaltungsbau zur Reduzierung der CO2-Emissionen, in: Gesundheits-Ingenieur*, München 1996

Herzog, Thomas, *Timber Construction Manual*, Basel Boston Berlin 2003

IndustrieBau, Zeitschrift, München

Lenze/Luig, *Gewerbebauten – Bauen für den Mittelstand*, Stuttgart 2003

Lignum, *Bauten für Industrie und Gewerbe*, Zürich 1985
Gewerbliche und industrielle Bauten, Zürich 1988
Gewerbehallen, Zürich 1991
Zweckbauten, Zürich 1995
Hallen: Produktion, Lager, Veranstaltungen, Zürich 1998

Lorenz, Peter, *Gewerbebau – Industriebau*, Leinfelden 1991

Öko-Zentrum NRW (Ed.), *Umweltverträglicher Industrie- und Gewerbebau*, Hamm 1997
ProHolz (Ed.), *Brandverhalten von Holzkonstruktionen*, Wien 1990
Hallen im Industriebau, Wien 1991

Rockwool (Ed.), *Industriebaurichtlinie Handkommentar*, Gladbeck o.J.

Ruske, Wolfgang, *Holzskelettbau*, Stuttgart 1980
Gute Industriearchitektur machen!, in: Baumarkt, Gütersloh 1983
Structures en bois, Denges 1984
Ausbau und Innenausbau im Detail, Kissing 1987
Glas, Kissing 1988
Holz-Glas-Architektur, Kissing 1988
Industrie- und Gewerbebau – Holzarchitektur als Teil der Unternehmenskultur, in: DBZ, Gütersloh 1989

Holzarchitektur als Teil der Unternehmenskultur, in: Holz-Zentralblatt,
Leinfelden 1990
Holzbau als Corporate-Design-Aufgabe, in: Baumarkt, Gütersloh 1993
Zukunft Erde - Solarstrategie und Neues Holz-Zeitalter,
Mönchengladbach 1995
Praxissammlung Holzbau, Mönchengladbach 1996
Holzbau heute, Mering 1999
Ebene Flächentragwerke, in: Bauhandwerk, Gütersloh 2000
Fassadenkonstruktionen, in: Bauzeitung, Berlin 2000
Ökologie und Innovation im Holzbau, in: Deutsches Architektenblatt,
Stuttgart 2000
Sichere Ausführung von Holz-Glas-Fassaden, in: Bauhandwerk,
Gütersloh 2001
Das Neue Holzzeitalter, in: DBZ Themenheft Holzbau, Gütersloh 2001
Brandschutz im Holzbau, in: IndustrieBau, München 2001
Fachwerkträger und Raumtragwerke aus Holz, in: Bauhandwerk,
Gütersloh 2001
Innovationen für das Bauen mit Holz, in: Bundesbaublatt,
Wiesbaden 2001
Industrie- und Gewerbebauten, in: Holzbau Handbuch,
Düsseldorf 2001
Holzwerkstoffe, in: Mikado, Kissing 2002
Bauen mit Nagelplattenkonstruktionen, in: Bauhandwerk,
Gütersloh 2002
Holzkonstruktionen für Industriehallen, in: IndustrieBau,
München 2002
Holzbaukultur, in: Mikado, Kissing 2002
Distributionszentrum in Bobingen, in: IndustrieBau, München 2002
Holzwerkstoffe als Fassadenbekleidung,
in: Normgerechte Bauausführung im Zimmererhandwerk, Kissing 2002
Hölzerne Dachtragwerke, in: Bauhandwerk, Gütersloh 2002
Corporate Design, in: Holzbau Magazin, Leinfelden 2002
Fassaden aus Holz, in: Holz-Zentralblatt, Leinfelden 2002
Brandschutz im Holzbau, in: Bauhandwerk, Gütersloh 2002
Das Werkhaus in Raubling, in: IndustrieBau, München 2002
Moderne Holzarchitektur in Europa, in: Holz-Zentralblatt,
Leinfelden 2003
Gewerbe- und Verwaltungsbau: Unternehmer setzen weltweit auf Holz, in: Mikado, Kissing 2004
Ökologisches und wirtschaftliches Bauen in der Praxis,
Mönchengladbach 1996

Sommer, Degenhard (Ed.), *Industriebauten gestalten*, Wien 1989

Unternehmensgrün (Ed.), *Umweltverträglicher Industrie- und Gewerbebau*, München 1996

Wilkhahn (Ed.), *Der Wilkhahn*, Bad Münder 1988

Picture credits

Abbadie, Hervé, Paris 47, 51
Acton Johnson Ostry, Vancouver 167
APA, Tacoma 15, 72, 75 (top)
Baufritz, Erkheim 145, 146, 148, 149, 150,
    151, 152
Braun, Heinz, Darmstadt 46 (right)
Coelan, Coesfeld 36, 37
Derix, Niederkrüchten 28
Deutsche Amphibolin-Werke, Ober-Ramstadt
    63, 64 (left)
DGfH/EGH, Munich 32, 33
Dold, Buchenbach 38 (right)
Ekler, Dezsö, Budapest 114, 115, 116, 117
Frahm, Klaus, Boernsen 83, 85, 86, 87
Fujitsuka, Mitsumasa/Helico, Tokyo 52, 53
Gestering, Bremen 10 (top)
Glunz, Hamm 12
Grau, Tobias, Rellingen 138, 139, 140, 141
Hellinger, Reinhold, Graz 43 (top)
Herzog, Thomas 10 (bottom)
Iida, Yoshihiko, Kanagawa 66, 67, 68, 69, 70,
    71
Inauen, St. Gallen 155, 157
Kaufmann, Reuthe 39 (top)
Kordina/Meyer-Ottens, Munich 43 (bottom)
Kündig, Bickel, Zurich 158, 159, 161
Küttinger, Munich 13, 30
Leenders, Krefeld 14

Lignatur, Waldstatt 118, 119, 121
Lignotrend, Weilheim-Bannholz 31, 40, 42,
    93 (bottom)
Lux, Georgensmuend 41 (left)
Meickl, Gerhard, Vettelschoß 24 (right), 25 (top)
Merk, Aichach 39 (bottom)
Ortmeyer, Klemens / architekturphoto,
    Duesseldorf 122, 123, 127
Ravenstein, Klaus, Essen 99, 101, 103, 106,
    107, 109, 111
Richters, Christian, Muenster 18, 76, 77, 78,
    80, 81, 129, 133, 134
Ronacher, Herwig, Hermagor 162, 163, 164,
    165
Rubio, Cesar, San Francisco 112, 113
Ruske, Wolfgang, Moenchengladbach 16,
    24 (left), 25 (centre), 34, 38 (left/centre), 73,
    75 (centre), 75 (bottom)
Schmidt, Jürgen, Cologne 91, 93 (top), 94
Strenger, Osnabrueck 17
SYNERGIE HOLZ-Bildarchiv, Moenchenglad-
    bach 11, 20, 21, 22, 23, 26, 29, 41 (right)
Tessler, Martin, Vancouver
Wakely, David, San Francisco 55
Wetzel, Martin, St. Georgen 25 (bottom)
Wilkhahn, Bad Muender 8, 10 (top/left)
Wilson, Chris, Hobart 56, 57, 59, 61

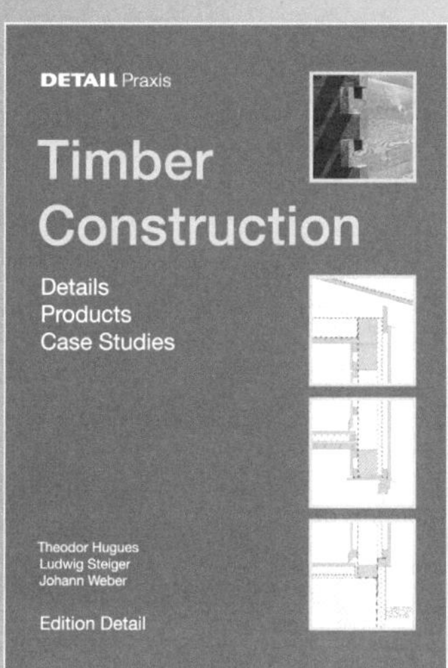

Detail Praxis:
Timber Construction

Details, Products,

Case Studies

Theodor Hugues, Ludwig Steiger, Johann Weber

2004. 110 pages,
53 colour, 4 b/w ills and
79 drawings
23 x 29.7 cm / 9.2 x 11.8 inch
Paperback
ISBN 3-7643-7032-7 English

A CONCISE SURVEY OF MATERIALS AND TECHNIQUES IN MODERN TIMBER CONSTRUCTION.

Timber construction has experienced a renaissance in recent years. A greater sensibility for ecological issues on the part of clients, planners and legislators has contributed to the ongoing boom and helped timber reassert itself as a building material.

The development and use of new materials and stricter energy-saving requirements have brought major changes to the industry. This publication is designed to give readers an up-to-date survey of modern wood products and construction technology. Whether prefabricated or built on-site, all details are explained in texts and sectional drawings, illustrated by two exemplary case-studies and additional documentation of nine built structures.

Extensive information on a wide range of wood products, insulating materials, and joints and fasteners is also provided.

Timber Construction is the first volume in a new series of expert, concise, attractively priced Detail Practice guides.

A COMPREHENSIVE GUIDE TO ALL ASPECTS OF TIMBER CONSTRUCTION FOR PROFESSIONALS.

With more than 840 photos, and 4000 plans and drawings, the *Timber Construction Manual* is a comprehensive, indispensable reference work in the specialist literature on timber. Materials, architecture and engineering, as well as regulation norms and standards – every subject is covered.

The opening chapters treat the basic principles of working with wood and provide detailed information on subjects such as thermal performance, sound insulation, fire protection, ecological aspects, load-bearing properties, and new methods of prefabrication, joining and erection.

Following this, more than 120 mainly modern built examples, ranging from heavy-duty bridges to multi-storey residential buildings, present exemplary solutions, complete with detailed illustrations and plans. Facades receive particular attention.

All plans and drawings have been carefully produced to ensure the details and methods of construction are clear and comprehensible.

Timber Construction Manual

Thomas Herzog, Julius Natterer, Michael Volz

2004. 375 pages,
179 colour, 630 b/w ills and
4000 drawings
24 x 33 cm / 9.5 x 12 inch
Hardcover
ISBN 3-7643-7025-4 English

For more details please visit our website
http://www.birkhauser.ch
or contact
promotion@birkhauser.ch

Birkhäuser – Publishers for Architecture

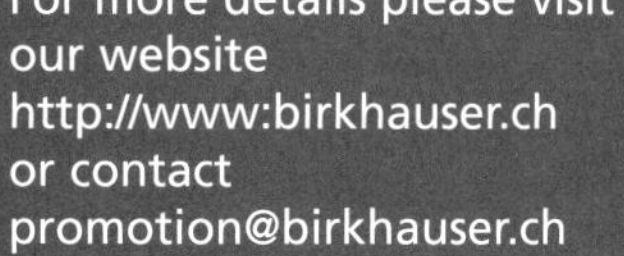